The Women of Paris and Their French Revolution

Studies on the History of Society and Culture

Victoria E. Bonnell and Lynn Hunt, Editors

The publisher gratefully acknowledges the contribution provided by the General Endowment Fund, which is supported by generous gifts from the members of the Associates of the University of California Press.

The Women of Paris and Their French Revolution

DOMINIQUE GODINEAU

Translated by Katherine Streip

University of California Press

BERKELEY   LOS ANGELES   LONDON

Originally published as *Citoyennes tricoteuses: Les femmes du peuple à Paris pendant la Révolution française*
© 1988 Editions ALINEA

University of California Press
Berkeley and Los Angeles, California

University of California Press, Ltd.
London, England

© 1998 by
The Regents of the University of California

Library of Congress Cataloging-in-Publication Data

Godineau, Dominique.
   [Citoyennes tricoteuses. English].
   The women of Paris and their French Revolution / Dominique Godineau ; translated by Katherine Streip.
      p.   cm. — (Studies on the history of society and culture ; 26)
   Includes bibliographic references and index.
   ISBN 0-520-06718-5 (alk. paper). — ISBN 0-520-06719-3 (pbk. : alk. paper)
      1. Paris (France)—History—1789-1799—Women.   2. Working class women—France—Paris—History—18th century.   3. Women—France—Paris—Social conditions.   4. Women in public life—France—Paris—History—18th century.   I. Title.   II. Series.
   DC731.G6313   1998
   944'.36104'082—dc20   96-31744
                                              CIP

Printed in the United States of America

The paper used in this publication meets the minimum requirements of American National Standards for Information Sciences—Permanence of Paper for Printed Library Materials, ANSI Z39.48-1984.

Excerpts from "The Hands of Jeanne-Marie" (epigraph) from *Arthur Rimbaud: Complete Works*, translated from the French by Paul Schmidt. Copyright © 1967, 1970, 1971, 1972, 1975 by Paul Schmidt. Reprinted by permission of HarperCollins Publishers, Inc.

Dedicated to Hélène and Henri Quinque

In these turbulent times when our city is thrown into an uproar, we cannot conceal from ourselves that women have played the part of firebrands.

Comité civil de la section du Nord,
15 Messidor Year III (3 July 1795)

The Hands of Jeanne-Marie

Jeanne-Marie has powerful hands,
Dark hands summertime has tanned,
Hands pale as a dead man's hands.
Are these the hands of Juana?

. . . .

These are the benders of backbones,
Hands that have never done wrong,
Hands fatal as machinery,
Strong as a horse is strong!

Shaking like bright furnaces,
Their flesh cries out the "Marseillaise,"
Shakes shivering to silences,
And never quavers Kyries!

They'll break your necks, you whores,
Strangle you, daughters of night;
Crush your hands, you countesses,
Your hands painted red and white.

A stain, a splash of populace,
Darkens them like yesterday's breast;
The back of these Hands is the place
All your ardent Rebels have kissed!

Marvelously pale in the sun's
Love-provoking light, they hauled
The bronze barrels of machine guns
Across Paris in revolt!

. . . .

Arthur Rimbaud, 1871

Translated from the French by Paul Schmidt

Contents

Illustrations

Preface: Marianne's Hands

The hands of Jeanne-Marie, the hands of Marianne, the hands of women revolutionaries, and the hands of knitters: we unite them deliberately here, these hands of the simple working-class people who rebelled during the French Revolution and those described by the famous poet almost a century later in one of the most beautiful poems about French women revolutionaries. "Dark hands, pale hands"—but are these hands so different, the hands of the woman revolutionary of 1871 and those of 1793, these hands that "sing the Marseillaise" and those of the idle noblewoman? Rather than shading their pale skin from the sun under the shadows of bronze rifles, Marianne's hands would cry to the president of the Convention: "Beneath these delicate hands have glided the barrels of those bronze entities—those mouths of fire that could make even a king hear thunder in his ear—the augur of change and all destinies!"[1]

And the bloody Revolution, which at long last succeeded in solidifying the political organization of French society: wasn't its memory illuminated primarily by the "sun's love-provoking light?"—to the displeasure of all the tortured spirits that frequent hate-gatherings and would much rather define it according to the number of decapitated heads and drops of blood spilled than try to understand what values the Revolution brought to light? "Love for oneself [is] love for others," wrote one historian on the revolutionary mentality.[2]

Marianne's hands were tender upon the forehead of a child, a spouse, or a lover—or raised before her face to fend off a violent husband's blows.

1. Speech by Hérault de Séchelles, 10 August 1793, to the "heroines of the fifth and sixth of October [1789]."
2. Michel Vovelle, *La Mentalité révolutionnaire: Société et mentalités sous la Révolution française* (Paris: Messidor, 1985).

They were damaged, "dark like yesterday's breast," by the cold water of the Seine where laundrywomen washed clothes, by the pricks of a needle if she worked in a tailor's shop, or by the spinning wheel if she worked in a mill. They polished metal or crafted fans, pearls, feathers, and other frippery. They sought provisions to feed her family. And they could shock, too—when they signed or marked a cross at the bottom of a petition, when their fingers followed the lines of a Declaration of Rights or of Robespierre's last speech, when they rose to beg for speech in a revolutionary assembly, when they strove feverishly to affix linen bandages upon the wounds of soldiers fighting on the Republican front line. Or, when they tugged upon a counterrevolutionary's uniform and spread to deliver a stinging slap to his cheek, when they carried their miserable rations of bread under the deputies' noses, only to transform into defiant fists a few minutes later. And, of course, when they knitted, in the tribunes of the National Assembly or before the guillotine.

This book does not describe some famous woman or the universal condition of Woman herself but the common women—the ones who didn't leave their names, the ones who shared in the quest for subsistence, and the ones who worked to earn a bare living, while still finding time every night to take their places in the tribunes of the National Assembly.

We hear of these women from time to time in general works on the Revolution. But even then—at the turn of a phrase, lost within a paragraph—they appear only briefly. Among which passages will they disappear next? What will become of these women when the revolutionary historians no longer cast them the slightest regard? From the moment that women were first granted citizenship, lengthy analyses and even complete chapters have focused on women's liberation, but these remain only parentheses disconnected from a general history. Women are presented apart from the Revolution or beside it; they are not included in the revolutionary process, conceptualized as it is without reference to their involvement. And once we do start to become more particularly interested in the women of the Revolution, it is a Revolution that, despite its richness and complexity, exists only as a backdrop. Women do not seem attached to it in any way—rather, they seem to transcend the social classes and political groups. Although women have become subjects worthy of historical interest, they are denied status as active subjects of Revolutionary history and their actions play more importance in the history of women than in the history of the Revolution. It is as if women constructed their stories alongside the "big story," which remains masculine and in which they are merely the eternal victims.

Yet the merging of the history of women and the history of the Revolution is possible, so long as we remain attentive to the pitfalls of anachronism. We must refrain from plastering our own historical and intellectual heritage ①
over the archives without taking into account Revolutionary thought, the population, and the social and political contexts of the period. We must not ②
neglect the occasion to point out the frequent willingness to inferiorize women in the sexual, social, economic, and political spheres during the Revolution, although we acknowledge that women were only one of many aspects that formed society and history. To know that women were present ③
in the course of a certain episode, that they did or did not share a certain attitude of the revolutionary mentality—these statements have no fundamental importance unless they illuminate the specific contexts and gender relations of women during the revolutionary movement. Studying women during the Revolution allows us to enrich our comprehension of the revolutionary phenomenon, to put in relief the parts that up till now have rarely been taken into account. The last stipulation is that we must resist drawing ④
the separation between a story that would view ordinary women (and men) only through the distorted prism of their ways of living and of being and their passions, and another that would study the ideas and concepts that belonged to only a few so-called enlightened men at the time. The history of ideas—of the production of thought—would after all be quite incomplete were it limited only to the elite, even if the elite were revolutionaries.

In the police records from the Revolution we find traces of ordinary *police*
women: laundrywomen, shop owners, working-class women, unemployed *records*
women, and the wives of artisans or merchants. We see them struggling
with everyday obstacles but also supporting and participating in the Revolution—forming a women's revolutionary movement. We hear their hopes, their fears, and their despair clamoring through the statements of interrogators, police accounts, and reports—hear them utter their loves, their disillusions, their bitterness—all while the democracy was forming. Their violence completely terrifies us at times—their violence of words, actions, and feelings in which enthusiasm and hate, vindictiveness and altruism, brush dangerously close to one another. It is the revolutionary moment that is in question—the powerful moment where mannerisms and behaviors are embittered—pushed almost to their paroxysms. The point is not to hush or hide the "ferocity" or the "angry impulses," as it was once said. Nor is it to judge, but rather, to try to understand them without losing sight of the stakes that motivated these women to act.

Tricoteuses, or "knitters," they would be called, because they knitted while they followed the assembly debates. An appellation seldom used during the Revolution but often used by their adversaries after the fall of Robespierre's party—and even surpassed by another term: "the furies of the guillotine"—this word survived as a way to designate the popular militants. But how did such a docile word, a word so inoffensive and so feminine, become charged with such a repulsive ferocity?

A woman who knits conjures images of warmth, rest, tenderness, and love; in the calm of the living room she works for others. The *tricoteuse,* however, evokes feelings of violence, hate, death, and blood; before the eyes of everybody and in the public tribunes, she ignites. The antinomy between these two associations assured the success of this word, which evoked the image of a feminine being dominated by anguish but harboring contradictory elements, allying the most delicate tenderness with the most extreme violence. *Tricoteuse* also evokes another stereotype of the woman who disguises herself—a dangerous woman beneath her domestic appearance. The word that is used to designate the activist, *sans-culotte,* which means "without pants" or "who does not wear pants," alludes to her dress, her appearance. Her clothing designates her social and political affiliations; her fetish, the needle, is really a weapon. As soon as you pass to her other sense, however, everything smudges, everything darkens— the activity indicated by the word *tricoteuse,* the activity of a peaceful mother of a family, is positive. Upon leaving the foyer to pass into the public scene, displaced, *tricoteuse* develops a negative meaning. And in the imagination needles are always symbolic of this sort of disloyalty; they can become dangerous; weapons without names; tools for labor tinged with bloody tips.

It is all just a question of deviance in the end. In transforming an image of warmth into an image of death, in characterizing a symbol and its opposite at the same time, *tricoteuse* has the advantage over *furie de guillotine* of being not only able to describe a political code but also daring to cross the thresholds between the private and public domains. The female political activist is described by a word that, in evoking once again the private sphere, communicates the awkwardness of her presence in the public arena. Tender, and thus feminine, women can only be that way at home; upon clearing the doorsteps of their houses they become ferocious. Although they have left the private sphere, there is nevertheless no place for them in public because they are still branded with their domestic roles—they penetrate only into an "elsewhere" where nothing is defined, or which the imagination and fancy distort.

At the end of the eighteenth century, women were conceptualized according to their roles as mothers and spouses; their existence was only conceived under the domestic roof. They were thus immediately placed outside of the public and hence outside of the city.[3] In his *Encyclopedia*, Diderot, although we can't really accuse him of misogyny, considers the word *citoyen* (citizen)—which is defined according to the possession of political rights—to be a masculine noun and explains: "One only attributes this title to women, young children, or to servants as one would to the members of a family of a citizen in the strict sense of the word; they aren't really citizens." Other dictionaries that treat *citoyen* as a political entity also designate it a masculine word but cannot help but use at one time or another its feminine form in order to refer to the spouse. Only the dictionaries that give a more limited sense of the citizen as a simple resident of a city officially welcome the feminine *citoyenne* into their pages.[4] Thus women, symbolic of private spheres, could not be considered as political individuals—only their spouses could grant them any sort of political existence.

The French Revolution, in declaring the Rights of Man and the Citizen, would make the latter a holder of rights, and not just the resident of a country. Would the female citizen *ever* find true recognition?

This book attempts to answer this question. Through the labyrinth of archives and their fruitful abundance, it measures the interval that exists between a singular image of the woman as a symbol of the private sphere and the real women of everyday life in the street, in the family, in the studio, in the tribunes, and in clubs. Here is where the knitters lived; this is where they wove and unwove their relations to the sansculottes. Here, other portraits of women during the Revolution appear, as they negotiate, confirm, reject, or superimpose upon the stereotype of the domestic being.

And this book would like to show, despite all of the missed rendezvous and relentless searches for recognition, their encounter with citizenship.

3. Lynn Hunt, "Révolution française et vie privée," in Philippe Ariès and Georges Duby, eds., *Histoire de la vie privée*, vol. 4, *De la Révolution à la Grande Guerre* (Paris: Seuil, 1987), pp. 21–51.

4. For a more precise definition, see Dominique Godineau, "Autour du mot citoyenne," *Mots* 16 (March 1988): 91–110.

Abbreviations

A.N.   Archives Nationales

Census: F^{20} 123–F^{20} 124 (Pluviôse Year V), F^{20} 255 (1807)

Spinning Workshops: F^{15} 3572 to F^{15} 3603–3604

"Correspondance relative à des échanges d'assignats contre du numéraire en 1790 et 1791 en faveur des fabricants et commerçants de Paris": F^{30} 115–F^{30} (boxes classified by sections)

Alphabetic series, Committee of General Security: F^7 4477–F^7 4575[53]

Military Commission: W 546, W 547, W 548, F^7 4429

Revolutionary tribunal: series W (particularly W 76, W 77, W 78, the Hébert case, and others)

Babeuf case: F^7 4276–F^7 4278

Prisons Seine: F^7 3299[14]–F^7 3304

Register and minutes of the comités révolutionnaires of the section and of the comités de surveillance d'arrondissements: F^7 2471–F^7 2526, F^7 4776–F^7 4779, AF^{II} 50

Addresses sent to the Convention: series C, unavailable for January 1793–Frimaire Year II

Reports of police informants:

    AF^{IV} 1470: March–June 1793 (anonymous)

    F 1c III Seine 27: May–June 1793 (Dutard, Terrasson, Perrière)

    F^7 3688[3]: May 1793–Nivôse Year II

    DXLII no. 11: September 1793–Nivôse Year II (Prévost)

    W191: Pluviôse Year II

W 112: Ventôse Year II

W 174: 1– Germinal Year II

F11 201 (a): 20 Frimaire–9 Germinal Year II (reports of Grivel and Siret on the food supply)

F 1c III Seine 13: end of Year II

F 1c III Seine 14: Vendémiaire–Frimaire Year III

F 1c III Seine 15: Nivôse–Ventôse Year III

F 1c III Seine 16: Germinal–Fructidor Year III

A.D.S.   Archives départementales, Seine

Registers of the comités civils: VD* Registres 794, 948, 980, 987

A.P.P.   Archives de la Préfecture de Police

Minutes of the police captains: series A, AA 48–AA 264

Archives de l'Assistance Publique

Registers of the comités de bienfaisance

B.H.V.P.   Bibliothèque Historique de la Ville de Paris

Various minutes in the manuscripts, particularly Ms. 932, Register of the comité civil of the Halle-au-Blé section

B.N.   Bibliothèque Nationale

Nouvelles acquisitions françaises, N.A.F. 2638–2720

B.V.C.   Bibliothèque Victor Cousin

Minutes of the general assemblies of the sections: Manuscrits 117–120

1

PARISIAN LIFE IN THE FRENCH REVOLUTION

1   Passersby

Paris at dawn. Shadowy figures with blackened faces, dressed in dark pants and jackets, unload wagons of coal in front of restaurants at the still silent Palais-Royal. In the dim light, one can barely distinguish a young woman bent beneath a sack; her name is Louise Catherine Vig-not, nicknamed *La Charbonnière* (the coal woman). An orphan at fifteen, she first lived with her sister. They both worked at unloading coal, dressed as men because women's clothes hampered their movements. After her sister married a fellow worker, Catherine rented a room from a family of coal sellers in the Faubourg Saint-Antoine, and daybreak after daybreak, sack after sack, she carried coal along with her brother-in-law. Around 5 A.M., when the cart was empty, she would return, exhausted, to her room, dressed in the colors of the departed night and pursued by the cries and laughter of those who now began to fill the streets, open their shops, and greet each other in the new day. In her room, Catherine ate her soup and slept until midafternoon. After a quick chat with her landlady, she would check if the coal cart had arrived; not seeing it, she would drink a pint of wine with a friend her own age who had just finished her work. The two young girls strolled in the neighborhood, hailing one acquaintance, laughing up their sleeves at each other's jokes. Then *La Charbonnière* would return to her coal. Except for one fine day in Prairial Year III (May 1795), when a gang of female rebels, demanding bread and the Constitution, crossed her path and Catherine, crowned with a three-cornered hat and armed with a saber, placed herself at their head.[1]

1. A.N., W 547 no. 46, F^7 4775^{45} d. Vignot.

Revolutionaries were not only to be found in insurrections, in political assemblies, or standing in line outside bakeries. Before examining the role of women in the French Revolution, I wish to portray them in their day-to-day, private lives. We will have greater insight into their social aspirations and political practices if we understand the difficulties of their domestic, emotional, and working lives. A human being, although composed of many facets, still constitutes a single being, and it is this unity of experience that we wish to apprehend. What was the life of a working-class woman during the Revolution? What were her joys, her pains, her domestic concerns and satisfactions, her fears and aggravations over food shortages and the events of the Revolution?

At the time of the French Revolution, there were more women than men in Paris. Censuses were unreliable, but according to various estimates,[2] between six hundred thousand and seven hundred thousand people lived in Paris in 1789. The census of 1797, which underestimates the population but has the advantage of distinguishing between men and women, shows women as representing 53.84 percent of the Parisian population. Women were especially numerous south of the Seine, particularly in faubourgs such as Saint-Marcel and Saint-Jacques, as well as in the central and northeastern *quartiers* (districts or neighborhoods). This female majority reflected population movements that originated before the Revolution, when many young women came from the country to work as domestics in the capital. During the Revolution, men—including, for example, priests, or nobles who left their wives to look after the patrimony—tended to emigrate for political reasons more often than women. Above all, the departure of numerous citizens for the army depleted the Parisian male population.

During this period, Paris was divided into forty-eight sections. Like the *quartier* of the Old Regime, each served as an administrative, electoral, and political unit.[3] Their inhabitants gathered in the evenings in general assemblies where they would discuss problems of the Revolution and local political quarrels, men would vote, and private and social conflicts would be-

2. See Daniel Roche, *The People of Paris: An Essay in Popular Culture in the Eighteenth Century*, trans. Marie Evans in association with Gwynne Lewis (Berkeley: University of California Press, 1987); Jeffry Kaplow, *The Names of Kings: The Parisian Laboring Poor in the Eighteenth Century* (New York: Basic Books, 1972); Albert Soboul, *Les Sans-culottes parisiens en l'an II. Mouvement populaire et gouvernement révolutionnaire, 2 juin 1793–9 thermidor an II* (1958; reprint Paris: Flammarion, 1973); 1797 Census: A.N., F20 123, F20 124.

3. On the *quartier*, see Arlette Farge, *Fragile Lives: Violence, Power, and Solidarity in Eighteenth-Century Paris*, trans. Carol Shelton (Cambridge: Harvard University Press, 1993).

come public. As representative of the sovereign people according to popular conception, the general assemblies often made their voices heard in the form of petitions in the National Assembly (first known as the Constituent Assembly, then the Legislative Assembly, and later the National Convention). Each section had its own administrative and revolutionary personnel: the superintendent of police, revolutionary commissioners who were militant sansculottes, and civil commissioners who gained in importance after the fall of Robespierre and his followers, when twelve surveillance committees organized by arrondissement replaced the revolutionary committees.[4] Every section had its own distinct character, such as the bourgeois, moderate, and even royalist populations of the west (Tuileries, Palais-Royal), the revolutionary sections of Faubourg Saint-Antoine and Faubourg Saint-Marcel, and the popular central sections. Their names changed with new developments in the popular movement. In the Marais district, the Droits-de-l'Homme (rights of man) replaced the Roi-de-Sicile (king of Sicily); in the Faubourg Saint-Germain, the Croix-Rouge (red cross) became the Bonnet-Rouge (red bonnet), then the Bonnet-de-la-Liberté (liberty bonnet), to end up, at the close of the Revolution, as the cold and discreet "de l'Ouest" (the west end) (see maps 1 and 2 and appendix 2).

Revolutionary Paris possessed specific gathering places, permanently animated by groups discussing politics, where men and women would rush to gain information about rumors. The garden of the Palais-Royal, renamed the Maison-Egalité in 1793, played a prominent role during the months of June and July 1789. Its walks were bordered by dress and perfume shops, jewelers, and bookstores; fruitsellers and *femmes du monde* (prostitutes) promenaded through its galleries. But the political heart of revolutionary Paris was the Convention, which convened in a room of the Tuileries. Petitioners and demonstrators marched to this destination; all around it, in the National Garden (today's Jardin des Tuileries), on its steps and its terrace, men and women harangued passersby on whatever they thought was needed to preserve the Revolution. Revolutionary crowds also congregated, to a lesser extent, in front of city hall and at the Jacobin club on the Rue du Faubourg Saint-Honoré.

Police spies worked at these hot spots, in the sections, the streets, the cabarets, the markets, and the theaters. The goal of these informers was

---

4. See Soboul, *Les Sans-culottes parisiens.* A partial translation into English can be found in Albert Soboul, *The Sans-Culottes: The Popular Movement and Revolutionary Government, 1793–1794,* trans. Remy Inglis Hall (Princeton, N.J.: Princeton University Press, 1980).

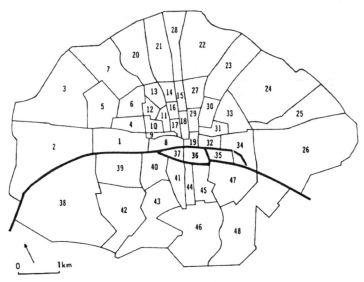

Map 1.   The forty-eight sections of Paris in 1790 (see appendix 2).

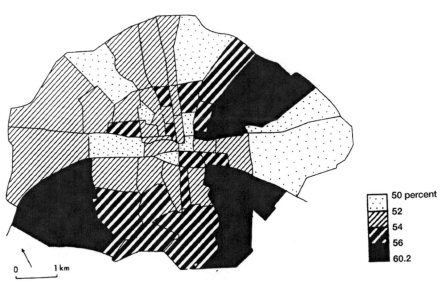

50 percent
52
54
56
60.2

Map 2.   Percentage of women in the total population. Source: Census of Pluviôse Year V.

not to aid the police by identifying thieves, criminals, and counterrevolutionaries but rather to study the mood of the public. Their job was to observe, without intervening, what occurred around them, and then to inform the minister of the interior on the state of public opinion. Their daily reports constitute a particularly rich resource for the historian.[5] For the most part, informers were intellectuals—teachers, lawyers, journalists, painters, and printers—frequently from modest backgrounds, who supported the Revolution.

Throughout the eighteenth century and during the Revolution, the division between public and private space was not as sharply demarcated as it would be later, nor had public space been identified as specifically masculine.[6] On the contrary, women of the people, wearing skirts and short gowns striped in the three national colors and caps "in the style of the nation," were often in the streets. Militant women proclaimed their political opinions by wearing medallions representing Marat or Robespierre around their necks, or a liberty cap. Hair cut short, *à la jacobine*, could indicate a political stance; tricolor cockades and ribbons were signs of revolutionary sympathy. And in this Revolution, which borrowed many of its symbols from antiquity, women dressed themselves *en amazone*. The costume of Louise Catherine Vignot, *La Charbonnière*, was not unusual: women preferred pants to heavy skirts for convenience, for security when they traveled, for deception when they wished to enlist in the army, out of habit when they returned from military service, or just out of whimsy. Dressed in this manner, housewives in search of provisions and workers trying to earn their living passed one another, jostled each other, and railed at one another in the streets of the capital.

Here in the streets were the washerwomen returning linen to their customers, hurrying with their irons and their small portable stoves to the washerwomen's boats moored on the Seine, and worrying about the price of soap or the difficulty of procuring it.[7] Their status was diverse. Some, to

---

5. These reports have been partially published in Pierre Caron, *Paris pendant la Terreur: Rapports des agents secrets du Ministère de l'Intérieur (27 août 1793–germinal an II)*, 6 vols. (Paris: 1920–1949), and Alphonse Aulard, *Paris pendant la réaction thermidorienne et sous le Directoire: Recueil de documents pour l'histoire de l'esprit public à Paris*, 5 vols. (Paris: 1898–1902). Examples without references are extracts from these police reports.

6. See Arlette Farge, *Vivre dans la rue à Paris au XVIIIe siècle* (Paris: Gallimard, 1979).

7. Soap, which cost 14 sous a pound in 1789, continued to increase in price until its price was set at 25 sous a pound (the legal maximum price on 29 September 1793). During the Year II, it was sold by coupon and delivered very slowly. Following the

their profit, laundered, mended, and ironed their customer's linen with the help of an apprentice or a charwoman. Some were specialists in the upkeep of fine linen. Some hired day laborers in the morning; others were small contractors who directed as many as twenty employees. The laundresses marked the physiognomy of the districts where they lived in great number: the Faubourg Saint-Marcel, le Gros-Caillou section of the Invalides, and the sections of the center that bordered the Seine. They were known for their bad character, their loose tongues, and their quick reactions. When, on the evening of 28 January 1794, a boat with approximately seventy laundresses on board broke loose and almost ran aground, the passersby who heard them cry at first shrugged their shoulders, convinced that the laundresses were arguing among themselves "as usual."[8] When necessary, women took advantage of the image of the virago, the label that society had given women who worked with other women and had an independent social life. The woman Marquet, accused of biting and kicking the corporal who interrupted her while she was stirring up a crowd against a pork butcher, responded "that she was born with an extremely violent character, that she is a laundress and that laundresses in general are not well-behaved people."[9] But make no mistake, laundresses' invectives targeted the privileged: merchants, the "rich," and the "moderates." And they were quick to leave their boats or their irons to defend an attacked sansculotte or lead a crowd of rebellious women. In a way, laundresses represented for women what shoemakers represented for men: they were a professional group with sansculotte tendencies. Thus, laundresses supported the spirit of one of the members of Babeuf's Conspiracy of Equals in Floréal Year IV (May 1796): "Salutations in democracy," he wrote, "yes, in democracy, because now we hear water carriers and laundresses say 'we are sovereign.'"[10]

When crossing the capital, it was difficult not to bump into one of the innumerable strolling female merchants who were inseparable from the Parisian landscape. At every street corner, they offered matches, tobacco, tinder, soap, thread, old hats, used clothes, canes, snuff boxes, stamped paper, cockades, ribbons, tisanes, coffee, rolls of bread, cakes, ginger bread, cherries, chestnuts, bunches of asparagus. . . . One could con-

---

suppression of the maximum on 4 Nivôse Year II (24 December 1794) and galloping inflation, the cost of soap increased in the Year III to the record price of 14 livres (one livre = 20 sous).

8. A.N., W 191, 9 Pluviôse Year II.

9. A.P.P., AA 136 f. 89.

10. A.N., F⁷ 4277.

tinue this inventory in the manner of Prévert, a reflection of the misery and the rage to survive of these women peddlers who lived "from day to day," ready to take advantage of the least opportunity, the smallest transaction that would enable them to pay their rent. Among them were workers without employment who sold their own belongings, rags, fruit, or anything else while they waited for better days. The riverside residents often complained of these peddlers whose cries troubled their tranquillity and whose displays of merchandise obstructed entry to their homes. In September 1793, the inhabitants of Rues Grenatat and Bourg-l'Abbé (a section of the Amis-de-la-Patrie), a gathering place for the merchants of pocketbooks, petitioned that these merchants be evicted because the "public road was interrupted" by their commerce and they were disturbed from five in the morning on by the "continuous uproar of the street fair."[11]

Some women possessed fragile wooden booths that, when bumped by a carriage, would fall and shatter. Hastily constructed, these booths were quickly demolished if they were built on another merchant's site. The widow Langlois, a vendor of bouquets and of oranges, had the habit of displaying her wares at the corner of the Quai de Gèvres and the Rue Planche-Mibray, an area that was forbidden to her many times because she blocked the thoroughfare. Thus she had the idea of constructing "a little booth" on the Notre Dame bridge; no sooner said than done, and at five o'clock in the morning, a carpenter showed it to her. Unfortunately, a merchant who had displayed rags for a long time on that spot, unable to "endure that anyone would set up a booth in her place," demolished it immediately with a hammer and the help of other vendors of the Notre Dame bridge.[12] These sorts of booths bordered the embankments of the right bank or were set against public monuments like the Louvre. In reality, these "booths" or "shops" were little more than a bit of tapestry for protection against the wind, a plank resting on wooden legs, a roof, or just a piece of ground to which merchants clung for economic and social reasons. These makeshift shelters represented integration into a community; they were proof that a merchant possessed her stable "place," that she did not have to "walk the streets" to sell her merchandise.

Dealers in secondhand goods were supposed to keep a book in which to write the names and addresses of people who had sold them their belongings, which they then resold. But many were quick to close their eyes on the

11. A.P.P., AA 49 f. 228.
12. A.P.P., AA 61 f. 151.

often suspicious origin of the merchandise offered to them; others, out of negligence or incapacity—many did not know how to read or write—did not keep their register up to date and ran the risk of arrest or severe reprimand.

Newspaper vendors shouted the titles of newspapers and pamphlets that they had gotten in the morning at the printer or the bookstore: "Robespierre has been arrested!" "The people are weary, they are dying of hunger, it is time that this ends!" These vendors, capable of moving public opinion and provoking gatherings by their announcements, served, voluntarily or not, the cause of various political groups. Thus, in the months after the fall of Robespierre, certain vendors contributed to the movement against the Jacobins by selling pamphlets hostile to them. In the Year III, many vendors were interrogated who, through militancy or ignorance, sold newspapers like Babeuf's *Le Tribun du Peuple*. On 23 Ventôse Year III (13 March 1795), the widow Vignon was questioned because she sold the insurrectional brochures *Peuple, réveille-toi, il est temps* and *Au Peuple des vérités terribles mais indispensables;* upon her release, she was arrested for the same offense two days later, and the authorities took care to note that her newspapers' ink was still fresh. Thérèse Pillet, who at the moment of her arrest two months later made certain that her newspapers rapidly disappeared, had the habit when announcing her titles of adding phrases judged to be "contrary to the preservation of public order": "Here is *Le Courrier républicain*, which screws us with hunger," "Discourse of General Pichegru, who is now getting his for having smacked us with his whip."[13]

In the center of Paris, la Halle, like all the other Parisian markets (at the Place Maubert, Saint-Germain-des-Prés, Patriarches, and so on), was a space populated by women. Female merchants and housewives contested the price of basic food items but had to come to terms with the great merchant monopolizers—those who hoarded products to increase their price or secretly resold goods above the maximum legal price. On the square paving stones of la Halle, women discussed the price of goods as well as the course of the Revolution; police observers noted with concern their "murmurings," the signs of their "bad humor." The women of la Halle were small re-

13. A.N., F⁷ 4687 d. Dumont and F⁷ 4775⁴⁶ d. Vignon; F⁷ 4775²⁶ d. Tessier and F⁷ 4774⁷⁵ d. Pillet.

tailers who sold their merchandise in small quantities to women who lived on the outskirts of Paris and came to sell their products on the Parisian market. As intermediaries in the market, these women had all kinds of problems; when it was difficult to get merchandise from the suburbs, as in spring of the Year II (1794), they were obliged to go out in the early morning before the provision carts, thus breaking the ordinances that forbade the circulation of merchandise at night. As retailers, they depended on larger, more important merchants and had to deal with them directly as consumers. The menacing crowd of fish merchants that formed on 25 Pluviôse Year II (13 February 1794) on the bridge of Saint-Paul exemplifies this aspect of their work. There was very little fish available at the ports on that day, and the retail merchants who had come to stock up threatened a wholesale dealer whom they accused of carrying fish in the night to large merchants and to caterers. Their complaints illustrate their position perfectly: "We who rush to sell in the streets, we cannot earn our living at all; when we come in the morning to get our merchandise we are told there is none, that the stock has already been distributed today. We know that the boats are still full. . . . This is a trick to support the hoarders."[14] These words are similar to the consumers' complaints. But, as "middlewomen," the merchants were often arrested for selling above the legal limit, which was too low for them to make the little profit necessary to buy bread. As members of the common people, wives or mothers of volunteer soldiers, they loved the Revolution and took pride in having "chased the tyrant out of his criminal lair, Versailles" on the fifth and sixth of October 1789. However, their trade inclined them to favor the rich who paid better, and it was convenient for them to adopt moderate political positions.

In the markets, very poor women shelled peas and grouped them by size, or peeled chestnuts for merchants. Female porters carried on their backs merchants' baskets that frequently weighed at least forty kilos. Other women passed in the street, bent under loads of charcoal, wood, or water for private clients. Ragpickers, practically beggars, rummaged through refuse with their hooks. There was probably not a single occupation in Paris in which women without work did not take part in order to gain the several sous that were still often not enough for their basic needs. Let the least accident, the least sickness, fall on the poorest families, and you would meet them "racing across Paris" to offer their services to whoever might need them.

14. A.N., W 191, 25 Pluviôse Year II.

Thus women were busy from dawn to twilight; the day passed, filled with the daily occurrences of work, the announcements and discussions of revolutionary events, interspersed with stops on the steps of the Tuileries, meetings of the Convention, or with breaks at the tavern when work became too onerous. In the evenings, the knitting women, their work under their arms, gathered in the galleries of the sections or the clubs. Households did not immediately fall asleep; when the weather was good, renters brought chairs into the courtyard or onto the doorstep, read the newspaper together, and gave their opinions on recent events. One example among others: on 5 July 1793, at 9:30 at night, Mazurier's wife and daughter enjoyed the coolness of the evening, "seated in the street at the door of their house" in the company of two neighbor women and a neighbor man, and "they discussed whether the section would accept the constitutional act" (the Constitution of 1793, submitted to popular referendum).[15] Then night fell and prostitutes took possession of the streets.

On 4 October 1793, city hall passed a decree that forbade "all prostitutes to gather in the streets, promenades, and public places and incite men to libertine behavior and debauchery, under pain of arrest and transport to the court of petty sessions as corrupters of morality and disturbers of public order." The police commissioners were instructed "to make frequent visits to the neighborhoods infected with libertine behavior," and the patrols were told to arrest "all the girls and women of bad life whom they found inciting to libertine behavior."[16] From this date on, the commissioners organized street sweeps of prostitutes.

Most arrests were concentrated in several neighborhoods. Almost 42 percent of the arrests were made on the border of the Seine, around the Place de Grève, in the sections of Arcis, and near city hall. In these streets, male and female lodging-house keepers, couples who acted as procurers and kept bordellos, "gave asylum" to the wretched "swallows of Port-au-Blé" in return for a percentage or an exorbitant rent. Toward the west, in the galleries of the Palais-Royal, in adjoining passages, or in the Jardin des Tuileries, patrols questioned women who denied being "public women" but admitted that they were kept by several "friends"; those who were arrested while soliciting were in a difficult financial situation. In happier times, though, they sometimes lived on a grand scale with several domestic ser-

---

15. A.P.P., AA 176, 6 July 1793.
16. *Moniteur,* XVIII, 41–42.

vants, gave elegant suppers, and were on a first name basis with young bourgeois and with fashionable actors and singers (the golden youth of the Year III), counterrevolutionaries who supported them. Outside of these two great centers, Paris sheltered other islands of prostitution: the garden and taverns of the Champs-Elysées; the Courtille; the streets of Champ-Fleuri, Jean-Saint-Denis, and Chantereine; Place Maubert; and the courtyard of the Palais de Justice.

For the most part, prostitutes were very young girls who lived outside the context of a stable family unit, as in the classic case of the young provincial woman arriving in Paris who, after seeking work in vain, was obliged to prostitute herself in order to live. An impressive number of "public women" admitted that they turned tricks "for lack of work." Many affirmed that poverty and need drove them to streetwalking, and that they preferred this work to stealing, adding sometimes that they hurt no one except themselves. When they were arrested, some expressed aversion for their circumstances. Admitted to the guard house of Arcis section in the night of 29 Germinal Year II (18 April 1794), Françoise Rousseau, a thirty-five-year-old dressmaker, explained that she was "a poor unhappy prostitute" who had spent the night outside and asked permission to warm herself; she declared to the police commissioner that without work and having sold all her belongings, "she had to do something in order to live" and addressed to him the following request: "Citizen Commissioner, please send me to the hospital where I will be much better off than in practicing this trade." She had worked as a prostitute for only one month. Others who had adopted prostitution as their trade were constantly repelled by it. Gabrielle Saron, a twenty-four-year-old prostitute, was found dead on 13 August 1793. The inquest suggested that this was a case of suicide, and her neighbors all affirmed that when she was drunk, she would repeat "that she was weary of her trade and wanted to kill herself."[17]

Although unemployment was usually the reason women became prostitutes, all prostitutes were not in the same situation. Some women completely abandoned their first occupation, whereas others solicited only periodically, as part-time work. A significant number of "women of the world" practiced another trade but solicited after their work was finished. Others had been sent to prison or to the hospital, for whatever reason, and

17. A.P.P., AA 60, 23 Pluviôse Year II, 29 Germinal Year II (Françoise Rousseau) and AA 249, 13 August 1793 (Gabrielle Saron).

had to prostitute themselves when they got out, lacking other resources to earn their living. Some prostitutes were arrested many times and incarcerated again only a few days after their liberation: Madeleine Deshayes was arrested on 1 April 1793; set free on 29 June, she was arrested again the next day, then on the first and the twenty-sixth of December 1793, and finally on 17 October 1794, although it had been only two days since she had gotten out of the Hôtel-Dieu.[18]

Prostitutes were often in contact with a milieu composed of thieves, gamblers, swindlers, and deserters. The men acted as pimps; the prostitutes sometimes gave their pimps almost all of their profit or the wallets stolen from customers, and warned them when they were about to be arrested. In contrast, certain prostitutes informed the authorities about thieves and deserters.[19] Others, out of patriotism or fear of being compromised, came of their own accord to denounce counterrevolutionaries whom they often met.

Believing that "the Revolution and liberty . . . could stand only on public morality," revolutionaries judged prostitution and prostitutes with severity.[20] In 1789, women proposed that prostitutes be forced to wear a distinctive badge or be restricted to specific neighborhoods.[21] Others, aware of the economic causes of prostitution, wished to remedy this through education that would mix reading and writing with professional apprenticeship.[22] In line with these projects, in September 1793, the Parisian club of the Société des Citoyennes Républicaines Révolutionnaires (Society of Revolutionary Republican Women) demanded that "prostitutes be moved to state-run houses in order to occupy them with useful work and, if possible, return these unhappy victims of libertine behavior, whose hearts were often good, and whom poverty alone almost always reduced to this deplorable state, to morality through patriotic lectures."[23] This was no longer simply a question of vocational training, but the club's demand was not just repressive;

---

18. A.P.P., AA 59, 30 June 1793, 11 Frimaire Year II, AA 60, 6 Nivôse Year II, AA 61, 26 Vendémiaire Year II.

19. See E. M. Benabou, *La Prostitution et la police des moeurs au XVIIIe siècle* (Paris: Perrin, 1987).

20. See note 17.

21. See for example *Pétition des femmes du tiers-état au roi*, 1 January 1789, or Olympe de Gouges's postface to her *Déclaration des droits de la femme et de la citoyenne*, in *Cahiers de doléances des femmes et autres textes*, ed. P. M. Duhet (Paris: Editions des femmes, 1981).

22. See, for example, *Vues législatives pour les femmes; Mademoiselle Jodin, Mémoire sur l'éducation des filles* (1790); or Bachelier, in *Les Femmes dans la Révolution* (Paris: Edhis, 1982), nos. 24 and 4.

23. *Moniteur*, XVII, 661, 679, 699.

[handwritten margin note: wish to reform prost. through civic and pol. edu. → seen as "good" victims]

it expressed the wish for a reformation of prostitutes through civic and political education. It took into account the condition of prostitutes, who were
not considered to be irrevocably lost—their hearts remained "good" but
they were the victims of poverty and needed to be educated. Thus, the Society of Revolutionary Republican Women demanded that they "be treated
with all the goodness and humanity that their sex and position required in
order that, when peace returned, they could be sent back redeemed into society, act as good citizens and become wives and mothers." Of this program,
the decree of 4 October 1793, taken from an indictment by the city prosecutor Chaumette, showed only the repressive side with not a word about
the poverty of prostitutes or their individual fates, or the possibility of rein-
tegrating them into society. They were no longer considered to be victims,
and incarceration, without any possibility of moral or professional rehabilitation, became the means envisioned to "save the country" by "purifying
the atmosphere of liberty from the contagious breath of libertine behavior." The concern was more to hide "vice" from the eyes of young men than
to fight prostitution. The exercise of prostitution was not expressly forbidden; rather, prostitutes were forbidden "to incite libertine behavior and debauchery" in public places.

[handwritten margin note: reality = lock them up, save the young]

After this decree, some prostitutes sought "honest" work to survive, but
this was difficult. The work crisis that affected many professions, salaries
for women that were often too meager to support a decent life, the departure into the army of men who could have helped them financially, and the
terrible situation of the Year III ceaselessly pushed women into the shadow
of the night.

Night and day, working-class women crossed narrow, dirty, and muddy
streets, sometimes brightened by red caps or allegories of Liberty that were
painted by inhabitants on the walls of houses. Violence was everywhere; it
was necessary to be on guard to avoid becoming the target of an individual's fury. Moreover, female passersby had to evade "indecent physical contact" and "fraternal kisses" demanded by drunken male citizens. However—a sign of the times—a coachman who accosted an unknown woman
with "hey honey, hey good looking, would you like a ride in my carriage"
was apt to be severely reminded by the police commissioner "that a lack of
respect is a violation of the law and the oath of republicans."[24] Women were

24. A.P.P., AA 92, 15 October 1793.

not only the objects but also the perpetrators of this day-to-day violence. Verbal violence was common—insults (whore, thief, fish, bitch) were standard fare between neighbors or coworkers. Death threats were fewer but expressive: a merchant of la Halle threatened to kill another "by saying that she wished to walk across her throat"; a laundress declared to her neighbor "that she wanted to eat her grilled heart."[25] Insults and threats quickly became blows. The official reports of police commissioners are full of examples of fights between women, which upset no one as long as they did not exceed certain limits. Usually, the female brawlers escaped with just bruises and scratches, but it was not uncommon for the plaintiff to put down a handful of her torn hair as evidence on the commissioner's desk. The relationship between the violence of social relations and revolutionary violence is self-evident. Why consider these insults as merely imaginative imprecations against an enemy, and then believe that the revolutionaries who were accused of "ferocious" or "bloody" words really had the intention of grilling the hearts of their enemies? Is it not fraudulent to invoke the (real) violence of revolutionary crowds without remembering the daily violence of the eighteenth century, which, moreover, is not restricted to the revolutionary period or to the working class? This is not to say that the men and women who created the Revolution were the ferocious brutes dear to counterrevolutionary historiography. The historian knows and must not forget that the behavior and gestures that expressed their sensibility is not immutable across the centuries.

Working-class women did not figure on the public scene as puppets, as articulate but soulless figures. They were stirred by all their human richness and complexity, their dreams and their wounds in which family relations often held a large place. Movement and violence, precariousness and solidarity, Revolution and daily life can be found in the realm of sentiment as well as in the theater of urban life.

25. A.P.P., AA 185, 2 July 1793, and AA 228 f. 213.

2 Family Relations of Women of the People

THE SEARCH FOR HAPPINESS
Union

"You know, citizen, that there is nothing in the world that is more precious than a husband, especially when you have the happiness to be well matched and to love each other."[1] The washerwoman who wrote these lines actually possessed what men and women of the people desired: a home, a haven of peace, love, regard, and stability, where they could be surrounded by the tranquillity denied to them by an often very uncertain life. We can see the search for happiness through a stable union in many remarks by young girls, remarks punctuated by words such as *happiness, household, friendship,* and *love.* The stable and happy family group, simultaneously dream and reality, was indisputably the ideal of the Parisian sansculottes, who made a political virtue out of the desire to found a family: the fifth reason for the arrest of eighty-three-year-old Angrand, a noble, the uncle of an *émigré,* and a former president of the Parliament of Paris, was that he had always been a bachelor and, therefore, a selfish person.[2]

Marriage represented both a promise of emotional security and a desire for economic security. Women saw it as a means of becoming established, both emotionally and socially. Two young girls who declared their pregnancy to the police commissioner had no qualms explaining, one, that she had agreed to her boss's request because "she expected to benefit from his proposition," the other, a dealer in used goods, that, desiring a business, she had "consented to marry" a young man who dazzled her by his

1. A.N., W 115 f. 1.
2. A.N. F⁷ 4580 d. Angrand.

17

station as a master in the trade of used clothes.[3] The married couple functioned as a partnership between workers and among working people whose sole property often amounted to honor, strength, and skill on the job;[4] men also chose their future companions according to whether they possessed these qualities. The young dressmaker Marie Madeleine Simon was asked for in marriage by a tailor who appreciated her "diligence at work and the regularity of her conduct." Another tailor had taught the trade of breechesmaker to a young worker whom he proposed to marry "in order to work together in the future and set up a household."[5] Marriage was a serious matter and not to be taken lightly. Parents often had their opinions, and interested parties sought to assure themselves that their sentiment was not ephemeral, the passion of a day that would lead to a commitment they might regret all their lives. "It is necessary to test oneself and know the object that one desires to possess before risking a proposal of marriage" responded a wise young girl to a suitor whose proposal she judged to be "too hasty."[6] The getting-acquainted period that preceded the nuptials was in certain cases pushed rather far, sometimes as far as living together without marriage.

Though marriage was desired by many women as the final goal of their relation with a man, free union was a common practice among Parisian popular milieus. Unmarried couples were like married couples in the eyes of their friends and relations, who did not see their unions as either tainted by debauchery or as gestures of defiance against society. The woman was, moreover, usually called by the name of her companion; this appellation could survive an eventual breakup, and unmarried couples spoke of their partner as their "wife" or their "husband." In fact, from the moment they began to live together, the existence of an official document was secondary. The militant revolutionary Bodson was not married, but he considered that

3. A.P.P., AA 77 f. 208 and A.N., F⁷ 4686 d. M. L. Dugardin.
After an edict of 1556 to prevent infanticide, single women had to declare their pregnancies to the authorities. These declarations were often accompanied by a complaint against the seducer in order to make him pay the costs of pregnancy and child support. In 1791, the declarations were implicitly suppressed (infanticide henceforth had to be proven), but the habit of making them remained at least up to 1795; all the declarations that have been found are in fact complaints against the seducer.
4. See Arlette Farge and Michel Foucault, *Le Désordre des familles: Lettres de cachet à Paris au XVIIIe siècle* (Paris: Gallimard, 1982).
5. A.P.P, AA 163 f. 278 and AA 186 f. 371.
6. A.P.P., AA 229 f. 193.

"it was as if he were married, with a wife and a child whom he had adopted." The actor Dieu asserted that "because of the freedom to worship, he did not believe that this question was important." Like numerous sansculottes, the police observer Perrière thought that "it was the publicity of the union that formed the chief characteristic of marriage" and that, consequently, one could not say that a female citizen, "known in her entire district for having lived for years with a man by whom she has had many children, is not the wife of this citizen."[7]

Sometimes one of the partners was already legally married. Frequently, the already married man did not tell his companion until several years had passed, when the ties of cohabitation had already been formed; they then continued to live together as a couple little different from a legitimate couple. Servants, employees, and companions also sometimes lived "maritally" with their bosses, in mutual affection. In contrast, there were couples, sometimes with children, who "lived together" in separate lodgings. Depending on their economic circumstances and disposable goods, a man and a woman could live together, take separate lodgings while continuing to see each other regularly, and then share the same apartment again "because it is easier for two to pay the rent than one."[8] Free union also represented an economic association. Couples set up a household together and would eventually work together.

In most cases, a consort recognized his children, if he were certain they were his. Some fathers, however, although continuing to live under the same roof with the mother, refused to give their name to their children. In this case, they often urged their companion to abandon their children at the Enfants de la Patrie, formerly the Enfants Trouvés (foundling hospital). Women did not always agree readily to this. Some couples eventually married, but it is remarkable how long it took for these marriages to occur. The majority declared that they were "intending to marry" and "on the verge" of marriage, sometimes giving as proof the legal steps they had taken at city hall, but marriage seemed only a formality—certainly not unimportant, but not urgent because it did not much change daily life. One had the impression that at the end of two or three years of communal life, if the partners saw that their union was happy and peaceful, that they got along well, they would decide to go to city hall, but not in a great hurry. And it seemed

7. A.N., F⁷ 4774⁸⁶ d. Raberaut; A.P.P., AA 240 f. 5; A.N., W 112, 11 Ventôse.
8. A.P.P., AA 174, 19 June 1793.

that, after this delay, even if they remained a couple, there was little chance that they would someday make their union legitimate.

[handwritten margin note: marriage = important, bc stability —> free union more common]

On 11 March 1793, Bastien Denand, a tobacco shredder who had engaged voluntarily to "fight the rebels of the Vendée," requested that the police commissioner of the Tuileries section "receive his statement that he regarded Marie Valard, a worker, as if he had married her, that he recognized the child that they had conceived together as his child, as well as the one whom she carried in her womb; that desiring that the said Valard with whom he had lived and shared the fruits of his labor for three years, would profit from the advantages given by the section to the wives of citizens who left for the Vendée," he asked to have his statement duly notarized.[9]

There are many statements like this in the archives, because, after the declaration of war on 20 April 1792, and the draft of three hundred thousand men on 24 February 1793, the government and the sections decided to give financial help to the families of volunteers and drafted soldiers. But was the unmarried female consort of a soldier part of his family in the eyes of the law? The sections, responsible for distributing this aid, had different responses to this question. For example, on 15 May 1793, the Museum section decided that the "respectable companion" of citizen Levasseur, Anne Lemaure, a lacemaker, could not claim the aid meant for soldiers' wives "because she is outside of the law since she is not married to citizen Levasseur"; also, continued the assembly general, "it is henceforth the responsibility of the section to provide for this female citizen; and in acquitting such a sacred debt, the section still does not make a great sacrifice." Anne Lemaure thus received forty livres a month taken from the four hundred livres that her companion would receive when he returned from the army.[10] Other sections adopted the same type of measure, a palliative for deputies' silence on the status of "natural" families of soldiers. In this state of indecision, the Bon-Conseil section complained at the Convention about the vagueness of the law, which "said nothing about those interested people who until now a barbarous prejudice has considered to be illegitimate" and which "is equally silent about female citizens who become pregnant out of a sentiment of tenderness before having fulfilled the desire of the law, that is to

9. A.P.P., AA 248, 11 March 1793.
10. A.N., F⁷ 4774²¹ d. Levasseur.

say, who omit the formality required by the law in order to authorize their union."[11]

Not all sections faced with these problems of lower-class life showed such understanding, and many refused all indemnity to unmarried women. Several police informers, citing public opinion, were indignant and demanded that the Convention issue a clear decree on this matter. They observed that it was illogical to recognize legitimate and illegitimate children as equal in receiving inheritance—by law of 12 Brumaire Year II (2 November 1793)—yet deny that all children were equally eligible for financial assistance. The Montagnards were also concerned with this question: on 8 Ventôse Year II (26 February 1794), Leonard Bourdon demanded that the Jacobins interest themselves in the fate of the "honest female citizens who found themselves living in poverty after the departure of their *natural* husbands for the army."[12] The Convention responded in part to these demands and on 13 Prairial Year II (1 June 1794), decreed that the beneficiaries of the law in favor of children, mothers, and widows of soldiers included "the children recognized by the defenders of the fatherland, who remained orphans or were reunited at their home as a family, as well as their mothers when they have faithfully fulfilled the duties of maternity by their continuous care before and after the father's enlistment."[13] This was a rather ambiguous, halfhearted measure, because it was not their right as "natural wives" but as mothers of natural children that allowed these women to receive aid; the case of women without children was not even addressed. In spite of this, we must emphasize that this measure was both significant and innovative. Having "forgotten" the numerous illegitimate families, the Montagnard deputies knew how to empirically adapt to the social reality of the working class. After the fall of Robespierre's followers, many sections taken over by the moderates revoked this measure and refused to give assistance to women and illegitimate children.

The problems faced by soldiers' companions illustrate that the state of free union, although a current social practice, did not have the same official value as marriage during the Revolution. Authorities easily grew suspicious of those who lived outside of the law. When the actor Dieu became

11. A.N., W 174, no date.
12. *Moniteur*, XIX, 590.
13. *Moniteur*, XX, 630.

furious after he was asked if he was "really married," the police commissioner retorted "that it is indeed true that freedom of religion is the law but that this same law requires a civil contract."[14] The expressions used by revolutionary committees in lists of inquiries about prisoners stated: "We suspect that there is no marriage between her and citizen Armé"; "A woman with whom Citizen Richelieu lives secretly."[15] The status of the unmarried female consort often brought an additional charge against a person under indictment. For certain commissioners, there was little difference between a consort and a prostitute. And the lower-class habit of calling a woman by the name of her companion, a sign of the social acceptance of free union, was considered illegal by the police commissioner of the République section. He added to the charge of complicity in theft the fact that the "girl Dallemagne" (who calls herself the wife of Deperche, a citizen whose bans of marriage have been published) "had deceived us by calling herself married and by taking a name not her own, a misdemeanor according to the law," a misdemeanor that could put her in prison.[16] Those who confuse legality with illegitimacy, beware! Companions who claim to be legitimately married spouses and risk making the law meaningless, beware! This conflict persisted, however, and authorities, willingly or not, put up with free union, which only became "suspicious" in the case of previous disputes between the law and the unmarried couple.

Many parents, who believed that only marriage was respectable, also rejected free union and reproached their children repeatedly or even cut off all ties with them. If the free union was prolonged, women often felt this to be a defeat, for most agreed to cohabitate with men in the hope that they would marry one day. For some, though not many, the admission that they were not married was a painful avowal, a secret wound jealously guarded and confessed in a final sigh. The death of one of the partners showed moreover that free union remained unsatisfying; death could bring about a rectification of the situation, sometimes posthumously, in memory of the deceased. Citizen Lankin, a jeweler from the Pont-Neuf section, told the police commissioner that the evening before, when he had declared the death of Madeleine Bénard, his servant, he had described her as a "children's governess." "His state of sorrow had not let him reflect on the title given to the said Madeleine Bénard," who had entered into his service two and a half years ago but with whom "he had soon formed closer ties," with whom he

14. A.P.P., AA 240 f. 5.
15. A.N., F⁷ 4775⁴⁷ d. Villot and F⁷* 2507 p. 31.
16. A.P.P., AA 228 f. 104–110.

had had a child that he had recognized, and with whom "he was going to link his fate . . . by the ties of marriage." In consequence, he corrected his first declaration and asked that the qualification of "lover and wife who had lived with him for more than two years" be substituted for that of children's governess.[17] More frequently, a marriage would be performed at the bedside of a dying partner, largely out of concern for the economic protection of the survivor. Having fallen sick, the painter Mathis called a police commissioner to his bedside, where "wishing to provide for the well-being of his child as well as for female citizen Rosier" with whom he had lived for seven years, he declared before two witnesses that he "took her for his wife and the little girl for his child."[18]

Marriage brought relative security that did not accompany free union. Although careful consideration occurred before marriage, the decision to live as a couple happened much more quickly. Marguerite Henry, a nineteen-year-old dressmaker, "explained that having met Citizen Ruyer, an employee at the post office, he appeared . . . a good citizen. Her youth and her lack of experience made her succumb to the propositions of this wretched man, who should have married her because he had promised her a happy condition. She had not hesitated before joining her fate with his and living with him."[19] These phrases express everything about women's expectations and marriage. Women saw cohabitation as a door to marriage, from which they expected happiness. If at the end of several months a young girl realized that her companion's conduct did not correspond to that of a good husband, she left him without much difficulty. Several months of life in common was only an experience, although an unhappy experience, but it might keep a young woman from linking her fate to a man who would have mistreated her all her life. However, it was rare that free union benefited a woman. Not all women whose companions behaved badly left after a few months. Some endured quarrels and blows for several years, hoping that the situation would eventually right itself, and if they finally decided to separate, it was because they no longer had any hope. The words of Anne Louise Paris have the bitter taste of the death of youthful illusions: "For eighteen years, she had lived with Thomas Pernet as his wife," but he was prone to such excess towards her that she feared for her life. Five days ago

17. A.P.P., AA 216 f. 246.
18. A.P.P., AA 186 f. 189.
19. A.N., F⁷ 4741 d. Henry.

he showed her the door, refusing to return to her the furniture that she had brought to him "when she had moved in with him in the hope of marrying him"; moreover, he had sold part of the belongings "that she had brought when she came to live with him in the hope of marriage and a household."[20]

On 11 Ventôse Year II (1 March 1794), the police observer Perrière, always attentive to the concerns of working-class women, requested a law that would punish "severely whoever lived openly with a woman and then abandoned her and her children conceived while living with him."[21] Of the women who declared their pregnancy to the police commissioner from 1793 to 1795, 16 percent had lived in free union with the future father. However, in 70 percent of the cases, the cause of the declaration was not abandonment but the fact that the father was at the army (25 percent) or already married (5 percent), or that the partners had decided to separate (15 percent). Furthermore, 25 percent of "natural fathers" recognized their children. That leaves 30 percent of known cases of abandonment of unmarried women. If we take into account those cases where the cause of the declaration is unknown, this percentage is reduced to 23 percent, because it is likely that a woman married to a man who abandoned her when she was pregnant would state this to the commissioner. This figure represents only 0.04 percent of the total declarations of pregnancy from 1793 to 1795. However, we only know about the abandonment of pregnant unmarried women. In addition, the breakup of an illegal union by a man shocked and outraged public opinion, for this was not just the act of a fickle man who left a young seduced girl to her tears, but that of an "unnatural" father of a family. Contemporaries sympathized with the fate of an abandoned woman with children whose wages would allow her to raise them only with difficulty. For women, free union was uncertain, without any assurance of economic security for themselves and their children. This led in part to a woman's search for marriage and contributed to the dislike that prudent parents had for this type of relationship, which left their daughter so vulnerable.

The archives also contain many statements from young girls who abruptly learned from their lover or through public knowledge that he was about to marry another woman, even though they had lived together for several years, and only several days before he had repeated a promise of marriage to her. These abandoned young girls did not represent "good"

20. A.P.P., AA 49, 25 Germinal Year II.
21. A.N., W 112, 11 Ventôse Year II.

choices for marriage: they were workers, strolling merchants, and often had no family in the capital. We know nothing of these women abandoned by their companions, but we can suppose that men (mostly artisans) would sometimes live for several years with poor women whom they cared for and probably loved, who recognized the children that they had together but preferred not to marry them legally and thus cut off their chances for a better alliance. These men were then free to return and seek with their previous companion a happiness that they did not always find with their legitimate spouse.

The Nurturer

Responsibilities were divided between men and women, as part of society's model of a good husband and a good wife, and were central to the definition of a couple, whether or not their relationship was legally recognized. Although the wages of a woman were not insubstantial, popular opinion believed the man should "provide for the needs of the household." Women expected their consort to assume this responsibility, which was recognized by all of society. The man who refused this obligation broke a tacit contract between him and his companion. Thus Marie Anne Maison preferred to risk living alone during her illegitimate pregnancy rather than continue to live with her consort who, she said, "instead of treating her maritally and humanely, refused her the daily expenses for food for the house, which she was obliged to provide by her work."[22] The man knew that he had to support his family, under pain of failure and emotional and social dishonor. During a quarrel, Marie Jeanne Boucher cried to her companion of sixteen years: "Tear my bonnet, Cadet, you are in no condition to give me another." This derisive insult showed the scorn she felt towards a man who did not know how to fulfill his responsibilities and completely overwhelmed Cadet who, mad with pain and humiliation, stabbed the woman he loved with his saber.[23]

As for the tasks performed by women in the family, they are described perfectly by the author of the *Lettres bougrement patriotiques de la Mère Duchesne*: "If I did not put my household into order, if I did not establish an exact agreement between receipts and expenses, I would suffer, especially with a husband who drinks like six men and who eats like four, and

22. A.P.P., AA 163 f. 296.
23. A.P.P., AA 185, 5 March 1793.

with a bunch of children who always have open mouths. Indeed, without boasting, I can say that Pétronille Mâche-Fer is one of the best housekeepers in the district."[24]

The housewife was responsible for managing the household money and so it was usually in her possession. Some husbands gave their wives a fixed sum per month, or what they requested; other husbands gave their wives everything that they earned. This seems like a handsome gesture. However, this was also a way to get rid of everyday calculation, to reject the daily anguish caused by an inadequate purse. In this division of labor, the man brought money home, and the women transformed it, no matter the amount, into good steaming soup on the table. The housewife as nurturer had to find the food necessary to nourish her household and to ensure that everything appeared on time. Quarrels broke out if dinner was not yet ready or if the soup was not hot when the man returned from work. When he could not come home at night, she brought his supper to him. If she did not have the time to prepare dinner because of her own work, she gave him money for his meal every morning. The role of nurturer was firmly anchored in public opinion and was used to defend women arrested for violence before the empty stalls of bakers or butchers. "The bad mood of this wretched woman arises from the fact that she could not procure food for her husband when he returned from his work" we read in the memoir of a woman imprisoned for a disturbance at a baker's door.[25]

These women worked at keeping their households alive rather than doing housework (a relatively rapid task in lower-class lodgings of one or two hastily furnished rooms). Household furnishings usually consisted of the marriage bed, children's beds, one or two tables, chairs, stools, and sometimes armchairs. Clothes, sheets, and dish towels were kept in a wardrobe, or more frequently in a chest of drawers. Sometimes there would be a chest, a trunk, a small trunk, or boxes for organizing the remainder or papers (ration cards for bread, baptism certificates, marriage certificate, parents' death certificates, letters, and so on). The stove spread warmth, helped at times by foot-warmers. The chimes of the clock were rarely heard; the watch on the mantelpiece marked time in many homes. Kitchen utensils (plates, spoons,

---

24. *Lettres bougrement patriotiques de la Mère Duchesne,* letter 4. *Lettres bougrement patriotiques* appeared every week on Tuesday and Saturday in Paris. We do not know whether their author was a woman, and issues were not dated.

25. A.N., F⁷ 4654 d. Cotte.

knives and forks, goblets, platters, saucepans, and coffee pots) were kept in the sideboard. Frames for quilting petticoats, irons, and spinning wheels showed the lodgers' work. The father's pike naturally had its place in the sansculotte house, perhaps beside busts of Voltaire, Rousseau, or Marat. Engravings or a mirror might decorate the walls.[26]

Her basket under her arm, the lower-class housewife, who was not at all a "lady of the house," accomplished her duties in the street, at the market, and by waiting in lines. Yet some revolutionaries believed that women were prescribed by nature to develop only in the private sphere. The only area where women, "divinities (of the) domestic sanctuary," were in their place was the inside of their homes, thought the city prosecutor Chaumette.[27] Rousseau had written that "nature and reason prescribe [them]" to stay "shut up in their homes" and to "limit all their cares to their home and their family," without passing "suddenly from the shadow of the enclosure and from domestic cares to the injuries of air, work, fatigue, and the perils of war."[28] The journalist Prudhomme, who explicitly recognized Rousseau's influence, implored women to "stay at home, to watch over their households," and to "never seek news outside of their home" but to wait for it and receive it "only from the mouths of their fathers or their children, their brothers or their husbands."[29] From this writing, which sought to undermine women's participation in politics, a vision of male and female roles in the family (and in politics) arose that differs from what we see in the archives. Even in the words of those who granted female citizens the right to inform themselves, we see a link between women and private life in the discourse of men of the lower middle and middle class. Although most of the more popular elements of the sansculottes affirmed that women should dedicate themselves above all to the "cares of their household," they never said that women should "return to the heart of their household." Their rejection of political participation by women was not synonymous with confinement in the home. Though the terms at first appear similar, there is a difference between the visions that bourgeois and lower-class men had of

26. On working-class furnishings in the eighteenth century, see Daniel Roche, *The People of Paris: An Essay in Popular Culture in the Eighteenth Century*, trans. Marie Evans in association with Gwynne Lewis (Berkeley: University of California Press, 1987).
27. Speech of 27 Brumaire Year II (17 November 1793), in *Moniteur*, XVIII, 450.
28. Jean Jacques Rousseau, *Emile ou l'Education* (1762; Paris: Garnier-Flammarion, 1966), pp. 476–477.
29. *Les Révolutions de Paris*, 185 and 213.

mentalités ——→ m/c /bouy goals ≠
lower class goals

women's place in society. The image of a housewife cloistered in a "domestic sanctuary" was a bourgeois vision that, because it did not take into account the real conditions of existence for women of the people, could only apply to women of the bourgeoisie with servants who could go out in their place. Here we witness a shift in the history of *mentalités* (collective mental attitudes)—and in the history of women—when a vision of male and female roles took shape and became diffused. This vision was at first only characteristic of the middle class but triumphed when the bourgeoisie established its political and economic power at the end of the Revolution and its ideological discourse became the dominant discourse.

Entrusted with nourishing the family and acutely concerned with the difficulties of finding basic necessities, women were also responsible for children. The lower-class housewife was often on the go and took her children with her for fear that the youngest, left alone at the house, would be burned by the stove or fall out the window. Thus you would see children at their mother's breast, in her arms, and holding on to her hand, in lines, in workshops, in the public areas of courts of justice, in political assemblies, and even in insurgent crowds. Some housewives, although not rich, preferred to send their children out to nurse in the environs of Paris for a year or two. Recourse to contraceptives, which spread little by little in the eighteenth century, can be seen in the remarks of a greengrocer who accused her neighbor of taking "medicines to excrete her children in the chamber pot."[30] However, women still had an impressive number of pregnancies: twenty-five! twenty-seven! (including miscarriages and stillborn children).

discourse!

Without entering into the debate on attitudes toward the child in past centuries,[31] we can nonetheless say that there are numerous traces in the archives of maternal and paternal love. The belief that a child should be protected was not restricted to philosophers of the Enlightenment such as Rousseau. Mothers guarded their children, and it was not uncommon that a dispute between children ended in an exchange of words or blows between their mothers. When mothers were obliged to abandon their children and to commit them to the Enfants de la Patrie, either because the couple could not nourish a new mouth or because the women were single and unable to

30. A.P.P., AA 228 f. 102.
31. See for example Philippe Aries, *Centuries of Childhood: A Social History of Family Life,* trans. Robert Baldick (New York: Knopf, 1962); originally published as *L'Enfant et la vie familiale sous l'Ancien Régime* (Paris: Plon, 1960); and Edward Shorter, *The Making of the Modern Family* (New York: Basic Books, 1975); both are discussed by Arlette Farge in *Fragile Lives: Violence, Power, and Solidarity in Eighteenth-Century Paris,* trans. Carol Shelton (Cambridge: Harvard University Press, 1993).

support their children, it was always heartrending. Many parents hoped to take their children back as soon as their means permitted it, and indeed, once times were better, made every possible inquiry to find them.

Revolutionaries valorized the image of the mother, for in the nation during the revolution and the war, women were not merely mothers but mothers of future republicans and revolutionary combatants. The future of the Republic, which needed soldiers, depended on them. The president of the Convention, Hérault de Séchelles, asked women "to give birth to a nation of heroes" to defend the Republic.[32] It would be absurd to consider the revolutionary mother as a producer of cannon fodder or of battalions of good little republicans. The Revolution was the birth of a new world that was intended to be eternal. In the imaginary, women intervened at these two levels and were thus at the heart of the "revolutionary sacred" that the historian Mona Ozouf defines as "a sacredness of birth."[33] Is it surprising that a revolution that used so frequently the word *regeneration* would represent the concepts of Reason, Liberty, Equality, and Fraternity as female, originally and intrinsically linked to its existence? *Regeneration, generate, generator*: the maternal image joins these words together.

If the mother was connected to the act of birth, she was also an assurance of continuity and of the future through the fertility she incarnated. When the Society of Revolutionary Republican Women swore after the death of Marat to "populate the land of Liberty with as many Marats as *they* could," they inscribed themselves in a problematic where the concept of immortality was the central figure. The heroes of the Revolution would continue to live through them.[34] Pregnant women, "allegories of the perpetuity of the Revolution," participated in numerous revolutionary festivals.[35] In a plan for a festival, Chaumette proposed that they be placed on a platform where these unambiguous words would be inscribed: "respect for pregnant women, the hope of the fatherland."[36] And when revolutionaries firmly reminded women that they were, above all, mothers, it was the "mothers of future generations" that they evoked, much more than women prosaically occupied with their children. Any analysis that views this insistence on the generative function of women as only a simple male desire to restrict women to the role of mothers—and this wish did exist!—would be a misinterpretation of the facts that omits a fundamental issue.

32. Speech of 10 August 1793, *Moniteur*, XVII, 367.
33. Mona Ozouf, *La Fête révolutionnaire* (Paris: Gallimard, 1976), p. 338.
34. See part 2 of this volume, chapter 6, "Light and Shadows, Summer 1793."
35. Ozouf, *La Fête révolutionnaire*, p. 135.
36. *La Gazette Française*, no. 703.

Giving birth to children was only the first act in the construction of a different and better world to which everyone aspired—it was then necessary to turn these children into good republicans. This was the principal task of the revolutionary mother. She was in charge of children during their earliest youth and, in these decisive years that formed the personality of the future adult, she had to imbue them with the republican ideal. "The proper character" of women was to "begin the education of men, prepare the mind and heart of children for public virtues, direct them at an early age towards the good, elevate their soul, and instruct them in the political cult of liberty,"[37] affirmed the deputy Amar. During the entire Revolution, women accepted and fulfilled this task with pride. Let us listen again to the words of Mère Duchesne: "If children must absorb with their milk the principles of the Constitution, who can and who must catechize them in this case? Who can develop the love of Liberty in their still tender hearts and minds, if not you, ladies? . . . If you only do this service for the nation, by my life! you will have done enough for the revolution."[38]

Infants were to "absorb with their milk" revolutionary principles and patriotic sentiments. We can see in this stereotyped formula, which occurs frequently in texts written by women, an affirmation of prosaic and symbolic nurturing, as well as an affirmation of women, the bearers of life.

Once her duties as housewife and mother were fulfilled, a woman had relative freedom of action. Some husbands did try to direct and supervise the conduct of their companions. Citizen Rouillère broke a broomstick in three on the head of his wife, who had gone into the street without him to celebrate the new Constitution with the section. He defended himself by accusing her of having left their crying child, but added "Besides, his wife was supposed to go to bed as soon as he did."[39] In spite of husbands' claims to authority over their wives, the general impression left by documents is one of relative, but on the whole actually rather large, independence for women, even though this was rarely affirmed in principle. Each spouse had his or her own sphere of activity, and when they attended to their own affairs, neither had to account for their doings.

> Both [man and woman] are equally destined to regenerate the ever-failing human species and to live happily in common felicity, to share their plea-

---

37. Report of 9 Brumaire Year II, in *Moniteur*, XVIII, 299.
38. *Lettres bougrement patriotiques*, letter 5.
39. A.P.P., AA 49 f. 10 and f. 593.

sures in order to double them, to lessen their pains by sharing them, to efface their sorrows by mingling their feelings, their ideas, and their desires, and to drown their sorrows in a common hope and in the merging of their souls; finally, called on to strew flowers reciprocally on their journey, in order to make it as happy as possible, it is necessary that both spouses are always independent, one from the other, in order always to live united; it is necessary that the same attentions, eagerness to please, and care that have formed the ties between them continue to strengthen these ties each day.

We would like to conclude with this beautiful and harmonious description by the Montagnard deputy Lequinio.[40] But unions were not always a refuge of tenderness. On the contrary, for some people, they were sources of anxiety, instability, and even torment.

SOUND AND FURY

The Dissolution of Couples

Couples often broke up as a result of abandonment by a spouse for economic reasons. A husband who left to earn his living or to try his luck elsewhere, who promised to return or to summon his family once he was established, would vanish sometimes in the mists of distance. If his wife learned, for example, that he had made a fortune in the United States at "Williamboury" (presumably Williamsburg), Virginia, the forgotten spouse could address her section's general assembly, which would then officially remind "that indifferent husband of the sacred duties he is guilty of forgetting."[41] More frequently, however, women were abandoned for emotional reasons. The unfaithful husband strayed not because of physical distance from his wife, but because his heart was drawn elsewhere. A wife then went to the police commissioner's office and complained that her household was ruined for another woman's advantage. The authorities did not hesitate to side with her and to overwhelm the unfaithful husband with reproaches. The secretary-clerk of the Bondy section, after urging the digger Millot to return to his wife and obtaining in response a categorical refusal, drew up on 26 March 1793 the following certificate for the wife (a copy of which he sent to the police commissioner of the section where Millot and his new companion lived):

> It seems that this man is debauched and has squandered his property with debauched women. He appears to be an unfeeling husband and an unnatural father. His wife, though, is completely different; consequently, he can blame

40. Joseph-Marie Lequinio, *Les Préjugés détruits*, 2d ed., (Paris: 1793), p. 146.
41. A.N., F⁷ 4774⁸⁹ d. M. Regnier, wife of Dormay.

her for nothing. This is all that we know and this is enough for right-thinking men to be concerned for this unfortunate woman, by dealing severely (against him) who has not feared to destroy this unhappy woman and who has concealed part of her household goods.[42]

This attitude of the authorities expressed popular animosity towards a married man who abandoned his wife and children, and perhaps still greater hostility towards the woman who led him astray. Her honor and reputation were stained, she risked receiving reprimands from friends of the forsaken spouse, and she incurred public reprobation, with sometimes fatal consequences. The young dressmaker Toinette Lafosse had been "deceived" by a married citizen, who assured her that he was a bachelor and that he would marry her. "Despairing to see that her district believed that she had debauched him . . . and not wishing to be the scorn of the neighborhood any longer," she tried to poison herself by swallowing verdigris.[43]

A deceived wife, who was defended and protected by the populace, was also in a much less precarious economic position than a woman who was not legally married. Husbands, even when they lived openly with another woman, often continued to support their wife and children. Thus, in spite of all potential dangers, the legal household was stable and enduring. For example, as soon as fortune favored him, citizen Coulonge, who lived with a woman who sold old clothes, returned to live with his family, while continuing to provide financial support for the clothes dealer.[44]

Another threat to domestic tranquillity arose from the Revolution and especially from the subsequent war. The return of the husband and soldier to his household could be accompanied by serious dilemmas. Occasionally, a wife sold the couples' belongings to ease the economic difficulties facing a single woman. Returning to his home, the soldier would find his room half empty. Sometimes his wife had left to move in with another. Even when she was there to welcome him, the indiscreet words of neighbors or her distant manner easily made a husband suspicious, and discord then grew within the household. Many women complained that their husbands tormented them endlessly after they returned from the army. One woman declared that "whether from jealousy or from bad counsel, he did nothing but insult her and mistreat her"; another stated that not only did he beat her but he sold her possessions, leaving her and her two children without

42. A.P.P., AA 59 f. 249.
43. A.P.P., AA 49, 16 Germinal Year II.
44. A.N., W 76, pl. 2, p. 71.

anything, and he threatened to oppose the pension that had been given to her as the wife of an invalid.[45] This suggests that, while remaining faithful to their husbands, women gained a spirit of independence during the months spent alone, which men did not appreciate when they returned.

The couple also represented a sexual union that could be broken, not by another attachment but by the transmission of a venereal disease, which seemed to be common. Fear of venereal diseases could bring a couple to separate. Marie Joyeux "had the misfortune to have a disease that she had caught" from a tailor with whom she had lived for six months. "When the disease progressed, they agreed to separate in order to cure themselves."[46] The Byard couple did not separate, but their marriage was damaged, and the Byard wife ended by demanding a divorce. Her husband did not cease to beat her because "since he had venereal disease . . . she did not wish to see him any more until he was cured." It was probably no accident that he would strike with the most fury at her womb.[47] There was no "feminist" demand during the Revolution for the right to dispose of one's body as one pleased, but rather a fierce desire not to catch "the sickness" from one's partner. In this way women of the people defended their health and the most intimate parts of their bodies.

We must note here that there existed at this time a kind of male fear or incomprehension of the female body.[48] We can see this fear in the official reports and petitions concerning women who were arrested for scandalous behavior in the street or for attacks of insanity. These documents often mention that the woman in question had her period or that she was menopausal, and thus it was necessary to excuse her excessive behavior. The insanity of Derrignon's wife was blamed on her "critical state": "It was possible that blood had gone to her head." In a memoir on behalf of an elderly woman, imprisoned for having participated in a popular insurrection in Prairial Year III, this deviation in conduct was attributed to a disorder "caused by the effects of drunkenness and fear" because, her defenders stated, "since the critical period for women her health was . . . weakened and . . . in all circumstances where she could receive lively impressions her spirit was so affected by her physiology that her mind appeared absolutely deranged." And the father of a young girl who threw herself out a window

---

45. A.P.P., AA 71 f. 255 and AA 70 f. 437.
46. A.P.P., AA 77 f. 208.
47. A.P.P., AA 250, 4 Fructidor Year II.
48. See Arlette Farge, *Vivre dans la rue à Paris au XVIIIe siècle* (Paris: Gallimard, 1979), p. 147.

"presumed that the sore throat and violent fever that she had for several days had been caused by the approach of her period, which had not yet appeared and which probably had given her a moment of dementia."[49] The menstruating woman thus became a stranger to the male world and was excluded from the rational domain. She was even an unhealthy stranger, if we are to believe a prostitute who asserted to a client: "It is five days since I have had my period, I do not have a pimple, I am perfectly healthy."[50]

The rare testimony that we possess on how women perceived menstruation and spoke among themselves of their sexuality suggests that there was a "natural" feminine understanding of these events, in which all false modesty was absent. Women told each other about their gynecological problems. When a woman's periods were very painful, they sympathized with her "uncomfortable state" and cared for her by making her drink sugared white wine. The mistress of the servant Marie urged her to go to bed, while taking care to spread a skirt upon the ground "so that her feet would not touch the tiled floor."[51]

"He Had to Break Her Heart through Her Womb" Grief, bitterness, vengeance, anger, and physical abuse were the lot of couples who were ill-matched or progressively alienated from each other by the difficulties of life. The complaints of wives mistreated by their husbands regularly appear in police commissioners' official reports. Certainly, these documents by themselves can be a source of distortion: women who were not beaten are unmentioned in these documents, and those who complained were exposed to the most excessive brutality. We must thus take care not to imagine all women of the people as covered with wounds and bruises. However, we can only be impressed by the fury of this violence, and, beyond the violence, we can perceive the outline of a network of support and a contrasting image of women of the people, who were often the victims of male brutality but rarely passive martyrs.

Cut foreheads, gouged eyes, torn ears, fractures, miscarriages, the marks of blows from fists, feet, wooden shoes, and tongs all bore witness to male violence. Possessed by fury, often under the influence of alcohol, violent husbands did not hesitate to strike their wives in the face, the belly, or the groin, to drag them by the hair, to throw them down the stairs, and to turn them out. Hatred entered into these violent acts when they were accompa-

49. A.P.P., AA 128 f. 98; A.N., F⁷ 4729 d. Gonthier; A.P.P., AA 63 f. 38.
50. A.P.P., AA 228 f. 80.
51. A.P.P., AA 92, 20 September 1793.

nied by death threats. The tailor Laurent yelled at his greengrocer wife "that he had to break her heart through her womb."[52] For some husbands, beating their wives was a regular practice. Blows were often most violent in these repeated offenses. Talbert, not content with having blinded his wife in one eye six years ago and having tried to poison her, cut her forehead with blows from a cane and struck her in the stomach with his wooden shoes. The wife of Gittet described to the police commissioner on 14 November 1793 the horrible treatment she had endured from her husband for eighteen months. "Last winter she had remained in bed for seven days from the blows he had given her"; on 9 November "he had hit her with tongs in the back and seriously wounded her"; on 11 November he had kicked and punched her in the back, she had fallen down the stairs and cut her forehead, he had become frightened at the abundant blood and had fled but today he had struck her several times in the face with his fist.[53]

But people were not indifferent to the fate of a battered woman. She could always find a defender, and in lodgings where everything could be heard, where everyone's private life became part of the collective life of the building, often an indignant female neighbor, awoken from sleep, intervened. On 21 September 1793, all the residents of 7 Rue Guérin-Boisseau were upset; their neighbor, the wife of Berton, at 47 Rue Guérin-Boisseau, "knowing that her husband was violent when he drank," had escaped to the stairway, where he chased her up to the sixth floor; there, her legs failing her, she had yelled "murder!" Immediately, the widow Dessieux came out of her room, saw Berton beating his wife, and said to him: "Good heavens, what do you mean by disturbing the peace in my house? I will make my deposition to the general assembly." He then turned against her, took her by the neck and hair, and grabbed her by the throat. Alerted by the cries, another woman came to their aid. He seized her also by the neck, but a third who had witnessed the scene "revenged them and struck him several times with her fist to make him let them go." He then fled, pursued by the widow Dessieux, who threw her clogs at his head. By his account, they said to him: "Ah! scoundrel, we've got you, we've been looking for you for a long time, now you have attacked your wife in our home."[54]

The female neighbor was always ready to welcome and offer a mattress to a woman who preferred to spend the night elsewhere while waiting for her husband to calm down, or to help a woman who had been thrown out

52. A.P.P., AA 186, 13 Pluviôse Year II.
53. A.P.P., AA 48, 1 April 1793 and AA 49 f. 266.
54. A.P.P., AA 49 f. 227.

of her home. These female neighbors never hesitated to respond to calls for help. And what about the male neighbor? He also condemned the man who "made a disturbance with his wife," remonstrated with him if he had the chance, but did not intervene directly in a quarrel. Hearing the wife of Bellanger being beaten one evening, the principal tenant of the house, who was responsible for keeping the peace, cursed but went up to sleep. It was a neighbor woman who, wakened by the "horrifying cries" coming from the Bellangers' home, got up, went out on the landing, and through the door "entreated the citizen to please not strike his wife and threatened to go get the police watchman."[55]

The police commissioner who received the complaints of mistreated women listened to them and summoned their husbands, whom he reprimanded severely and sometimes locked up for several hours "as paternal chastisement" or until they became sober. If their conduct was particularly violent or accompanied by another misdemeanor such as breaking furniture or insulting authorities, he sent them to prison. The wives often demanded their husbands' release. Their letters help us understand why women hesitated so long before lodging a complaint. The wife of Moisson explained that, with six children "such a heavy burden was too much for her" and that she "wished her husband to go free in order that he could go gather in the harvest so that by his work he could help his wife in her distress."[56] We again come up against this economic problem, the material impossibility for a wife to raise her family on only her wages.

Subject to the incessant persecution of violent husbands, some women "cracked" and threw themselves into the Seine. Others, in contrast, defended themselves and responded to blows with blows. When the husband passed certain limits, they declared this to the police commissioner. Often the woman who came to lodge a complaint had more than one reason to bear a grudge against her husband. Not only had he attacked her but he had taken her few belongings. He sold her goods, he stole her savings and her jewelry, he did not live up to his role as husband, he "did not give her a sou" and "left her in poverty." Again we must note here the not insignificant number of soldiers' wives who complained. Had the violence they suffered doubled since the return of their husbands from the army, as they insisted, or did they endure less patiently the blows that they were no longer accustomed to receive? A number of women on the verge of divorce, now sepa-

55. A.P.P., AA 188 f. 228.
56. A.N., F⁷ 4774⁴⁷ d. Moisson.

rated from their husbands, lodged complaints at the first serious blow. They had probably received worse when they lived with their husbands, but since the divorce proceedings had begun, they considered "that he no longer had any right over them" and wished to be able to "enjoy the advantages of the divorce law" in peace.[57]

At the end of the eighteenth century, violence and brutality were not just characteristic of men. Police commissioners often were called to put an end to fights between a male and a female citizen right in the street. Investigations revealed that it was not always the man who threw the first punch, nor was it always his blows that were the most painful. A citizen placed a piece of his nose on the desk of a police commissioner and explained that, while in a café, a woman he had lived with for ten years "had become excited and thrown herself on him like a fury, striking him with her fists, and that in an act he could not understand, she had bitten off a piece from his nose."[58] Female violence also occurred within the home. One woman took her companion by the collar and tried to stab him. Another tore the clothing of her husband who did not want to pay their debts and redeem their belongings from the Mont-de-Piété.[59] This violence was in response to specific situations rather than habitual. We cannot think that these two women mistreated their companions regularly. However, some men affirmed that their wives physically abused them several times, but these cases were rare. And, even if it was very likely that, out of concern for his "masculine honor," the beaten man did not report abuse to a commissioner, the violence of women toward their companions is not comparable to the violence of men toward women. However, once again we must place these violent acts in a larger context. Male brutality seems a little less fierce when we study the contusions, wounds, and black eyes inflicted by female combatants on one another during riots. Even so, these wounds were less frequently fatal. And there remains an essential difference. A violent fight between two enemies does not have the quality of repetitive and almost daily fury characteristic of a man's abusive behavior to his companion.

Separation   Weary of blows or simply tired of living with their husbands, some women left the conjugal home, taking with them their belongings, clothes, jewels, pawn tickets from Mont-de-Piété, furniture, merchandise, and savings. When he returned home after a day of work, stupefied, the

57. A.P.P., AA 188 f. 228.
58. A.P.P., AA 248, 12 August 1793.
59. A.P.P., AA 208, 8 March 1793 and AA 69 f. 495.

husband might find his lodgings half empty, his wife absent and, sometimes, a request for divorce in plain sight. Then he would go to find her, ask for an explanation for this precipitate departure that he did not always understand, and promise to reform. She would listen attentively to this man who spoke of his love and his esteem for her, who reminded her of all that she expected from marriage, and often she returned to live with him. But the disputes, cries, and blows would recommence, and she would leave him again. It was not rare that, during their life in common, couples would separate three or four times, for several days or several months. The case of the married couple Montuel provides a good example of these unions that combined love and rage, hope and fear. After Montuel tried to strangle his wife who was just up from childbirth, he turned her out but "continued to visit her" at her new residence—up to three times a day—"asking her to return to him and pleading that she should not remain lodged so poorly." Trusting his promises, she returned to the conjugal home after five days. She enjoyed only fifteen days of tranquillity before her husband took away her ring and her marriage certificate, "saying that he no longer wished her to bear his name," stole her savings, and made her sleep on the stairway. Once again she fled, but he then went to find her in her new lodgings and begged "that she let him eat at her home for thirty sous a day; a sentiment of friendship moved her to receive him, but at her home just as at his home, he continued to mistreat her."[60] This endless coming and going, these repeated, often stormy separations show an instability that, without being exaggerated, should nevertheless be taken into account when we imagine the emotional and psychological equilibrium of these women.

Others did not return and no longer wished to have anything to do with their husbands. Moved by a spirit of stubborn independence, sometimes they even refused the aid that they could claim as wives of soldiers. But the good relations they could not establish as long as they lived together sometimes developed from these separations chosen in common. The man continued to help his wife financially while she looked after him if anything happened to him. These ruptures often had a legal stamp, even when they were not accompanied by an official statement of the "separation of goods and bodies." A woman who found refuge with the police commissioner would declare that she intended to separate from her companion, legitimate or not, and the conditions of the separation—division of property, custody of children, a possible food allowance—would be decided in his office.

60. A.P.P., AA 264 f. 457.

Thomas Panet promised before a police commissioner to pay his concubine, Anne Louise Paris, "all that she had when she moved in with him, plus six hundred livres indemnity for the time that she had spent at his home; that as for the child he had with her, he would give it ten livres a month if she wished to keep it and, if she did not want this, he would keep it and care for it."[61] A police commissioner who played the role of mediator would urge a couple to separate when they troubled public order with their incessant quarrels. On 11 March 1793, a man and a woman who had been fighting were brought before the police commissioner at city hall. The woman, a fruit merchant, declared to him "that she had lived for three years with the individual . . . who had been arrested, that they had already had several quarrels and had always been reconciled by the commissioner, but two months ago, [when they were] once again brought before him, the commissioner had forbidden the aforementioned individual to return to her home, [been] given their declaration to stop seeing one another, and [responded to her request] for his mediation in dividing the property that had been left in the room where they had lived." (Because the man took no notice of the commissioner's prohibition, he was sent to prison).[62] These separations, even those between unmarried couples, thus assumed a quasi-legal character. After the adoption of the divorce law, this was the only possible way for unmarried couples to make their rupture official. Even legal couples, however, preferred to make a simple declaration before the commissioner rather than embark upon divorce proceedings, perhaps because, as a gunner recalled, "in order to divorce, you need money."[63]

The divorce law was passed on 20 September 1792. Married couples could separate by mutual consent, for incompatibility of temperament and character, or for seven "specific grounds": madness; condemnation to degrading punishment; serious crimes, cruelty, or injuries; licentious morals; abandonment for two years; absence without news for five years; and emigration. In Floréal Year Two (April 1794), an eighth motive was added: an actual separation for six months, verified by six witnesses. Divorce by mutual consent or for incompatibility of temperament was free. In other cases, the appearance before a tribunal required the paid services of a legal advocate.[64] In Paris, from 1 January 1793 to 17 June 1795, 5,987 divorces were

---

61. A.P.P., AA 49, 25 Germinal Year II.
62. A.P.P., AA 138 f. 350.
63. A.N., F7* 2482, 13 Thermidor Year II.
64. D. Dessertine, *Divorcer à Lyon sous la Révolution et l'Empire* (Lyon: P.U.L., 1981).

granted, and 71 percent of the requests for divorces came from women. Incompatibility was the cause most often cited (in many cases, it masked the third motive), followed by lack of news and abandonment.[65]

Rather frequently, perhaps out of fear, a woman who wished to divorce took advantage of her husband's absence to draw up her request and present him with a fait accompli. Then she left the conjugal home and took a separate room to protect herself from her husband's rage. This was not an unnecessary precaution. One woman who neglected this step heard her husband say the night when he received his divorce action "that the divorce would occur that night, that he had two pistols and that he would use them."[66] If she could, she would seek refuge at the home of a family member, hoping in this way to avoid all slander on her honor. Although it was very rare for a woman to divorce in order to live with another man, there were many husbands who would overwhelm their wives with insults during the divorce proceedings: "He called her a slut and a whore throughout her old neighborhood," "She was a slut and a whore with children by others," "She wouldn't act like prostitute any longer," and so on. The husband of the woman Sevrey, accompanied by several friends, made a "considerable disturbance" in the middle of the night before her father's house, where she had retreated, calling her a slut and yelling "that she was sleeping with someone."[67] Women went to complain to the police commissioner about these slanders that called their honor into question. And, just as the husband's friends were ready to help him "serenade" the wife who wished to divorce, her friends were ready to protect her and see that all went well for her. The misadventure that befell citizen Bellepaume shows this female solidarity. When he returned to the town hall intending to oppose the divorce demanded by his wife, she had stirred up against him "a considerable number of citizens of both sexes, but chiefly women who turned out in the town hall," who pursued him in the corridors, abused him, and tore his clothes. He recognized these angry women as merchants of the Quai à la Ferraille, acquaintances of his wife from work. In his account, he declared with barely veiled indignation that his wife "desired to free herself from the matrimonial bond."[68] Like him, most men had difficulty accepting that their wife could escape them in this way.

65. M. d'Auteville, "Le divorce pendant la Révolution," *Revue de la Révolution* (1883): 2, 206–473.

66. A.P.P., AA 48 f. 620.

67. A.P.P., AA 209 f. 131.

68. A.P.P., AA 139 f. 24.

The wife, who often requested divorce to escape from the hell of a bad marriage, enjoyed the liberty that the law gave her afterwards. A letter sent to the Convention in the autumn of 1793 by female citizen Govot clearly shows the delights of this refound independence:

> The female citizen Govot, a free woman, solemnly comes to give homage to this sacred law of divorce. Yesterday, groaning under the control of a despotic husband, *liberty* was only an empty word for her. Today, returned to the dignity of an independent woman, she idolizes this beneficial law that breaks ill-matched ties and returns hearts to themselves, to nature, and finally to divine liberty. I offer my country six francs for the expense of war. I add my marriage ring, which was until today the symbol of my slavery. Receive, legislators, this marriage ring, or rather these chains that have brought me bitter days. The day is more honest, I taste liberty without constraint. I will dedicate my existence to making myself worthy of enlarging the list of republicans who acquire honor through their regeneration and whose creed is entitled: morality, equality, and a universal and indivisible Republic.[69]

Although some husbands pursued their former spouses with vindictiveness and dissatisfaction at the women's newly recovered liberty, divorced women were not subject to public scorn. We find only husbands uttering remarks that brought grief to a wife at her divorce or compared her to a debauched woman. And when the carter Doublet said to a wine merchant whose home sheltered Doublet's former wife: "Wine merchant, this is a divorced woman, you should throw her out because she is a thief, she has stolen eight hundred livres from me, she is a divorcée, that is, a whore," the husband was the one who was obliged to leave.[70]

Divorced men often added the insult *thief* to the slander *whore*. This is because, at the time of the divorce, when the couple's property was divided, the woman took what was her due and the husband was forced to pay a food allowance to support their children. The economic situation of the divorced woman had little in common with the position of the abandoned woman with children, or even of the woman separated from her companion. From the moment when she no longer had to count only on her own earnings to raise the children, she was much less vulnerable economically. For this reason, women who were divorced savored their independence. If the law had not constrained their husbands to return their belongings and to help with the children, this independence would no longer have been attractive but probably would have meant economic disaster. The divorced woman and her

69. A.N., C 278 d. 739, p. 2.
70. A.P.P., AA 208, 6 March 1793.

belongings were protected by the law, and those men who believed themselves "authorized to go when it suited them" to the home of their previous wife to remove the possessions given to her at the time of the division of property found themselves called to account by the police commissioner.

Children were another source of discord between divorced and separated couples. When a woman left the conjugal dwelling, she usually took the children with her. The law stipulated that, afterwards, children would be entrusted to their mother at least until the age of seven years. Sometimes the couple would arrange that each had charge of a child. Normally, the one who obtained custody would permit the other to see the child when he or she wished. The latter, father or mother, held fast to this prerogative. There were frequent quarrels when one of the ex-spouses refused to let the other parent see their child. Parents who did not have custody were sometimes tempted to carry off the child "on their own authority."

When a husband asked for a divorce, there were similar difficulties. His wife could harass him angrily during and after the proceedings and even threaten him with death. She could also contest the division of property. However, it was much more common for men to ask for a divorce because they intended to remarry than for women. It was also not uncommon for a woman to turn her rage against herself and try to put an end to her life. In sixty-six cases where women asked for divorce, there is not a single husband who attempted suicide or who said he was unhappy that his wife wished to leave him. We can attribute this to male honor as much as to a lack of feeling, which expressed itself differently in the acts or repentance of violent husbands.

The study of the breakup of family relations has helped to strengthen the relatively weak evidence from the archives on the condition of lower-class family women. Some women had an eventful family life, the opposite of the peace and stability expected from marriage. But just as they knew how to respond to the blows that they received, they did not all allow themselves to be beaten and could take the initiative to leave the conjugal home with their children, to the perplexity of their husbands who were not always violent and did not always understand the motivations of their wives. Although some women were abandoned or fled their spouses to avoid crippling injury, other women chose to seek their way alone again. Did these women endure solitude or claim independence? Within all these personal histories, the two positions intersect. Moreover, all these women were conscious of being separate individuals who refused to accept positions of servitude vis-à-vis their companions. The liberty proclaimed by the Revolution also held a place in their private lives.

These women, whether single, widows, abandoned, or the spouses or companions of soldiers, constituted a significant female population without ties, a floating population that survived under often difficult conditions of existence, at the limit of marginality. We can add to this list the many young girls who lived outside the framework of a narrow family structure. Their problems were so specific that the question "independence or solitude?" deserves, in their case, a separate examination.

INDEPENDENCE OR SOLITUDE?

"To Seek a Life Elsewhere"

Orphans or young women abandoned in their childhood, who left the Enfants de la Patrie as soon as they were old enough to work, had always been alone. Others were driven out of their homes, like the young eighteen-year-old dressmaker who was thrown out by her father one evening when she returned an hour later than usual, having had more work to finish.[71] Still others had fled beatings, or more rarely, sexual aggression, that unique expression of violence, by their father or their mother's lover. Historians have clearly shown how the family could be a repressive environment for young people who earned their living but who were not granted autonomy.[72] Like their brothers, young girls of popular milieus would not submit to this oppression, and weary of small daily conflicts, they sometimes chose to leave home. After a fight with her brother, Angélique Dezereau, a twenty-two-year-old maker of espadrilles, slammed the door while saying to her mother "that she was going to seek a life elsewhere, that she would not return, and that she did not wish to yield to her with respect to her son."[73] A remonstration or a slap too many, a prohibition to see a lover who displeased their parents, could become the last straw that compelled numerous young girls to "escape from the paternal home." These departures were sometimes impulsive acts that the young woman might regret later while trying to find a neighbor "who would act as an intermediary" with her parents. They also could represent a real spirit of independence that took the form of a final abandonment of the family home. "Seeking her life elsewhere, weary of the

71. A.N., F⁷ 4668 d. Deloute.
72. See, for example, Farge and Foucault, *Le Désordre des familles.*
73. A.P.P., AA 177, 11 Thermidor Year II.

paternal home, moving to her own place, she did not always need her parents to take care of her."[74] This was how young girls expressed themselves when they felt that their lives were their own and found themselves confined in a family that repressed their vivacity and opposed the full development of their personality. They wished to breathe the air of the city at their risk and peril, like those young women, burning with desire to see the world and hoping for economic success, who left the countryside, often in the company of a sixteen- or seventeen-year-old female friend as young as they, to brave the life of the capital.

Women whose families had been established in Paris for generations or more recent Parisians, sisters, cousins, friends, or traveling companions moved in together. There were also many networks of relations that young women who lived alone could draw upon. Chief among these was the family network. A young person who arrived from the provinces could often go to a relative's home, where she slept for the first few nights and whom she would see again afterwards. Young female Parisians whose family home could not contain their overflow of spirits frequently renewed ties with their parents once their anger passed and the young women had affirmed their autonomy by renting a room. Their parents, who accepted their departure as an accomplished fact, would help them afterwards in difficult periods of unemployment or sickness. Then there were neighbors with whom these young girls dined and walked and who looked after them. The female citizen Stance tried to commit suicide because of her poverty and her solitude ("She did not know anyone in Paris"; she was not "friends with anyone"). However, she was discovered by a female neighbor who, not having seen her for several hours, became worried and knocked at her door.[75]

But these relations could remain superficial. Some women, in spite of everything, were really alone and miserable and had to beg to survive. On 4 Frimaire Year II (24 November 1793), Marguerite Ory, a twenty-five-year-old dressmaker, tried to be arrested by expressing unpatriotic sentiments "to procure for herself a stable lodging out of despair, having been abandoned by her relatives and friends and without any other resource for living."[76] These were certainly extreme cases of destitution. Nevertheless, very few of these young women were really settled. Rather, they were women who moved from furnished room to furnished room. During the two years that she lived in Paris, Catherine Carré, a seamstress from Liége,

74. A.P.P., AA 163 f. 35 and AA 93, 24 Pluviôse Year II.
75. A.P.P., AA 228 f. 196.
76. A.N., F⁷ 4774⁵⁹ d. Ory.

lived successively in the Rue de la Jussienne, in the Faubourg Saint-Denis with a female relative, in the Rue du Four Saint-Honoré for a year with a female citizen, in the Rue Neuve-Saint-Marc for three months, and finally in the Rue Roquépine for a month. The case of Victoire Robin, a breeches-maker from Orléans, is still more striking. In one year she lived in five different places.[77] Frequently these were hasty moves, for the woman took with her what she could find in the furnished lodging. Their living conditions were often so precarious and uncertain that, as soon as the opportunity to commit a small larceny appeared, they did not hesitate and only acknowledged afterward that it had been a "bad idea" to take a worthless blanket, a half sheet, or part of the wool stuffing from a mattress. Pocket picking was also common: a handkerchief glimpsed from the pocket of a passerby, a bonnet displayed in a shop window, or pieces of linen hung out to dry were resold by the thief for several livres, which allowed her to pay her debts or to redeem her belongings from the Mont-de-Piété. Such petty thefts show how difficult life was for these women. Most lived like tightrope walkers on a wire that served as the border between poverty and indigence. It only took sickness, a robbery, or several days without work for their fragile equilibrium to break. At such moments, their male friends, without actually supporting them, might help by giving them a little money from time to time, paying their rent, or finding them work.

Opportunities for amorous meetings were not infrequent. Neighborhood or professional ties often sparked lower-class loves. The godfather, son, or cousin of a dressmaker or an embroiderer quickly noticed the delicate silhouette of the young worker bent over her needle. Some courtesy, some joke or an exchange of glances, and the young man "asked to walk her home . . . and by his attentions, friendship developed."[78] More than once a carpenter had seen a washerwoman who brought linen back to his neighbors climb the staircase of their building with agility. In order to get to know her, he asked her one day to take care of his linen also. Ties of friendship were formed at dances. Marie Françoise Defailly "often went to a country ball at Belleville with a good female friend and there she met Aubert, who offered to see her home. Gradually they fell in love, to the point where having brought her home, he succeeded in going up to her room."[79] Then these lovers would take walks in the country or in Paris, would eat together, visit each other, give each other gifts, and seek out each other after work. They

---

77. A.P.P., AA 227 f. 136 and AA 61 f. 111.
78. A.P.P., AA 77 f. 127.
79. A.P.P., AA 77 f. 182.

wrote when they were separated, but also at the beginning of their relationship to prove their affection and their good faith. It was not until after
two letters from Citizen Guy that Marguerite Rousseau "let him come to
her home to tell her what he felt for her in all honesty."[80]

When the relationship progressed, the young girl did not usually go to
the home of her lover. Instead, he visited her. When his absence was pro-
tracted, the female lover worried because this could mean that he had abandoned her. It was not uncommon that, helpless, she did not know how to
find him. Many prudent seducers refused to give their address to their girl-
friends and tried in this way to protect themselves from prosecution by a
pregnant young woman with whom they did not wish to concern themselves. Young girls who lived alone and often had economic difficulties were
easily tricked by promises of marriage and the hope of an affectionate and
economic establishment. Their declarations of pregnancy bear witness to
these disappointed hopes and to the fragility of their unions.

Girls Become Mothers

We find numerous declarations of this sort in the reports of police commissioners—233 from January 1793 to July 1795.[81] The results are expressive: the average age of the informant is twenty-three and a half years. Statistics show a continuous progression from sixteen to twenty-five years,
then a sudden decrease up until around the fortieth year. It was indeed
young single girls who let themselves be seduced by promises of marriage.
The peak of eighteen years perhaps stems from the fact that this was the
age when the majority of young girls left their family homes and were thus
less experienced than their elders. These statements are generally dated in
the last months of pregnancy, when the young woman had no more hope.
Those made before the sixth month followed an event, such as the departure of the seducer or his marriage to another, which left the woman no
more doubt as to her abandonment. The great majority of complainants (65
percent) had no life in common with the father, 16 percent lived with him
in a free union, 14 percent were servants who were pregnant by their employer, and 4 percent were kept women. More than half were abandoned.
In 25 percent of the cases, they were certain that their pregnancy directly

80. A.P.P., AA 77 f. 171.
81. F. Fortuné, "Sexualité hors mariage à l'époque révolutionnaire: Les mères
des enfants de la nature," in *Droit et réalité sociales de la sexualité*, Actes du Col-
loque de Toulouse, 1987.

caused their abandonment. Slightly more than 12 percent of the fathers recognized their child. Finally 17 percent of the declarations were made because he had left for the army or had died.

Some of the declarations indicate the protagonists' trades. Unfortunately, the statements do not show the status of the complainant or of the accused within the professional hierarchy. In spite of this, we can draw some general information from this data. Tailors and beltmakers (professions employing considerable female labor), shoemakers, carpenters, masons, café-keepers, and, to a lesser degree, common laborers were frequent company for seamstresses, laundresses, breechesmakers, and charwomen. The absence of handicraft workers or merchants among the complainants is curious and difficult to explain (see figure 1).

Domestic workers chose their lovers among artisans or among their male coworkers. However, they usually became pregnant by their employer *master–servant relations* or his friend. For these masters, who thought quite simply that they had a right to their employees, all means, whether force, promises, or gifts, were fair. They emphasized "their rank as master" and profited from the promiscuity of life. Young girls, weary of their persecutions and afraid of losing their jobs, often gave in to their advances. Marie Anne Dhérongeville, raised at the Enfants Trouvés, went to work for a citizen who told the steward of that charity ward that he needed a servant:

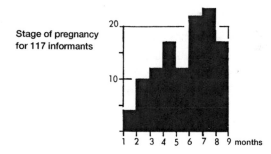

Stage of pregnancy
for 117 informants

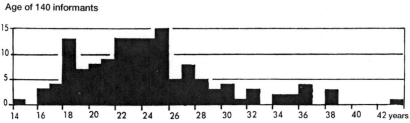

Age of 140 informants

Fig 1. Declarations of pregnancy (January 1793 to Messidor Year III)

> He did not hesitate to proposition her. . . . Wherever he found her he would repeat his cruelty by making her different promises. . . . She remembers especially that he expressly forbade her to meet anyone, or to attach herself to any lover. . . . Abusing her inexperience, as soon as he found her alone he said to her that she had to kiss him. Knowing all the respect that she owed to her masters but persuaded that she only owed them her respect and her diligence, she absolutely refused. Seeing that she was obstinate in refusing his caresses, he employed weapons that he believed would be more victorious. He spared nothing in order to satisfy his passions. . . . He gave her stockings, handkerchiefs, and other things of that nature. . . . He promised to make her the head of his household. Seeing that she persisted in her resistance, he made her sleep in the bed of his servant in a room through which he had to pass in order to enter his own room.

He finally succeeded, after several months of this game of cat and mouse, when she gave in to his entreaties.[82] When a master learned that his employee was pregnant by him, he usually did not want to hear anything more of her. However, at least 13 percent recognized the child: a not negligible statistic that mitigates the overly black portrait of relations between servants and masters and confirms that sometimes they could be the model of a stable free union. Thus, after having taken advantage of the fact that the kitchen where he slept was adjacent to the stable where his servant, Nicole Moricard, slept, Citizen Driancourt "recognized for all time . . . that she was pregnant by his doing . . . and that he did not want her to work so hard and took on someone to help her."[83] And these declarations of pregnancy should not make us forget that the majority of masters left their servants alone.

After the declaration of pregnancy, a seducer was forced by the police commissioner or the justice of the peace to pay a certain amount to the complainant for "trouble, expense, and interest."[84] This measure was still enforced in 1795, in spite of the implicit suppression of declarations of pregnancy in 1791. The lover of Michèle Gambert, who had first promised to give her fifty livres a month during her pregnancy and then forced her to sign a declaration denying his paternity, was condemned in March 1795 by the justice of the peace to pay the promised sum, which he paid the day after the judgment.[85] The majority of complainants were content with financial help, but some demanded that the father recognize his child so that the child could inherit. Impressed by the complaint or taken by remorse, se-

82. A.P.P., AA 139 f. 404.
83. A.P.P., AA 219, 2 Ventôse Year III.
84. A.P.P., AA 159 f. 136.
85. A.P.P., AA 96 f. 150.

ducers assumed their paternity before the authorities. After Catherine Martin's declaration of pregnancy, her lover, who had refused up until then to keep his promises, "acknowledged that he had frequented her and promised to have full consideration for her and to view his child always as a natural and legitimate child."[86]

The authorities believed these pregnant women and helped them pursue whomever they named as the father. The anonymous authors of a "project for legislation and administration in general" were indignant at this.[87] They proposed that "when a girl had the weakness to let herself be seduced," the nation give her monthly aid until her child came of age in order to increase soldiers and avoid "these difficulties that occur every day through the declarations that the law requires of pregnant young women." They continued: "We must agree that this law is indeed unjust to men. And if we believe a woman's word, doesn't this encourage those who are of bad faith to make false declarations?"

They asked if it was just for a woman who had known several men to have the "effrontery" to ask for reparations from the richest among them.

> To require that a man prove that a girl has had dishonest commerce with another is almost to require the impossible. . . . It suffices . . . to prove in these kinds of difficulties that the girl does not enjoy a good reputation and that she is frequented by libertines. . . . To prevent these difficulties, it is necessary that a girl not be allowed to make a declaration about a man unless she has a written promise of marriage from him. . . . With these precautions, young men will be more circumspect and will only frequent people of their station, whom they would not be reluctant to marry in case of an accident. Girls who are weak enough to be surprised without having taken these precautions will have nothing to claim. They can indeed make their declaration about those whom they have known, but they will have no right over them.

These wishes were partially granted, although young women did not benefit from any allocation of the state, when the "right-thinking" morality of young men of good families triumphed. In 19 Frimaire Year III (9 December 1794), during its meeting over the elaboration of the civil code, the Convention decreed that "the law will not admit the investigation of unadmitted paternity. It reserves to the child disowned by the mother the right to prove its filiation against her" (Article X). Pons de Verdun, a member of the National Convention, asked that this article be revised, for in its

86. A.P.P., AA 200.
87. A.N., W 76 pl. 1 f. 55.

present form "it would present grave inconvenience. It would force a mother to take care of her children alone. The father could clear himself of all responsibility by a denial." Mailhe fought this proposal because "he thought that one should require written proofs of paternity. It would be contrary to propriety to give too much latitude to the inquisitorial investigation of paternity." Finally Article X was adopted under its original form.[88]

In fact, these declarations were a source of abuse, but this seems to have been relatively rare. Complainants never hid that they had been seduced more by the social situation of a man than by his person, or that they had been seduced because they did not have work. In addition, they often proposed to bring as proof the testimonies of neighbors or passionate letters that promised marriage.

In contrast to the Year III, during the Year II the revolutionaries followed a policy of protection of unmarried mothers. On 7 Pluviôse Year II, in the political club of the Lepeletier section, a citizen "announced that a fifteen-year-old girl had given birth to a republican and was destitute. He asked that the club take into account the state of this female citizen." A collection of 160 livres was taken and four commissioners were charged with "discovering the father and making him recognize the child and contribute to its support."[89] The Convention also was interested in the fate of unmarried mothers, and the law of 13 Pluviôse Year II (1 February 1794), which gave ten million in aid to the city halls of the Republic, included as a second category of "ill fated individuals" "the children born or conceived outside of marriage whose mothers took the obligation to nurse them." It specified that, whatever the stage of her pregnancy, if an unmarried mother asked for help, the law wished it to be given—a measure that was not always followed.[90]

These examples should not mislead us. Except for special social measures and those citizens who wished to struggle with "barbarous prejudices," there was not a policy of "rehabilitation" of unmarried mothers during the Revolution. To escape from public scorn, many young girls preferred to hide their pregnancy from their friends and relations.

Independence or solitude? The question is perhaps poorly put, and therefore we must speak of a hazardous independence. No doubt the desire to be free of parental custody motivated many young girls who chose to

---

88. *Procès-verbaux de la Convention nationale . . .* , vol. 51, p. 88.
89. B.N., Mss. NAF 2662 f. 104.
90. *Circulaire aux 48 sections de Paris*, A.N., F[15] 3581.

live autonomously. For some this was also a necessity, and they thus knew a solitary and miserable life. However, the majority were not adrift and were surrounded by their friends, their family, their neighbors, their fellow workers, and their lovers who might marry them some day—but these happy endings are outside the scope of our documents.

There is a vast distance between young girls' hopes for a happy union and their condition when they were seduced and abandoned. Their dream of happiness and a life built on affection crumbled. These brutal circumstances gave rise to anxiety. Historians have noticed this anxiety in literary texts and in the traditions of religious sentiments and have believed it to be a "privilege of the elite."[91] But can this anxiety be divided into a quasi-metaphysical condition for the elite and a material anxiety for the people? Men and women of the people have left scarcely any written trace of their sentiments, but the archives suggest feelings of insecurity, of instability, and of anxiety that, far from being purely material, spring much more from a slippage perceived between their self-consciousness and their ideal life. The numerous cases of madness and suicide in the police commissioners' reports show the violence and the material and psychological insecurity that were often the lot of women (and men) of the people, as well as the difficult search for harmony between oneself and the world, and also within oneself. Eighteenth-century literature is partial to suicides. Suicide often occurred among the lower classes, not because of a lack of work or money, but out of loneliness, rejection by family, or even simply weariness of oneself: "Having suffered greatly, lost her parents, and finally grown tired of everything, having no other preoccupation but a continuous boredom with her own person . . . she thought she would end her weariness" by drowning, explained a twenty-five-year-old servant. And a thirty-five-year-old brushmaker, also "weary of life," a woman with an apparently tranquil life, threw herself from a roof.[92] Depression and existential anguish are not just modern maladies or "privileges" of the elite.

However, they were not common for women of the people. In contrast to anxiety, we see adaptation to circumstances, perseverance, and above all the desire to march with head high in the family as well as elsewhere. We see the search for happiness, a search that was tenacious and sometimes, often, much more frequently than our documents let us see, fruitful. Do happy people have no history? In any case, they leave less trace in the archives.

Interesting thought . . .

91. See, for example, Michel Vovelle, *Ideologies and Mentalities*, trans. Eamon O'Flaherty (Cambridge: Polity Press, 1990); originally published as *Idéologies et mentalités* (Paris: Maspéro, 1982); and Michel Vovelle, *La Mentalité révolutionnaire: Société et mentalités sous la Révolution française* (Paris: Messidor, 1985).
92. A.P.P., AA 220, 6 June 1793, and AA 80, 6 Vendémiaire Year II.

3 Women at Work

During this period, there was no doubt in anyone's mind that women had a place in the world of work. In addition, it was taken for granted that a woman of the people was a laborer. Although the collective *mentalité* assigned the task of supporting a family to the father, lower-class conditions of existence made the mother's work indispensable as well. In many households, her labor represented that critical difference between poverty and indigence. It was often impossible for unskilled workers, manual laborers, masons, and artisans who were no longer apprentices but not yet masters to support their families on a single salary. In the case of unemployment or an accident, families would have been unable to survive if women did not work. It was also absolutely necessary for women and young girls who lived alone to work for their livelihood. Thus, employed women were the norm in popular milieus and played a constitutive role in the social and familial landscape.[1] A sick-nurse identified herself as belonging to the "sansculottes class" because she and her husband had no "other means of support than their arms," and a female fanmaker, mar-

---

1. Raymonde Monnier estimates from different sources that there were forty-five thousand female Parisian wage earners under the Empire, a number that represents about a fifth of the adult female population. But the author has carefully specified that this statistic is only a minimum; see Raymonde Monnier, "L'Évolution de l'industrie et le travail des femmes sous l'Empire," *Bulletin d'histoire économique et sociale de la Révolution française* (Paris: Imprimerie Nationale, 1979). Large numbers of working women were to be found not only in Paris. Maurice Garden has noted that "widespread female labor was one of the striking features of Lyonnaise society in the eighteenth century," in *Lyon et les Lyonnais au XVIIIᵉ siècle* (Lyon: Bibliothèque Faculté des Lettres, 1970), p. 139. The same remarks could be made about Rouen: see Claire Le Foll, *Les Femmes et le mouvement révolutionnaire à Rouen, 1789–1795* (Master's thesis, Université de Haute-Normandie, 1985).

ried to another fanmaker, described herself as a woman "who needed to work to live and support her family."[2]

But women's wages did not merely supplement their family's income. If a woman worked, her family was not necessarily in desperate financial straits. Neither the young girl married to an artisan able to provide for all their needs, nor the woman whose husband earned his living with relative ease, would always give up her profession.

Women's work was not a subject of polemics or demands. Neither men nor women regarded it as abnormal or as a sign of an unjust society exploiting its weakest members. This is in contrast to the nineteenth century, when women's work, occurring under deplorable conditions, was thought by progressives to reflect the misery of the proletariat and to be one of the disastrous consequences of capitalism, an unnatural phenomenon that threatened to destroy the institution of the family.

We also do not find that people of this period linked women's right to work and women's emancipation. Women's work was not seen through a feminist perspective during the Revolution. There was no specific discourse on women's work as a social phenomenon. Instead we find discussions and complaints about the ratio of men to women in a profession and the work conditions for women in certain branches of labor. These discussions did not invoke or proclaim the existence of "female labor" as a global concern. Female workers affirmed many times the right to work, as stated in the Declaration of Rights of 1793, but they asserted a right possessed by everyone, whether man or woman, to provide for his or her existence.

Female workers fought to obtain more equitable remuneration for their labor, but even though women's wages were generally half of men's salaries, we do not find demands for "equal pay for equal work." Instead, from the beginning of the Revolution, female workers asked not be restricted to subaltern tasks and that poor young girls be apprenticed without cost to professions more lucrative than sewing. For this to occur, traditionally male professions with higher salaries had to be opened to women. Government initiatives were taken to achieve this end. These initiatives were favored by the war and made possible by the suppression, on 2 March 1791, of corporations whose strict rules had forbidden women to enter certain trades during the Old Regime.

Unlike the war of 1914–1918, the revolutionary wars did not bring about progress in female employment, for the simple reason that, when the Rev-

2. A.N., F⁷ 4678 d. Dolgof and F⁷4774 d. Lottin.

[margin note: when revo began, most & have jobs]

olution began, most lower-class women in Paris already had jobs. However, the wars may have encouraged this phenomenon by pushing women who had lived up until then by their spouse's work to seek employment to ensure their own and their children's subsistence. Moreover, in this pre-industrial society, the departure of farmers for the army was viewed as a threat to the economy. Agriculture lacked manpower, and one often heard how senseless it was that vigorous men should be occupied by "sedentary" tasks when they would be more usefully employed in the fields. Thus the authorities welcomed attempts to open the "mechanical" trades and artisanal or industrial professions to women, even though these occupations were high in the hierarchy of professions.

What is new here is not the introduction of women into the artisan class but their increasing access to more qualified and thus better paid work. We would be wrong to imagine that women were only employed in the so-called female activities of laundering or sewing. On the contrary, during this period female labor was characterized by its diversity. Professional mobility was equally surprising. Depending on the circumstances and opportunities for work available to the female laborer, the same women might make buttons in a workshop, display her merchandise at the marketplace, or bend over her sewing in her room. The crisis of labor that raged during the Revolution aggravated this incessant movement from one branch of employment to another and forced qualified female workers to seek "odd jobs" because there were none available in their professions.[3]

[margin note: Prof. mobility and Diversity]

[margin note: → lots of movement btw jobs]

FROM FASHION RETAILERS TO CHAIR MENDERS
Sew, Serve, Instruct, and Nurse

We have already seen some of these female workers, washerwomen, and merchants make their way through the streets of the city. But among the professions, sewing was women's primary work. There were many female linenworkers and needleworkers, women who labored for male tailors, breechesmakers, and menders. Not all of them had served as apprentices, and unemployed women could easily pass themselves off as textile workers. They might work at home, on consignment for specific individuals, or work on materials made up on the premises for important merchant-

3. The crisis of labor began before the Revolution, particularly in the textile industries after the trade agreement with England in 1786. During the Revolution, the luxury industries, which employed a large female workforce, were affected by emigration, and female unemployment became even worse.

manufacturers of linens and clothing who employed about a hundred female workers. Some dressmakers directed small workshops of from one to
ten female employees. These seamstresses were usually paid thirty sous a
day, the minimum necessary for a single person to survive, if they were paid
daily wages. (One livre equaled twenty sous.) They did not always receive
this much, however, and thus we can appreciate the financial difficulties of
these women.

Merchants and seamstresses in women's fashion, who belonged to the
aristocracy of female workers, were not as concerned about how to provide
for the next day. The fashion seamstress received an expensive, lengthy, and
painstaking apprenticeship that trained her to handle a brush and a needle
with equal skill, and later, to earn her living successfully, even if she lacked
the capital to open her own women's clothing store. The fashion seamstress
often had connections to the richest levels of society because of her profession, and, although she was not a counterrevolutionary, she did not take an
active part in the Revolution.

The domestic servant was another traditional type of female worker. At
the turn of the century, women represented more than 80 percent of
Parisian domestic servants.[4] Female servants, who were often of peasant
origin, had different responsibilities and status depending on whether they
worked for the aristocracy or the upper middle class in a wealthy home that
included several servants, or worked as the "all-purpose maid" in a family
of more modest means where they were the single servant. In great houses,
where a subtle but well-established domestic hierarchy reigned, servants,
cooks, nurses, and chambermaids worked side by side. Chambermaids were
at the top of the domestic hierarchy. These women, who were cultural
intermediaries between the elite with whom they were in permanent contact and the popular masses from whom they had sprung, were more often
found by the side of their masters than with the patriots during the Revolution. Earning relatively high wages, enjoying material advantages, and
economizing on their lodging and clothes, they could amass a modest fortune and leave their original sphere of birth not just ideologically but also
financially.

The many female "cooks" or "all-purpose maids" (*cuisinières* and
femmes de confiance—two terms that implied the same responsibilities and
were employed indiscriminately), the single domestic servant of a lower-
middle-class or middle-class family, were more representative of popular

4. Monnier, "L'Évolution de l'industrie."

milieus. They helped their mistresses with the housework, with marketing, and with the children and occasionally worked in the store, the workshop, or the cabaret. They lived in the same rhythm as their employers, shared their intimacy and their leisure, were in their confidence, and knew of their concerns. Sometimes they were the lovers of bachelor employers. If these women were patriots, they jeopardized their positions with employers hostile to the Revolution who dismissed them out of fear of denunciation for counterrevolutionary activities. When they were employed by a sansculotte household, which preferred to call them "partners in work" rather than domestic servants, they went in the evening with their employers to the section or the Jacobin club. Whereas some female domestic servants went from job to job out of economic necessity or a desire for independence and ended in poverty, others stayed several years with the same employer and were able to put away substantial savings to provide for their old age.

At the bottom of the domestic hierarchy were charwomen and sweepers, who were often either unemployed female laborers or women trying to add to the insufficient wages from their regular employment. These domestic servants did not live with their employer and were not paid by the year but were paid according to the amount of work finished in a day.

Domestics of both sexes were held in low esteem during the Revolution. Hanriot, the sansculotte commander of the Parisian national guard, was "galled that his mother did not want to leave her position as a domestic servant," and did not wish to see her again.[5] For a populace whose ideal was a society of small independent producers, there could be no worse state than to be under the direct domination of a master to whom one sold oneself for the year. Revolutionaries had to mistrust these workers who were dependent on and influenced by counterrevolutionaries. However, several domestic servants became famous in the women's revolutionary movement: the wife of Dubouy, called the Mère Duchesne, a "satellite and missionary to all women under Robespierre's orders" according to her enemies, attended all the revolutionary assemblies and was known to the Jacobins; the wife of Dubreuil, secretary in 1793 for the Society of Revolutionary Republican Women, wrote several times to Marat and rebelled against the "marital despotism" of men; Constance Evrard, another member of the Revolutionary Republican Women, was a friend of Pauline Léon, with whom she participated in several revolutionary activities, and an assiduous reader of various patriotic newspapers. She was honored in 1791

5. A.N., W 77.

by the *Révolutions de Paris* for having proposed to join the "battalion of tyrannicides."

These were not the only professions that employed women. For example, female teachers were not uncommon in Paris. Under the Old Regime, the education of artisans' and shopkeepers' daughters was conducted in part by nuns of charitable religious orders. Similarly, women held classes at their homes and taught young children who sometimes boarded with them. One of the major preoccupations of the revolutionaries was education (the Declaration of Rights of 1793 stated that education was "necessary for everyone"). But, in spite of several projects that envisioned a primary education for girls and boys—Condorcet's and Lepeletier's plans and the law of 29 Frimaire Year II (19 December 1793)—the revolutionaries did not have time to organize primary education at a national level. Initiatives by sections to keep the old charity schools in operation, or, if necessary, to create primary schools, multiplied in Paris in response to the sansculottes' hopes. In these establishments, which were controlled by the sections and free to the poor, students learned the rudiments of reading, writing, and sometimes arithmetic. The female teachers used examples from the Declaration of the Rights of Man or from the Constitution and dictated to little girls that "nations formed a single family, to defend a single cause against the oppression of tyrants."[6] In some schools children were taught rules of hygiene or received a professional apprenticeship from workers who were hired for this purpose.[7]

Women cared for the mind and for the body. The men of the Revolution often pictured women as the first "natural" teachers of their children, as well as the comforters of suffering invalids. But did women, who were traditionally responsible for the task of relieving suffering, find professional employment among men who kept official medical knowledge to themselves? Under the Old Regime, nuns served as nurses in the hospitals. During the Revolution, there was an attempt to replace them with "good female patriots" whose responsibilities were usually reduced to distributing food to patients. Sick-nurses, who watched over ailing patients at their homes, were old women whose failing strength or vision made it difficult for them to continue in their original profession. At the other extreme of the chain of life, midwives (more than two hundred in Paris, according to Louis Sébastien Mercier) practiced their trade at their patients' homes or took in as boarders women who were about to give

---

6. A.N., F⁷ 4774⁸⁷ d. Raucourt, F⁷ 4774⁶⁶ d. Pellier.
7. A.N., F⁷ 4635 d. Casin.

birth.[8] There were not many wet-nurses in the capital, and they tended to live in areas that were still quite rural in character, such as Chaillot. We should also point out the unique presence in the archives of an "oculist" whose "skill in curing diseases of the eye" was attested to by several authorities.[9]

Gardeners, usherettes, actresses, singing instructors, music teachers, foreign language instructors, landladies, store managers, bookkeepers: these are still more examples of the many occupations open to women at this time. Finally, women were an important part of the workforce among artisans.

Female Laborers

The artisan class is often represented as a male world, where the master's wife was the sole female presence. Indispensable to the workshop, she assisted her husband and could direct the workers, look after the administration and the bookkeeping, and ensure that the business ran smoothly in the event of her husband's absence or death. Seated behind her counter, she sold what was produced. In small, family shops, she helped with the labor; in larger shops, she was the privileged target of coworkers who were antagonistic toward the master.[10] But she was not the only woman in the artisans' world. Some women were true contractors and employed from twenty to two hundred workers. Women were proprietors in textile, clothing, and other female trades, as well as owners and directors of such varied businesses as breweries and soap, faience, and porcelain factories. Female workers of the artisan class were even more numerous and representative, although they are little known and often "forgotten" by historians, perhaps because it is difficult to perceive traces of them in the documents from which historians work. One source for the revolutionary period gives a good account of the importance of this female workforce: the lists of males and females provided in 1790 and 1791 by their employers, who wished to exchange large assignats (French paper money from 1789 to 1797) for small notes or metallic currency to pay their employees. These lists give striking evidence of the importance of female labor in workshops and industry and allow us to map precisely the geography of labor in Paris at this time.[11]

8. Louis Sebastien Mercier, *Tableau de Paris* . . . , vol. 5 (Hambourg: Virchaux & Compagnie, 1781), p. 47.
9. A.N., F^7 4774^{87} d. Rapigeon.
10. See Arlette Farge, *Fragile Lives: Violence, Power, and Solidarity in Eighteenth-Century Paris*, trans. Carol Shelton (Cambridge: Harvard University Press, 1993).
11. "Correspondance relative à des échanges d'assignats contre du numéraire en 1790 et 1791 en faveur des fabricants et des commerçants de Paris," A.N., F^{30} 115 to

Production was still organized in an artisanal manner. Two kinds of organization predominated: the independent artisan and scattered manufactories. In the first, labor occurred in workshops of medium size, under the direction of the master-artisan, who sometimes also sold the products of female employees who worked at home. In these workshops, men and women often labored together. In an atmosphere that exuded fashion and luxury, women cut, combed, pasted, and sewed the shimmering fabric and skillfully prepared those trinkets dear to coquettes and seducers, such as feathers and artificial flowers destined to adorn the heads or the hats of elegant women, or pearls that shone at their necks. Female cutters, applicators, finishers, mounters, gluers, wood gilders, printers of sheets of paper, painters of sheets of paper or of texts, embroiderers of taffeta or of paper, braid embellishers, and illuminators of sheets of paper were among the many female workers in fanmaking (four thousand women to two thousand men) and the production of small wooden objects (chess sets and so on).[12] Buttonmaking was another profession that primarily employed women. Because metal and fabric were both necessary for the production of buttons, women made frameworks for buttons and worked as polishers, inserters, and winders in button workshops.

The fabrication of these products of fashion and luxury took place in the center of Paris, in the narrow crooked streets of the sections of Réunion (Beaubourg), Temple, Gravilliers, and Amis-de-la-Patrie, where shops of wholesale dealers of fashionable accessories can still be found. Female workers labored in groups of one or two dozen people in workshops that were often directed by women, who might be married to the owner or themselves the proprietor in trades such as making artificial feathers, flowers, and pearls. Work at home was also important. Besides the women and men who labored in the workshop, owners often also employed women who worked on raw materials at their home for one or several manufacturers. Work, whether in the workshop or at home, was accomplished by families. Masters employed mothers and daughters,

---

F[30] 159 (the correspondence is filed by section). This discussion on female workers of the artisan class is based for the most part on this source, along with women's declarations in police reports (principally the alphabetic series of the Committee of General Security at the A.N. and the collection of the A.P.P.) and requests for admission to the municipal spinning workshops (A.N., F[15] 3579, 3580, 3582, 3588, 3589, 3603–3604).

12. The figures for the number of men and women employed in fanmaking come from Monnier, "L'Évolution de l'industrie." In addition, Monnier estimates at "25,000 or 30,000, at least, the number of women employed in Parisian luxury industries," which was about 12 or 13 percent of the female population.

brothers and sisters, and husbands and wives. A woman born the daughter of fanmakers or specialists in woodwork was taught the trade (family apprenticeship was encouraged by work at home) and then married a coworker in the same branch of employment. The specialist in woodwork Ducray worked with her husband and her mother in the workshops of another woodworking specialist in the same home where they lived in the Gravilliers section.[13]

Before adorning the neck, finger, or wrist of a beautiful lady or pricking the finger of a daydreaming woman or covering the head or hanging at the sash of a defender of liberty, these jewels, needles, helmets, and sabers first passed through the hands of female metal workers who polished, burnished, plated, and gilded them. All jewelers employed one or more female polishers (the polishing profession consisted almost entirely of women), cutters, and gilders, and the workshops that produced gold leaf also welcomed women. Female polishers could be found at armorers, pinmakers, and brass manufacturers. More than a fourth of the workforce (107 people, including 47 apprentices) of the celebrated Firmin-Didot, bookseller and printing type-founder, consisted of women, who sometimes were related to other workers. Didot himself recognized that work conditions were very unpleasant in his foundry. His establishment was a veritable furnace permanently lit by a hellish glare escaping from the furnaces, which illuminated the faces of female workers who bent over small letters that they polished on a sandstone mill.[14] The women in the goldsmith's or silversmith's trade worked either at home or in workshops of four to ten people situated in the city center or on the Ile Saint-Louis (an important area for jewelry), near which they lived. A female metal worker should not have been burdened with financial worries because her wages (two or three livres a day in the Year II) were not a poor salary, even if they were ridiculously lower than the wages of male workers in the same trade. However, since the production of all luxury items had slowed down, those who worked for jewelers sometimes had no more than a day's work per *décade* (the ten-day week of the republican calendar, instituted in autumn of 1793). Whereas some women then became beggars, others were able to apply their skills to manufacturing products necessary for the war.

Other independent artisans employed women. Shoemakers and bootmakers hired women to decorate shoes with embroidery and to line wooden

13. A.N., F⁷ 4685 d. Ducray Claude.
14. A.N., F³⁰ 151.

shoes with fur. Espadrilles and pocketbooks were made in workshops of women directed by men. Wigmakers employed women to fashion wigs. At furriers and peltmakers, women did needlework and were paid at the same rate as seamstresses and female beltmakers. For carpenters, women did small jobs of finishing work, such as polishing, and caned and stuffed chairs (two occupations where women predominated). In upholsterer's workshops, men and women worked side by side. These workshops also employed many women at their homes, particularly in the Faubourg Saint-Antoine. The saltpeter-makers of the faubourgs included among their workers women who sold ashes for scouring.

Dispersed manufacturing linked to merchant capital also left its mark on the world of female labor. A merchant-manufacturer, who was not an artisan, furnished raw material to female workers who labored alone in their homes or for master-artisans who employed a small number of people. These "master-workers" (*maîtres-ouvriers*) depended on the merchant-manufacturers who paid them and retailed their work.

Fine fabric, gauze, and silk work were all organized according to this model. The seventy-four employers who wrote to request small notes of assignats were mostly very large merchant-manufacturers; among them, twenty had to pay from fifty to one hundred people, and eleven paid more than one hundred. The ones with the fewest workers lived in the section of the Observatoire. The others, who had their headquarters in the fashionable quarters in the north, frequently directed the chain of production from top to bottom and included embroiderers among their female workers. They bought and distributed raw materials among many small workshops spread out among several areas of the capital (or even in the villages of Picardy) and then sold the raw gauze or distributed it among several embroidery workshops. From half to three fourths of the workers that they paid were women; the operations of winding, cutting, and warping were executed almost solely by women. The gauzemaker partners Bellanger and Dumas Descombes (Amis-de-la-Patrie section) employed 225 women and 205 men. More than half of their workers lived in the Faubourgs Saint-Marcel (seventy-two) and Saint-Antoine (fifty-eight); twenty-six lived in the faubourgs of the north; and only thirty lived in the center sections.[15] The Faubourg Saint-Antoine is completely absent from the map that shows the distribution of merchant-manufacturers, but it appears clearly in the

15. A.N., F^{30} 138.

map of their workers, whereas the section of Bon-Conseil, situated in the central districts, disappears. Female winders often lodged in the Faubourg Saint-Antoine, where the majority of them worked alone in their room, and cutters directed family workshops located in the Faubourg Saint-Marcel. As for gauze embroiderers, we find them only in the north of Paris, near the fashionable districts. Family labor was frequently the rule: forty-three of the ninety-six workers of the manufacturer Lamotte worked with their families (seventeen couples including one with their dauhter, two with their mother, one with a female worker, plus two sisters and twice two brothers).[16] The same Lamotte notes the amounts that he had to pay his workers: a woman earned on average about half of a man's salary (six livres thirteen sous to thirteen livres five sous for a six-day week); some women, however, earned fifteen to sixteen livres a week. Moreover, there were men who were paid less than women but never less than their own wives. If we add that the highest paid employee was a man and that the lowest paid were women, we will have a good general sense of the disproportion between male and female wages.

Female and male gauzemakers rarely found work during the Revolution because this industry was one of the most strongly affected by the economic crisis within the luxury trades. As early as 1791, the administrators of municipal workshops for the indigent painted an ominous picture of the fate of these female workers, who were "reduced to sleeping on a little straw on the floor and living on bread and water." Requesting liberty for her husband, a female worker of the Faubourg Saint-Antoine wrote to Fouquier Tinville: "I will not describe my distress to you. It suffices to say that for two years I have not had work because I am a gauzemaker."[17]

The lace trade, where the workforce was four-fifths women,[18] was another luxury industry that depended on merchant capital and was strongly affected by the crisis. The organization of labor within this trade was pyramidal. At the top, the merchant-manufacturer dealt with ribbonmakers, fringemakers, and gold and silver lacemakers, who often worked for several wholesale merchants. These "master-workers," who were frequently women, executed part of the work with the help of their family and one or two employees and distributed the rest to female workers who worked

16. A.N., F^{30} 127.
17. A.N., F^{15} 3579 and W 159 d. Boullay.
18. In "L'Évolution de l'industrie," Monnier gives the statistics of one thousand male workers and four thousand female workers.

alone at their homes. They were intermediaries between their workers and the wholesale merchants. The merchant-manufacturer paid each of them an amount that corresponded to their wages and the wages of their workers.

Many women also worked for merchant-manufacturers in the glove trade and hosiery business (stockingmaking). Women in the stocking trade, who often received wretched pay, were not employed as weavers but worked in preparing the product, as winders, and in completing it, as sewers, liners, and embroiderers.

In dispersed manufacturing, the artisans were wage earners who owned ②
their own tools and employed several workers. Production remained artisanal and familial. The employees of the merchant-manufacturer did not work in the same place but labored in small dispersed workshops. There was no concentration, except for products made by the employees of the merchant who was responsible for selling them. Even so, wholesale merchants often called their enterprise a *manufacture* (factory), meaning by this term all the workers employed by them rather than a specific site. Many merchant-manufacturers resided in the central districts, whereas their female and male employees frequently lived in the faubourgs. Thus the residents of the Faubourgs Saint-Antoine and Saint-Marcel were far from being composed only of independent artisans, and the central sections were not the "worker" neighborhoods that such historians as F. Braesch and George Rudé believed; they took the word *factory* in its modern sense and assumed that a merchant-manufacturer's employees worked in the same place and lived in the same section as their employer (which was, however, often the case for independent artisans.)[19]

Examples such as embroidery and lacework, professions where merchant-manufacturers declared an enormous workforce, clearly show how necessary it is to correct these historians' studies of the topography of labor in Paris. Female embroiderers or lacemakers worked either for fashion retailers, who might eventually make them partners, or for important merchant-manufacturers. Those merchant-manufacturers who made lace or "blonde" lace (that made from silk, particularly prized by Marie Antoinette) were very large-scale wholesale merchants employing 150 to 800 female workers, most of whom lived in the provinces. Parisian lacemakers disdained the Faubourgs Saint-Antoine and Saint-Marcel;

19. F. Braesch, "Essai de statistique de la population ouvrière de Paris," *La Révolution française* 63 (July 1912): 289–321; George Rudé, "La Population ouvrière de Paris de 1789 à 1791," *Annales historiques de la Révolution française* 187 (January–March 1967): 15–37.

most lived northwest of the Seine. The bourgeois sections of the west, where in general few female workers lived, welcomed lacemakers and embroiderers who were relatively skilled and well paid. Embroiderers also resided south of the Seine, where the section of Croix-Rouge sheltered the Rue des Brodeurs. During the Revolution, embroiderers, along with gauze workers and lacemakers, were the female workers most harshly affected by the labor crisis. The organization of the embroidery trade depended completely on merchant capital at two levels. A very large-scale merchant, often a purveyor of gauze, muslin, and lace, divided his orders between different intermediaries who were in business with several merchants at the same time. In turn, they distributed work to embroiderers who worked alone at their homes, or in small workshops of four to five people. These intermediaries, often women, were not dependent artisans directing small familial workshops, but true contractors employing a hundred female laborers who worked at home. Thus Mlle. Desays, proprietress-embroiderer of the Croix-Rouge section, took orders from various wholesale merchants, then had the work executed by eighty-six female embroiderers, "indigent day-laborers" whom she paid herself and most of whom worked at home.[20] Yet small workshops could also labor directly for the wholesale merchant.

In his study of the Parisian working population, E. Braesch has not taken this organization into account. Thus he describes the Oratoire section (Garde-Française), in the center of the capital, as a "female worker" section with an extremely high average number of workers per patron (21.8). However, the three employers who declared the largest work forces in this section were "embroiderers." These "embroiderers" were actually merchants who dealt with female contractors or master-artisans who lived, not in this section, but in the Faubourg Saint-Marcel, which then still appeared to be a "worker" center. The Oratoire section, on the contrary, was noteworthy as a district where important wholesale merchants of luxury products resided.

Similarly, because of his misinterpretation of the meaning of the word *factory*, Rudé believes that there were more than fifty concentrated factories in Paris, each consisting of more than one hundred workers, creating a total of "14,500 factory laborers," particularly in textile industries.[21] These so-called factories were, in fact, mostly the total of small workshops

20. A.N., F^{30} 153.
21. Rudé, "La Population ouvrière."

directed by dependent master-artisans and scattered across the entire city, or even in the country. This is probably the case for that "factory" of eight hundred workers in the declaration of a manufacturer of blonde lace. Since we know how the manufacture of lace was organized and that the majority of workers declared by merchant-manufacturers lived in the Ile-de-France or Normandy, we must be skeptical about the existence of this "factory" in Rudé's sense. Certainly, we can see here a "stage in the evolution of the great capitalist industry of the future," as this historian writes, but a stage that was more destructive than constructive because it was still dominated by merchant capital. As these workers were not "crowded together in greater enterprises," we do not see, at least in gauzework, lacemaking, embroidery, or ornamentation, "the sketch of an industrial way of life and relations between workers and patrons that were no longer that of artisanal production." On the contrary, inside the different small workshops laboring for the merchant-manufacturer, production was organized in an artisanal fashion. Relations between the employer-owner and his fellows and the female workers remained traditional. The former was barely richer than the latter, and they were linked by familial and neighborhood ties, doubled by a probable solidarity among themselves against the merchant-manufacturer.

Despite the fact that the independent and dependent artisan class was dominant in Paris, there were indeed workshops where a hundred or so workers gathered, which were closer to small concentrated factories (although there was no mechanized production in these workshops) than to artisanal workshops, marking an intermediary stage in economic development. Here the employer was more distant. Replaced by the foreman, he no longer worked alongside the female employee every day and directed her labor. She could no longer feel solidarity with her employer's wife when he drank, beat her, or cheated on her. In these large workshops, slowly, in small stages, the female worker of the artisan class gave way to the woman worker of "large" industry. During the Revolution, this transformation was far from complete and the outline of the female worker was still very blurred. Thus spinners, who lived especially in the Parisian suburbs, might work in true concentrated factories, at home, or in workshops with modest workforces. The same organization can be found in blanketmaking, which occupied an important place in the Faubourg Saint-Marcel. The blanketmakers were all large manufacturers employing from 40 to 250 workers, among whom were many women who did the preparatory tasks for weaving and were paid half as much as men, who alone had the title of "workman weavers." In blanketmaking we see again the transition toward a true manufactory production. On the one hand, the manufacturers assembled some of their workers in their workshops, but on the other hand, they employed families working at home, perpetuating the conditions of division. Thus merchant capital and industrial capital coexisted without the former clearly prevailing over the latter.

The hat trade represented another form of transition, where merchant capital did not intervene. Large-scale artisans (or their descendants) became true manufacturers who employed a hundred or so workers at the same place, but there remained a majority of small independent master-artisans who owned their shop of about ten employees. A fourth of the workforce of hatmakers, residing around the Beaubourg section (Réunion), was composed of women. Like woman workers in blanketmaking and many other Parisian female laborers, women in the hat trade were restricted to the subaltern tasks of preparation or of finishing, where wages were predicated upon a standard of relatively insignificant qualifications.

Such concentrations of female workers were equally evident in other trades, such as wallpapermaking, which took place predominantly in the Faubourgs Saint-Antoine and Saint-Marcel. The foundry of Firmin-Didot provides another example. It is striking to see that the majority of these concentrated factories were situated in the faubourgs—the northern faubourgs whose "worker" character Braesch and Rudé have emphasized, as well as the Faubourgs Saint-Marcel and Saint-Antoine. It is, moreover, in this last neighborhood that the April 1789 riots occurred against the wallpaper manufacturer Réveillon. This struggle is considered by historians as the only "insurrectional movement by wage earners" as a social group during the Revolution.[22] It seems astonishing that this unique disturbance over wages took place in a faubourg whose worker character has been denied by Rudé as well as by Braesch. Instead of denying this character, we must seek in these three faubourgs the rare workmen and workwomen in Paris at this period—"workers" not in the sense of *wage earners* but in a sense closer to the contemporary meaning, although we cannot speak here of the modern proletariat; such workers are to be found in these faubourgs rather than in the

22. See George Rudé, *La Foule dans la Révolution française* (Paris: Maspero, 1982), p. 55 (published in English as *The Crowd in the French Revolution* [Oxford: Clarendon Press, 1959]); Albert Soboul, "Problèmes du travail en l'an II," *Annales historiques de la Révolution française* 28 (1956): 236–254.

central sections populated by a large number of wage earners of the artisan class.

The "Miasmas of Hope"

In bookmaking, female laborers did not work only at type casting. Before work took place at the printing establishment, women were employed in workshops or at home doing the sizing and spreading necessary for manufacturing paper. Then, in the workshops of the Latin Quarter, female workers folded, stitched, and bound printed sheets and passed the edges of the pages through gold. Folding and stitching, executed only by women, and bookbinding, where women represented about half the workforce, were the least "noble" and well paid tasks of the profession. Here as elsewhere, men reserved for themselves the more specialized and well-paid positions of engravers and printers. *♀ get worst jobs in profession*

Nevertheless, women were employed in other areas of publication and were much sought after for all jobs that required the delicate and artistic labor of drawing. They were skillful at providing contrast for geographical maps and at coloring and illuminating engravings. Martinet, an engineer and engraver for the king's natural history collection who had worked with Réamur, Buffon, and Brisson, employed more women than men. They "were all trained by him and habituated from their earliest childhood to his works of natural history, where the correction of drawings and particularly the fidelity of colors are essential."[23] Women painters, who found they could not earn enough money through their paint brushes, went to work for printers from whom they gained "a good sustenance."[24] *still could get good jobs*

Moreover, women—in particular, widows—directed printing establishments. For example, Anne Félicité Colombe, proprietor of the Henri IV print shop, located in a suite of rooms on the place Dauphine, was an ardent militant and a member in 1793 of the Society of Revolutionary Republican Women. In December 1790, her press published Marat's *L'Ami du Peuple*. Harassed by the authorities, who seized her newspapers, and dragged into a libel lawsuit, she refused to tell the commissioner where Marat could be found. As the proprietor of the shop where *L'Ami du Peuple* was printed, she was one of four women arrested on 17 July 1791, after the Champ-de-Mars fusillade. Unfortunately, we have little information about this woman, who was well known at this time, although we can guess that she was a colorful character and that she was generous (having finally won the

23. A.N., F^{30} 155.
24. A.N., F^7 4774^{42} d. Mencelle.

libel lawsuit brought against her, she gave to the poor of her neighborhood the twenty thousand livres that her accuser Etienne was condemned to pay her).[25]

Typography remained, however, a business of men. But in this period of change, Madame de Bastide started in 1791 the Project for a Free School of Typography on Behalf of Women (*Projet d'une école gratuite de typographie en faveur des femmes*). She pointed out that "no one could say: 'I am not made to work,' because everyone is born to exist" and that "no establishment offers any resources to women . . . ; however, everyone knows that the work ordinarily given to women is not sufficient to provide for a family." For Madame de Bastide, typographical composition suited her fellows, who were "naturally sedentary, adroit, and patient." To gain admission to this school, apprentices would have to know how to read and write well, be of irreproachable morals, be from fifteen to thirty years old, and undertake to educate two students: "With good will and a little intelligence, a few months would suffice for them to arrive at the level of perfection necessary to assure their independence." This program would be completed by the creation, at the same place as the workshops of the printing establishment, of a "civic school for women" where students "would learn without expense the knowledge necessary to their work": languages, history, geography, ethics, drawing, painting, engraving, and music. A library would be open "where they could come to consult works at all hours of the day." This instruction would be free for "the indigent class of the sex who is of greatest concern to our establishment." Those better off financially had to pay the modest sum of three livres a year.[26]

This typographic school for women was indeed opened, probably in spring 1793. The establishment, which also operated as a printing press, was placed under the direction of citizen Deltusso, a "writer-translator of the National Convention sessions." His program differed little from the one proposed by Madame de Bastide. However, the "civic school" was suppressed and the typography apprenticeship, which lasted six months, cost four hundred livres. The students had to know how to read and write and be at least twelve years old, and they were not accepted until "the strictest inquiries" had been made about them. The total number of students was limited to sixty. Those who, at the end of their apprenticeship, wished to remain attached to the establishment were paid according to a rate equal to printers—about seven livres a day

25. A.N., F⁷ 4624 pl. 1 pp. 52–69.
26. A.N., F¹⁵ 1861.

according to the legal maximum of the Year II—an important measure considering the inequality between male and female wages! This corresponded to the school's objective, developed by the citizen Bastide and described in the prospectus that the school sent as an advertisement to section authorities, for distribution to Parisian women.[27] Its goal was to give female citizens sufficient qualification so that "the most worthy half of the human race" was not "reduced to dependence on the other half." The authors of the prospectus were convinced that the exclusion of female workers in typography resulted from the unequal education of the two sexes and not from the nature of women, whose great dexterity, assiduity, zeal, and intelligence they praised. Consequently, the school and the printing establishment was placed under the aegis of the regeneration of morals.

The revolutionary authorities appreciated the enterprise. The Committee of Public Safety became a client and on 11 Prairial Year II (30 May 1794), Grégoire made a favorable report to the Committee of Public Instruction and asked that the program be extended to "many types of work that suited [women])," so that both agriculture and the arts could benefit from "a large group of men who would be advantageously occupied in these two areas, which suffer from their absence."[28] Encouraged by this support, the director requested on 27 Prairial Year II (15 June 1794) at the Convention that their prospectus be posted everywhere at the nation's expense, that a financial indemnity and premises in different districts be granted to them, and finally, that part of the printing of official work be reserved for them.[29] Only the Representative Poultier spoke against the enterprise, giving as pretext the risk of women being poisoned by miasmas from the ink in type cases. Female workers mocked this hypocritical concern in a petition: "He does not want to poison us. He prefers to see us die of hunger and of cold. Men are not so affected by these miasmas for they have nothing to fear. . . . It is wrong that people have always wished to reduce us to uselessness. The miasmas of hope have yet to upset our health."[30]

27. B.N., 16° Q, document 36; A.N., F7* 2472, p. 45.

28. Extract from the register of deliberations by the Committee of Public Instruction, reproduced in the *Pétition à la Convention nationale pour l'Ecole typographique des femmes*, published in *Les Femmes compositrices d'imprimerie sous la Révolution française en 1794, par l'ancien typographe M. Alkan aîné* (Paris: Dentu, 1862), and in *Les Femmes dans la Révolution* (Paris: Edhis, 1982).

29. *Archives parlementaires* 91, p. 634.

30. *Lettre des Citoyennes typographes, à tous les Représentants du Peuple, Excepté Poultier*, A.N., AD VIII 20.

don't want competition [handwritten marginalia]

However, the initiative was not welcomed by workers within the profession. They were alarmed by the prospect of competition from women, which went against received ideas. The director of the school, ridiculed and attacked "by those interested in perpetuating abusive practices," described the enterprise as "bold." He cleverly associated the hostility of the typographers with the privileges of the ancient guilds. Prudently, he asked that the "courageous" printers, who, with an open and egalitarian spirit, had agreed to teach their trade to women, be employed by government printing establishments in case of failure. Otherwise, they would be condemned to die of hunger because all printers would close their doors to them. "The workers of the Old Regime would never forgive them for lending themselves to his views and working with him at a plan that would partially abolish the privilege that printers had enjoyed until now."[31]

We do not know what became of this enterprise, which continued to operate at least until Germinal Year III (April 1795) under the name of the Imprimerie des Femmes and under Deltusso's direction.

The antagonism that the typographic school must have encountered is indicated by a conflict that occurred in wallpaper manufacturing, another branch of the printing industry. Laborers in wallpaper worked in concentrated factories. The famous Réveillon employed from two hundred to three hundred people. Among his employees were female gluers and draughtswomen but only male printers. When, at the beginning of the Year II, the wallpaper manufacturers Arthur and Robert engaged women in their workshops in the Piques section as printers, they provoked the anger of workers in the profession.[32] On 20 Brumaire Year II (10 November 1793), Val, an overseer of Arthur and Robert, received the following threatening letter:

> Scoundrel, how dare you place women at the printing table. You must wish to have your face smashed by printers of the Fabrique Républicaine, by citizen Legrand's printers, by Réveillon's printers and by printers in all the other factories, who mutter against you for bringing women into the profession. See, tyrant, how angry the printing guild is at you. You would do better to dismiss the women and to give higher wages to the workers or you will have your face kicked in by the workers. We have written you a first letter, you

31. See notes 28 and 29. A small epistolarly novel had, for example, been published by the Imprimerie des Femmes: *Triomphe de la saine philosophie, ou la vraie politique des femmes*

32. The account of this conflict can be found in A.P.P., AA 209 f. 214–223 and AA 248, 23 Brumaire Year II.

say you have wiped your ass with it and that you don't give a damn about whoever wrote it. Here is a second letter of good paper and good ink. It is your responsibility to watch over your actions. We will not say more.

Signed by all the printers in Paris factories.

In this violent reaction of male professional chauvinism, we can see the fear of a decrease in wages brought about by employment of a possibly less well paid female workforce. If the letter reports the truth, the "muttering" of the workers of Réveillon in the Faubourg Saint-Antoine and of Legrand in the Faubourg Saint-Marcel, both fairly distant from the Piques section, shows simultaneously the strong feelings aroused by this act and the existence of relations between different wallpaper printers that probably stemmed from the old guilds mentioned in the text.

The next day, the Fabrique Républicaine, a neighbor of Arthur and Robert's factory, was in complete agitation. A worker named Auguste showed his fellows an insulting letter signed by Val that told of his intention to continue to employ women. After comparison, it was noticed that the letter sent to Val and the one supposedly from him, sent to Auguste, were in the same handwriting and thus proved concerted activity. The director of the Fabrique Républicaine became anxious "about the fatal results that could arise from a gathering of workers intent on opposing the employment of women in paper manufacturing." He decided to engage in a test of strength by also admitting female workers to his factory, but, suspicious of the reception that these new recruits might receive, he prudently asked the section authorities for protection. On 23 Brumaire (13 November), the revolutionary commissioners of the Tuileries section pointed out to the male workers that the guilds had been abolished and "that it was their duty in all justice to let female citizens work who could compete with citizen workers of different factories in Paris. Moreover, by employing women, a great good would result for all of society." The police conducted an investigation in the factory to find the author of the letters. In spite of these precautions, three days later, the workers of Arthur and Robert were taken to task in the street by a printer of the Fabrique Républicaine: Arthur and Val were knaves and beggars, and so were their workers, who could expect their colleagues of the Fabrique Républicaine "to bankrupt them" in a short time. The printer threatened that Val would "play with a hot hand" (would be guillotined), and allegedly added that the controversial letters had been written by the printers of his factory. He "repeatedly insulted" one of Arthur's female workers "by calling her a whore and telling her that all her fellow-workers were not worth any more than she."

The documents do not tell us if the wallpaper printers finally won. However, the attempt to introduce women as typographers in the printing establishment failed, and the care with which male printers watched jealously to prevent any female intrusion in their profession was legendary. The "miasmas of hope" could not resist male exclusivity.

All that remained were the "miasmas of misery" for a female worker population restricted to the worst and least profitable employment—labor that also exhausted them. And when vision faltered, when the hand trembled, when the fatigued body refused to respond to the demands of trades that were often physically taxing, when old age could not be ignored and their children were too poor to care for them, the women were reduced to begging. Younger women wore themselves out in order to earn enough to feed and shelter themselves. In the professions where women were more skilled, their salaries were higher but were still less than the wages of male workers. In some cases this did not mean unequal salaries for the same work, but lower wages for less qualified tasks, and it was maintained resolutely that these conditions should not change! Besides, even during the Revolution, wages of female trades did not show the same general increase as the wages paid by the trades of many male workers.[33] These same female trades were often among those first directly affected by the crisis in the production of luxury items. Occasional lack of employment increased the difficulties of many female workers. To suppress this unemployment, which was endemic in certain professions, and enable this female population to survive, the revolutionary authorities created public assistance work.

Women Working for the Section

Thus soldiers' relatives and unemployed female workers were employed to make clothing needed for the army. In practice, the sections were at first responsible for the enterprise, which was centralized after 1793 by the office in charge of clothing for troops. This office on the one hand made business agreements with large private subcontractors free from any supervision, and, on the other hand, opened six local offices where its agents distributed work to women in the capital. This was not appreciated by all female workers. Many preferred that work be distributed in the sections. During the summer and autumn of 1793, women formed tumultuous assemblies,

---

33. Saint-Aubin, *Tableau comparatif des prix des principales denrées et marchandises ainsi que de l'industrie et de la main-d'oeuvre tels que pris existoient avant les assignats, tels qu'on les a vus du 5 au 15 prairial, et . . .* (Paris: Maret, Year III [1796?]), p. 28.

wrote petitions, and intervened with section authorities, popular clubs, and general assemblies, relieving each other—without concerted planning—at the Convention witness stand. The protests culminated on 29 August, when female workers read to the members of the National Convention a petition approved by more than 4,675 women that demanded that work be returned to the sections: "It would be more glorious for us to fight the traitors [the administrators] and to denounce them than to allow ourselves to die in our homes without daring to dispute with them the rights in which we should share."[34]

The Convention was ready to accede to the demands of the female workers but was unsure which position to adopt because of a lack of agreement among the women. Finally, at the end of autumn, the work was entrusted to the sections, and there were no more complaints on this subject. Most sections then named two commissioners, usually militant sansculottes, who were responsible for bookkeeping and for cutting the cloth in order to distribute it to female workers whom they paid. They kept a profit from the business but were subject to the authority of the general assembly of the section, which could dismiss them. The female worker who was the victim of an injustice would present her case to the general assembly.

Complaints and petitions resumed, however, inspired by lack of work and the rate of pay. Although work was being done in the sections, government committees continued to form agreements with private subcontractors to the detriment of female workers, who often found themselves without employment. A petition drawn up by the popular club of the Unité section on 4 Pluviôse Year II (23 January 1793) asked "to abolish and suppress all the private subcontractors of the Republic," "leeches of the people" who monopolized the markets and paid dirt-cheap wages to "penniless female workers." Because of private subcontractors, "the workshops were not stocked at all and female workers in this section did nothing." Thus it was necessary that the Convention divide all work among single workshops, where, because they were managed by good sansculottes, the female workers would "receive a fair salary for their work." The exorbitant profits taken by the private contractors were denounced even more forcefully.[35] In the days that followed, the petition circulated in all Parisian popular clubs, provoking a "great uproar" and the applause of women in the galleries. During Pluviôse, this petition was talked about throughout Paris,

34. *Archives parlementaires* 73, p. 176. See also *Archives parlementaires* 72, pp. 516 and 836; A.P.P., AA 139 f. 37, AA 72 f. 100, AA 227 f. 52; A.N., F⁷* 2488 f. 70.
35. A.N., D III 155–156¹ d. 9. On the hostility of the sansculottes toward the private contractors, see Soboul, "Problèmes du travail."

and in streets and cabarets agitated female workers condemned the profits of private purveyors and even of section tradesmen. Women received only fifteen sous for making a shirt that the nation then bought for double! And what would be left for female workers once they had paid five sous for the thread?[36]

These complaints about pay ceased soon afterward. However, protests about the lack of distributed work continued all through the period. On 1 Ventôse Year II (19 February 1794), the inhabitants of the Tuileries section even asked the revolutionary committee for "permission to advertise loudly in order to assemble female citizens who wished to ask for work from the Convention."[37] The further we advance in time, the less labor the sections could give to female workers, who were, however, more and more numerous. In the Year III (1795), the situation grew worse and workers' complaints multiplied. When the climate was explosive and Parisian authorities feared a popular uprising, a woman who had the misfortune to assert too openly that there was no more work in the sections and that "for several days she had not eaten for lack of work" was immediately arrested.[38] With the failure of the insurrection of Prairial Year III (May 1795), section workshops disappeared in favor of single private purveyors.

Aside from sewing for the sections, women worked for the clothing supply office or for the municipal government. Thus, in the Bonne-Nouvelle section, about a hundred female workers lived in an old convent where the office of clothing supply had established workshops for making tents and frock coats.[39] At the municipal flour warehouse on the Rue du Temple, two to three hundred women, who were paid twenty-five sous a day in workshops of sixty to eighty people, mended sacks for the office of provisions. Even in the middle of winter, these workshops were not heated; when an employee remarked that it was cold and that a fire was necessary in order to work, she was told that "if she made similar proposals again, she would be fired." She retorted that male and female workers were the sovereign People, "that the municipal officers and the authorities were only their agents, and that it was indeed astonishing that the Sovereign lacked wood when its agents were abundantly provided with it." This woman was dis-

---

36. A.N., W 191, reports of 4, 7, and 24 Pluviôse; B.N., Mss., N.A.F. 2662 f. 104.
37. A.N., F7* 2471, p. 127.
38. A.N., F 1c III Seine 14, 23 Frimaire and A.P.P., AA 61 f. 189.
39. A.P.P., AA 77 f. 5–9.

missed, as well as her daughter who, at the end of this incident, had read the Declaration of the Rights of Man in the workshop. They did not admit defeat and turned to the popular club of their section for defense (which it undertook).[40]

Social demands relied on revolutionary political principles (the sovereignty of the people, the rights of man) and appeals to popular clubs by female workers drawn up against the municipal government. These characteristics call into question the images of docile and submissive female workers and help correct the idea that the wage-earning population had little interest in the Revolution, only retaining from it the "cursed maximum" for wages.[41] The following events in municipal spinning workshops illustrate this on a scale not seen in other conflicts. Although these events did not change the course of the Revolution, they constitute one of the most significant work conflicts of this period.

WOMEN WORKERS AS CITIZENS

Spinning Workshops and Their Personnel

The predecessor of these workshops was the Office of Spinning by the Poor, created in 1779, which supplied hemp for spinning to the destitute throughout the parish. In February 1790, Bailly, the mayor of Paris, created on his own initiative a spinning workshop for the indigent, an enterprise quickly taken over at his request by the Department of Public Works. Spinning workshops were then established in execution of the Constituent Assembly's decree of 30 May 1790, to give work to old men, women, and children without any resources. These mills were active from the following month of July.

In two "workshops" (here meaning concentrated manufactories), women spun cotton, hemp, and linen. One was established in the old Jacobin convent in the Rue Saint-Jacques (the section of Thermes-de-Julien, then of Beaurepaire, and finally of Chalier, not to be confused with the Jacobin convent in the Rue Saint-Honoré, where meetings of the club of the same name were held) and was called in the Year II the "Atelier du Midi"

---

40. A.N., F⁷ 4775²⁰ d. Six.

41. In September 1793, a "general maximum for essential goods and wages" was established. Its revision in 1794 lowered real wages. Therefore, when workers saw Robespierrists on their way to the guillotine on 11 Thermidor Year II, they booed at them and jeered the "cursed maximum."

(South workshop). The other workshop, in the faubourgs north of the city, first occupied the premises of the old Récollet convent (section of Body), then moved in the Year II to the Faubourg Saint-Denis (section of Nord) under the name of "Atelier du Nord" (North Workshop). A general warehouse (the old Office of Spinning by the Poor) was in charge of accounting and retailing the thread made in the two workshops. Until 9 Thermidor Year II, the municipality was responsible for their administration under the control of the department of Paris (the regional government of Paris); after provisional management by the department, the workshops came under the direction of the National Commission of Agriculture and the Arts, then the National Commission of Public Assistance.

From August 1790, the workshops were overcrowded. In September 1790, there was no more room at the Jacobins; in February 1791, three hundred people waited for places to open. From the end of 1790, only women filling a maximum number of the following conditions were accepted into the workshops: they had to have been born or have resided in Paris for a long time, be burdened with infant children, have lost their job in "consequence of circumstances" (the labor crisis), be aged (first more than fifty years old, then more than sixty years) or handicapped, and from 1792 have a husband at the front.

The Jacobin establishment had seven workshops, including one for young men; the Récollet establishment had only four workshops, including one for young male spinners. In the two factories, the number of female workers varied every week, then every ten days. Thus the actual workforce of the Jacobins oscillated between 1,139 and 1,862. For the months of Pluviôse Year II to Vendémiaire Year III (February to October 1794), the average number of female workers was 1,798, of which 1,091 worked inside the factory—but we can find up to 1,130 female workers assembled on the premises of the spinning workshop. The others were employed at home by the workshops, which supplied them with raw materials and sometimes a spinning wheel in exchange for the guarantee of a solvent citizen. Each Jacobin workshop thus held on average two hundred or three hundred people, a completely extraordinary statistic for the period. At the Récollets, the minimum number of workers recorded was 360 men and women and the maximum was 1,312. An average calculated over the first six months of 1793 gives the following statistics: 78 young male workers and 646 female workers, of which 437 were on the premises and 209 at home—the men all worked in the precincts of the Récollets. The female workers in cotton spun in a workshop of about 150 people, and those in hemp were in two workshops of around 100 people each. The female pickers, about 100 old women, worked in the men's workshop.[42]

Each workshop was under the direction of a foreman (a man for male workshops and a woman for female workshops) and one or more assistant managers, who were often foremen's daughters. Besides spinners, each factory also included several female wool-combers and folders, various office clerks, and a director.

Female workers were first employed by the week (six working days) and then by the *décade* (nine working days) and collected their wages on Saturday, then on *nonodi* (the ninth day). Only apprentices and folders received a fixed amount; the others were paid by the task, according to quantity and quality (estimated by the foreman) of thread produced. For days of twelve hours (7 A.M. to 7 P.M. or 6 A.M. to 6 P.M.—a schedule sometimes prolonged until 9 P.M. at the request of the female workers) with two hours of break for meals (10 A.M. to 11 A.M. and 2 P.M. to 3 P.M.), most female workers earned the ridiculously low amount of ten to sixteen sous a day, inferior by about half to average female wages. Moreover, administrators did not hide that "the goal of the establishment was to pay a price lower than the factories, in order not to deprive the private factories of their female workers."[43] To increase these miserable wages, spinners engaged their little daughters, children of less than ten years, as apprentices who were paid four sous a day. In 1790, two servings of soup a day were added to the amount earned. These were quickly replaced by bread, when the women complained that this meal was "not worthy to enter the human body." So from 5 March to 1 October 1791, six pounds of bread per week was distributed to each worker. After this date, the administrators of the public establishments, alleging as pretext the high price of bread, reduced this ration to four pounds a week, brought to six pounds per *décade* when the revolutionary calendar went into effect. During the Year III, the scarcity of bread drove the administrators to replace it by eighteen sous per *décade*; theoretically, bread in Paris cost three sous per pound. By this standard, it was not a decrease, but in reality no Parisian woman could buy at this date such a quantity of bread for this amount of money.

underpaid &
underfed

---

42. Results are calculated from bookkeeping accounts of workshops, which unfortunately contain many gaps: A.N., F[15] 3586, 3571, 3564, 3561, 3566, 3567, 3569.

43. A.N., F[15] 3575–3576, "Rapport sur la filature des Jacobins fait dans les assemblées des sociétés populaires de l'Ami du Peuple et de Chalier les 16 et 21 floréal an II."

To apply for a place in the spinning workshops, women had to present proof of residence and of indigence. Six boxes in the National Archives contain 4,514 requests for entry to the workshops by women.[44] Some certificates inform us of the age of the destitute woman, her occupation and that of her husband, and the reason for her request, but most only give her name and her section. Thus the statistics available are only the minimum.

These women lived in the same neighborhoods as spinners and gauze workers, districts where the factories were also located. These were the faubourgs of the north and especially Faubourg Saint-Marcel (45.6 percent of the requests originated from here) and other districts on the left bank, which together add up to 74.56 percent of the requests (and even 78 percent if we add the Iles de la Cité and Saint-Louis). However, the sections of the center and of the west on the right bank had very little representation, which is remarkable considering the number of their residents.

All ages, from four to ninety-three years, were represented in the spinning mill. However, certain groups occurred more often than others: young girls from ten to fifteen years, whose mothers usually also labored in the workshop, and women from thirty to thirty-four years, mothers of families burdened with young children, whose husbands were at the front. Finally, there was a rather large proportion of women aged more than sixty years who cleaned cotton in the workshops (see Fig. 2). Those who gave their original occupation were mostly workers in the textile trades: 21 percent were spinners and workers in cotton, 19.5 percent were workers in linen, and 10 percent were gauze workers. We can add to these last most of those women, very numerous in the sections with many recruits, such as Observatoire or Jardin-des-Plantes (Faubourg Saint-Marcel), who without formally stating their trade explained that "their occupation was no longer viable." Then follow unemployed servants (15 percent), merchants who were too poor to procure the capital necessary for pursuing their trade (11 percent), and washerwomen without business or no longer physically able to continue their trade (7 percent). There were not many workers of the artisan class (6 percent), which is consistent with the few requests for entry from central sections. Among their fathers or husbands were fellow artisans, unskilled workers, unemployed men, or invalids in the care of their wives, and from 1792, soldiers. Lack of employment remained the principal reason female workers wished to be admitted to the workshops: at least

 *make-up of workers*

---

44. A.N., F[15] 4579, 4580, 4582, 4588, 4589, 3603–3604.

351 requests came from women who were without work for six weeks to two years.

"Some Are Terrible, Especially among the Women" The director of Récollets, in the months following the opening of the workshops, anxiously reminded administrators "that there are several cases of revolts instigated by women."[45] This proved to be premonitory, for up until their closing the municipal spinning workshops were ceaselessly agitated by explosions of anger among the female workers. From 1790, they petitioned to obtain wage increases and were already little inclined to "the submission and respect due to superiors" stipulated by the rules. "You have no orders to give me and I will not obey you," a female worker replied to her foremen as she threw her portion of kidney beans that she found too meager.[46]

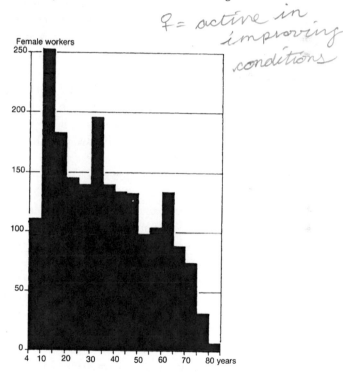

Figure 2.   Age of 1,976 female workers
in the spinning workshops

45. A.N., F15 3581.
46. A.N., F15 3575–3576, letter by the wife of Suberbier.

On Friday, 27 May 1791, a "revolt" took place at the Récollet workshop accompanied by "violent threats and assaults" against one of the workshop foremen "in regard to the price of work." The next day, payday, everyone was in a ferment. On 3 November 1791, while about sixty female workers of Récollets went to complain to the municipality about the decrease in bread rations established a month previously, approximately twenty workers urged their coworkers at the Jacobin workshop to insurrection. Some workers were dismissed after these troubles, but tension increased during the following days. A female worker even asserted "how abominable it was that the administrator punished women who had done nothing but good, and how formerly at the Saint-Denis warehouse where she had been employed, if as much had been done to them, they would have rebelled until their fellow-worker was restored." But although this fervor was caused by the suppression of two pounds of bread, the female workers nonetheless let themselves be manipulated by their director, who made them believe that an employee whom he wished to dismiss was at the origin of the decrease in bread.[47]

On 2 April 1792, the spinners of the Jacobin workshop protested against their wages in a petition sent to the mayor of Paris. They did not sign the petition because they had been told that "for the least step they took to prove the horrors that happened daily" they would be "put in an underground dungeon."[48]

These disturbances grew in magnitude during the winter and spring of the Year II (1794). The political situation at that time was at its most confused. After what has been called "the Indulgent offensive," led by Danton and Desmoulins in Pluviôse (January to February 1794), the Cordelier club, directed by Hébert, reacted and violently denounced in their turn the Indulgents, the moderates, and the "Endormeurs" (the "people who tried to lull public opinion to sleep"). The two large Parisian clubs, the Jacobins and the Cordeliers, opposed one another in Ventôse (February to March); the Cordeliers veiled with black crepe the Declaration of the Rights of Man and called for "insurrection." This political crisis reached a climax in Germinal (March to April) with the execution of the Cordelier leaders, followed shortly after by the execution of the Dantonist Indulgent leaders. This profoundly disoriented the populace, who were also worried by food shortages. The crisis of spring Year II, when the political and the social were indissolubly linked, had repercussions in the world of female work, notably in the

47. A.N., F[15] 3567.
48. A.N., F[15] 242.

large municipal spinning workshops. A series of movements, emerging from old demands believed to be forgotten, exploded and gave an impression of general insurrection in the spinning workshops, but this insurrection must be situated in a larger movement. The struggles of female workers were not labor disputes that formed an extraneous body grafted onto a Revolution of small independent artisans. On the contrary, they were an integral part of the crisis of spring Year II, which was so dramatic for the Revolution's future.

[handwritten: spinner's unrest part of Revo.!]

It all started in the Jacobin manufactory around the middle of Frimaire (December 1793), when the wife of Janisson and several of her colleagues in the hemp workshop decided to send a statement to the administrators to complain of the loss in 1791 of two pounds of bread per week. At the same time, their foreman, the female citizen Neuve Eglise, was denounced by four of her associates as being "very aristocratic." In fact, most of the supervisors and managers of the spinning workshop had been appointed at the time of the establishment's creation by the authorities then in place and, gradually, as the Revolution progressed, became openly counter-revolutionary. Subject to persecution, patriotic male and female workers were reduced to silence. Learning of the denunciation, Janisson's wife and two of her coworkers, the female citizens Beaugros and Fougeret, who were emboldened and had overcome their fear of dismissal, went to make a declaration about the female citizen Neuve Eglise's unpatriotic statements.[49]

Although she was threatened in her workshop, Janisson's wife did not let this affect her, and once the affair of Neuve Eglise had followed its course, she took up her proceedings again on the subject of work conditions and wages. On 19 Pluviôse (2 February 1794), she accompanied the female citizens Bariolles and Bussières, workers in the cotton workshop and bearers of a petition demanding the two pounds of bread withdrawn in 1791, to the popular society of Ami-du-Peuple (Marat section) and then to the society of the Chalier section.

> We experience the most extreme oppression and our demands presented to the administration at different times have been in vain. . . . No more demands, they have all been useless, no reply, except for dismissal, we have had to keep silent. Here, citizens, are the men who have been appointed to govern

49. A.N., W 351 d. 717, female citizen Neuve Eglise.

the unfortunate poor. You should not doubt that these men are highly indifferent to the fate of the sansculottes wives. They have no honesty and still less pity. You are just, republicans, we hope for everything from you, that you will do all you can to alleviate our fate. You can count on our gratitude.[50]

Just as interesting as these complaints about withheld bread and the abuses of administrators is the fact that this petition was presented by female workers in different workshops (cotton and hemp) and read to popular societies of the sections, organizations that were closest to the social stratum of the poorest of the female sansculottes movement. And if it was entirely justifiable that the female workers appealed to the popular society of the Chalier section, where the manufactory was located, the choice of the Marat section—a section siding with the Cordeliers in the crisis that then traversed the revolutionary movement—was not perhaps merely because the female citizen Bariolles lived there.

The popular society of Marat effectively took the affair into its hands: without warning the director of the workshop, it sent commissioners to visit the different workshops and record the complaints of female workers. Besides the grievance over the two pounds of bread, most complaints concerned wages: insufficient pay scale, the elimination of two hours work in the evening, and no payment for carding. The spinners also asked that the upkeep of spinning wheels, which had been assigned to them recently, would again be taken over by the administration, for this maintenance lowered their salary of ten by twelve sous per month. They refused to consider themselves beasts of burden and insisted on their right to work in decent conditions. They asked for the restoration of the stairwell lamps, which had been replaced by candles that provided insufficient light. They complained that the workshops' lack of good insulation and tile flooring was unhealthy and demanded an increase in wood for the stove. The sansculottes *mentalité* can again be seen in their declarations: they were indignant that women who were not in financial distress were appointed foremen and assistant managers, to the detriment of mothers of indigent families, and were anxious at clandestine removal of cotton, suspecting the clerical employees of stealing from the nation.[51]

In fact, from the final *décade* of Pluviôse, agitation was the rule in the workshops. On 25 Pluviôse (13 February 1794), a bobbin was introduced for

50. Ibid., and F⁷ 4748 d. Janisson, F¹⁵ 3603–3604 "Mémoire des victimes de Coquet."
51. See note 43.

reeling silk, and the reel was used to calculate the price to pay female workers for their thread. This proved disadvantageous to some and caused a "movement": the female workers of one workshop went through the workshop, insulted the administrators, and threatened those who were ready to accept this tool, which was finally broken.[52] About fifteen days later, two spinners of the Jacobin workshop went to the Récollets. The doorkeeper, however, prevented them from dragging the female workers of that spinning workshop into their movement, and the spirit of insubordination that reigned at the Jacobins did not overtake the Récollets.[53] On 16 Ventôse (6 March), the wife of Janisson spoke to Hébert and proclaimed afterward with confidence in the workshops that their concerns went well since Père Duchesne looked after them.[54]

It is interesting to note that insubordination took place at the same time in the Salpêtrière spinning workshops. At the beginning of the evening on 28 Ventôse (18 March), a dozen workers threatened their superintendent (a moderate), then locked themselves in their workshop and refused to come out upon the arrival of the revolutionary commissioners of the Finistère section, who had been hastily called. They were arrested and defended on the spot by the popular society of the section. But the movement did not continue and they were released in Fructidor Year II (August 1794).[55]

Nevertheless, in the Jacobin workshop the disturbance was so great that on 28 Ventôse (18 March) the director resigned. To respond to this insubordination, on 4 Germinal (24 March) the committee on the administration of public works observed: "The movements that for several months have occurred in these workshops and the agitation that continues to reign there require that their management be confided to a firm man, who knows how to maintain order and who guarantees by his energy the success of the rigorous measures that the administration intends to take, in order to recall those who have strayed from their duties."[56]

The new director, Coquet, the previous director of the Récollets, was indeed firm! It mattered little if he scorned sansculottes, abused female workers, and dismissed them without a shadow of remorse. However, it took time for him to impose silence on the workers. The day after the citizen

---

52. A.N., F15 3581 and F15 3603–3604, written statements of the female citizen Douteau.

53. A.N., W 77, pl. 1, no. 7.

54. A.N., F7 4748 d. Janisson.

55. A.N., F7* 2516, pp. 45–46 and F7* 2517 f. 233, 235, 238.

56. A.N., F15 3575–3576.

Neuve Eglise was condemned to death by the revolutionary tribunal, a female worker "known for creating disorder" rejoiced in the workshop that
soon all foremen would be guillotined.[57] And in several petitions sent to the
Convention or to administrators, female workers persisted in loudly demanding two additional pounds of bread, as well as the return of two well-
loved foremen who had been transferred to the Récollets by Coquet and replaced by "his creatures." Coquet then exercised rigorous repression: after
having threatened the wife of Janisson, he decreased the quantity of spinning material given to female workers (six pounds instead of eight), which
represented a loss of wages for them. Then, on 28 Floréal (17 May) the
workers sent the administration a petition in which they stated that they
only earned ten to twelve sous per day, complained of the elimination of
two hours work in the evening, and demanded their eight pounds of hemp
every ten days, and even nine pounds if that was possible. Finally, they
asked not only for the reestablishment of two additional pounds of bread
per week, but even the reimbursement of all that had been "withheld" from
them for two and a half years, as well as all that they had spent since the
maintenance of spinning wheels had been their responsibility.[58] On 29
Floréal, the wife of Janisson and her coworkers delivered this petition to
Collot d'Herbois, a member of the Committee of Public Safety.

At the same time, the popular societies of Marat and of Chalier went to
announce their "investigation" at the department of Paris on 11 Floréal (30
April) and visited the workshop the next day accompanied by the president
of the department, Concedieu, who seemed to wish to resolve the conflict
in favor of the women workers, much to the director Coquet's dissatisfaction. On 16 and 21 Floréal, the report on the Jacobin spinning workshop was
read in the meetings of the popular societies of the two sections. But
Coquet, whom all testimony presents as a skillful intriguer, knew how to
win friends among the members of the department and the sansculottes of
the Chalier section—particularly the support of Lambin, a relatively
important individual in the section, who was recompensed by the appoint-
ment of his wife as assistant manager of a workshop. As a result, this report, which was completely against Coquet and supported the female
workers and their demands, was not taken seriously, for Coquet's friends
presented the members of the commission as calumniators.[59]

57. A.N., F[15] 3603–3604, written statement of the wife of Douteau on 11 Prairial, Year II; see also note 54.
58. A.N., F[15] 3603–3604.
59. See note 43 and F[15] 3603–3604, letter of Ruffié.

Moreover, a short time after his visit to the Jacobin workshops, Concedieu lost his office at the department, which, after having first congratulated the popular societies, made them understand that it would henceforth be solely responsible for this affair. However, on 20 Floréal (9 May) the societies made a final effort, drawing up an official report that in bitter tones marked the growing split between the revolutionary government and the politically disabled sansculottes: "Female citizens have demanded bread allowances that have been taken away from them, and asked for increases in pay for their work. Should these acts be seen as agitation and disturbances? Shouldn't a true sansculotte be able to make her voice heard when she suffers without being regarded as an agitator?"[60]

We are far from Saint Just's affirmation, in his report of 8 Ventôse Year II (26 February 1794), that "the unfortunate are the powers of the earth. They have the right to speak as masters to governments who neglect them." The study, still to be undertaken, of administrative personnel during the Revolution should enable us to understand the deviation between Saint Just's declaration and the question posed by the sansculottes two months later.

As for Coquet, certain that he would be successful, he "reestablished order" and dismissed the last rebels—in particular, their ringleaders. The widow Fougeret was among these and, moreover, had the misfortune to point out to Coquet that a mother of a family could not live with only six pounds to spin every ten days and that "certainly, if he had no more than that to live, he would not be satisfied." In a petition, she explained the consequences of her words:

> Then he regarded me obliquely, while saying to me that I looked like those two or three counterrevolutionary women. Then I said to him that he resembled an aristocrat, and that he should prove to me what he had asserted— that I, the wife of Fougeret, I would go to the revolutionary committee. He made me stand up. I sat down again because he had said that he was going to seek the guards who doubtless would have been new witnesses. I said to him "Moreover, I will go to the Convention to ask for bread." "Go to the Convention," this same Coquet said, "you will be heard as you have been for your writings" and from that moment it has been twelve days since I had anything to do.

Then she was definitively dismissed with her two children.[61]

60. See note 56.
61. See note 58.

This response, coupled with the loss of the rapid growth that the sansculottes movement had known, bore fruit, and the agitation ceased little by little, although we can still sporadically find petitions by female workers.

In Messidor, the department of Paris seemed more attentive to the demands of "Coquet's victims" and sent two of its members to visit the workshop. On 28 Messidor (16 July), Coquet, having fulfilled his mission to "reestablish order," resigned. On 19 Fructidor (5 September), the department reinstated the women dismissed by Coquet, and a commission was charged "with examining all the acts of oppression that might have occurred in the workshops." But the new director wrote to the National Commission of Agriculture and the Arts, which had been responsible for the workshops since 14 Fructidor (31 August), that these measures "gave [him] some anxiety for the tranquillity of this workshop." So, on 22 Fructidor (8 September), after expressing its surprise in not very pleasant terms that the department had taken such a resolution, the Commission of Agriculture and the Arts annulled the decision to set up an investigation.[62]

The North Workshop (formerly Récollets), which had gone through the crisis of spring Year II without visible excitement, took up the torch again. On 17 Messidor (5 July), when hemp, which was scarce at this time, was reduced, female workers threatened to close their workshop and to expel the foremen. At the beginning of the Year III, spinners complained of the poor quality of the hemp, which ruined the spinning wheels, bloodied their fingers, and made them lose time. Paid by the job, they saw their wages decrease in consequence. After learning that they would be received by the Commission of Agriculture and the Arts, several spinners in the North Workshop threatened to whip others if they refused to accompany them to the commission. On 7 Vendémiaire (30 September), the director of the spinning workshop twice asked the commission for help and told it "that for some time it has been hell to be with these women."[63]

Female workers in cotton also made demands. Because cotton was then difficult to obtain, the quantities given to them to spin were greatly diminished, and they earned absurdly low amounts at the end of ten days. Finally, an indemnity was granted them.[64]

On 17 Brumaire Year III (7 November 1794), female workers in hemp at the North Workshop addressed a petition to the Commission of Agri-

---

62. A.N., F[15] 3567.
63. Ibid., letters by Gantier on 18 Messidor and 22 and 29 Fructidor Year II.
64. See note 58.

culture and the Arts. They asked that their wages follow the rate of inflation ("everything having risen in price, what they earned from their work
was now insufficient to procure basic necessities"), stressed the poor quality of the raw material they received, and demanded that their thread be
assessed according to a single scale.[65] Four days later, the director presented his side to the commission about the atmosphere that reigned in
his workshops. Female workers "had previously plotted among themselves. They equip themselves at an excessive price and say openly that if
they are not paid as they should be, they will go to the Convention and
will close the workshops and turn out their foremen—that the workshops
belong to them."[66] Indeed, not having obtained satisfaction, the workers
addressed several petitions to the Convention. On 21 Frimaire Year III (11
December 1794), the Commission of Agriculture and the Arts responded
to these demands, saying that the base wages of the spinners were indeed
"faulty, but in a contrary sense to the claims of the female workers," and
that, in fact, the wages should be lowered. Finally, it proposed to dismiss
the ringleaders.[67]

The administrators openly stated their intentions: they wished to make
at least a minimum profit, and they wanted, above all, to avoid disturbances.
To achieve these goals, on 15 Nivôse Year III (4 January 1795) they passed
a decree ordering all their employees to work at home. A slightly later report is, for this reason, particularly eloquent: "The great number of individuals of all ages that the workshops assemble each day having on several
occasions given way to disturbances or to riots alarming to public tranquillity, it has appeared expedient to suppress work within the factory and to
substitute work at home" that combines the advantages "of avoiding large
gatherings of individuals . . . and of procuring the most beautiful spinning
for the establishment."[68]

But work at home was often not practical for indigent women who lived
in poor lodgings where they lacked room to set up a spinning wheel—a female worker even affirmed that she was "obliged for lack of any other place
to spin in a courtyard." Others were given notice by their landlords, who
were disturbed by the noise of their work. The female workers also stated
in their petitions that most of the spinners did not know how to card raw

65. Ibid.
66. A.N., F[15] 3567, letter by Gantier on 21 Brumaire Year III.
67. See note 58.
68. A.N., F[15] 3600–3601.

cotton and that no landlord would be responsible for providing the security necessary for the raw material and the spinning wheels for "women who did not possess a sou."[69]

In the South Workshop this process seemed, in spite of the petitions, to be carried out in relative calm. This was not the case for the North Workshop, where workers in cotton refused to take their spinning wheels to their homes and were opposed to their leaving the premises. The ringleaders asserted that they were not to be driven out from the workshops. On 23 Pluviôse (11 February), about fifty cotton spinners went to the director's office, who was compelled to call the civil committee of the section "to restrain them and make them listen to reason." The cotton spinners contacted the linen and hemp spinners, who then declared that "if workers in cotton remain, they would return with their spinning wheels to the workshop." The Commission of Agriculture and the Arts was obliged to yield and accept most of the demands.[70]

In Ventôse and Germinal of the Year III (February to April 1795), the scarcity of cotton led the Commission of Public Assistance, which was now responsible for the spinning workshops, to convert female workers in cotton to hemp work, employment that was less well paid and accomplished at home. During their apprenticeship, cotton spinners would receive an indemnity. In spite of this, after a trial period, cotton workers refused to continue the hemp work because of the difficulty of this conversion and because spinning cotton was more lucrative. They brought back to their workshops the tools and the raw material that had been give to them to work on at their homes. The Commission of Public Assistance, after having estimated that it was "prudent" to keep a cotton workshop in one of the establishments, finally asked the following question on 18 Germinal (7 April 1795), only a few days after the failure of the popular insurrection of 12 and 13 Germinal: "Should the demands of cotton spinners and their resistance . . . stop the Commission and oblige it to yield to their wishes?" The commission recalled that, after all, these women were only the indigent "who cannot procure work elsewhere and that this was a resource offered to them." "Does one who comes to ask for this work have the right to choose the work that suits

69. A.N., F[15] 3603–3604, petition of 19 Pluviôse Year III; F[15] 3567, petition of 26 Pluviôse Year III.

70. A.N., F[15] 3567, letters by Gantier on 21, 24, and 25 Pluviôse Year III, letter by the commission on 22 Pluviôse, report of the civil committee of Faubourg-du-Nord section on 23 Pluviôse, letter by Mars on 24 Ventôse.

her the most or that pleases her more? The Commission does not think so."[71]

A page had been turned. The time was finished when the nation had a responsibility to help the relatives of its defenders to survive. The time was over when, even in theory, the interests of female workers would be considered. This report is characteristic of the Year III and of the new society that the members of the National Convention strove to create through the new Constitution. The spinning workshops were no longer either the charitable institutions of the Old Regime or places of employment for women whom the Republic had the duty to assist because the Declaration of the Rights of Man and of the Citizen of 1793 considered aid to be a "sacred obligation." Now it was affirmed without evasion that these were enterprises that must be profitable. As for the women who worked there, they were no longer either "paupers" assisted by Christian charity, or wives of sansculottes and revolutionary soldiers, indigent women to whom "society owed a livelihood . . . by providing work for them" (article 21 of the Declaration of Rights of 1793). They were merely female workers who must content themselves with listening silently to the rules of their employers and who should be grateful to be given work. In this way, the administration of spinners during the Year III brings us directly to the famous speech of Boissy d'Anglas to the Convention on 21 Ventôse Year III (11 March 1795), when the deputy developed the fundamental principles of French economic liberalism. Thus, during the Revolution, and more precisely and not at all by chance, during the Year III, theories on the respective positions of worker and employer were developed that would be applied throughout the nineteenth century. We can find signs of these theories during the eighteenth century, but they emerged victorious from the Revolution.

Female workers preferred the Declaration of the Rights of Man and the Citizen to d'Anglas's speech. How could they have reconciled their working conditions with the determination affirmed in the Year II to create a more just society founded on the rights of the people? Why should this dignity, of which the Old Regime had supposedly wished to deprive the people, continue to remain absent from the workshops? Why did this idea of common happiness, "the goal of society," disappear at the sound of spinning wheels? By what mysterious operation were speeches heard the evening before in clubs, societies, or the street forgotten once past the door

71. A.N., F[15] 3603–3604, reports of the commission on 26 Ventôse and 18 Germinal Year III.

of the workshop? For these female workers, the right to a living, inherent to the popular *mentalité*, did not depend only on price controls on essential goods but also on just wages for their work. The rights of the people should also be the rights of male and female workers. They were not just women but citizens who worked.

The popular consciousness of a right to a life with dignity did not emerge abruptly from the cannons fired at the Bastille. The protest movements of female workers did not begin with the Revolution. Spinners and administrators referred several times to movements dating from the Old Regime. But the Revolution, in declaring the Rights of Man and of the Citizen, had opened a space that, drawing on the Declarations and on the law, strengthened these aspirations. Thus female workers often referred to their rights as female citizens. We may recall here that in a struggle with her foremen, a worker read the Declaration of Rights in the workshop. And among the many demands of workers in spinning workshops, there appears at the beginning of Thermidor, Year II (July 1794) a request for a public reading in the workshops of the *Bulletins de la Convention nationale.*

Before thinking of themselves as producers, these women thought of themselves as citizens, members of the Sovereign People. Thus a female sackmaker was astonished in Pluviôse Year II that "the Sovereign (the female workers) lacked wood when its agents (the municipal inspectors) were provided with wood in abundance." Thus the female workers of the North Workshop asserted one year later that the workshops belonged to them. These are affirmations by female citizens who considered themselves owners of what belonged to the municipality and to the nation rather than declarations by female workers demanding the ownership of the means of production.

That work conflicts were expressed in political language stemming from the Revolution corresponds to the mental attitudes of these female workers. Their value and their rights were related, in their conception, to their membership in a political body, the Sovereign People, and not to the value of their work. We could see this as a conceptual deficiency, but it is far from evident that a limitation of outlook is implied by the reference to the rights of man and citizen (or of woman and female citizen, in making abstract the ambiguity attached to the second term during the Revolution) rather than to the value of their work. Can we even speak of a conceptual deficiency without risking anachronism? The development of the workers' movement, which had not yet entered its first stage, would give to nineteenth-century workers a new conceptualization that integrated the value of work.

We can also see here the relatively high degree of politicization of the Parisian population, or at least the predominance of structures of political thought (to think in political terms is not necessarily synonymous with politicization, in the sense of reflection on political problems or political engagement). This predominance of political thought appears still more striking in that this was not a question of the traditional female sansculottes, recruited from the independent class of artisans, and that these workers, even the ringleaders, were not those conspicuous female militants that we find from the beginning to the end of the Revolution.[72] In a society where politics dominated, the popular masses applied what we now consider political notions to domains that were not strictly political, because their tools of conceptualization, and thus their arms of defense, led to such a formulation. *Revo = tool of conceptualization* (handwritten)

The link between work and politics can be seen in the female workers' modes of action. They all took their complaints and demands before the sections' popular societies. The chronology here is equally revealing, for all these work conflicts are framed by the months of Pluviôse and Ventôse Year II, marked by the crisis between the Cordeliers and the Jacobins. Moreover, the municipal administrators wrote on 10 Germinal Year II (30 March 1794) to the revolutionary tribunal that they were convinced that the agitation in the spinning workshops was related to the Hébert affair.[73] Without imitating the administrators and seeing a "Cordelier disturbance" in the insubordination of female workers—whether spinners, sack menders, or female workers in the sections—we can, however, place this agitation in the more general context of a Parisian revolutionary movement and remark once again on the multiple and complex aspects taken by the crisis of winter and spring of the Year II.

Were women thus spearheading social struggles? We must beware of such rapid conclusions. Only a minority of women made the link between revolutionary principles and their productive use. And these women worked under very peculiar conditions, distinct from the traditional and artisanal organization of work in Paris, where workshops of

72. The ringleaders were a part of what we call "female grassroots militants" or "female sansculottes." See "Birth of the Female Sansculottes Movement, 1789–1793," this volume.

73. A.N., W 77 pl. 1, p. 5.

more than one hundred people were not common. We must not be deceived by the figures of the ringleaders whom we have encountered. Outside of periods of heightened disturbance, a large portion of female laborers in the workshops followed without much resistance the orders of their foremen, either through lack of consciousness or fear of losing their jobs. We will seek in vain for traces of organization or coordination between female workers. The ties between different workshops in the same manufactory were loose, and collective petitions were usually made under the name of a single manufactory. The rare examples of alliances among female workers are insufficient to destroy the general impression of fragmented protest movements, disconnected for the most part from one another. There were no permanent relations among female workers in different workshops, and even in the most critical moments there were no initial signs of an organization created with the goal of defending their rights. At this time, popular societies partially filled this void.

We seem to be in the presence of the initial stammerings of a female worker population, on the whole left relatively powerless before the (new) rules of the game in the world of work. These women, unlike men or female workers in other branches of production, had been rejected by corporations and trade guilds in the Old Regime. Although dissolved during the Revolution, the guilds left habits of organization and solidarity among their old members. In addition, work conflicts among the male population that we glimpse by chance during research, even if these conflicts were less acute, violent, or resolute, almost always had a more structured and unified character than the struggles of female workers. Male workers "league together and always stand firm through number and strength," and when necessary stopped work and formed true strike pickets.[74] However, these were skilled artisans unhaunted by the specter of unemployment, not indigent elderly women or female workers of economic sectors in crisis. It was different in the sexually mixed occupations, where wage-workers were more organized. In these occupations, female workers also participated fully in the formation of protest movements. Thus on 30 Nivôse Year III (19 January 1795), a woman distributed leaflets at the doors of the type-founders workshops,

74. A.N., F^{30} 152, the printer Didot the elder on 14 April 1791. This was not just the practice of printers. There were strikes or threats of strikes for wage increases, along with occasional "strike pickets" and the distribution of "leaflets" to workers in the profession, among wheelwrights, saltpetermakers, stonecutters, brushmakers, and glassmakers.

urging the workers to demand wage increases.[75] It is necessary to compare the different forms of "worker's" struggles during the Revolution,
but the work conflicts that traversed it are still relatively unknown. And
yet, in all those discussed here, whatever their peculiarities and their
limitations, behind the female worker there always appears in profile the
shadow of the female citizen.

75. A.N., F 1c III Seine 15, report of 1 Ventôse Year III.

worker → citizenship

2

ASPIRING CITIZENS

4 Birth of the Female Sansculottes Movement, 1789–1793

CROWDS AND WRITINGS

—*Marie Jeanne Trumeau, wife of Bertin,* fish merchant, was condemned to hang for inciting to arson and looting while crying "Long live the Third Estate" during the riot against the manufacturer Réveillon on 28 April 1789.

—*Marie Charpentier, wife of Haucourt,* washerwoman from the Faubourg Saint-Marcel, the only woman among the official "Conquerors of the Bastille," was crippled during the siege of the fortress.

—*Marie Françoise Williaume* joined the crowd that took the "abominable Bastille," her hands blackened by the gun powder that she had seized that morning at the Invalides.

—*Marguerite Piningre, wife of Vener,* ran on 14 July to wine merchants whom she forced to fill her apron with broken bottles to use as grapeshot for the beseigers' canon.

And there are still others, whose names are lost to history, who have only left a trace in the archives, but who show us that, without strident heroism, women of the people were part of the Revolution from the very beginning.[1] It is unimaginable that these active women, a vital part of social life, would have remained unmoved by these occurrences. On the contrary, Parisian women followed carefully the events that occurred so precipitously after the opening of the Estates General at Versailles on 5 May

1. George Rudé, *La Foule dans la Révolution française* (Paris: Maspero, 1982), pp. 56, 257 (wife of Bertin), 75 (wife of Haucourt); A.N., C 285 d. 829, p. 12 (M. Williaume), F 1c III Seine 27 (wife of Vener).

1789, and they participated in the movements of crowds that made the Parisian summer of 1789 a summer unlike any other.

In these predominantly male crowds, women were not particularly conspicuous. They were neither leaders nor led, neither noticed nor rejected, but simply present, as sensitive, conscious, rebellious, or hopeful individuals. However, the heat of summer was scarcely over when they burst overwhelmingly onto the political scene and drew attention for the first time in revolutionary history as a group of women, outlining the characteristics of a revolutionary female practice and highlighting male-female relations in the popular movement.

The events of 14 July had provisionally saved the young National Assembly, but concerns remained.[2] In September, there was no bread and people were haunted by the legend of the "famine pact," supposedly organized by aristocrats hostile to the Revolution in order to reduce them to powerlessness. The gatherings of women who besieged the Hôtel-de-Ville began to attract attention. The food shortage was accompanied by a political crisis, when the king refused to approve the decree on the abolition of privileges (4 August) and the Declaration of the Rights of Man and of the Citizen (26 August). Patriotic newspapers asked that Louis XVI leave Versailles to live among the people of Paris, protected from court intrigues. The news that the king's bodyguards had trampled the tricolored cockade during a banquet at Versailles touched off an explosion. On 4 October, the Palais-Royal was lively with groups of women who spoke of going to Versailles. The next morning, the female merchants of la Halle and the inhabitants of the Faubourg Saint-Antoine rang the alarm and, gathering before the Hôtel-de-Ville, demanded bread and arms. Six to seven thousand women and some men forced their way into the Hôtel-de-Ville and then began to march toward Versailles, led by Maillard, the head of the "Bastille volunteers." On the way, they seized the cannons of Châtelet and forced female passersby to accompany them. Arriving at the end of the afternoon, they entered the National Assembly and sat on the benches by the deputies, to whom they gave a petition demanding bread. Six representatives were sent to the king, who promised them wheat and bread. After the women had left, the citizens who had organized in Paris as a national guard gathered at the sound of the alarm and in turn went to Ver-

2. On 17 June, the deputies of the Third Estate of the Estates General took the title "National Assembly." On 20 June, they swore not to disperse before establishing a Constitution. On 23 June, they refused to obey the king, who on 27 June was forced to order the nobility and the clergy to rejoin the National Assembly.

sailles, where they arrived during the night. The king then accepted the decrees of August. The next day, incidents occurred between the protesters and the bodyguards, but the national guard reestablished order. When the royal family appeared at the balcony, the crowd cried, "To Paris!" and that evening, under a driving rain, "the baker, the baker's wife, and the little baker's boy," escorted by the national guard and women, entered Paris, followed by wagons of grain. A few days later, the National Assembly moved from Versailles to Paris.

From this first intervention by a female crowd in the Revolution, we can identify characteristics that became increasingly distinct during the following years. Women took the initiative and were soon followed by men organized in armed groups. In a tense political situation, the need for bread mobilized women and created a female mob but did not blind them: "They wished for bread, yet not at the price of liberty," wrote the author of *Les Révolutions de Paris*, who described how the women overwhelmed a royalist with abuse when he "perfidiously" assured them that they would not lack bread if the king recovered all his authority. We cannot speak of a clearly developed female consciousness in 1789, but already the question of subsistence is inseparable from political concerns.

Even before Parisian women intervened so concretely in revolutionary events, other women had begun to write, moved by the hope sweeping over the country. Ever since the announcement of the meeting of the Estates General in 1788, women had written—audaciously, timidly, moderately— to express their wish not to see half the human species forgotten in the great changes that were to bring about the happiness of humankind.[3] The scourge of prostitution haunted many of these texts, whether their authors—bourgeois, respectable, and severe—condemned the "women of the world" in the name of a morality they wanted to uphold or saw these women as victims of poverty. To allay prostitution, they paid much attention to the question of education for girls and the economic survival of poor women. Another theme frequently addressed is the plight of women who had married badly—young girls sacrificed to the pecuniary advantage of their families, "slaves" for life to their husbands, who could regain liberty only through a law authorizing divorce. Pamphlets demanded that regional laws be abolished, particularly the Norman law, which divested girls of all

3. *Les Femmes dans la Révolution* (Paris: Edhis, 1982); *Cahiers de doléances des femmes et autres textes,* ed. P. M. Duhet (Paris: Editions des Femmes, 1981).

inheritance and placed wives and their goods under the legal guardianship and authority of their husbands. The Old Regime made women into legal minors (it was impossible for them to go to court or sign contracts). The Revolution recognized their civil existence and legal rights. Local laws were abolished in favor of a single law applicable to all subjects. The equal rights of women and men to inherit were recognized, and marriage was declared a contract that could be dissolved by either party in the divorce law of 22 September 1792.[4] The *Mère Duchesne* could then write: "Be proud of yourself, Mére Duchesne, for bloody hell, you should be. In the past, when we wanted to speak, our mouths were shut while we were told very politely, 'You reason like a woman'; almost like a goddamn beast. Oh! Damn! Everything is very different now; we have indeed grown since the Revolution . . . Bloody Christ! How liberty has given us wings! Today we can soar like eagles."[5]

This statement was a little too quick to take wishes for reality; even though women were—with some difficulty—recognized as members of civil society, there was never any question of giving them political rights. The Constitution of 1791, which inaugurated a voting system based on the poll tax, distinguished between active and passive citizens: the first paid at least three days of work as tax and possessed the political rights of a citizen to vote and bear arms; the second did not have these rights. As for female citizens, who were neither "passive" nor "active," it was apparently so evident that women could not enjoy political rights that the issue was not even raised.

Evident to some people, but not to all: the most radical pamphlets by women denounced the violation of principles that meant that women were excluded from their natural rights, as guaranteed by the Declaration of Rights. They demanded that women have restored to them, like men, their dignity and "the rights inherent to their being." Otherwise "the fundamental principles that supported the majestic edifice" that the deputies established "for the happiness of the French" would be overturned.[6] These views were expressed with particular force by Condorcet in his article "Sur l'admission des femmes au droit de cité" (July 1790) and by Olympe de

4. Elisabeth Guibert-Sledziewski, "Naissance de la femme civile," *La Pensée* 238 (March–April 1984): 34–38; C. Le Foll, *Les Femmes et le mouvement révolutionnaire à Rouen, 1789–1795* (Master's thesis, Université de Haute-Normandie, 1985).

5. *La Mère Duchesne*, eighth letter.

6. Madame de Cambis, *Du Sort actuel des femmes*, 1791 and Etta Palm d'Aelders, *Adresse des citoyennes françoises á L'Assemblée nationale*, 1791. Both texts are available in *Les Femmes dans la Révolution*.

Gouges who in September 1791 wrote a *Déclaration des droits de la femme et de la citoyenne*. But these various texts, in spite of their profound theoretical significance, remained individual responses by authors who were unfamiliar with the revolutionary movement by women in October 1789.

Can we claim, then, that there was, on one hand, a female elite who were enlightened and aware of the inequality of the sexes but who preached in the void, and on the other hand, women of the people who were only concerned with having enough to eat and navigating the dangers they were exposed to by the Revolution? It is too easy to answer yes, as others have often done—not so much out of bias but because it is difficult to avoid stereotyped explanations that appear true on the surface. That surface is most often presented in the accessible prose of the elites: in this situation, women of the people are always the ones who lose. To reestablish a balance, we must go beyond texts that are clearly protests and plunge into the revolutionary whirlwind, become familiar with concepts that were active then, and restore the coherence and meaning of the frequently ignored activity of women of the people. "And we too, we are citizens," wrote Mademoiselle Jodin, daughter of a Genevan watchmaker and encyclopedist in 1790.[7] Women who participated in the revolutionary movement inscribed this phrase in history and tried consciously to give it force.

To Unite for the General Good

Women wanted to be female citizens: the word *citoyenne* recurs constantly in pamphlets by women. In these revolutionary times, the word was not restricted to the neutral meaning of the inhabitant of a country.[8] Under women's pens, it resounded with civic sentiments, sometimes as the demand for rights, but more often, it was primarily when stating the duties of citizens that women, timid and prudent, tried to insert in the political space opened by the Revolution that strange individual, a female citizen without citizenship. The very words *female citizen* linked women to the polis, to the nation, and thus they tried to give meaning to these words when working for the general good. For revolutionaries, the greatest good could

7. *Vues législatives pour les Femmes, adressées á l'Assemblée Nationale par Mademoiselle Jodin, fille d'un citoyen de Genève* (Angers: Mame, 1790), available in *Les Femmes dans la Révolution*.

8. See Dominique Godineau, "Autour du mot citoyenne," *Mots* 16 (March 1988): 91–110.

be expected by acting in unison. Thus, during the years 1789–1791, women gathered together in clubs.

We should note here that these meetings were much more significant in the provinces than in Paris. We do not have records of each of these clubs of women, but even if some towns lacked such a society, the list of the approximately thirty known clubs during the period from 1789 to 1793 is certainly not exhaustive. Many were situated in the southwest of France: Bordeaux, Beaumont (Dordogne), Damazan, Casteljaloux (Lot-et-Garonne), Montauban, Caraman (Haute-Garonne, created in 1793), Vic-en-Bigorre (Hautes-Pyrénées), Bayonne, and Pau. We can add Civray-en-Poitou (Vienne), Aulnay (Charente-Maritime), Ruffec (Charente), Cognac, Angoulême, and Saint-Junien (Haute-Vienne). To the East, we find Nancy, Châlons-sur-Marne, Dieuze (Meurthe-et-Moselle), Besançon, Tonnerre, Mont-Cenis (Saône-et-Loire), Dijon, and the surrounding villages. In the center were Orléans, Blois, Cusset (Allier), and Clermont-Ferrand. In the southeast, clubs met in Lyon, Yssingeaux, and Alès. In Normandy, we find Breteuil (Eure), Avranches (a club of royalist women), and Le Mans; in the Parisian basin, Creil, and in the North, Lille.[9] In other towns, women met occasionally but without really forming clubs. Still elsewhere, they did not meet separately but were members of the sexually mixed clubs in their town.

Women's clubs had rules, a president, and secretaries for different committees. They rarely had more than sixty active members, but their total membership was significantly higher (227 at Ruffec, 400 at Dijon). From 1790 to 1791, the clubs were mostly composed of women from the middle class, who were relatives of notable local revolutionaries. Subsequently,

9. This list was taken from Marc de Villiers, *Histoire des clubs de femmes et des légions d'amazones* (Paris: Plon-Nourrit, 1910), and from addresses sent to the Convention (series C of the A.N.). Marc de Villiers unfortunately does not give the dates these clubs existed (were they created in 1790–1791, or in 1793; did they exist during the entire period, or were they short-lived?). See also Henriette Perrin, "Le Club de femmes de Besançon," *Annales révolutionnaires* 9 (1917): 629–653, and *Annales révolutionnaires* 10 (1918): 37–63, 505, and 645; G. Langeron, "Le Club des femmes de Dijon pendant la Révolution," *La Révolution en Côte-d'Or* (Dijon: 1929), p. 5 and following; "Registre des Amies des vrais Amis de la Constitution de Ruffec (Charente), 1791–1792," *La Révolution française* 46 (January–June 1904): 245–278, and "Les Soeurs de la Constitution de Breteuil" (a club of unmarried young women), *La Révolution française* 56 (January–June 1909): 531–536. One can ask if there is a relation between the importance of the southwest in the number of women's clubs and the origin of Olympe de Gouges (Montauban) and of Claire Lacombe (Ariège).

their membership became a little more democratic, but their relations with the men's clubs of the towns remained close, although not without conflict. In their first years, the clubs were concerned primarily with philanthropic tasks. They replaced the nuns of the old charitable congregations in overseeing the instruction of young girls, in taking care of sick people, in helping the indigent, and so on. The clubs of Dijon and Besançon opened charity workshops for poor women in the city. We could view ironically the activities of "lady patronesses" who were not at all revolutionary, who did not question the status of women, and who reflected the social composition of these clubs, and we would not be wrong. But then we would forget that it was the acceptance and even the demand for a traditionally female role that allowed women to assemble and to take an interest in political life without risking public opprobrium. For besides these charitable activities, these club meetings were filled with readings of the Declaration of Rights, the decrees of the National Assembly, newspaper articles, and so on. In 1791, they mobilized to defend the constitutional clergy to women of their cities and hunted down priests who did not take the oath.[10] After 1792, most clubs became radical and took an active part in the political life of their city or region and sent petitions to the Convention.

The formation of a network of women's clubs was envisioned many times: in 1791 the Ruffec club corresponded with the Bordeaux club, and the clubs of the Dijon countryside were affiliated with the club of Dijon. In this city, as well as in Cusset, a project to form a national confederation of patriotic French women was proposed in September 1792 (see map 3).

In Paris, the attempt to organize women who belonged to clubs at the beginning of the Revolution did not meet with unqualified success. The initiative came from Etta Palm d'Aelders, a Dutch woman living in the capital who was known for her speeches on the political rights of women. In March 1791, she founded the Société Patriotique et de Bienfaisance des Amies de la Verité (Patriotic and Beneficent Society of Female Friends of Truth) for women, the counterpart of the male Féderation des Amis de la Vérité (Federation of Friends of Truth), an offshoot of the Social Circle of Abbé

---

10. After the property of the clergy was nationalized in November 1789, the Constituent Assembly adopted the Civil Constitution of the Clergy on 12 July 1790, to which priests were forced to swear allegiance and which the pope condemned. Those who accepted it were called *assermentés* or *constitutionnels;* the others, supported by part of the population and in particular by many women, were called *réfractaires.*

Map 3. Women's clubs and sexually mixed popular societies (1789 to 1793).

Fauchet. Etta Palm d'Aelders wanted each Parisian section to sponsor a patriotic club of female citizens who would unite with the provincial clubs under the watchful eye of the male Friends of Truth. These were ambitious hopes, but her Society of Female Friends of Truth, in spite of its wish to arrange apprenticeships for poor young girls and various interventions in favor of the law on divorce, stagnated for a year, unable to join the revolutionary female movement.[11] Together with Etta Palm and Olympe de Gouges, Théroigne de Méricourt, an engaging woman surrounded by a legend woven of blood, madness, and hysteria against a background of battalions of amazons, formed the trinity of female personalities of the Revolution. More inclined to revolutionary action and less elitist than Palm or de Gouges, de Méricourt also wanted women to organize in clubs and helped to found two sexually mixed clubs; both were ephemeral and disappeared for lack of participants.[12] The large Jacobin or Cordelier clubs were not open to women, who could only attend meetings in the public galleries.

This does not mean that women of the people did not meet in Paris. In February 1790, the primary school teacher Dansart created a sexually mixed club that attracted a large female membership and in 1791 took the name of Société Fraternelle des Patriotes des Deux Sexes Défenseurs de la Constitution (Fraternal Society of Patriots of Both Sexes Defenders of the Constitution). After this, other fraternal clubs for men and women appeared in the sections of les Halles (les Marchés), the Place-Royale (l'Indivisibilité), and Gobelins (Finistère). A neighbor of the famous Jacobin club the Fraternal Society of Patriots of Both Sexes held meetings in one of the rooms of the old Jacobin convent on the Rue Saint-Honoré. Women in the Fraternal Society had membership cards and debated and voted like men. They were not completely equal, however, since the office of president was reserved for a man. Of the six positions for secretaries, two were by law reserved for women, who were particularly in charge of the "sisters" of the club.[13] The other offices were occupied either by women or by men. Female representation in the proceedings of the club did not have to envy our modern political parties. The mixture of men and women was not just a formal concession to the equality of the sexes. The "sisters" truly animated the life of the club and were not pushed gently aside during important initiatives. In this place, where they could gather and speak, militant women of the popular classes, the future knitters, took their first steps in revolution. Louise Kéralio was the most conspicuous woman in the club,[14] but at her side were other notorious women: Pauline Léon, the wife of Boudray, the wife of Timbal, and later Claire Lacombe. Most of these women were also

---

11. *Discours sur l'injustice des lois en faveur des hommes, au dépend des femmes,* and other texts of Etta Palm d'Aelders.

12. O. Ernst, *Théroigne de Méricourt* (Paris: Payot, 1935).

13. Regulations of the club (Fraternal Society of Patriots of Both Sexes) can be found in B.H.V.P., 12760 no. 1 (rules of 2 June 1792), 672 no. 53, 67681, 958576.

14. Louise Kéralio was one of the first female journalists. With her husband, François Robert, she wrote the *Mercure national et étranger.*

spectators at meetings of the men's clubs, or were members of the fraternal clubs of their district.

The Fraternal Society was as patriotic as its name.[15] From the very first, along with the most advanced revolutionaries, it rebelled in the name of the Declaration of Rights against the distinction between active and passive citizens and opposed the right of the royal veto. It was close to the Cordelier club, with whom it created in May 1791 a Central Committee of Parisian Fraternal Societies. After the king's attempt at flight on 21 June 1791, the Cordeliers and the Fraternal Society of Patriots of Both Sexes led a common campaign for the abolition of the monarchy. On 22 June, the Cordeliers sent to the Fraternal Society their republican petition; for a whole month, the two clubs multiplied antiroyalist pamphlets and speeches. On 14 July 1791, a petition named "Of the One Hundred" was signed jointly by 135 male and female members of the two clubs.[16] This movement climaxed on 17 July 1791, when the Cordeliers called the populace to sign their petition at the Champ-de-Mars on that day.

In the good-natured, familial, and rather poorly dressed crowd who responded to the invitation on 17 July, nothing distinguished among their fellow citizens the two twenty-three-year-old women or the older woman who accompanied them: Pauline Léon, a member of the Fraternal Society; her mother, a widow who made chocolate; and their friend and neighbor, the cook Constance Evrard, a compulsive reader of revolutionary newspapers. All three were assiduous members of the Cordelier club and had participated in several patriotic demonstrations. Further along in the crowd strode another adherent of the Fraternal Society, the wife of Boudray, who had left her café of Bains-Chinois for a few moments in order to sign the petition. Then the gunfire of the national guard commanded by La Fayette rang out: fifty people were killed while others fled. Paris was in a state of shock. Men and women who, like Constance Evrard and Pauline Léon, insulted the national guards for their "glorious deed" were held and interrogated. Anne Félicité Colombe, the owner of the printing press of Marat's *L'Ami du Peuple,* was also arrested, along with Etta Palm d'Aelders (as a foreigner), Danton's female cousin, and the wife of the president of the

15. The term *patrie* was not limited during the Revolution to a nationalist and chauvinistic meaning. The homeland was not just the country, or the land (the word *France* was rarely used as synonymous with *patrie*), but the nation, all the citizens joined together in revolution. Thus *patriot* was synonymous with *revolutionary.*

16. F. Braesch, "Les Pétitions du Champ-de-Mars," *Revue historique* 143 (1923): 192–209; Albert Mathiez, *Le Club des Cordeliers pendant la crise de Varennes et le massacre du Champ-de-Mars* (Paris: H. Champion, 1910).

Cordeliers. The subsequent repression was severe. Most of the Parisian clubs were closed until the end of July, their revolutionary leaders arrested or forced into hiding, and the democratic party was disrupted.

THE ARMING OF FEMALE CITIZENS

After the king's flight and the fusillade on the Champ-de-Mars, the republican ideal, which was only held by a minority in 1791, grew stronger in 1792. It helped that war had been declared with Austria on 20 April 1792, and that Louis XVI, refusing to take measures necessary for victory, appeared to be a traitor allied with the enemy in order his regain his power. The revolutionary movement became more radical and the sansculottes made their appearance on the political scene. The spring and summer of 1792 were punctuated by various armed parades that united national guards, active and passive citizens, women, and children. The most important of these demonstrations occurred on 20 June 1792. The inhabitants of the Faubourgs Saint-Antoine and Saint-Marcel, armed and demanding the return of the patriot ministers dismissed by the king, marched before the deputies and then before Louis XVI, who was forced to put on the liberty cap. All descriptions of the event, whether writings or drawings, show that the demonstrators were men and women, the women sometimes armed with sabers or pikes, their children by their sides. With this mixture, the artificial division between active and passive citizens fell while the image of the Sovereign People, composed of all citizens and the sole possessor of legitimacy, transcending social and sexual differences, became crucial.[17] The overthrow of the throne and the abolition of the distinction between active and passive citizens are part of the same movement. The revolutionary vanguard worked for the disappearance of a narrow conception of a citizenship that excluded the poorest individuals. Officially still reserved to the "actives" but expanding to include everyone through revolutionary action, "citizenship" appeared during this period as a concept in active redefinition. Little by little, the Parisian sections rejected the distinction between active and passive citizens and allowed the latter to join the national guard and to vote in the general assemblies. On 30 July 1792, the Legislative Assembly recognized this by decreeing the admission of passive citizens into the national

17. Darlene G. Levy and Harriet B. Applewhite, "Women, Radicalization and the Fall of the Monarchy," in *Women and Politics in the Age of Democratic Revolution,* ed. Darlene G. Levy and Harriet B. Applewhite (Ann Arbor, Mich.: University of Michigan Press, 1990), pp. 81–108.

guard; after the insurrection of 10 August 1792, it voted to convoke a convention elected by universal male suffrage.

Women, also excluded from political rights, became part of this process of redefinition and struggled to acquire real citizenship. Through their political action, a movement was born that was inseparable from this other process. The militant woman wished to be a citizen, behaved as a citizen, and demanded the rights of a citizen, which would allow her to carry her political struggle to a successful conclusion. This is how we must read the petitions by women in 1792. For beyond their struggle in common with men, these women were conscious of the need to specifically affirm the status of the female citizen that they were in the process of forging through their political struggles. The right to bear arms was at the heart of their demands. Their demand for arms cannot be reduced to a patriotic sentiment of protection for the country, but exceeds it and must be inscribed in a problematic of power and citizenship. "To be armed for their personal defense is the right of all men indiscriminately; to be armed for the defense of the country is the right of every citizen," affirmed Robespierre on 27 April 1791, on the exclusion of passive citizens from the national guard.

On 6 March 1792, Pauline Léon, at the head of a delegation of female citizens, read at the bar of the Legislative Assembly a petition signed by more than 319 women who demanded permission to organize a female national guard.[18] Among them were several members of the Fraternal Society and about twenty women who, in their district or in the future Society of Revolutionary Republican Women, continued their political commitment for several years. It should be noted that this petition, which constituted the "official" birth of the Parisian female militants in their first public gesture, was specifically a demand for arms. This constellation of women's demands concerning issues of power, citizenship, and political struggle contributed to the hatred, fear, and phantasms that the word *tricoteuse* (knitter) later evoked. Affirming themselves to be citizens because they were related to free men and because they were interested in the fate of the homeland,[19] the petitioners concluded by demanding one of the attributes that made a female citizen: the right to bear arms, a natural right "possessed by every individual to provide for the defense of life and liberty," in the name of the Declaration of Rights that applied to men and to women. This last demand, quickly slipped into the petition, turned out to be full of consequences.[20]

18. A.N., AE II 1252 C I 90, microfilm AE II 37.
19. See Godineau, "Autour du mot citoyenne."
20. Speech published *Les Femmes dans la Révolution.*

Twenty days later, in a speech given to the Fraternal Society of Minims (Place-Royale section), Théroigne de Méricourt, more clearly conscious of the consequences of her actions, more explicit about her goal, and thus more radical, called on female citizens to organize themselves in army corps and developed the same themes point by point. The apostrophe *female citizens* recurs insistently in this speech. Like the authors of the petition of 6 March, the orator linked this word to the homeland and to the ideal of cooperating for the general good ("Female citizens, do not forget that we must devote ourselves completely to the homeland"). She also posited the natural right to "repel the attacks of the enemy." But she went even further, for from the natural rights of each individual, she progressed to the reality of what women were in society ("Compare what we are with what we should be in the social order") and ended with an appeal: "Break our chains; it is finally time that women emerge from their shameful nullity, where the ignorance, pride, and injustice of men have kept them enslaved for such a long time."

Four months later, eighty female citizens of the Hôtel-de-Ville section again demanded that the Legislative Assembly decree that "true female citizens" be armed.[21]

As the Revolution radicalized and concern over danger to the homeland grew at the very heart of the popular movement, the conception dominant in 1789 of female citizens cooperating for the good of all was progressively complemented by the idea that the female citizen must also enjoy the same rights as the male citizen. Certainly Olympe de Gouges and Condorcet had already affirmed this, and with much greater power, but with the force of only one individual's words. In 1792, this was no longer a question for individual voices; it was a question to be voiced by groups of women—moreover, women who were part of the popular movement. What their formulation lost in acuteness and clarity, it gained in weight. It was now women of the people, although doubtless not the poorest, who demanded their rights: besides the chocolate maker Pauline Léon and her inseparable friend the cook Constance Evrard, the wives of a shoemaker and of a servant, a female haberdasher retailer, and a dressmaker signed the petition of 6 March 1792.

At the same time as the sansculottes, the popular female militants came to the fore. This does not mean that the sansculottes defended the rights of these women; it would be false to say that after the period of theoretical feminism supported by the isolated elite the popular movement became the champion of equality between the sexes. Militant women had to take their

21. A.N., C 154 d. 292 bis, p. 1.

interests in hand, but they did so within the popular movement in which they formed the female component. Their need to make specific petitions for specific demands (the right to arm) but also for more general issues (in June, women demanded from the National Assembly "the punishment of all conspirators") was significant.[22] These women's petitions, where the names of many who would later distinguish the revolutionary female movement appeared for the first time, created a network of women with ties that were still rather loose and that remain vague because of gaps in the archives. Did they meet in the street, on the Terrasse des Feuillants before the National Assembly, in the Jacobin and Cordelier galleries, or within fraternal clubs? We do not know and must limit ourselves to the fact that there was a small group of Parisian women who knew where and how to meet when it became necessary. Reduced to suppositions, we can also guess how this incipient female sansculottes movement could not fit itself within the frame of existing clubs, even the sexually mixed clubs. The reason was simple: to make their opinion heard on political problems, to proclaim their wishes and demand their rights, revolutionary militant women had to meet separately.

At the end of July, the sections and the *fédérés* (confederates) from the provinces who had come to Paris to celebrate 14 July demanded the deposition of Louis XVI. In the night of 9 to 10 August, the alarm sounded; Parisians and *fédérés* marched on the château of Tuileries where the royal family resided. After a violent and bloody conflict, the insurgents were victorious. The monarchy was at an end. If 10 August 1792 was a day for men, women also took part in the assault, just as they had participated in the overthrow of the Bastille. A witness recounts: "I saw, an instant before the combat, an amiable and still young lady with a saber in her hand, standing on a rock, and I heard her harangue the multitude. Suddenly, thousands of women hurled themselves into the fray, some with sabers, others with pikes; I saw several kill Swiss guards there. Other women encouraged their husbands, their children, their fathers."[23]

This account is an exaggeration—there were not "thousands of women" among the assailants but several women who, here and there, saved the life

22. On the women's demand for the punishment of all conspirators, see A.N., C 152, p. 2. The names of signers make us believe that this petition was probably instigated by female members of the Fraternal Society of Patriots of Both Sexes.

23. *Moniteur*, XIII, 538.

of their fellow citizens and tore guns from the hands of the Swiss guards who defended the Château. Some women were wounded, but more often they were held back by their companions than by the prospect of danger. The misfortune that befell Pauline Léon speaks eloquently here. After passing part of the night in her section, the young girl, armed with a pike, took her place in the rows of the battalion that went to the Tuileries, but she had to give up her arms to a sansculotte "at the request of all these patriots." Now that a citizenship without social exclusivity was about to be legally established, now that what had been constructed and acquired through struggle was going to take legal form, women were again excluded. And we can already sense the paradox in the fact that women, who were admitted to be members of the Sovereign people when the populace tried to recapture their rights, did not enjoy all those rights, inasmuch as they were women. However, women proved their courage on 10 August. To honor their conduct during the attack of Tuileries, the *fédérés* awarded a civic crown to three women. The first was none other than Théroigne de Méricourt. The second, Louise Reine Audu, hit by a bullet in the thigh, had already attracted official attention during the women's march to Versailles in October 1789 and was imprisoned at the end of that month. As for the third, her name still did not mean very much in the summer of 1792: unlike the first two, the twenty-seven-year-old actress Claire Lacombe had only lived in Paris for five months. Originally from a family of merchants in Ariège, she had, up until March 1792, successfully practiced her profession in Marseille, Lyon, and Toulon. Attracted to Paris by its fame as both a revolutionary and a theatrical capital, she had not remained a spectator, and on 25 July 1792, dressed as an amazon (a style of dress common to both Théroigne de Méricourt and Louise Reine Audu), she had read an address to the Legislative Assembly, offering to combat the tyrants and asking for the arrest of General Dumouriez. Without work, she lived on her savings, regularly attended Jacobin meetings, and was a member of the Fraternal Society of Patriots of Both Sexes.[24]

The tenth of August marked the end of the distinction between active and passive citizens. There was now only a single class of citizens who enjoyed all the rights attached to citizenship. However, the women who contributed to this democratic advance did not benefit from it. They remained citizens without citizenship, while from 1793 to 1795 all men possessed

24. A.N., T 1001 (1–3) d. Lacombe; *Archives parlementaires* 47, p. 144.

civic rights.[25] This situation made the injustice all the more glaring and influenced the actions and words of women.

WOMEN OF THE POPULAR MOVEMENT

During the three previous years, women had participated in the Revolution individually or as a group distinguished from men by differences that were cultural, social, and political rather than biological. They did not appear at the margins of the popular movement but were included in it, forming its female component, which could remain distinctive or merge into a larger group but at any rate never separated from it, remaining fundamentally a part of the larger group. Not an isolated element, this female component maintained ties with other elements of the popular movement, whether they were political (Jacobins, Cordeliers, *enragés*, and so on), social (for example, "the workers"), or sexual (men in general). Let us take the image of mathematical sets: the totality of the "popular movement" was constituted of different subsets defined by different political, economic, and social criteria, including gender. The subset "women" that the historian necessarily isolates in order to study it, intersects with others: among the women who composed it, some belonged to the subgroup "*enragé*" because of their *enragé* opinions, whereas others, or even the same women, belonged to the subgroup "workers" because of their position in the labor force. The image is moving rather than frozen and follows the twists and turns of historical sequences.

Those who distrust mathematical order and history reduced to monolithic blocks should be reassured. The popular movement and its female component were plural. Behind this general designation, individual women breathed, thought, and acted. To take this group of women as a whole would not allow us to understand their motivations and interventions in the Revolution. The women who participated during the first three years of the Revolution did not all experience the same degree of political engagement and did not figure in the same place in the revolutionary scene. Yet, a historian who seeks to determine the guiding lines and to find a meaning from collective behavior cannot work without categories. Thus three groups can be seen among women of the popular movement: "outstanding" militant women, "grassroots" militant women or the female sansculottes, and the women of the popular masses.

25. Without using the terms *passive* and *active*, the Constitution of the Year III (22 August 1795) returned to suffrage based on the poll tax.

It is necessary to clarify the term *militant woman*. Revolutionary historiography ordinarily uses *militant* to describe those listed as present in the general assemblies. This criteria cannot apply to women since they did not vote. Nonetheless, some female revolutionaries who engaged in action are very conspicuous. Women who fall under different criteria can thus be identified as "militant women": women who belonged to revolutionary clubs or who were one of the "gallery regulars" in revolutionary assemblies; women who participated in at least two insurrectional days; women who showed certain characteristics of the sansculottes *mentalité*. The militant woman was thus a woman who more or less followed a political line or who showed a more or less sustained political interest. Her presence in the archives is not just a result of simple and limited indignation over the words of counterrevolutionaries, the cost of living, food shortages, or the greed of merchants.

Among these militant women, a small number of female citizens emerge who were particularly active and conscious and who show all the characteristics of our various criteria. These "outstanding" militant women regularly attended revolutionary assemblies, possessed a thorough knowledge of politics, and handled with ease the concepts borne by the Revolution. Their existence is clearly documented. We can find them in different archives and at different periods. These individuals did not form a separate group of women but rather an aggregate of figures of women whose engagement was scarcely different from that of men. Present by definition even in the archives, we can find only around fifty to a hundred of these women in all of Paris (see appendix 3, "Portraits of Militant Women," in this volume).

The "grassroots" militant women, or patriotic female citizens, fit only one or two of these criteria. We can find in the documents a group of women who attend the assemblies occasionally—not every night, but when they had the time, when the subject held their attention, or during a period of strong popular mobilization. They were aware of the stakes of the Revolution that they defended in the street, the cabarets, and on their doorsteps. They appeared as a group in police reports, where they were not distinguished as individual women but as "patriotic women," "female Jacobins," "the furies of the guillotine," the "knitters," and so on. Their names are revealed only by chance, in relation to an incident, their figures glimpsed briefly before returning to the shadow.

"Outstanding" and "grassroots" militant women formed the female sansculottes movement, a vague but important group, whose actions and reactions often depended on the social and political status of women.

Not all women of the people who intervened in the Revolution were militants. Many Parisian women who never engaged in any pronounced revolutionary acts were nonetheless strongly attached to the Revolution, adhered to its ideals, and were interested, even from afar, in political life. They sometimes took part in riots or insurrections such as the march to Versailles. The popular female masses, composed of these women and militant women, thus had a less recognizable political identity than the female sansculottes movement—although these latter form part of their group.[26] The transition from "women of the people" to "popular female masses" occurred through the dynamic of gathering for common goals, collective participation, and formation into a female popular movement.

THE ASSEMBLY OF REPUBLICAN WOMEN AND THE PRICE OF FOOD

The issue of subsistence was often at the origin of female crowds. Subsistence, politics, citizenship: from this triptych that drove women to act during the Revolution, historiography has generally recorded only the first. Let us take care not to sin by doing the reverse: the birth of the female sansculottes movement during the years 1789–1792 and its full emergence in the spring of 1792 has until now captured our attention, but we can no longer suppress the fact that several months earlier the entire female popular masses had been mobilized by the rising price of commodities. In January and February 1792, prices were lowered by force in the popular districts at the center of Paris and in the Faubourgs Saint-Antoine and Saint-Marcel: the rioters, often rounded up by women, forced the grocers to sell them merchandise at prices determined by the crowd.

Beginning in the autumn of 1792, the economic crisis intensified again. There was no separation between the economic, the social, and the political spheres in the popular movement, and men and women of the people lent a favorable ear to the *enragés,* who demanded price controls and severe measures against the monopolizers, the merchants, and the speculators, especially those who speculated on the rate of the assignat and thus aggravated inflation. The *enragés* did not form a political group, properly speaking, but were represented in Paris by Jacques Roux, Varlet, and Leclerc and were well established in the sections. At the beginning of 1793, the price of basic commodities, such as sugar, brown sugar, candles, and soap, was exorbitant, bread was hard to get, and people became increasingly aggravated. On 12 February, a deputation of forty-eight Parisian sections demanded bread and price controls at the Convention.

---

26. There remain, of course, women of the people who, deliberately or out of indifference, took no interest in the Revolution, even if they did not rise up against it.

Ten days later, female citizens of the Quatre-Nations (Unité) section asked the Jacobins to lend them their hall in order to discuss monopolies. Despite the commotion caused by women in the galleries who accused the club of accommodating monopolizers, the Jacobins refused. Finally, around three hundred female citizens gathered in the hall that the Fraternal Society of Patriots of Both Sexes allowed them to use. Their first act was to gather as a club under the name of the Assembly of Republican Women. They then wrote a petition, which they presented on Sunday the twenty-fourth to the Convention. While groups of women demanded bread and soap in the halls of the legislature, the wife of Wafflard, "Vice President of the Assembly of Republican Women," explained that as "mothers and wives of the defenders of the homeland, they were frightened by the manipulation of monopolizers" and demanded "insistently the revocation of the decree of the Constituent Assembly that declared money to be a commodity." Moments before, a deputation of washerwomen had presented another petition on the cost of soap. They asked that the death penalty be applied to monopolizers and speculators, who alone were responsible, they felt, for the high price of soap. The Convention listened to them coldly and sent the two petitions to its committees, adjourning them until two days later. The female petitioners said angrily as they left the Convention: "We have been adjourned until Tuesday, but we adjourn ourselves only until Monday. When our children ask us for milk, we do not adjourn them until two days later." Thus they decided to meet the next day before the Convention.[27]

Indeed, the next morning approximately forty women gathered at the Place du Carrousel and demanded a drum from the regiment of guards in order to "assemble all women and to present themselves as a group to the National Convention in order to ask them to execute their petition." Two ringleaders were questioned. One, a young unemployed cook, had proposed to climb a steeple and ring the alarm with her clogs or a hammer because it was finally time to demand a law that punished the monopolizers with death. Moreover, she had preached the dismissal of the Girondin deputies, for "she had believed it useful for the general good" to renew this motion heard the day before in the Jardin des Tuileries.[28]

---

27. Alphonse Aulard, *Les Société des Jacobins*, vol. 5 (Paris: 1889–1897), p. 37; *Moniteur*, XV, 555, 543, 544; *Archives parlementaires* 57, p. 151 and *Archives parlementaires* 59, p. 180; *Les Révolutions de Paris* 65; A.N., AF IV 1470, C 247 d. 367 f. 16.

28. A.P.P., AA 248 f. 67. The two women were released by the superintendent of police "under the condition that they would be more circumspect in the future."

Thus during the winter of 1793, the gatherings of women (the female sansculottes) assumed for the first time the appearance of a club, still in embryonic form. Though a subsistence crisis had given birth to their initiative, their conception of the "general good" was not just of an economic order. These women linked the struggle to reduce the cost of living and the purification of the Convention. But the female citizens who presented themselves to the Convention on the twenty-fourth did not return on the twenty-fifth. Their petitions were forgotten during renewed rioting over prices in Paris.

Disturbances broke out in the morning of the twenty-fifth in the central sections of Paris, where there were many large grocery shops. All day and even late into the night they spread in more or less concentric circles. As in the previous year, rioters besieged the grocers and forcibly set the price of soap, sugar, brown sugar, and candles.[29] Unable to prevent the mob from taking and distributing merchandise, police commissioners watched over the progress of these forced sales. When the people demanded that the home of a merchant suspected of monopolizing be visited, the commissioner led the search, either to prevent any trouble or to give the illusion of a semblance of authority—or even because he was forced by the rioters to accompany them. This presence of the authorities, even though completely overshadowed by the mob to which they had to submit, shows that most rioters were not looters. They were not engaging in illegal practices but limiting themselves to the distribution of commodities, which they felt had been monopolized, at a price that they judged to be fair.

Journalists presented the riot as a demonstration by women among whom were several provocateurs dressed in skirts who had not "even taken the precaution of shaving!"[30] The commissioners' statements and the reports of police informers, which were less fanciful, give us a more nuanced image of the facts. Women were, for the most part, a majority in the crowd, particularly in the bourgeois districts of the west and in the first section affected by the riot that they had started. Even more than by their virulent words against grocers whom they threatened to hang, women of the market were noteworthy for their expressive behavior: ironic before the guard,

---

29. According to the sections, the prices fixed by the rioters were eighteen to twenty-five sous for a pound of sugar, ten to twelve sous for brown sugar, twelve sous for candles, and ten to twelve sous for soap. The description of the riot section by section can be found in statements of police superintendents at the A.P.P.; see also G. Rudé, "Les Émeutes des 25, 26 février 1793 à Paris," *Annales historiques de la Révolution française* 25 (1953): 33–57, and *La Foule*, pp. 135 and following.

30. *Les Révolutions de Paris* 65.

under whose nose they sang with insolence; pathetic when a pregnant woman struck her womb while saying "I need sugar for my child," showing by this gesture, as clearly as by a long speech, that the right to existence takes precedence over the right to property.[31] But men, more often than women, took the initiatives by smashing in the doors of grocers, asking for searches, and so on.

At this time, these events were blamed on a plot by counterrevolutionaries or by Marat, according to whether one supported the left or the right side of the Convention. Albert Mathiez and George Rudé see here instead the work of Jacques Roux and the *enragés* as organizers of the riot.[32] That the watchword *enragé* encouraged a climate favorable to the riot is undeniable; that the *enragés* orchestrated it behind the scenes is debatable and not very convincing. And there is no direct relation between the riot and the Assembly of Republican Women that gathered on the twenty-fourth. The two petitioners arrested on the morning of the twenty-fifth near the Tuileries had absolutely no intention of proceeding to set prices by force but wished to go to the Convention to obtain a response. Their words were far from announcing, even indirectly, the events that unfolded during the day. Then, after the riot, there is no more talk of these two petitions. It is likely that female citizens preferred to have them forgotten so that no connection would be made between their deeds and the forced price-settings. The two petitions had simply contributed to the state of agitation, a prelude to the popular disturbance of the twenty-fifth.

The historiography of the Revolution has "preferred" to present only the image of apolitical female rioters, thus "forgetting" the attempt by women to form a club. It has also "forgotten" that, on 1 May 1793, before a deputation from the Faubourg Saint-Antoine declared to the Convention that if the deputies did not take vigorous measures concerning the organization of the army and price controls,[33] the faubourg would consider itself to be in insurrection, it had been preceded at the witness box by a hundred women from Versailles. With a drummer and a pennant at their head announcing that "we demand price controls on grains," they had read a petition demanding general price controls on grains and flour. The women from Versailles and the people from the faubourg were received curtly, and after the women were heard, the deputies rushed to close the meeting, to the

31. A.P.P., AA 153, 25 February 1793.
32. Rudé, "Les Émeutes."
33. The sansculottes were against free market pricing and demanded a general legal maximum price for commodities.

great anger of the petitioners. Several deputies were insulted and women occupied the hall, asserting that they were going to spend the night there and that they would not leave before "the Convention had done justice to their request." The mayor succeeded in making them "hear reason" and they were lodged by the neighboring sections.[34] After this day, the Convention finally capitulated and on 4 May decreed a regional maximum price for grains and flour.

Certainly, the subsistence riot of 25 February had more important repercussions than the gathering of several hundred women the evening before. Certainly, the threat of the Faubourg Saint-Antoine, the revolutionary faubourg par excellence, had an impact far more decisive than the pennant of the Versailles women. There are, however, repeatedly "forgotten events" that are important to fill in.

After the deputation of the Versailles women left Paris, a young girl, feeling "very deprived" about not being able to go to the Jacobins like her parents, allegedly told the police informer Dutard: "It is necessary that things change; we will still wait for a while, but if the rightists [Girondin] do not convert, things will go very badly for them."[35]

Indeed, during the entire month of May the attention and activity of militant women was centered on the struggle between the Girondins and the Montagnards. In addition, their actions gained a new resonance, for some organized in a female club, the Society of Revolutionary Republican Women.

34. *Les Révolutions de Paris* 199, p. 237; *Moniteur,* XVI, 287; A.N., C 255 d. 479 p. 3, C 355 d. 1864 p. 19, AF IV 1470, F 1c III Seine 27.
35. A.N., F 1c III Seine 27.

5 Women as Guardians of the Nation

The Société des Citoyennes Républicaines Révolutionnaires was officially created on 10 May 1793. On that day, "several female citizens went to the office of the secretary of the municipality and, in order to obey the municipal police law, declared that they intended to assemble and form a club for women only. The club planned to oppose the projects of enemies of the Republic. It would be called the Society of Revolutionary Republican Women and would meet at the library of the Jacobins on Rue Saint-Honoré."[1]

Two days later, the women read to the Jacobin club a speech that was a true declaration of faith, in which they asked for "prompt and vigorous measures to save the country"—the extermination of "all villains" and the arrest and disarming of "all suspect citizens."[2] They encouraged the formation of "companies of amazons" armed to fight against the "enemies within." They were applauded when they declared that they did not believe "in the patriotism of wives of deputies who did not want to disturb a pin, who did not wish to deprive themselves of anything."

But things went downhill quickly when the women claimed to respect only "female citizens whose heart burned with the fire of patriotism." An uproar began in the hall. The speaker continued nevertheless to invite the Jacobins to sign a petition that the Finistère section had asked them to present, which called "for the imposition of an enormous tax on the rich in order to assure the subsistence of the wives of defenders of the Republic." We read in the report that the "noise" began again. *Noise* is a modest term for

1. *Moniteur*, XVI, 362.
2. *Journal des débats et de la correspondance des Jacobins*, no. 412.

the tumultuous response by men who disapproved of the apparently too forceful spirit shown by the female citizens. The men's hostility grew to such a degree that the speaker, her voice broken by sobs, said, "We will save the country, citizens, do not believe that you can discourage us." The president of the meeting cut the incident short by affirming that "The Society (of Jacobins) is impressed by the heroic courage that you show." The speaker then concluded by calling upon all female citizens to unite with them in order to save the country and by asking that "women's caps become liberty caps." A rupture was prevented, but this incident was a bad omen of the difficulties the club was to encounter.

The structured group that the female sansculottes had hoped for during the past year was now, in May 1793, finally achieved. Following the rough model of the Assembly of Republican Women, which had created a precedent in February 1793, popular female militants led by Pauline Léon had met more or less regularly before officially informing the authorities of their meetings on 10 May.

Once it had begun, the women's club functioned like any other Parisian club. It held its meetings in the library of the old Jacobin convent on the Rue Saint-Honoré, and after the end of July and the beginning of August, under the charnel house of Saint-Eustache. A president, vice president, and four secretaries were elected for one month, and a treasurer with two assistants and an archivist for three months. Two assistants were nominated by acclamation to help the officers. The club had three committees—administration, charity, and correspondence—composed of twelve members each. Elections were by roll call. Each applicant for membership had to be presented by a member and seconded by two more members and to be at least eighteen years old for "the society felt that it could not refuse the right to speak to any member and that young female citizens could, with the best intentions, compromise the society by motions that had not been carefully thought out." "High moral standards" were "the most essential condition" for admission, and their absence one of the chief reasons for exclusion. New candidates had to take a standard oath: "to live for the Republic or . . . die for it" and "to obey the rules." Female citizens who were not members were permitted by the club to attend meetings, on condition (only in theory) that they were vouched for by two members.[3] This club of and for women was not open to men, who could only attend meetings on exceptional occasions

---

3. *Règlement de la Société des Citoyennes Républicaines Révolutionnaires de Paris*, 9 July 1793: B.H.V.P., 9589.

in the public galleries, but who could appear in delegations to the club. Although they tried to preserve their autonomy and identity within the popular movement, the Society of Revolutionary Republican Women were not entirely isolated from other clubs. Several times they acted in common with other revolutionary societies, and they asked to be affiliated with Jacobin, Cordelier, and other popular Parisian clubs.

The club was composed of a little more than 170 women, but only about one hundred regularly attended meetings. The information we have about them is rare and incomplete. Aside from the names of about sixty of the members and sympathizers, we know the age of nine: two thirds were rather young (twenty-five to thirty years old); the other third was aged (sixty to seventy years old). If these figures reflect the composition of the club, its members were women who were relatively free from family responsibilities, with either one or no children, or no longer responsible for their children. We know the professions of nineteen members and can see here the different fields in which Parisian women worked. The trades listed include commerce, clothing, crafts, domestic service, and even acting![4] Their level of education is high: a little less than a third of those women about whom we have information on this subject (seven out of twenty-two) did not know how to sign their name; the others had perfect mastery of handwriting. However, it is necessary to emphasize that most women on record were the "executives," the club president, vice-president, and secretaries. The other militants discovered by chance in the archives are usually wage earners or street merchants rather than shopkeepers or the wives of artisans; moreover, these were the illiterate women. Although the directors belonged to the petite bourgeoisie, the club recruited or influenced women of a lower class. Whatever their social background, most lived in revolutionary families. Mother and daughters sometimes attended meetings together, where they rubbed shoulders with the wives of sansculottes militants and section officials.

The goal of the militant women at the start of the club was to participate actively in safeguarding the Revolution. For these women, who could not really express themselves within the regular men's clubs and popular societies of the sections, the existence of a club for women made it possible to work actively for the Revolution's success. Nothing was more foreign to

4. The list includes one chocolate merchant, two cake merchants, three haberdashers, an elderly hosier, a secondhand dealer, a washerwoman, two linenworkers, a dressmaker, the wife of a gasman, a gold polisher, a printer, a shoe mender, the wife of a saddler, two cooks, and an actress.

their spirit than the thought of women assisting men. Their initial intention, as expressed to the Jacobins on 12 May, was to form armed corps of women to combat the "enemies within": "We have resolved to *protect the interior*, while our brothers protect the borders." The Revolutionary Republican Women, at least at the beginning, had a bipartite conception of tasks in the revolutionary movement. Repeating the division between woman-interior and men-exterior, they transposed it onto the defense of the Revolution and defined two areas of intervention, one for each sex. Men were to combat the *exterior* enemies of the Revolution, while women were to fight its *interior* enemies.

Are women, wives and mothers, interior beings? Very well then, but let us not forget that in the symbolic language dear to the Revolution, the nation is nothing but the family of citizens. Thus it is the responsibility of women to "protect the interior" of the country, to hunt down all who within the borders (of the house) threatened the revolutionary family, figuratively and literally. Emphasizing the fact that the "tender mothers" could not let their children in their arms have their throats cut by "enemies within" while their husbands were at the borders, on 12 May the Revolutionary Republican Women asked women *to arrest and disarm suspect citizens*. This was what it meant to "guard the interior" during the Revolution. The traditional guardians of the hearth were thus to become the *armed* guardians of the nation during revolution. "So what if our husbands leave, we are here," the Revolutionary Republican Women asserted frequently, with such insistence that we must ask if beyond an affirmation of their public spirit and their courage, we should not also read a secret desire for the absence of men, favorable to the full development of their revolutionary spirit. This is what worried some men, who were afraid that the end of their exclusive political power would signal their enslavement by the other sex.[5] This meeting between the traditional image of women and revolutionary familial symbolism had unexpected consequences! But the Revolutionary Republican Women realized quickly that their idea of the division of revolutionary duties between the two sexes (a profoundly original conception not formulated by other militant women) was far from receiving unanimous acceptance; without totally abandoning this idea, they no longer presented it so peremptorily as they did on 12 May to the Jacobins.

5. See "Sexual Difference and Equal Rights" in this volume.

As a corollary to their desire to defend the Republic while occupying political space, the Revolutionary Republican Women wanted to bear arms. This is not surprising: requests to arm women had constituted the first common action of militant women and were inseparable from their wish to achieve complete citizenship. The Revolutionary Republican Women insisted on this point, always within this double perspective of revolutionary engagement and struggle for political rights. Two weeks after having proposed to the Jacobins—with the reception we have seen—that "companies of amazons be formed" in order to arrest and disarm suspected citizens, they committed a second offense by reaffirming before these same Jacobins their desire to gather in "phalanxes to destroy the aristocrats."[6] The first article of their regulations stipulated that the club had "as a goal to arm itself in order to work for the defense of the homeland"; but the rule that dated from 9 July is less categorical than their first and leaves "female citizens free to bear arms or not." With the beating of a drum, an unfurled flag, and the eye of vigilance (a revolutionary symbol), the Revolutionary Republican Women marched on parade, all wearing red caps as headdresses and some donning amazonian garb. Journalists employed military vocabulary to report on the club's demonstrations and mix mockery and fear in describing the powerful impression left by these parades, which recall the displays of the national guard—with one important difference: the Revolutionary Republican Women were not an armed corps. The "truly military ceremony" described by journalists consisted only of the glorious clothes that adorned, in a burst of pride and stubbornness, a hope that had been reduced to moon dust.[7] Two days before the club was banned, the Revolutionary Republican Women prepared to go to a section ceremony with only four miserable pikes.[8] This pathetic number leads us to believe that these pikes were symbolic accessories rather than an attempt at genuine armament and proves that these female citizens had given up their original claim.

Yet they never renounced their desire for political engagement within the revolutionary movement, in order to save the homeland by any appropriate means. Thus, during the first phase of their activity (May to June 1793), they mobilized their forces in the battle against the Girondins.

6. Alphonse Aulard, *La Société des Jacobins,* vol. 5 (Paris: 1889–1897), p. 212 (meeting of 27 May).

7. *La Gazette française,* nos. 514, 533, 534.

8. *Les Révolutions de Paris* 215, pp. 207–210 (minutes of the meeting of 7 Brumaire Year II).

"HORDES OF FURIES" AGAINST THE GIRONDINS

The conflict that had gradually developed between the Girondin and Montagnard deputies since 1792 dominated political life during May 1793. The Girondins (Brissot, Roland, Vergniaud, and so on), supporters of economic liberalism, remained hostile to the measures for a controlled economy demanded by the sansculottes. Indeed, they planned that after 10 August 1792, the people were no longer to play a part in politics. The Montagnards (Robespierre, Saint-Just, Marat, Danton, Desmoulins, and so on), advocates of a plan for society that resembled the female sansculottes' project, favored an alliance with the popular masses. From the Montagnard point of view, this was the only way that a revolution assuring everyone's happiness could triumph.

The popular militant women—the "patriotic women" as they were called by police informers, the "knitters" as they were later to be known—supported the Montagnards. At the beginning of May, police informers began to take an interest in these women who, before the Convention, called for insurrection against the Girondins and asserted "that it is necessary to renew the spirit of 10 August and assassinate and cut the throats of all the rich," "insult citizens, call them cowards and craven," and spit scornfully on the "notary clerks" who were not eager to defend the Revolution at the front.[9] The informers had previously noted that there were many more women than men in gatherings. From mid-May on, while some women organized in clubs and the conflict between Girondins and Montagnards intensified, these women played a daily part in police reports just as they did in the speech of their contemporaries. Thus they were perceived as a specific group within society and a specific part of the popular movement. This sudden and intense interest by police informers reflects a female push forward within the Parisian sansculottes movement. Contrary to the assertions of many historians, who rely too much on the attention paid to the relation between women and subsistence, the confrontation between Girondins and Montagnards during May 1793 is one of the revolutionary episodes in which women are conspicuous by their presence.

Every day militant women—Revolutionary Republican Women and others—gathered in groups at the Tuileries, near the legislature. Like the cake merchant nicknamed Mère Duchesne by a police spy "because she

---

9. A.N., AF^{IV} 1470, 4 May; F 1c III Seine 27, 5 May; F^7 4775^{14} d. Saunier. A.P.P., AA 248, 5 May 1793.

resembles Père Duchesne in her opinions and how she expresses them," they inflamed the crowd against the Girondins.[10] On 13 May, the police informer Terrasson described the Revolutionary Republican Women as the driving force behind the anti-Girondin opposition: "Women persist in demanding the removal of twenty-two deputies (the most notable Girondins). . . . They even hope that they will be helped by men."[11]

The new arrangement of the Convention's meeting room angered several women, who complained that the public could no longer hear anything from the public galleries. The galleries were filled with men and especially women who encouraged the Montagnards by their applause or by booing their adversaries. For this reason, the Girondin deputies reserved some galleries for the citizens of regions that supported them. To enter these galleries, it was necessary to show a special authorization and present a pass provided by the deputies. On 13 May, "many female citizens" asked the Convention for permission to enter these reserved galleries, but the Convention passed on to the agenda. Outraged by this "despotism," the Society of Revolutionary Republican Women passed a motion at one of their meetings to impede this discriminative measure. From nine in the morning, they kept guard before the door of the galleries, prevented male and female citizens with passes from entering, tore up their complimentary invitations, and insulted and threatened them. Armed with one of these entry cards, Théroigne de Méricourt was brutally whipped on 15 May by the Revolutionary Republican Women and called a Girondin; they released her only because Marat intervened in her favor.[12]

DEPUTY:	What are you doing here? Who has given you permission to be here?
FEMALE CITIZEN:	Equality—are we not all equal? And if we are all equal, I have the same right to be here as any other.
DEPUTY:	You are here to disturb the assembly, and I will certainly find a way to make you leave.
FEMALE CITIZEN:	Go, sir, it is not your place to be here, your place is in the main hall, and in spite of all your efforts, we will stay here and fight your iniquities.[13]

10. A.N., F 1c III Seine 27.

11. Ibid.

12. A.N., AF II 45 pl. 351, 16 May; AF[IV] 1470, 15 May; F 1c III Seine 27, 20 and 21 May. *Moniteur*, XVI, 375. This episode marks the end of Théroigne's political career; she was arrested shortly thereafter and imprisoned as insane at the Salpêtrière.

13. A.N., F 1c III Seine 27, 21 May.

This little dialogue between a Girondin deputy and a member of the Revolutionary Republican Women guarding the door illustrates clearly the atmosphere that reigned in the Convention. As this deputy complained, militant women frequently disturbed the meeting of the Convention by activity in the galleries. On 18 May, shouts were heard in the hallways of the assembly, interrupting the deputies. Several Girondins rose, crying that this tumult degraded the Convention. One deputy asked that the female sentries "make sure that there are never more than two people in the hallways"; another denounced the Montagnards and demanded the arrest of all those who stood guard at the entry to the galleries and the immediate forced exit of spectators who indulged in insults and boos. Several moments later, there was more noise in the passage; a woman entered one of the galleries reserved for Girondin supporters and tried to make a young man leave. Her cries disturbed the Convention, which became "very agitated." Several representatives rushed to the office of the president, Isnard. In the confusion, the young man rather than the woman was arrested. During the general turmoil, several Girondin deputies threatened to leave. The incident was followed by a debate between Girondins and Montagnards, during which Isnard warned his colleagues of a planned revolt: "Women will begin this action; they have even enlisted for this deed of iniquity. At the moment when their wild arms will stab the fatherland, they are persuaded that they are heroines who must save it. Men will come to the aid of the women."[14]

Two days later, "violent mutterings" and cries of "Down with him! Down with him!" from the galleries interrupted a Girondin's harangue. Larivière asked that the meeting be adjourned "to show that there was no freedom." Marat replied ironically, "What does this panic over several outbursts of disapproval by women mean? *The experience ought to have cured the Convention.*"[15]

The spirit of these women, particularly the Revolutionary Republican Women, was not felt only at the Convention. From the beginning, the women's club was linked tightly to the Cordeliers club, which, along with the Jacobins, supported the Montagnards. Thus the Cordeliers let the women speak in their meetings. On 22 May, men and women spoke against

14. *Moniteur*, XVI, 414, 420, 421.
15. Ibid., 429.

the Girondins. "A woman spoke with all the energy of her sex," exhorting the sansculottes "not to stop before they had passed decrees to save the Republic and bring down the enemies of the Revolution." She called on citizens to take to the Convention the petition written in common several days before by the Revolutionary Republican Women and the Cordeliers, which demanded the arrest of suspects, the creation of revolutionary courts and a revolutionary army, the indictment of the Girondins, and the purging of administrative offices.[16]

The Revolutionary Republican Women also attempted to persuade other women to adopt their point of view. On 19 May, they tried, without success, to rouse the women of Versailles:[17] "Down with the Twelve! Long live the Montagnards! To the guillotine with the Brissotins! ['Brissotins' was another name for the Girondins, from the name of Brissot, one of their leaders.] Long live Marat! Long live Père Duchesne! Come with us, female citizens, we are going to crush the new despotism." We see the Revolutionary Republican Women again, at the head of three hundred women, "arranged in order of battle" with their flag and their drum, demonstrating in order to free Hébert.[18] Hébert was a leader of the Cordeliers and the director of the newspaper *Le Père Duchesne,* arrested by the Commission of Twelve (a commission of inquiry consisting of twelve Girondins) for an issue of the newspaper containing a violent anti-Girondin campaign.

The Convention was not the only place where there were opposing opinions. In the sections, the sansculottes, who were pro-Montagnard, and those called "moderates," the pro-Girondins, also fought over power. In these hours of crisis, female citizens, who normally were only spectators at the section assemblies, declared themselves to be full participants and left the galleries to join their fellow citizens. The women eventually voted with them and became involved in struggles where sansculottes and moderates battled. They gave and received blows and were sometimes wounded by chairs thrown at their heads. On the evening of 22 May, one hundred to one hundred and fifty women and some men gathered before the distinctly "moderate" section assembly of Butte-des-Moulins, which had twice refused to support the petition by the Cordeliers and the Revolutionary Republican Women. Despite the threat of a sixty-man patrol, the residents of

16. *Brochure de Bergoeing à ses commettants et à tous les citoyens de la République,* 28 June 1793, Caen.

17. Ibid.

18. Ibid.; *La Gazette française,* 28 May 1793; A.N., AF[IV] 1470.

the section, backed up by representatives from the women's club, urged on groups that were hostile to the section moderates. A crowd gathered around the women and a lively discussion commenced. A passing butcher's apprentice bragged that he did not get mixed up with anything, that he did not frequent either clubs or popular societies. His words provoked the sighs of a "little woman": "Such men are indeed to be pitied for not being enlightened!" On 29 May, under the influence of its President Fielval (a "gangrenous aristocrat"), the Mont-Blanc section used the pretext that the room was too crowed to pass a motion forbidding female citizens to attend the meeting of the section assembly. This excuse did not fool anyone: women were excluded by the moderates because they helped the sansculottes. The women refused to be defeated; adopting the tactic used at the Convention, a dozen stationed themselves at the entrance to the meeting hall and asked each citizen who appeared if he was an aristocrat. When Fielval left, he was "assailed, attacked, threatened, and insulted in the most outrageous manner" by these female citizens, who promised him that they would tear off his epaulets "and even hang him."[19]

At the Convention, in the clubs, in the sections, and in the street, whether they took the initiative or supported the sansculottes, female patriots played an important role in preparing the revolt against the Girondins. On 24 May, a police informer noted that "there was general agitation" and that "women were the instrument used by (the agitators of the people)"; on 27 May, another reported that the "considerable gathering" held the day before at the Tuileries "consisted mostly of women put forward for political reasons by men who did not themselves dare to make proposals or attempt blows." Many women were arrested when they advocated revolt.

The author of a linguistic study on *Le Courrier des 83 départements* of the Girondin Gorsas, P. Huetsch, has compiled tables of lexical fields of the network of Gorsas's "enemies"; in almost all of these tables, women occupy an important position. Thus Anarchy "used women," and more than half of Marat's "workforce" was composed of women. The Jacobins counted among their "political allies" Robespierre's "devoted female followers," "Marat's bacchantes," and the "group of shrews of the Montagnards."[20]

19. A.N., AF^{IV} 1470, 22 May; F^7 4707 d. Fielval.
20. P. Huetsch, "*Le Courrier* de Gorsas (25 May 1793—31 May 1793)," *Bulletin du Centre d'analyse du discours de l'Université de Lille III*, no. 2 (1975).

In a *Précis des événements* that led to the fall of the Girondins, this same Gorsas elaborated at length on the importance of women's role during the end of May: "A tremendous agitation reigned moreover in Paris. Women gathered, doubtless excited by the furies. They armed themselves with pistols and swords; they arrested people and rushed to various city crossroads, carrying before them the standard of licentiousness . . . ; they wanted to put an end to the situation; they wanted to purge the Convention; above all, they wanted to make heads fall and to become drunk with blood."[21]

Blood, armed women who ran through the city and whose standard could only be that of licentiousness: Gorsas knew how to find frightening images. However, beyond the imaginary mobilized by the Girondin for political ends, his account, partially confirmed by other documents, testifies to the importance of the female sansculottes' role in late May.

Women participated in the revolt that they had called for so fervently. On 31 May, when the tocsin rang and the sansculottes were called to arms, the spokesman for the Commission of Twelve at the Convention was booed by galleries filled with women. Shortly after, the deputation of Parisian sections asked that the Girondin leaders be excluded and the economic and social programs of the female sansculottes be enforced. During this time in the city streets, women supported the rebels. A sixty-two-year-old female linenworker begged the national guards of the Butte-des-Moulins section to rejoin their comrades; when they told her to go on her way, she drew a knife from her pocket and affirmed "that it is for them as well as for aristocrats because they were aristocrats." She was arrested and escaped prison only because of a deputation of Revolutionary Republican Women led by Constance Evrard, in whose custody the police superintendent released her.[22]

The club as a whole took part in the day of revolt: at the start of the afternoon, a deputation presented itself to the city council and asked to be admitted to deliberate with the joint committee of the sections that led the uprising. The council congratulated the women for "their republican zeal" but "regretted that they could not be admitted to the revolutionary committee of men" because this was no club but a meeting of deputies from the forty-eight sections. However, the women were invited to watch the

---

21. Antoine Joseph Gorsas, *Précis rapide des événements qui ont lieu à Paris dans les journeés de 30 et 31 mai, premier et 2 juin 1793* (Paris: Imprimerie de la Veuve d'Ant. Jos. Gorsas, 1793?).

22. A.P.P., AA 90, 31 May 1793.

meeting. They followed the deliberations attentively and even on occasion intervened, proposing on 1 June that the sansculottes volunteers be given food supplies so that they could stay at their posts.[23]

The day of 31 May ended in failure. On 2 June, the movement resumed: the insurrectional committee of the sections surrounded the Convention with national guards, whose cannons prevented the deputies from leaving. The Convention had to yield and order the arrest of twenty-nine Girondin deputies. Although not a part of the insurrectional committee, the Revolutionary Republican Women were at the Convention with the deputation from the sections and presented their own petition, which, like that of the insurgents, asked for the immediate arrest of the Girondin leaders. In his *Précis,* Gorsas describes the "ferocious vow [dismissal of the Girondins] expressed by the furies" and how, when the rioters prevented the outlawed deputies from escaping, "they were supported by a troop of women calling themselves revolutionaries, a troop of furies, avid for carnage"; armed, these "women without shame . . . held the deputies captive"—it even seems that "one of [the deputies], pursued by five or six of these shrews, had to jump out of a window."

On 2 June, a young female linenworker was arrested in the courtyard of the Convention and "believed to be armed with daggers and pistols": after she was searched, it turned out that she did not have any weapons. This phantasm of women armed to the teeth can be found in the accounts of the rebellion given by the Girondins: Gorsas, Bergoeing, and Lanjuinais all insisted on this point, in a veritable delirium.[24] It is true that the Revolutionary Republican Women had decided to organize in "companies of amazons" to fight the Girondins and that the rebels had armed themselves with the first weapons at hand, such as work tools or the knives that women of the people carried in their pockets. Thus the phantasm of women carrying weapons probably had a real basis that was encouraged by the Girondin deputies' desire to frighten their readers by describing the arming as horrible, anarchic, and indecent. But this also suggests an unreasonable male fear that goes beyond concrete reality and touches on the domain of *mentalités.*

Far from being absent from the revolutionary movement during the spring of 1793, women were among its most active participants. They had

23. *Moniteur,* XVI, 527, 543.
24. Gorsas, *Précis; Brochure de Bergoeing;* Lanjuinais, *Dernier crime de Lanjuinais aux assemblées primaires, sur la constitution proposeé en 1793.*

already taken part in militant action and so were ready for the insurrectional days of 31 May to 2 June. The means of action are clear: create permanent agitation; intervene at all levels and in all areas of political life, such as the Convention, the sections, and the street; counterattack all moderate or Girondin initiatives; and call the populace to revolt. The Revolutionary Republican Women triggered many initiatives, inspiring not only action by women but the larger popular movement. However, women's activity was not limited to this club. The female citizens who filled the galleries, attacked the moderates, called the populace to insurrection, or supported the sansculottes in the sections were certainly not all members or even sympathizers of the club. They belonged to the group of grassroots militants, the female sansculottes. The frequent interventions of the club probably inspired these women, even if only indirectly. However, we cannot account for the upsurge of activity by women during the spring of 1793 with this single explanation, which can moreover be turned around: perhaps this upsurge of activity inspired the creation and key work of the Revolutionary Republican Women. After all, did the club not draw from the general insurgent activity of women the power necessary to declare itself the equal of men and ensure its recognition by the revolutionary movement?

The equal of men? The Revolutionary Republican Women were in fact considered a leading force in the revolutionary movement, by Girondin deputies as well as by police informers, clubs, and revolutionary authorities. Nevertheless, although women formed part of the insurrection, the revolutionary club for women could not be admitted to the insurrectionary committee of the sections, and on 2 June at the Convention they were not among the insurgents but on the sidelines, obliged to present a separate petition in order to make their voices heard. Organized in a revolutionary club, the members of the Revolutionary Republican Women could express themselves and work toward the fall of the Girondins, but their group, which had to overcome the limitations imposed on female militancy in the sections, found itself once again helpless to assert a real equality when the representatives of the Sovereign People took charge of the revolt. A police informer claimed that, before the rebellion, women had hoped for the support of men. Gorsas wrote that, during the revolt, women supported the rioters. Once again we encounter the essential question of the place of women in the Sovereign People, of the nature of their citizenship.

MILITANT WOMEN AND THE MASSES, OR HOW TO
PERSUADE THE PEOPLE OF THEIR OWN BEST INTERESTS

The Girondins were eliminated from the Convention. But when the deputies drew up the new Constitution, some regions of the country supported the Girondins and rebelled. Even in Paris the moderate opposition was far from being reduced to silence. And economic problems continued.

As early as the middle of June, Parisian women complained about the absence or expense of commodities. Rumors of a monopolizer's plot resurfaced. On 25 June, in a threatening petition, the *enragé* Jacques Roux asked the Convention for the enforcement of price controls, for "liberty is only a vain phantom when one class of men can starve another with impunity. Equality is only a vain phantom when the rich, by monopoly, have the right of life and death over their fellows." The same day, around six o'clock in the afternoon, a "large group of female citizens" stopped two vehicles full of soap on the Rue Saint-Lazare. Believing that the merchandise was meant for monopolizers, they seized the crates and sold the soap at twenty sous a pound.[25]

The next day, the disturbances resumed even more forcefully and extended to the neighboring sections. Rumors spread that boats from Rouen were to return there with their cargo. At six o'clock in the morning, a crowd of neighborhood women gathered at the Saint-Nicolas and de la Grenouillère ports (the Royal and du Carrousel bridges) and forced the soap to be sold at fifteen or twenty sous a pound. City hall summoned soldiers in the affected sections and sent elected municipal representatives, who finally succeeded in calming the rioters. At the same time, two hundred female citizens besieged a house on the Rue de Provence that they believed held soap and forced the police superintendent to search it. In the afternoon, more than a thousand women set the price for the contents of a cart of soap near the Champs-Elysées.[26]

On the morning of the twenty-seventh, women attacked the boats moored at the Quai de l'Ecole near the Pont-Neuf. The disturbances no longer had the local character of previous days. Now Parisian women from all the city districts gathered at the Quai de l'Ecole. However, at noon many armed men gathered and patrolled the Seine. The men were taken to task by female passersby; a dressmaker called them "damn idiots" and spat on them "while showing disdain and scorn." In spite of this hostility, the

25. A.P.P., AA 226, f. 311, 329, 330 and AA 174, 25 June 1793.
26. A.P.P., AA 248, 26 June; AA 174, 26 June; AA 127, f. 179–184; AA 148 f. 182–188. *Moniteur*, XVI, 754.

guards succeeded in preventing further looting. The same day, washer-women presented a petition "against the excessive cost of soap, candles, and other commodities" to the Convention.[27]

The female rioters—washerwomen who worked by the day, women who worked as merchants in the food market at la Halle, street merchants, dress-makers, and the wives of small artisans, masons, and water carriers—were clearly of popular origin. Not only did they not feel guilty, but they took pride in being members of the sansculottes and accused the guards and hos-tile passersby of being monopolizers, bourgeois, and aristocrats, thus link-ing the political and the social. Indeed, these days stemmed more from the fear of a plot to deprive revolutionary Paris of essential supplies than from indignation over the price of commodities, as had been the case in February 1792 and 1793. At the outset, female citizens stopped vehicles and gathered in crowds around boats in order to ensure that their cargo would not leave the capital.

The Hébertist city hall and the Montagnard Convention explained that the riot was the result of a counterrevolutionary plot meant to show "that the people were incapable of governing themselves," to make departments (regions of the country) believe that the Convention was never peaceful and safe in Paris, and to prevent the acceptance of the Constitution adopted by the Convention on the evening of 24 June. However, they differentiated between "distraught" rioters and "malevolent" agitators. There was a de-sire, which bore fruit, to persuade "the people" that they acted against their own interests. The Revolutionary Republican Women devoted all their en-ergy to this end, using their influence with women. By their account, they succeeded "in redeeming several lost female citizens from their errors."[28] Warned of a gathering, city hall sent deputations to the people who were fixing prices and often succeeded in showing "the trap" laid by the "malevo-lents" to encourage the revolt of the departments against Paris, civil war, and food shortage. City hall placed "the property that the malevolents wished to loot" "under the protection of the people,"[29] that is, the rioters, whom the deputations went to persuade of their "error." Most of the "looters" had approved the events of May and June, supported the Montagnards, and were consequently sensitive to political arguments

27. A.P.P., AA 185 f. 245–250 and AA 59 f. 274. *Moniteur*, XVI, 759.
28. *Moniteur*, XVI, 762.
29. Ibid., XVII, 1–2; A.N., F⁷ 4661 d. Darcel and F⁷ 4710 d. Faucher.

about the distribution of food and popular price fixing. Although certain of their rights, they did not wish to weaken the Revolution, which was being attacked on all sides. Nor did they wish to foment dissension when the union of all revolutionaries was desperately sought.

The still weak Montagnard Convention felt it was necessary to weld together all the forces of the country. The acceptance of the Constitution by the French people was to demonstrate the unity of the country, in which women meant to participate. In fact, the summer of 1793 was unquestionably the period when militants and authorities accepted women's participation in the popular movement with the most indulgence, and even enthusiasm.

6 Light and Shadows,
Summer 1793

WHAT IF WOMEN WERE MEMBERS OF THE
SOVEREIGN PEOPLE?

The Acceptance of the Constitution

The Constitution was adopted by the Convention on 24 June and then submitted to referendum. Female citizens did not have the right to vote, but in many (electoral) primary assemblies, they refused to be excluded from the nation and voted alongside men in the case of vote by acclamation, or after men in private ballots when voting by name took place. Women also often took oaths along with men.

The Parisians assembled on 2 July, and during the following days, different sections came to announce their vote and congratulate the Convention. Female citizens participated in all of these processions. Most of the time they played the same role that they had performed in festivals: they threw flowers and civic wreaths, and the President embraced them. Their presence was "ornamental" but also demonstrated the unity of the nation. Here we see the ambiguity of the place reserved for them in the revolutionary movement. They were citizens who were excluded from the political body, but whose presence was necessary in demonstrations of unity, for, after all, women represented half the country. In addition, they were saluted as (future) mothers who ensured the prospects of the Republic.

Women were not content with this passive role. Their presence in the section processions that marched to the Convention at the beginning of July reflected their desire not to be phantoms of revolutionary political life. Whether intervening in person or asking the speaker of the section to act on their behalf, they asserted that "although their sex did not permit them to vote," "they could not remain insensible to the republican feelings that their husbands, brothers, and friends had expressed" and that they also accepted the Declaration of the Rights of Man and the Constitution. They swore to raise their children in the principles of liberty and equality, to marry only true republicans, or to die "if necessary to better consolidate the bases of a truly republican constitution."

Other women presented themselves apart from section processions, alone or as a specific group, such as flower sellers or wives of Convention gendarmes. After having given "their assent" and announced their joy and their support for the Montagnards, these deputations of women sometimes asked for the immediate organization of national education, price controls, and a severe law against monopolizers.

As flower sellers asserted that "tranquil in their places, they actively watched over an honest trade and wished to return, full of satisfaction, to their duties as mothers and wives," a female citizen from the Beaurepaire section became indignant that these women "did not count in the political system" and demanded the right to vote: "You have given a Constitution to men, they now enjoy all the rights of free men, but women are very far from this level. We ask you for primary assemblies, and as the Constitution rests on the Rights of Man, we demand today the full use of these rights." (She was applauded.)[1]

The Revolutionary Republican Women also congratulated the Convention for the Constitution. Their presence on 24 June in the official procession was noted by a journalist: "In the entire procession, about one hundred Revolutionary Women constantly stayed beneath their flags; they had about ten or twelve, and were led by men who directed their march and their movements."[2]

The female citizens of the provinces did not lag behind in this movement. Since 1791, their clubs had grown increasingly radical and now supported the Montagnards, whom they urged to stay at their post. At Besançon and Bordeaux, they mobilized against Girondin federalism ("federalism" was the name given to the anti-Montagnard rebellion in certain departments); at Casteljaloux (Lot-et-Garonne) they even gathered in clubs for women to better "declare their support for the National Convention and their aversion for a subversive and disorganized system"

1. *Archives parlementaires* 68, pp. 139 (Bondy), 251 (flower sellers), 254 (Beaurepaire), 283 (Croix-Rouge), 286 (Marchés), 314 (Théâtre-Français), 381 (Bon-Conseil), 383 (Nord). A.N., C 261 d. 572 f. 29 (Bondy), d. 573 f. 12 (flower sellers), f. 57 (Croix-Rouge); C 262 d. 574 f. 5 (Théâtre-Français), f. 22 (female citizen Baillard), f. 30 (female citizen Willaume); C 263, 11 July (wives of gendarmes).
2. *La Gazette française,* nos. 540 and 542.

(federalism). The female citizens of Muret (Haute-Garonne) and the women's clubs in Damazan, Clermont-Ferrand, Le Mans, Nancy, and Beaumont (Dordogne) voted their own acceptance of the Constitution. Women in the last three clubs reproached the Convention in scarcely veiled terms for excluding them from the "right to express their suffrage"; thus the Republican Women of Beaumont asserted in a preamble that "female citizens also have the right to ratify an act to which they have so effectively contributed" and that the Rights of Man "are also *their rights*." The wife of Thiefaine of Valognes (Manche) was even more precise: after congratulating the members of the Convention for 31 May and the Constitution, and for putting an end to abuse and "countless" prejudices, she continued: "But injustices to my sex must still be overcome; they irrevocably seem to take away from us all public administration and forbid us even to express our feelings about the great interests of the country."

The Besançon women's club also demanded the right to vote.[3]

We could say that the previous examples of two women and three women's clubs who asked that women be included in the political body are not many, and we could add that the revolutionary militants were thus insensible, or even totally unresponsive to their exclusion from political rights. And yet in so doing, we would fail to see that besides a clearly developed feminist consciousness that was indeed in the minority during the Revolution, the political form of these interventions could hide a "feminist" dimension.

More than a mere minority voiced these demands for political equality. This is even more true of the veiled reproaches for exclusion from political rights. But above all this wave of addresses by women who declared at the Convention that they supported the constitutional act or even that they had gathered to vote for its acceptance reflect more than political commitment and support for the Montagnards. Nothing had been asked of them; their vote when they gave it was largely symbolic. It was not illegal, but it had no legal weight, and women knew this. In gathering and making their assent part of the Convention, they transformed a private act—support for the Constitution by an individual excluded from political rights—into a public act whose authors, female citizens, belonged to the political body. These addresses by women—their insistence on solemnly informing the

3. A.N., C 262 d. 577 f. 1–3 (wife of Thiefaine), d. 583 f. 8 (Nancy); C 266 d. 629, pp. 13 (Damazan), 15 (Clermont-Ferrand); C 267 d. 631, p. 19 (Beaumont), d. 635, p. 10 (Le Mans); C 280 d. 765, p. 12 (Muret). H. Perrin, "Le Club des femmes de Besançon," *Annales révolutionnaires* 9 (1917); G. Langeron, "Le Club des femmes de Dijon pendant la Révolution," *La Révolution en Côte d'Or*, vol. 5 (Dijon: 1929).

legislators that they also ratified the Constitution that was "presented for the sanction of the sovereign people" (female citizens from the Marchés section), even if "the law deprives them of the precious right to vote" (Faubourg-Montmartre)—demonstrated their desire for integration with the Sovereign People and the right to exercise popular sovereignty despite their legal exclusion from the electoral body. By this very step they acted as citizens and reappropriated a natural right to which they were entitled.

RECOGNITION OF THE REVOLUTIONARY WOMEN'S MOVEMENT

Parallel with these more or less implicit demands representing acceptance of the Constitution by female citizens, the summer of 1793 was marked by the attention brought by revolutionaries to the place of women in society and in the popular movement.

On 17 June, the police informer Perrière remarked that the word *equality* produced "a pleasant impression . . . especially on women. Born slaves of men, they apparently have a greater interest in its reign." That this police informer used these terms to evoke the fate of women reveals the interest then taken by both men and women in the social and political status of women. During the summer of 1793, a global project for women's emancipation did not come to fruition, but throughout the country the vision of women as wives confined to their homes was questioned.

Thus at the beginning of July, female citizens of the Droits-de-l'Homme section asserted in a speech given at the Society of Revolutionary Republican Women that "the declaration of rights is common to both sexes."[4] "Offended and humiliated" by neutrality, they refused to be considered "passive and isolated beings" relegated "to the narrow sphere of their household." They wished "to have their place within the social order, . . . working toward the common good" and asked: "Why women, gifted with the faculty of feeling and expressing their ideas, should hear their exclusion from public affairs stated?" They recognized that their "first obligations [were] private responsibilities" and remarked that a "thousand minute details" brought about by domestic tasks left them less leisure than men. Nevertheless, they continued, "It is possible to reconcile what nature imperiously demands and what the love of the public good commands." The rules of the popular club (of both sexes) of the Arsenal section, which stipulated

4. *Discours prononcé à la Societé des Citoyennes Républicaines Révolutionnaires par les citoyennes de la section des Droits-de-l'Homme en lui donnant un guidon sur lequel est la Déclaration des Droits de l'Homme* (Paris, end of June–beginning of July 1793).

in the name of the "principles of social Equality" that "the right to acquire and to spread education and knowledge useful to the Republic belongs indiscriminately to both sexes," is specifically dated 17 July 1793. One month later to the day, the Hommes-Libres Society in the Pont-Neuf section became open to women, who until then had been relegated to the galleries.[5]

On 30 June, the department of Paris and the section representatives, who had led the anti-Girondin revolt and continued to meet at the Archbishopric, paid homage to the Revolutionary Republican Women. By virtue of their "zeal," their "activity," their "audacity," and their "courage" in May and June, they "are indeed worthy of the fatherland." This text outstrips the circumstances: it is an affirmation of the right—and even the duty—of women to participate actively in the Revolution. Its authors thought, contrary to the opinion of most revolutionaries, that "their homes cannot contain the abundance of republican wives' and mothers' affections." They recognized that women had not been created only for the pleasure of men, but that they belonged to all of humankind: "Yes, female citizens, there is in you a virtue when each man tells you that you must love no one but him; when his jealous egoism requests of your spirit the virtue of faithfulness, it is also a virtue to love the homeland, and to let your spirit flower for the happiness of humanity."

They blamed the past order of things for the image of "woman as commodity," to use a modern expression. While most revolutionaries asked women to be sweet, modest, and reserved, these men congratulated them for their "passions": "Female sex insatiable in desires, female sex filled with an immense love, no, your heart does not fool you when it is never satisfied."

After having assured them that "their post was under the tricolored flag," these men exhorted women to continue their deeds. "Dissembling royalists, intriguers, people who had been bribed, and finally traitors of all sorts" were still active. Women should pursue and arrest them, monitor faithfulness to oaths, and inspire defenders of principles.[6]

These words must have pleased the Revolutionary Republican Women. Here the Parisian authorities only repeated their initial credo. The times of tears provoked by male hostility seemed so distant! Storms would soon darken on the horizon, but for the moment the sun shone

---

5. *Règlemens de la Société de l'Harmonie Sociale des Sans-Culottes des deux sexes Défenseurs de la Constitution;* B.N., Mss., N.A.F. 2713 (Minutes of the Société populaire des Hommes Libres Amis de la Constitution).

6. *Les Autorités constituées du Département de Paris, et les Commissaires des Sections, Aux Républicaines Révolutionnaires,* A.N., T 1001 (1–3) d. Lacombe.

and only praise was heard about the Revolutionary Republican Women. On 21 June, the *enragé* Jacques Roux spoke highly of them at city hall. His speech reflected the state of grace of June 1793 and not the privileged connection that existed subsequently between the *enragés* and the Revolutionary Republican Women. At the end of June, the Revolutionary Republican Women took a position inside the *enragé*-influenced Cordeliers society against Jacques Roux (who had already been attacked by the Montagnards, the Jacobins, and the Hébertist Cordeliers) and contributed to his expulsion. On 30 June 1793, a Revolutionary Republican Woman criticized the *enragé* to the Cordeliers, thus supporting the delegation of Jacobins presided over by Collot d'Herbois, who had come to attack Jacques Roux. The next day Collot d'Herbois reported to the Jacobins that the women "had prepared people to welcome us."[7] This was indeed a honeymoon between the women's club and the Montagnard and sansculotte authorities, who were conscious and grateful for the help that women had given and could still give them.

This warm harmony was not just a political tactic; it also expressed the revolutionary movement's recognition of women's participation and, more profoundly, the society's interest in the question of women's roles during the summer of 1793. The reasons for this overture are to be found in the revolutionary movement. The first reason, external to the female sansculottes movement, was the French people's desire to regain the sense of unity that had been undermined by the counterrevolutionary enemy. The Constitution provided that sense of unity. Through their integration in demonstrations of acceptance and congratulations, such as processions and speeches, women from the provinces as well as the capital asserted themselves implicitly as members of the Sovereign People and aired their demands. The Festival of Unity on 10 August 1793 concretized this unity: "With this festival, we witness the creation of the totality of the French people," wrote the historian Jacques Guilhaumou.[8] The second of four stations of the procession was a triumphal arch that commemorated the days of October 1789. One of the faces of the arch read: "They have chased the tyrant before them like a vile prey." The "heroines of 5 and 6 October" sat on cannons beneath the arch. The president of the Convention, Hérault de Séchelles, recalled that "these bronzes, these mouths of fire that made the

7. Alphonse Aulard, *La Société des Jacobins,* vol. 5 (Paris: 1889–1897), p. 283; *Le Journal de la Montagne* 32 (3 July).

8. I thank Jacques Guilhaumou for sharing with me his unpublished work on the Cordeliers during the summer and autumn of 1793.

ear of the king hear thunder and augured the change of all destinies, rolled under delicate hands." "Instead of flowers that adorn beauty," he offered these women "the laurel, the traditional emblem of courage and victory"— although he added that they must pass this laurel on to their children. Then, turning their cannons, the heroines "reunited with the Sovereign People" and joined in the procession.[9]

Women could not be excluded from the pursuit of unity during the summer of 1793. They were part of a unified people, and this was a given of all the festivals. Nonetheless, even though Hérault de Séchelles's speech insisted powerfully on the maternal role, the festival on 10 August differed from most other festivals by presenting women more as active members of the popular movement than as maternal or allegorical figures. They were integrated with the revolutionary people, the Sovereign People, because of their revolutionary activity.

Here lies the second reason for the overtures of summer 1793: the Revolutionary Republican Women and the entire female sansculottes movement's spirit made possible the glorification of the heroines of October 1789. In this context of unification, which had to include women, the strength of the revolutionary women's movement enabled women to be represented as members of the Sovereign People. In addition, within the female population itself, this strength encouraged awareness. The confidence that their role in the popular movement gave to militant women caused some to question and challenge women's social and political status. And the existence of a revolutionary club for women, valued by the sansculottes authorities, played the same role. It was indeed because women had contributed to the victory of the revolutionary movement that some asked to be entitled to the same rights as "free men."

Only a Cassandra could have troubled the atmosphere of unity and the glorification of revolutionary heroines that permeated the atmosphere of the 10 August festival by questioning the choice of heroines: the festival did not honor the Revolutionary Republican Women, the female sansculottes active in 1793, but female merchants of the Halle who strongly disapproved of clubs for women and whose revolutionary intervention was part of the past. By glorifying the women of times past, the festival relegated the women of the present to the shadows. The participation of women in the revolutionary movement, if it was to be celebrated, was depicted as

9. Jacques Louis David, *Rapport et décret pour la fête du 10 août*, B.N., 8° Le(38) 334.

pages of a history that had already been turned. Was this glorification or embalming? Cassandra would have wondered, but there was no Cassandra among the militant women, who were joyful to see themselves recognized, even through interposed women. And they still had much work to accomplish, for the summer of 1793 was not easy for them.

A TROUBLED SUMMER

Female Jacobins and Revolutionary Mourners

The mobilization of women did not decline during the summer of 1793. However, unlike during the spring, women no longer formed a separate part of the revolutionary movement, but had merged with it. As soon as the revolutionary struggles shifted to the general assemblies of the sections, female citizens became more like active spectators than full-fledged actors and could not assert themselves as a specific force, although this does not mean that they were not part of the popular movement. As in the spring, women took part in physical and verbal struggles between the sansculottes and the moderates. On 25 August, the Fraternal Society of Patriots of Both Sexes took the initiative in forming a central committee of popular clubs, a committee that Albert Soboul believes directed the popular movement.

In the street and in private conversations, patriotic female citizens fiercely defended revolutionary politics. On 5 July, three neighbors, who since the fall of the Girondins had not stopped quarreling, came to blows on the subject of the Constitution. Two of them who were moderates remarked with bitterness that women had not been invited to sign its acceptance and that the Constitution "did not lower the price of things in the least." The third became enraged, called the others aristocrats for not having accompanied the section to congratulate the Convention and threatened to summon several women "to beat them up."[10] In another example, when they returned from the sexually mixed Arsenal club, female militants were addressed sharply by their neighbors, who jeered, "Jacobins, bitches, crazy crones." Insults followed insults, the mood grew incensed, and people threatened to "kick one another's ass," until the only man who was present took the militant Anne Rose Berjot by the hair, hit her, and sicced his dog on her.[11]

10. A.P.P., AA 187, 6 July 1793.
11. A.P.P., AA 70 f. 44. See appendix 3, "Portraits of Militant Women," in this volume.

The death of Marat on 13 July was one of the most outstanding events of the crisis of summer 1793. The historian Guilhaumou has shown that what constitutes "the Death of Marat as a discursive event" is "not the assassination itself, but the manner in which the death of Marat became a spectacle as of 15 July."[12] Through the mediation of these ceremonies, the desire for defense and vengeance, at first inexpressible, could be expressed in the revolutionary slogan "put the Terror on the agenda" (that is to say, turn the terror of the other, the enemy, back against himself). This terror is "inscribed through" the bloody wound "in the very body of Marat,"[13] which was identified, through the funeral, with the body of the Republic. Grassroots female militants who gathered around the club of the Revolutionary Republican Women played a major role in this apotheosis of Marat's body. They held a wake over his body, and on 16 July, the day of the funeral, they carried his bathtub, collecting the blood that continued to flow from his wound and throwing flowers on him: "The body of Marat decomposes, putrefies in order to be reborn, thanks to women, as a sublime form."[14] Several journalists remarked on the many women at this burial. The Revolutionary Republican Women read an "ode," during which they laid a crown of everlasting flowers on Marat's head.[15] During the night of 16 July, they paraded the bloodstained shirt and bathtub of the Friend of the People through the streets of the city. On 28 July, during the ceremony of the transfer of Marat's heart, they again played a major role, both numerically and symbolically. Once more they surrounded the bloody remains of Marat, wept for him, and threw flowers over him.

The importance of women derives from several phenomena. Women, responsible for birth, also frequently assume the task of witnessing death. These weeping Revolutionary Republican Women were not just a memory of antiquity, nor was their gesture only political; it was also part of a process of immortalization. Through women, the cold cadaver of Marat

12. Jacques Guilhaumou, "Description d'un événement discursif: la mort de Marat à Paris (13 juillet—16 juillet 1793)," *La Mort de Marat,* ed. J. C. Bonnet (Paris: Flammarion, 1986).

13. Ibid.

14. Ibid.

15. A.P.P., AA 77, 17–28 Prairial Year III (wife of Despavaux). This "Ode" or "Republican poem" can be found at the end of the "Adresse de la Société des Républicaines Révolutionnaires séante à la bibliothèque des ci-devant Jacobins," read on 17 July 1793 at the Convention: A.N., C 262 d. 580, p. 2 (see also *Archives parlementaires* 69, p. 84).

disappeared in favor of the immortal hero Marat. The discursive event "Death of Marat," set off by the two statements "Marat is dead" (13 July) and "Marat is not dead" (16 July) would have been impossible without the figure of woman, symbolically indispensable to this immortalization, to this re-nascence. "Sexual act? Fertility rite?" wonders Guilhaumou about the women who, on 16 July, collected the blood flowing from Marat's wound. The speaker from the Republic section cried "May the blood of Marat become a seed for intrepid republicans." The next day, the Revolutionary Republican Women swore at the Convention to "people the soil of Liberty with as many Marats as they were capable."[16] The blood that flows from the wounds of the dead hero, assimilated to male semen, also recalls the blood that flows each month from the female body as a sign of its fertility.

Was the role of women in these ceremonies also in line with the recognition of the female revolutionary movement during the summer of 1793? In a certain sense, it appears to be a consecration. However, we can also see here an unconscious desire to limit its development or even to end it by restricting it to the symbolic. In part, the Revolutionary Republican Women were victims of this limitation.

The Revolutionary Republican Women

Symbolic Commitment and Political Absence   After their struggle against the Girondins and the honeymoon of summer 1793, the death of Marat opened a third stage in the life of the club. For a month, the Revolutionary Republican Women were completely absorbed by the event. Not only were they present during the funeral ceremonies, where they spoke each time, but they swore on 24 July at city hall a vow that an obelisk be raised in memory of the hero, courtesy of a collection among the sansculottes. Until the middle of August, their activity was focused on this initiative. The club, as well as the sections and the popular societies that supported their project, wanted the inauguration of the obelisk to coincide with the festival of 10 August, but it did not take place until 18 August. The bathtub in which Marat had been assassinated, carried by four citizens, recalled the horror of the crime and the wounded body (that of Marat and, by extension, that of the Republic). The chair, the table, the writing case, and the pen and paper he had used, carried by four female citizens, symbolized the immortality of

16. Guilhaumou, "Description."

Marat and his presence among the sansculottes. These objects thus evoked the vigilance of the Friend of the People.[17]

In the evening, after the festival, the Revolutionary Republican Women announced to the Jacobins that they were going to concern themselves with national security.[18]

While for almost a month Hébert and the other Cordelier leaders, assuming a position at the head of the revolutionary movement, demanded measures of national security, the Revolutionary Republican Women, busy with their obelisk, remained silent on this subject—at least if we trust the few texts about them that we possess. On 17 July, in a speech in honor of Marat, they indeed asserted at the convention that "there is oppression against the social body when a single one of its members is oppressed. In this case, we are oppressed, legislators, the Friend of the People is no more."[19] The defense of the social body was a reaction against its oppression, but instead of asking for repressive measures that could logically be expected after this observation, the Revolutionary Republican Women repeated their famous statement about the Marats that they would engender. It is tempting to see here a limit to the female revolutionary movement, dominated by the maternal and reproductive function. In fact, we depend here on suppositions. If, as seems probable, the text presented on 17 July at the Convention had been written before 16 July, and therefore before the apotheosis of Marat's body, we only witness the impossibility of announcing rigorously the "desire for the Terror." Thus the Revolutionary Republican Women called implicitly for the defense of the social body, the body of the Republic, but this call remained in suspense, and in its place occurred a statement by which the Revolutionary Republican Women became part of the process of Marat's immortalization, which was then the order of the day.

Before the inauguration of the obelisk on 18 August, the club did not actively participate in the demands for the exclusion of nobles from employment, a general draft, and the arrest of suspects, which would lead to the slogan "put the Terror on the agenda." However, on 19 May, in a petition made in common with the Cordeliers, the Revolutionary Republican Women had demanded the arrest of suspects, the formation of revolution-

17. Speeches on the life of Marat: *Moniteur*, XVII, 229, 281, 299, 429, 432; *Journal de la Montagne* 57, 62, 78; *Archives parlementaires* 72, p. 384; Aulard, *Jacobins*, 5: 314; B.N., Mss, N.A.F. 2713 f. 32. Description of the inauguration of the obelisk on 18 August in *Annales de la République française*, no. 234.

18. Aulard, *Jacobins*, 5: 356.

19. See note 15.

ary tribunals, and the drafting of a special revolutionary army; and on 10 July, Pauline Léon had presented to the Jacobins a petition from the club demanding the exclusion of nobles from all employment—in particular, from military command.[20] Although they were leaders and spokespeople in May, June, and the beginning of July, the Revolutionary Republican Women did not take part subsequently in what became the very essence of the revolutionary movement, the expression of vengeance through the demand for a legal Terror. The club had not known, at the time, how to free itself from the event of Marat's death. It remained focused for a month after that date on the apotheosis of Marat's body, while the most advanced revolutionaries made clear the finality of this event. It was not until 18 August, just after the festival in honor of Marat, that the Revolutionary Republican Women took responsibility for what had actually been one of the founding premises of the club, which had never ceased to concern them until 13 July: the implementation of measures for national security.

It is true that when they presented on 24 July their project for the obelisk, they certainly did not expect that it would take so much time to finish. City hall, which could only applaud their initiative, did not welcome it with warmth, and in fact delayed its completion. As for the Jacobins, they were not enthusiastic about sharing the cost of construction. We can read the club's impatience in their actions: the speed with which they announced their return to political life scarcely several hours after the inauguration of the obelisk shows how weighty their enterprise must have been for them.

The club's inability to transcend the "Death of Marat" should probably not be overlooked if we wish to understand its last days, which were marked by a complete reversal of revolutionary leaders' opinion about the club and ended with its prohibition on 30 October 1793. The future of the club seemed to play itself out during the weeks of 13 July to 18 August, a period of obscurity where historians stumble, without knowing if their questions are only a result of the scarcity of documentation. The series of events does not stand out, the Revolutionary Republican Women are on the margins of political life, hidden by the shadow of Marat, and yet this is where we must search for the roots of subsequent events. How did the attitude of the important clubs such as the Jacobins and the Cordeliers, which had been warm toward the Revolutionary Republican Women in June, become reserved in July and August and turn overtly hostile in September? It is difficult to un-

20. *Journal de la Montagne* 41.

derstand this progression. Did the power of the club's symbolic engagement in the ceremonies of 16 and 28 July make some revolutionaries wary and others appreciative of the fact that women limited themselves, after the funeral of Marat, to a symbolic role in the revolutionary movement? Did the absence of the club from the political scene permit a heretofore contained suspicion to declare itself little by little? We would love to answer these questions clearly, but the historian must recognize an inability to explain everything.

The Political Identity of the Revolutionary Republican Women   In this shadow show, some figures return more frequently, such as the body of Marat, which dominated all others, and Claire Lacombe, who stood out as the chief leader of the club. After 10 August 1792, the young woman took an unceasing interest in political life; she attended all the meetings of the Jacobin club, where on 3 April 1793, she proposed to take aristocrats and their families as hostages.[21] That same day, she signed an advantageous contract (three thousand livres a year) with the director of a theater troupe in Mainz to play "leading roles, in tragedy as well as in comedy and drama." The experience would have been wonderful for an actress in love with revolution: Mainz in 1792 was stirred up against its bishop-prince and French troops had entered the city, which had become the center of German Jacobinism. It is pleasant to imagine an eventual meeting between the young French actress who would mark the future of the women's revolutionary movement and the future queen of German romanticism, Caroline Michaelis.[22] There are destinies that we would love to see cross. But the meeting did not take place, because Claire Lacombe did not go to Mainz, which was besieged and then retaken by the Prussians in the spring of 1793. Remaining in Paris, she invested all her energy in the club of the Revolutionary Republican Women. We do not know if she was among the original members or if she joined later; her name does not appear in documents until 31 July 1793, when she is the speaker for a deputation of the women's club at city hall. Then, on 18 August, she announced to the Jacobins that the Revolutionary Republican Women were (finally!) concerned with national security. Later, she led all the important initiatives of the club and became

---

21. *Archives parlementaires* 47, p. 144.

22. This woman, who later married August Schlegel and then Schelling, was for the time being just Caroline Michaelis, the widow of Böhmer, "Dame Lucifer," who had taken up the Jacobin cause at Mainz. See M. Cl. Hoock-Demarle, *La Femme au temps de Goethe* (Paris: Stock, 1987).

successively secretary and president. Gifted with a strong personality, she led the club to defend opinions that were close to those of the *enragés*. Here the third shadow appears, that of the *enragé* Leclerc.

Linked with Claire Lacombe (who was accused of being his mistress) and the future husband of Pauline Léon, Leclerc influenced the positions taken by the Revolutionary Republican Women. However, the women's club cannot be reduced to a militant group entirely devoted to the *enragé*, as historians usually do. Things are not so simple, and it is useful to define more accurately the place of the club on the political revolutionary chessboard. At the beginning, as we have seen, the Revolutionary Republican Women were close to the Cordeliers club, and in June 1793 they helped exclude from that club the *enragés* Jacques Roux and Leclerc. Their commitment to the side of the enragés—and, in particular, Leclerc—which appeared powerfully at the end of summer, dates from July and August. On 4 August, Leclerc addressed the women in these words in his newspaper:

> It is especially for you to sound the alarm, Revolutionary Republican Women, generous women who are truly above all praise. . . . As there is within you neither room for giving nor for receiving, a vile interest has not suffocated in your souls the sentiments of nature. . . . By your examples and your speech, go reawaken republican energy and reanimate patriotism in faint hearts! You must sound the alarm of Liberty! The time is urgent, the peril extreme. You have merited priority, glory awaits you!

This call resembled an appeal launched at female militants in March 1793 by another *enragé*, Varlet. Jacques Roux was also a partisan of intervention by women in political life.[23] Thus, the *enragés* were rather favorable toward participation by women in the popular movement, an attitude that would have permitted a reconciliation with the women's club. As section militants and grassroots politicians, they were probably in a better position than deputies to appreciate interventions by women.

23. On 16 March 1793, before the Convention, Varlet wished "that the apathy of the Jacobins be replaced by the energy of the women of 5 and 6 October" (A.N., AF[IV] 1470). Jacques Roux wrote on 23 August 1793: "Victory is certain as soon as women become involved with the sansculottes. They have the double advantage of conquering men by the brilliance of their charm and their intrepidity," cited by Albert Mathiez, *La Vie chère et le mouvement social sous la Terreur*, 2 vols. (Paris: Payot, 1927), p. 332.

Because of these observations and the personal connections between Leclerc and the two most important figures in the women's society, the historiography has presented the club as an *enragé* by-product. This view conveys the idea that women cannot have autonomy, in politics as elsewhere; that it is not reason but feelings, the love or fascination inspired by a man, that directs their actions; that they can only be the playthings of a man who thinks for them. This viewpoint also does not see that the steps that the Revolutionary Republican Women took toward and with the section militants distinguished the outward activity of their club from its creation to its prohibition. Sections and popular societies had quickly supported the project of the obelisk. Later, when the Revolutionary Republican Women were personae non gratae to the Jacobin and the Cordelier clubs, they acted in concert with the sections, which still welcomed them. We are struck by the community of opinions, the regular reports of reciprocal assistance, without apparent misunderstandings, that existed between the Revolutionary Republican Women and the section militants, much more than by their ties with the *enragés*.

Several remarks are essential concerning the club's anchorage among the sections. The *enragés* Jacques Roux and Varlet made a practice of looking for support from their respective sections of Gravilliers and Droits-de-l'Homme. However, we would not agree with Soboul that "Leclerc tried to act upon the sections through the mediation of the Revolutionary Women."[24] Intervention within the sections was a distinct practice of the women's club from its origin and not a means of action copied from the *enragé* militant. In addition, Jacques Roux and Varlet were well-established individuals in the section they inhabited, whereas the Revolutionary Republican Women were a group of people from separate sections who intervened in different sections of the capital. To be precise, this was a group *of women*, and as separate individuals they could not participate fully in the political life of their respective sections. United, they could intervene in the sections—but not specifically in their own sections. In this sense we can almost say that they constituted the forty-ninth section or popular society of a Parisian section. Their political practice—the presentation of demands to the general assemblies, joint decrees, and so on—was indeed that of a Parisian section, but their "section" was without

24. Albert Soboul, *Les Sans-culottes parisiens en l'an II. Mouvement populaire et gouvernement révolutionnaire, 2 juin 1793–9 thermidor an II* (1958; reprint, Paris: Flammarion, 1973), p. 228.

geographic foundations and could not claim the same political status, because it represented only its assembled members and not a part of the Sovereign People.

The repeated interventions in sections dated mostly from the last months of the club's existence. Before the period inaugurated by the death of Marat, they were not so systematic. Hence our second remark: this club of women calling itself such—a Parisian club certainly, but one that sought and achieved national scope—evolved into what we can call a Parisian popular society (like those in each section for men) composed of women, which presented itself as sexually neutral (they no longer demanded after July that women be organized into armed corps), and withdrew into Parisian political life. This withdrawal was forced on them by the initially reserved and then openly hostile attitude of the important clubs. We must also take into consideration the internal divisions within the Revolutionary Republican Women's club.

Curiously, this club has always been thought of as a monolithic whole, whose members all shared the same opinions united behind Claire Lacombe, who was under Leclerc's direct influence. Yet this was the only women's club in the capital, *the only place* where revolutionary women could develop their ideas and exercise a militancy not limited by male leaders—as was the case in the sections and even in sexually mixed clubs—whether their political sympathies went to Robespierre, Hébert, or Leclerc. Several tendencies, more or less close to the Jacobins, Cordeliers, or *enragés*, thus existed within the club, and depending on the period, one or the other dominated. Disagreements broke out between the Revolutionary Republican Women who were pro-Robespierre and those who, headed by Claire Lacombe and Pauline Léon, supported the *enragés*. When Pauline Léon asked that the Convention be revised and quoted Rousseau's assertion that "the prolongation of power is often the death of liberty," she did not obtain the assent of all members, some of whom remarked that "doubtless Rousseau did not mean to speak of a revolutionary era." At one meeting, a female citizen lost her temper with the "blasted Jacobins." "This indecent language caused great commotion" and the expulsion of the woman was requested by some members, without success. The *enragé* tendency prevailed only with difficulty. Within the club, Claire Lacombe was accused of lodging Leclerc at her home and asked to vindicate herself. According to a later denunciation made by a former member, "the general staff [of Claire Lacombe] composed of many women was sent to all corners of the hall to influence the club" during meetings.[25] In the autumn, the *enragé* group dominated the club only by means of excluding other members—and not lesser ones, but people like female citizen Colinger, who had been president in July.

These internal divisions were caused by the fact that as the only Parisian women's club, the Revolutionary Republican Women united female citizens who were of course all revolutionary but of different political sympathies. This weakened the club and partially explains the ease and rapidity of its disintegration once the first blow was struck against it from outside. This also allows us to understand its sometimes contradictory positions in favor of various groups of the revolutionary movement.

A Program of Public Safety   Its political program defined the club's chief characteristics: a political group close to the female sansculottes movement, predominantly *enragé* but sensitive to other currents of the revolutionary movement. To fight effectively against their principal target, "the enemy within," they demanded terrorist measures on several occasions. By "terrorist measures" they meant the arrest and trial of the Girondins, the arrest of suspects, the creation of revolutionary tribunals, the exclusion of nobles, and the trials of aristocrats and Marie Antoinette. The *enragés* and the Cordeliers had become the spokespeople for such demands, which were for the most part spelled out in the petition presented to the Convention by the Revolutionary Republican Women on 26 August 1793. This petition, whose importance Soboul has emphasized,[26] marked the return of the women's club to the political scene and is one of their only remaining complete texts. The shibboleth of general mobilization, which was an essential demand during the month of August, did not appear in the petition until the end, as an addendum. Until the end of August, the club had been absent from most revolutionary activities. Their disinterest can be linked to the attention focused by these women on enemies within; moreover, the measure for general mobilization had already been decreed three days before. The Terror, linked to the idea of a levy en masse in August, was placed on the agenda at the end of August, as part of revolutionary justice. The Revolutionary Republican Women, who asked on 26 August for the creation of a rather large number of extraordinary tribunals to annihilate "all conspirators within," participated in this movement.

25. A.N., F⁷ 4756 d. Claire Lacombe.
26. A.N., C 267 d. 638 p. 22; B.N., Lb(40) 2412. Soboul, *Les Sans-culottes parisiens*, p. 150.

The theme of the exclusion of nobles, presented in this petition, was developed by the *enragés* during the spring of 1793 and reintroduced by Hébert on the political scene after the death of Marat. The "Hébertist" Cordeliers made it of paramount importance to their program for national security. Leclerc enlarged upon it in his newspaper as early as 17 July. As we recollect, it was also the object of the last intervention on 10 July by the Revolutionary Republican Women before the death of Marat.

The question of executive power was central to the petition, just as it was central to the political debate, under two forms. The first theme, already taken up by the club on 19 May, was set out here along the "Hébertist" Cordelier line. The Convention had made good laws ("You have passed a decree, by which all suspect people must be arrested"), but the political conduct of its executants invalidated these laws in advance ("But I ask it of you, isn't this law laughable when suspect people themselves are supposed to execute it?"). Four days later, the Cordelier Royer raised the question of future executants of terrorist measures.

The request for the organization of executive power in this petition also resembled a Cordelier statement. On 26 August, the Revolutionary Republican Women stated: "Organize the government according to the Constitution. In vain we have been told that France is lost by this measure. It cannot be lost when the responsibility of agents is no longer a vain word, when the corrupt minister would be certain of losing his head to the scaffold." As issue number 275 from Hébert's newspaper, *Père Duchesne*, said on 22 August: "It is necessary to organize promptly a government as the Constitution sets forth. Then basic necessities will become abundant because ministers will be responsible and fear for their heads."

Here end the resemblances that signify the Cordelier influence at the end of August and the beginning of September and a probable compromise between the different tendencies of the women's club. Already, the threatening tone of the petition recalls the tone of Jacques Roux or of Leclerc. Later, the club resolutely took the side of Leclerc; indeed, until the end of summer it multiplied its interventions with the sections and clarified themes presented on 26 August in a manner sometimes opposed to Cordelier positions.

Thus, while the Cordeliers did not link the organization of executive power with the inevitable dissolution of the Convention, in September the Revolutionary Republican Women, dominated by the *enragé* tendency, linked the two points intimately, just like Leclerc. On 15 September, they asked that all existing authorities be replaced—including the Convention—

and asked for "the functioning of executive power." If we are to believe their adversaries, Claire Lacombe and Pauline Léon repeated the same words as Leclerc, the former by asking for "the Constitution, the whole Constitution, and nothing but the Constitution," and the latter by stating that the members of the Convention have "hung onto their benches" for too long.

The Revolutionary Republican Women never separated the need to purge administrators from the question of control and the responsibility of agents of the state, which were recurrent terms that followed from the sansculotte concept of direct democracy. On 6 September, they proposed at the general assembly of the section Sans-Culottes (here the name of the district) the writing of a petition "to ask that the responsibility of ministers and all agents and public civil servants no longer be a vain word," that the minister of the interior, Garat, subsequently be arrested, and "that all the public functionaries who had left their place or who were going to leave them are made to give a categorical account of their management and administration and, until the purging of their accounts, be under arrest."[27]

Though the Revolutionary Republican Women made the question of executive power central to their conception of the Terror, as did the Cordeliers, their posing of this question was radically different. The Cordelier theory assumed a revolutionary executive, whose function was to put into practice the laws of the Convention, which had been "denatured" by administrators. The Revolutionary Republican Women imagined an executive under popular control, which was in their opinion the way to save the homeland from "enemies within," because only the people were uncorrupted and worthy of confidence. Thus whereas the Cordelier leader Vincent confided to the revolutionary committees the responsibility for watching over the administrators, the Revolutionary Republican Women, close to the sansculottes, entrusted this responsibility directly to the people, who were sovereign in their sections.

Moreover, on 21 September, the Revolutionary Republican Women suggested before the Croix-Rouge section the "nomination of a central committee composed of deputies from all sections." This initiative was identical to that of the central club of the Paris department. That very day, it announced the resumption of its meetings at the Archbishopric and invited sections and popular societies to each name two commissioners to take part in its deliberations.[28] Once again we see links between the

27. B.H.V.P., Mss. 746 f. 145.
28. A.N., F⁷ 3688³, report of 22 September. Soboul, *Les Sans-culottes parisiens*, p. 194.

women's club and the Parisian sansculottes movement. Its positions in favor of section autonomy from existing authorities, at a moment when federalism represented one of the great dangers for the Revolution, could only further estrange the revolutionary leaders (of the Convention) from the club. Within this perspective, we can wonder if the prohibition of the Revolutionary Republican Women stemmed as much from government hostility against the autonomy of the sections and against the principles of direct democracy dear to the sansculottes as from the club's *enragé* positions or their status as women.

Nonetheless, although the political tendencies of the Revolutionary Republican Women corresponded to those of the Parisian female sansculottes, they differed from them in paying little attention to the problem of basic necessities. Not that they had no interest in this question, but they did not take it up except in a limited or marginal fashion in their essentially political interventions, at least until the middle of September. During the first four months of their existence, they only referred twice to this issue! And the first time was with the Cordeliers in their common petition of 19 May. Espousing the thesis of a "famine plot" directed by "the mercantile aristocracy of an insolent caste who wanted the same status as royalty and wished to monopolize all riches," the female petitioners asked for measures against "the speculators, the monopolizers, and the selfish merchants." However, in order that "there be no unhappiness in the Republic," they demanded not a general maximum on prices but a purge of the executive council!

During the summer, in the middle of the subsistence crisis, the Revolutionary Republican Women intervened only a single time on this subject. On 24 July, among other requests, they asked at city hall that the monopolization of coal be stopped. Curiously, nothing was said about the expense of commodities and the scarcity of bread that then constituted two of the principal concerns of the working class.[29]

This characteristic, extremely surprising in women close to the *enragés*, illustrates perfectly the political nature of the Revolutionary Republican Women. However, it is surprising only in regard to the stereotype that women participated in the Revolution solely as housewives, concerned only with food problems. Since the group first appeared in the spring of 1792, the most committed militant women had been mobilized largely because of political questions: female citizenship, the defense of the Revolution, and

29. *Moniteur*, XVII, 229.

later, during the summer of 1793, the organization of executive power. The club's originality on the revolutionary scene (given that its first uniqueness was as a club for women) stems from the fact that it maintained much closer ties to the sections than the men's clubs, while giving less importance than sansculottes militants to the question of basic necessities. This paradox reveals how difficult it was for women interested in politics to present themselves as equals among the revolutionaries.

A SUMMER WITHOUT BREAD

The originality of the Revolutionary Republican Women acquires a still greater dimension when we realize that during the summer of 1793 Paris was poorly supplied with flour and bread was scarce. Bakers were accused of putting it aside for the rich, who paid them more. And every day, in one district or another of the city, incidents took place in front of bakeries.

City hall ordered that the distribution of bread not begin before six o'clock in the morning, but from 2 to 3 A.M., scarcely awake, women gathered before bakeries and waited for hours, complaining of the fatigue caused by these long night watches. And for a female worker, who put in not a double but a triple day's work, was it better to wait at the baker's door and lose money or go to work and not obtain bread? This was an insoluble dilemma, which particularly affected the female merchants of la Halle. To arrive at one o'clock in the morning at the baker's doors, but "obliged in order to have bread to go to work to earn it," a female merchant would ask her neighbors in line to keep her place while she went for stock at la Halle; unfortunately, when she returned, there would be no more bread. In August, when the situation was particularly critical, the gatherings began the evening before. The line became a place of conviviality, even if forced. All night, the women gossiped and also quarreled, they had their places saved in order to go to work or to nurse their child, and they awakened the baker's neighbors who complained of the "awful noise" that prevented them from sleeping. Journalists and police spies saw these nocturnal gatherings as places of debauchery where young men and girls, during warm summer nights, had amorous meetings. But the majority of women and men scarcely thought of dalliances; tired and worried, they easily became upset, and these lines were a source of potential riots. Despite the presence of the section commissioners and armed soldiers, the gatherings sometimes became unruly. As soon as the bakery opened, there was such a scramble that female citizens were crushed. A young worker in linen even dressed as a man "to get bread more easily, since in her district men pushed women aside and were the only ones who obtained bread at the bakers' doors."[30]

Many female citizens refused to "take their place" at the end of the line, which occasionally caused a general uproar. The possible consequences of these upheavals frightened the authorities in charge of distribution. Nothing worried the commissioners more than these women who provoked people by their cries. On 28 July, a housewife was questioned for having "preached insurrection by complaining about the scarcity of bread." On the evening of 8 August, a female beltmaker was interrogated for having cried "with all her might" "that she and her child had not eaten today—[and] that it was abominable to make female citizens pile up at his [the baker's] door, one of whom had had her arm broken."[31]

Some of these women even made counterrevolutionary speeches, such as the woman who on 7 August, three days before the festival that was to display the unity of the nation, said to the national guards: "This is a damned awful nation. I curse this nation of dogs, I have been up since three o'clock [in the morning] looking for bread and have not been able to get any."[32] There were more women, however, who linked the crisis to the political situation and expressed their fear of a "famine plot." On 14 August, the wife of Tillard contended that one "of the most powerful means" employed by the enemies of the Republic "to murder it and reduce it was to create famine."[33]

Scarcity of bread was not the only consequence of the crisis: working-class women were equally concerned by the lack of coal, which was necessary for many trades, and were especially worried at the beginning of autumn by the price of commodities. They connected these issues to the popular demand for an economic program, a complement to the political Terror, that would suppress monopolies and implement fixed prices. This program arose from the aspiration of the lower classes for the right to existence and equality of rights: the greater fortune of some should not deprive others of products necessary to their existence.

The crisis broke out on 4 September, two days after the incredible news that Toulon had been surrendered to the English by the royalists. On the morning of the fourth, workers gathered to demand bread at city hall. After procrastinating, city hall planned a demonstration for the next day.

---

30. A.P.P., AA 216, f. 286.
31. A.P.P., AA 163 f. 26 and AA 209 f. 109.
32. A.P.P., AA 176, 7 August 1793.
33. A.N., F⁷ 4657, d. Croisil.

On 5 September, the sections went as a group to the Convention, which decreed the arrest of suspects and the creation of a revolutionary army, measures that had long been demanded by the sansculottes. The Terror was put on the agenda—political Terror, for the Convention had still not voted for a general maximum on prices for commodities. However, prices continued to rise. On 21 September, a group of women complained at la Halle of the price of food. "This cannot continue," and so they themselves set a price list because "the Convention feels no concern for their misery." Tired of the situation, women moved to action. On 28 September at la Halle, potatoes were taken and distributed at twenty sous a bushel.[34] The very next day, the Convention finally voted for a general maximum on prices for the most necessary commodities and for wages. The situation thus calmed down little by little, in spite of continuing difficulties until the end of December 1793. From this time, and up until the end of the Year II, there was no more talk of bread.

34. A.N., F^7 3688^3.

7 Citizenship Denied, Autumn 1793

Parisian women took part in the demonstrations of 4 and 5 September. On 5 September, the Revolutionary Republican Women joined with the popular clubs that accompanied the commissioners of the sections.[1] Women were also among the crowd that invaded the Convention without violence.

The popular upsurge continued throughout the month of September, and, according to Albert Soboul, became full blown in mid-September during the episode of the "war of the cockades," which was "a significant expression of the popular mentalité" and directly concerned women.[2]

THE WAR OF THE COCKADES

On 3 April 1793, the Convention declared that wearing tricolor cockades was compulsory, but it was unclear if women were also obliged to wear them. Female militants made it a point of honor to hang cockades from their bonnets as a sign of patriotism. Two days after their club was officially established, the Revolutionary Republican Women asserted at a meeting of the Jacobins that it was necessary that "women wear the tricolor cockade." They decreed that all members of the club should be so adorned and sent an address to the forty-eight sections inviting female citizens to follow their example.[3] The commissioners who met at the Archbishopric affirmed on 30 June that, for these free and revolutionary women, their cockades were their diamonds. But a woman who drew at-

1. A.N., C 271 d. 665 p. 33.
2. Albert Soboul, "Un Épisode des luttes populaires en septembre 1793: la guerre des cocardes," *Annales historiques de la Révolution française* (1961): 52–55.
3. *Journal des débats et de la correspondance de la Société des Jacobins*, no. 412.

tention to herself by her cockade was thought to be a Jacobin and risked mistreatment by men and women who scarcely appreciated that a women might become involved in politics and appreciated still less that she took one of the most radical sides. In June 1793, the club members complained of having been struck because they wore cockades. In August, the sexually mixed popular club of the Pont-Neuf section became concerned that its female members were being "insulted and extremely mistreated by some women" for wearing cockades.[4]

This issue unleashed violent passions in September. The first blow was struck by female citizens of the Unité (previously Quatre-Nations) Fraternal Society, which had already complained of insults they had suffered by wearing their cockades on 25 August at city hall. At the beginning of September, these women wrote a petition urging the Convention to pass a decree punishing "the shrews who mistreated female citizens who wore the national cockade" and obliging all women to adorn themselves with this "sign of Liberty." They circulated this petition in the sections and popular societies, which often supported it and forbade women to enter the general assembly without cockades. After hearing the women on 12 September, the Cordelier club recognized "that female citizens who share our labor must also share this benefit." The movement gained in scope. On 13 September, the women read their petition before the Jacobins, and the city government forbade women to walk in public promenades without cockades. Finally, the Unité Fraternal Society read their petition on 16 September at the bar of the Convention. It was signed by an exclusively female committee and twenty-three female citizens who were members (including the wife of Monge and her three daughters), as well as by the Revolutionary Republican Women and the sexually mixed popular societies of the Pont-Neuf and Amis-de-la-Patrie sections. The Cordeliers, the Jacobins, and twenty-eight sections supported it. However, the members of the Convention did not pronounce themselves either for or against the petition.[5]

But the female citizens of the Unité section had already taken their initiative to the streets. On 13 September, they threatened women who were not wearing cockades and clashed with "fishwives" who did not want to hear any talk of them. From this moment on, brawls multiplied between

---

4. *La Gazette française*, no. 533; B.N., Mss., N.A.F., 2713, 20 August 1793.
5. A.N., C 271 d. 670 f. 18 (text of the petition and signatures); *Archives parlementaires* 74, p. 285; B.H.V.P., Mss. 746 f. 145; B.N., Mss., N.A.F., 2713; *Moniteur*, XVII, 679.

women of the markets and partisans of the compulsory wearing of cockades. The former were hostile to this adornment, for they said, "Only whores and female Jacobins wear cockades." Women "should be concerned only with their households and not with current events," and the cockade should be reserved for men.[6]

On 18 September, an old woman was whipped and her clothing torn because she did not wear a cockade, while women who wore them were chased at la Halle. Fights erupted throughout the city. "Some districts trample the cockade underfoot, others respect it more than ever," wrote the informer Béraud on 20 September. The female merchants of la Halle tore off bonnets decorated with a cockade but maintained that they would wear them if decreed by the Convention. The disorder grew to such an extent that on 21 September, police administrators asked the Convention for "a decree that penalized anyone who tore or profaned the national colors in any sort of clothing or on any person." The Convention gave in and ordered that "women who do not wear the tricolor cockade will be punished, the first time by eight days in prison. In case of repeat offense, they will be labeled suspect. As for those women who tear it from another or profane the cockade, they will be punished with six years of imprisonment."[7]

Several days later, police spies acknowledged unanimously that "the cockade was worn almost uniformly by all women" and that the fights had stopped.

However, the brawls soon began again, this time over the question of how and where to place the cockades. Should they be worn on the right, the left, in front, in back, on the bonnet, or on the chest? Female patriots reproached those who submitted to the decree with bad grace by hiding them under handkerchiefs, ribbons, or pompoms or by making them ridiculous objects of coquetry and luxury surrounded by tassels, green leaves, bouquets, clusters of feathers, and so on. By the beginning of winter, police reports of incidents concerning cockades had dwindled. Women who were questioned were usually released by the authorities, who recognized that they were without cockades because of forgetfulness and not out of ill will. However, some women still refused to wear them because of their political convictions. When questioned why she was without a cockade, one woman asserted "that she would never betray her way of thinking and that she was an aristocrat."[8] As for women of "high society," the wife of a business agent

6. A.N., F⁷ 3688³, 14 and 19 September; DXLII no. 11, 13, and 18, 25 September.
7. *Archives parlementaires* 73, p. 571.
8. A.N., F⁷ 4735 d. Guérin.

became their spokeswomen by crying on 27 Prairial Year III (15 June 1795) that "wearing the cockade made a woman look like a bar maid."[9]

The "war of the cockades" might seem to involve only women and be a comic aspect of the popular movement, during which knitters and women of la Halle "tore each other's hair out" under the amused eyes of men. But Soboul, with his knowledge of the Parisian sansculottes movement, has recognized that these incidents were significant and does not hesitate to describe these confrontations as central to revolutionary struggles.

It is true that the cockade provoked fights between women in the streets, and men did not intervene. This is because men never interfered in physical confrontations between women. However, although the issue of wearing cockades concerned women directly, it also interested the entire popular movement. For proof, it suffices to consult the minutes of the section assemblies, to notice the support of the Cordelier and Jacobin clubs for the petition on compulsory wearing of cockades by women, or to notice how women wearing cockades were attacked as "female Jacobins."

As always when women are concerned, *mentalités* and politics are closely linked. To the extent that female militants were revolutionaries, all overtures to participation by women in political life during 1793 became integrated with struggles of the revolutionary movement. The decree of 21 September was a victory *for* female citizen patriots and a victory *of* the popular movement. The powerful rise of women within the sansculottes movement during the preceding months made a demand by women a demand by the entire popular movement. Moreover, this episode of the cockades shows a posteriori that the place of women during the spring and summer was the consequence of the power of the female sansculottes movement and not just the activism of the Revolutionary Republican Women. Female militants of the sections started the war of the cockades, in which the women's club, although already implicated since 16 September, intervened very little, and as support rather than as a driving force.

The Convention passed the decree of 21 September only because popular pressure supported a balance of power in favor of the male and female sansculottes. But although it capitulated on this point, its moderate elements did not mean to go any further and encourage a revolutionary female movement to develop as part of the popular movement. Not only did

9. A.P.P., AA 241 f. 161.

the Convention refuse any other measure that could have appeared ultimately as a step on the road to an eventual political equality between the sexes, but it even forbade women to form political groups.

REVOLUTIONARY REPUBLICAN WOMEN—
"ALLEGED REVOLUTIONARY WOMEN"
OR "COUNTERREVOLUTIONARY BACCHANTES"?

On 16 September, the Jacobin club openly attacked the Society of Revolutionary Republican Women for the first time, under the pretext that Claire Lacombe, their president, had threatened to expel a female citizen and member who was hostile to Leclerc. Chabot asserted that it was "time to tell the whole truth about these supposedly revolutionary women." Bazire supported him. The two men, deputies who had just been expelled from the Committee of General Security under pressure from the revolutionaries, violently attacked the women's club and its president for allegedly seeking to free two counterrevolutionaries. Their fellow members laughed along with them when they departed from political discussion in order to depict women as typically frivolous and so on. Claire Lacombe was accused of making counterrevolutionary statements (such as the claim that men should not be kept arbitrarily in prison, and as Leclerc had written, that "the Constitution, the whole Constitution, and nothing but the Constitution" must be applied), of having called Robespierre "Monsieur," and of having lodged a former noble and notorious counterrevolutionary, the *enragé* Leclerc. She tried to defend herself, but women seated at the sides of the gallery threatened her: "Down with the new Corday! Leave, unhappy woman, or we will tear you to pieces!" Lacombe was hard to intimidate. She mocked the courage of her adversaries by boldly asserting that "never would anyone force her to leave against her will." At these words the fury doubled, and Lacombe threatened to teach the first man or woman who dared to advance "what a free woman can do." The determination of this woman who was known to be armed with a knife had its effect. Calm was reestablished, but the club was accused of having encouraged the "looting" of sugar in February and soap in June. The Committee of General Security, having been notified, arrested Claire Lacombe, who was released the next day because the revolutionary committee of her section had found in her home only papers "that breathed the purest patriotism."

In an account of this meeting read to the Revolutionary Republican Women, Claire Lacombe denied part of the accusation, particularly that of having called Robespierre "Monsieur."[10] Refusing to put "the Citizen Robespierre" in the same category as the moderates of the Convention, "the Bazires of the day," she urged him to be wary of their manipulations: "Beware, Robespierre! I perceive that those who have been accused of corrupt practices believe that they will escape this denunciation by accusing those who denounce them of having spoken ill of you. Beware that those who need to protect themselves through your virtues don't drag you with them over the precipice."

The Jacobins had attacked the political participation of women on 16 September through the Society of Revolutionary Republican Women, whom they blamed for all the troubles that had happened in Paris. Their next step was to adopt unanimously a proposal to encourage the Committee of General Security to arrest "suspect women." The Revolutionary Republican Women continued their activities, and two days later they presented to the Convention a petition about wives of *émigrés* and women who were prominent in public. But from this moment, they were on the defensive and were attacked on all sides. On 23 September, *La Feuille du salut public* dragged Claire Lacombe through the mud: "The woman or girl Lacombe is finally in prison and can no longer cause harm. This counterrevolutionary bacchante can now only drink water; it is known that she enjoys wine a great deal. She equally likes a good table or men, as the intimate fraternity between her, Jacques Roux, Leclerc, and company demonstrates."

Claire Lacombe was not imprisoned at that time, and she promised to "beat with a stick" those who printed this false report.[11] Her bravado could not hide the decline of the women's club in this final period of its existence. With its back against the wall, the club abandoned the political terrain to intervene only on the issue of basic necessities, which until then had been merely secondary in its program of activity. On 21 September, five days after the Jacobins' attack and for the first time since their return to politics after Marat's death, the Revolutionary Republican Women included in their program for national security "price controls on all commodities used by the people" (the general maximum). And after the paragraph in the *Feuille du salut public*, all the club's interventions featured only basic necessities, marking their definitive abandonment of politics. On 30 September, a deputation led by Claire Lacombe asked city hall to search homes in order to enforce the maximum voted the previous evening and stop mer-

10. A.N., T 1001 (1–3) d. Lacombe; see also *Moniteur*, XVII, 694.
11. *Le Courrier française*, 27 September.

chandise from leaving Paris. On 9 October, the club "showed [city hall] its concern" about the lack of enforcement of the legal maximum price and "compared the people to the blind to whom light has been promised, and who carry to the tomb the regret of having made a poor choice of doctor." On 25 October, the club worried about the scarcity of commodities, which, it thought, "resulted only because monopolizers hide the most necessary commodities to make us regret the disastrous freedom of commerce," and again invited city hall to search homes in order to find monopolizers.[12]

The club's retreat into social questions was complete. The problem of basic necessities seemed to dominate not only the club's interventions but also its internal deliberations.

Nevertheless, no matter what their activities, the Revolutionary Republican Women were henceforth considered suspect. The counterrevolutionaries tried, without success, to attract them to their side.[13] The revolutionaries tried to distinguish themselves from the club, leaving the women increasingly isolated. On 20 September, the Cordeliers refused them affiliation. On 25 September, the female citizen Boudray asked the *Moniteur* to no longer confuse the Fraternal Society of Patriots of Both Sexes, of which she was secretary, with the Revolutionary Republican Women.[14] Only Jacques Roux, forgetting that the club had renounced him three months earlier, defended them. In number 267 of his newspaper, *Le Publiciste de la République française par l'ombre de Marat*, he grew indignant that "The Revolutionary Women's Club, which has given so much service to Liberty, has been denounced within the Jacobins by men who have had recourse to their courage and their virtue a thousand times" and that "the most enthusiastic female republicans have been treated as intriguers."

In number 268 of his paper, he referred again to the club, denouncing their opponents: "The scoundrels, the hypocrites! They used the like of Leclerc, Varlet, Jacques Roux, Bourgoin, Gonchon, and so on. They used the revolutionary women, such as Lacombe, Colombe, Champion, Ardoins, and so many other republicans to break the scepter of tyrants."

But these lines written in prison compromised the club more than they helped it; they reinforced the idea that the Revolutionary Republican Women were suspect.[15] On 6 October at the Convention, the Hommes-

12. *Moniteur*, XVII, 229 and XVIII, 81, 217.
13. A.N., F⁷ 3688³, 25 September.
14. *Moniteur*, XVII, 755.
15. Jacques Roux was arrested on 5 September 1793 and wrote his newspaper in his cell (where he committed suicide on 10 February 1794). His incarceration was

Libres Society of 10 August denounced "the uncivic intentions of several woman who call themselves revolutionaries" and asked "that women not be allowed to form any separate society henceforth." The club had to wait until the next day to justify itself at the bar, where Claire Lacombe asserted that "their rights were those of the people" and that "if they were oppressed, they would know to resist that oppression."[16] On 8 October, Claire Lacombe justified herself before the Jacobins, refuting the accusations made against her and the club on 16 September, and claimed that the "true friends of Liberty and Equality were not present" that day. She was applauded. But the reconciliation was only superficial, and on 23 October the Hommes-Libres Society of the Pont-Neuf section "groaned over the division that existed" between the club of women and the Jacobins.[17]

Events speeded up. The club divided between those who were ready to follow Claire Lacombe, henceforth the club's true leader, down an increasingly isolated road, in open opposition to the Convention, government committees, and the Jacobins, and those who did not wish to cut themselves off from the revolutionary movement. At the end of October, the female citizens Lecouvreur and Colinger (the president in July) were expelled; they were probably not the only members to undergo this fate. Other Revolutionary Republican Women chose to address their comrades not at club meetings, which were probably stormy, but in letters to newspapers.[18]

The Banning of Women's Clubs

The liberty cap, the ancient symbol of freed slaves adopted by the sansculottes as free men, demonstrates the flat refusal of all emancipation for women.

Part of the population—women as well as men—only grudgingly accepted the decree that made the wearing of the cockade compulsory for women; they feared that this was but a first step. Why would the Convention stop now? Wasn't it also going to decree the compulsory wearing of the red cap for women—then that women must wear their hair short, that

---

only the first blow aimed at the *enragé* opposition: after the attack against the Revolutionary Republican Women on 16 September, Varlet was sent to prison on 18 September. Leclerc, also threatened with arrest, ceased to publish his newspaper on 21 September.

16. *Moniteur*, XVIII, 62, 69.
17. *Journal de la Montagne* 130; B.N., Mss., N.A.F., 2713.
18. B.N. Mss., N.A.F., 2713, f. 50; *Journal des débats des Jacobins*, no. 302.

they must be armed, that they had the right to vote in assemblies, that they would be drafted into the army, and even that marriages first celebrated under the Old Regime must be renewed? The most fantastic rumors spread through Paris.[19]

The rumors may have been fanciful, but they show how, in the context of a strong women's movement that was partly based on protest, the 21 September decree concerning the cockade was perceived as a step forward to the double goals of recognizing the participation by women in the popular movement and recognizing the equality of men and women. This first step would be followed by others, leading finally to full citizenship and political rights for women—the right to bear arms and the right to vote. In the context of summer 1793, compelling women to wear the cockade was tantamount to recognizing their political existence. It was the logical conclusion to their glorification on 10 August 1793, as members of the Sovereign People. Politics was wrested from its masculine exclusivity—*wrested* in the truest sense. A real fear on the part of the masculine population that their supremacy might be called into question in all areas was, at the end of summer and the beginning of autumn 1793, centered around the issue of the cockade.[20] The reference to short hair—like men's hair—in the preceding rumor reveals the fear of an end to inequalities between the two sexes, as it developed in the imaginary.

Moreover, a woman with short hair was said to be coifed *à la jacobine* (in the Jacobin style). The decree of 21 September was the result of a double movement: the strength of the popular movement and the upsurge of the female sansculottes within the popular movement. The widespread wearing of the red cap, symbol of the female sansculottes, could have gone in a logical progression: a woman wearing the cockade would claim to be a citizen; thus, a woman wearing a red cap would claim to be a revolutionary citizen. As a second step on the road to sexual equality, this would soon have been followed, some thought, by the right to bear arms; it would also have been an affirmation of popular strength. So future events developed around this issue.

On 13 October, the female merchants of la Halle attacked women who sold liberty caps, asserting that they had already been forced to wear the cockade "and that was enough." On 4 Brumaire (25 October), a rather tipsy man and woman tore the headdresses called "bonnets" from the heads of

---

19. A.N., F⁷ 3688³, 21 and 28 September; DXLII no. 11, 22 Vendémiaire and 8 Brumaire Year II.

20. See "Sexual Difference and Equal Rights," this volume.

female passersby while crying, "Down with `bonnets' because they lower the head, we want no more `bonnets' and long live the national cockade!" These rather obscure words of drunks show how the issue of the red cap upset people.[21]

The Revolutionary Republican Women frequently wore liberty caps, at least during their meetings. Based upon this fact, the female merchants of la Halle concluded that the club wished to make all women wear the caps. They arrived at this conclusion too quickly, for the Revolutionary Republican Women, who were on the defensive and aware of danger, had decreed to expel "those among them who committed violence against women on this subject."[22]

On 7 Brumaire Year II (28 October 1793), the Réunion section invited the club to the inauguration of the busts of Lepeletier and Marat. The Revolutionary Republican Women thus gathered in their meeting place, some wearing red caps. But when they prepared to leave, the women in the galleries cried, "Down with the red cap, down with Jacobin women, down with Jacobin women, down with Jacobin women and cockades! These villains are responsible for the unhappiness of France." The turmoil increased, and a female citizen announced that there was "a plan afoot to dissolve the club." The justice of the peace of the Contrat-Social section arrived and told the troublemakers that "there should be no fuss about the red cap," that the women were "free to coif themselves as they saw fit." He invited the president to give up her cap—which she placed on the head of the judge—and then declared that the club was not in session and that everyone could enter. At these words, "a crowd of countless women rushed into the hall and overwhelmed the members with the most filthy invectives." The Revolutionary Republican Women were struck and dragged, and several lost consciousness. They took refuge with the revolutionary committee of the section, who asked them to hide to appease the fury of their enemies. They refused. But then an officer came to warn them that "heads are heated, the crowd . . . immense" and that one "is now crying, 'Long live the Republic, down with the revolutionaries!'" They agreed to leave by a secret passage.[23]

The same day, two female citizens who were walking in the neighboring section of Guillaume-Tell had their "police caps" torn by a woman, who was applauded by men who had gathered, saying; "Tear their police caps from

21. A.N., DXLII no. 11, F⁷ 4775¹⁷ d. Leverbe, wife of Senert.
22. B.N., Mss., N.A.F., 2713 f. 50.
23. *Les Révolutions de Paris* 215.

them, which only men [should wear], only whores and women paid by the aristocracy wear them."[24]

The brawl provoked by the female merchants of la Halle turned against the club and sounded its death knell. That same day, the deputy Léonard Bourdon rendered justice to the "purity of their institution," but asked that the club "be requested to confine itself within the boundaries of the law" (when had they ever broken it?) and to no longer "trouble public order by making revolutionary female citizens wear tokens by which they seemed to wish to distinguish themselves." On 8 Brumaire (29 October), the Committee of Public Safety printed a public notice stating that the incident was "a ploy by Brissot's partisans" (the Girondins).[25]

The female merchants of la Halle had known for a month that the wind had turned. Without further delay, the day after the incident they asked the members of the Convention "not to give any support to the red cap" and at the same time to abolish the Society of Revolutionary Republican Women because "the unhappiness of France was only introduced by means of a woman" (Marie Antoinette or Charlotte Corday).

Fabre d'Eglantine then began to speak. Taking into account the anguish expressed for some time by part of the male population, he put his colleagues on guard. There had been troubles because of the cockade, and there were now difficulties because of the red cap, thus "beware especially that after having obtained a decree on this last subject, they do not stop there. You will be asked for the belt, and then two pistols on the belt." He linked the recurrent phobia of armed women, nourished by the fear that women would obtain political rights, to the present economic situation. "You will see lines of women going for bread, [armed and ready to fight] just as we go to the trenches." He relegated women to the status of frivolous minors. In order to cause trouble, the "malevolents" attacked "the most precious object for women, their clothing," and they knew well how to use the arms that women themselves were incapable of using. He remarked that members of women's clubs are not "busy with the care of their household, are not mothers inseparable from their children, or girls who work for their parents and take care of their younger sisters; but they are a sort of knights-errant, they are emancipated girls, female grenadiers." Fabre had no fear of using powerful images such as stray soldiers or female laborers stuck to their hearths! He ended by calling on all

24. A.N., F[7] 4774[20] d. Lesage and Laundry, F[7] 4727 d. Godeau, F[7] 4728 d. Godot.
25. *Moniteur*, XVII, 285; A.N., BB[3] 8.

the fears of Convention members: "Women wearing the red cap are now in the street."[26]

The next day, Amar, spokesman for the Committee of General Security, gave an eloquent speech to the Convention. He began by distorting facts through a narrative that, in a few days, became the official version of the incident. This story presented the Revolutionary Republican Women as the instigators of the brawl through their fierce wish to force women to wear red caps and pants! But his report quickly surpassed this anecdote by posing two fundamental questions:

1. Can women exercise political rights, and take an active part in government affairs?
2. Can they deliberate and gather in political associations or popular clubs?

With a great many arguments, he explained why the committee had responded negatively to these two questions. He based his explanation on nature, emphasizing that women possessed neither the physical nor the moral and intellectual qualities necessary for the exercise of political rights. From this natural and unchanging order, he created a social order: "The private responsibilities to which women are destined by nature itself extend to the general order of society."

Women could not leave their role of sweet and modest mothers and wives: "This question is essentially linked to morals, and without morals, there can be no Republic." "The modesty of a woman" does not allow her to show herself in public and struggle with men. Thus she should not "leave her family to immerse herself in the affairs of government."

Then he developed a political argument: "If we consider that this is the dawn of the political education of men, that all principles are not developed, and that we still stammer the word *liberty*, all the more reason that women, whose moral education is almost nonexistent, are less enlightened in principles [than men]. Their presence in popular clubs would thus give an active role in government to people who are more vulnerable to error and seduction."

His conclusion was clear and precise: "It is not possible for women to exercise political rights."

Only the deputy Charlier rebelled, not against excluding women from political rights but against prohibiting them to assemble in clubs. The Con-

26. A.N., C 280 d. 761 p. 28; *Archives parlementaires* 78, pp. 20–22; *Moniteur*, XVIII, 290.

vention did not support him and decreed that "clubs and popular societies of women, under whatever denomination, are forbidden." The second article of the decree prepared the offensive against section clubs, which were to follow the prohibition of women's clubs: "All the meetings of popular societies must be public."[27]

The Revolutionary Republican Women tried to defend themselves, but the decision was irrevocable. When they presented themselves to the Convention on 15 Brumaire (5 November) to protest the decree of 9 Brumaire, based on "a false report," all sides demanded the order of the day, and the women had to leave "hastily under boos and mockeries."[28] And on 27 Brumaire (17 November), when a deputation headed by women wearing red caps entered a meeting of the municipal council at city hall, a "violent demonstration" occurred in the galleries. Chaumette took advantage of this by vituperating women who left their households to participate in political life.[29]

Thus officially ended all political activity specifically by women. There was even a return to the image of women forbidden from the public domain, which had been put in question for a time. The rapid change of opinion about the club, and also more widely about the participation of women in the revolutionary movement, may seem surprising. However, even if the chronology seems to lend support to them, it would be caricatural to draw up stereotyped schemas: the leaders made use of women when women were useful to them and asked women to retreat to their hearths when they had no more need of the women's help. More than a simple question of strategy, it is necessary to see in this about-face an intricate interweaving of politics and *mentalités,* or else we wind up with a simplistic and complicit image of women as victims of male misogyny and power. To make women into a passive and isolated entity negates the existence of militant women who participated effectively in the Revolution and contributes to a refusal to recognize the role of women of the people within the popular movement. This perception results in a conception of a "history of women" that has been constructed, negatively, by men. These men say that it is only because they were women that women were forbidden to gather. We say that they

---

27. *Moniteur* XVIII, 299; *Archives parlementaires* 78, p. 49. See "Sexual Difference and Equal Rights," this volume.
28. *Archives parlementaires* 78, p. 364.
29. *Les Révolutions de Paris* 216; *Moniteur,* XVIII, 450.

were forbidden to assemble because they were women who were part of a revolutionary process riddled with struggles. We do not wish to deny the reality of the lower status of women. But it is more meaningful, both for the history of the Revolution and for "the history of women," to research the causes of this brusque about-face in the total revolutionary context and within the female revolutionary movement itself.

Moreover, this about-face was not complete, for the elements closest to the sansculottes movement sang the praise of the Revolutionary Republican Women during the summer, whereas the deputies of the Convention were the first to turn against them in the autumn. And not just any deputies, but Chabot, Bazire, and Fabre d'Eglantine, three moderate Montagnards and future "Dantonist" Indulgents. The cries of the adversaries of the club were also eloquent: "Down with the female Jacobins!" "Long live the Republic! Down with the Revolutionaries!"—and the woman who, after having booed the Revolutionary Republican Women because the word *revolutionary* "displeased" her, called the sansculottes "pimps" and "demeaned" the popular clubs.[30] The Revolutionary Republican Women had clearly seen the counterrevolutionary tendency of their opposition as early as 14 June, when they assured city hall: "The counterrevolutionaries do not want us to get involved in political affairs."[31] We can measure the extent of their retreat from politics after their heyday at the end of summer, when female militants who, in order to wear the cockade, suffered the insult of "female Jacobins," silenced their adversaries, and imposed the compulsory wearing of this cockade.

The moderates' offensive of autumn relied on *mentalités* that the most politically advanced revolutionaries also shared, as well as on the isolated position of the club. Denigrated on all sides, increasingly cut off from the revolutionary movement, having demanded measures of Terror but not accepting those that resulted from the decision to declare "the government revolutionary until peace returned" (10 October 1793),[32] the Revolutionary Republican Women brought disfavor on the entire female sansculottes movement. And the latter were not strong enough, not even to demand the compulsory wearing of the red cap by women—there was never a question

30. A.N., F⁷ 4582 d. 2 p. 32.
31. *La Gazette française,* no. 253.
32. The application of the Constitution was officially postponed until the peace; the executive power was placed under the surveillance of the Committee of Public Safety.

of this—or even merely to give a political meaning to this episode and prevent its adversaries from presenting it as a typically feminine problem of coquetry, a depiction that already excluded the female militants from the political domain. This retreat by the revolutionary female movement allowed views to be expressed that were hostile to the political participation of women. Certain male fears (of violence by women, of having their supremacy questioned, and so on) were thus exorcised by dwelling, like Amar in his report, on images of ideal women.

This report stemmed simultaneously from numerous political causes and *mentalités*. The most fundamental was the retreat from the entire sansculottes movement, and in a clear manner from the women who were a part of this group. Through the Revolutionary Republican Women, it was aimed specifically at women, but also at political groups to which the club of Parisian women was or had been linked, such as the *enragés*, the Cordeliers, and the militant members of the sections (see the second article of the decree of 9 Brumaire).

The Revolutionary Republican Women were particularly vulnerable in that they were women within the revolutionary movement and they supported political positions that were increasingly isolated within the women's movement. They unleashed passions and were placed in the front lines when the question of the political rights of women was posed. In the previous months, the rise of the female sansculottes movement was accompanied with questions and demands concerning the status of female citizens. As long as the pressure of the female sansculottes asserted itself, this movement in favor of a new place for women in civil and political society gained an advantage over its adversaries, in spite of lively opposition: thus the members of the Convention were driven to pass the decree of 21 September on the cockade. Isolated from its context, this movement could appear insignificant. Two police reports, dated 21 and 22 September, clearly reveal that this was part of a more general trend deeply affecting the populace: "Malevolent people. . . inspire women with the desire to share the political rights of men [and] seek to persuade them that they have as many rights as men in the government of their country, that the right to vote in the sections is a natural right that they should demand, that in a state where the law consecrates equality, women can claim all civil and military jobs."

The anxiety expressed by some men resulted not only from their imaginations! Thus, as soon as the female sansculottes showed signs of weakness, the opponents of political rights for women (the majority of the population and the deputies) took advantage of this weakness to end a debate that had gained too much importance; they attacked the most well-known and the most vulnerable female militants. Significantly, the Amar report—the only legislative text in the entire Revolution that theoretically raises the question of the political rights of women—is dated autumn 1793. It inscribes itself negatively and preemptively in the diffuse debate that had obtained importance from the power of the female sans-culottes in the summer. But the weakness of the movement by the fall of 1793 permitted the debate to come to an end. If misogyny expressed itself overtly at the National Convention on 30 October 1793, it is not at all because the Montagnards were more phallocratic than the Girondins; it is because of a sense of urgency. The Legislators could no longer ignore the clearer and clearer demands of the women's revolutionary movement. To put an end to these demands, they were forced to openly raise the question of women's rights.

But had this banned club of Parisian women put on its own agenda the revalorization of the social and political status of women? Its members did not reject the social functions of housewives and especially of mothers, but they did not accompany this with a rejection of public life. They refused to be "servile women, domestic animals," and considered themselves revolutionaries in their own right.[33] They never demanded openly the least political equality with men. Not once did they become publicly indignant over their exclusion from the electoral body. Their only official demand for equality of rights was for the right to bear arms. During the Revolution, to demand the right to organize in armed corps was also to demand one of the foundations of citizenship. For many, this right would be followed by its complement: the right to vote. Can we thus speak of feminism? The word is anachronistic, but it is indisputable that the Revolutionary Republican Women aspired to equality between the sexes. They meant for women to be true citizens, active members of the Sovereign People. If this was "feminism," it was a feminism that expressed itself in the political language of the Revolution. "Feminism" and politics were, for these women, inseparable.

In any case there is no doubt that they were conscious of their specificity as women in the revolutionary movement. A witness who can be believed recounted that he had attended a meeting of the club, in which the agenda bore "on the usefulness of women in a republican government."

33. Aulard, *La Société des Jacobins*, 5: 212 (meeting of 27 May).

"Sister Monic" concluded a long speech with these words:[34] "Women deserve to govern, I would say almost more so than men. I ask that society, in its wisdom, examine the rank that all women must hold in the Republic, and if it is necessary to continue to exclude them from all positions and administrations."

One of the secretaries of the club, the wife of Dubreuil, wrote in the autumn of 1793 that those who criticized it were men attached to their "marital despotism," unworthy republicans who wished to maintain women in a state of degradation. Moreover, the club applauded Article II of the matrimonial code, "which permitted women to inhibit the squandering of their husbands," and rebuked the deputies who were opposed to it.[35] These rare indications make us believe that the Revolutionary Republican Women at heart wanted to improve the condition of women, a subject that might have been broached in their meetings more often than their public interventions, which are unfortunately all that remain to us.

If they remained conscious of their condition as women, the assertion of their specificity in the revolutionary movement rapidly decreased in their public interventions. In fact, before they encountered opposition, the Revolutionary Republican Women reduced their referential horizon. At its beginning, the club affirmed itself as a specifically female political force, yet it subsequently presented itself only as a sexually neutral political force. Initially of national scope, it withdrew into the Parisian terrain and then abandoned the political to restrict itself to the social, before being dissolved.

However, it had its importance. It constituted an attractive pole for Parisian women who refused to limit themselves to the cares of housework and ardently desired to participate in the "common good." And its members helped the Montagnards to triumph. Women and revolutionaries: this double quality, at the very origin of the club, was difficult both to live and to accept. The women who gathered to struggle against "suspects" ended their careers as suspects.

34. Proussinalle, *Le Château des Tuileries* (Paris: 1802), 2: 35.
35. *Journal des débats des Jacobins*, no. 302.

8 The Search
for Basic Necessities,
January–July 1794

In spite of the Amar report, women from popular milieus, as "thinking" and social beings, continued their interest and participation in revolutionary political life. Although they could no longer express their thoughts and demands in a club for women, only a minority had belonged to this club, and its prohibition did not end the presence of women of the people in the revolutionary movement.

"IF THIS IS NOT THE RIGHT AMOUNT FOR YOU, IT IS ACCORDING TO THE LAW" (JANUARY–FEBRUARY 1794)

From the end of autumn and throughout the winter of Year II, food was indisputably more available to lower-class Parisians. The issue of bread was almost settled and problems over food disappear in the archives, only to reappear hesitantly at the end of Nivôse (January 1794)—no longer in complaints about the scarcity of bread but about "the egoism" and "cruelty" of butchers. Paris was poorly supplied with meat, which became extremely scarce in the middle of Pluviôse (the beginning of February 1794). On several occasions, police informers compared the situation to the former scarcity of bread, particularly at the end of Pluviôse (middle of February), when the lines before butcher shops began in the middle of the night. However, although they noted in a general fashion the number and unruliness of these lines, commissioners' statements contain no accounts of women questioned for their conduct at a butcher's door.

In contrast, documents overflow with examples of butchers' lack of consideration and infractions against the law. Butchers were reproached for scorning their lower-class customers and for not respecting the legal maximum price. Police reports are full of anecdotes about butchers who refused to wait on women of the people or gave them poor quality meat if they could not or did not wish to pay above the legal maximum price. It was said that butchers kept their good cuts for the "rich," who were not afraid to pay more. "They wish to push poor people to the breaking point," complained women. "All these villainous butchers, large grocers, and other merchants loved and respected the legal maximum price of 1790 as a god, because this maximum price was set under tyranny. Now that it is set for republicans, they no longer want it."[1] Housewives, who felt that the government favored them, energetically protested these "vexations" against equality and did not hesitate to stand up to merchants or to present at commissioners' offices the "delights" (cheap cuts) that butchers put aside for them. On 1 Ventôse (19 February) on the Rue de la Montagne Sainte-Geneviève, a woman "asked for the amount of meat that she needed, and calculating the sum for this quantity based on the legal maximum price, she presented this amount to the butcher and asked him if this was the right amount. 'No,' said the man; 'Well then,' replied the woman, 'if this is not the right amount for you, it is according to the law.' At that point she left, in spite of the cries of the meat merchant who was obliged to put up with this."[2]

Beginning in Nivôse (the end of December 1793), police reports mentioned the rarity or expense of eggs and vegetables. However, the situation was far from catastrophic, and even though one finds here and there mention of a hostile speech to merchants or turbulent lines, by the middle of Nivôse quarrels over food ended again with embraces and cries of "Long live the Republic!"[3] One month later, the situation was more disquieting. The scarcity of meat continued. More seriously, vegetables and eggs became increasingly rare and could only be found at "insane prices." At the end of Pluviôse (the middle of February), the situation grew still worse. "In the markets we see women who grow desperate and return with tears in their eyes over not having found the things they need or only finding them at prices that are much above their means," wrote a police informer on 29 Pluviôse (17 February).

"RUMORS SEIZE THE WOMEN" (MARCH 1794)

At the beginning of Ventôse, informers reported almost daily that they had seen women lamenting over their empty hands when returning from the

1. A.N., W 191, report of Bacon on 10 Pluviôse.
2. A.N., W 112, report of Perrière on 1 Ventôse.
3. A.N., F⁷ 3688³, 14 Nivôse.

market, one woman in tears, another calling for death. There were not enough butter and eggs, and the cost of vegetables was exorbitant. The legal maximum price was, in fact, no longer observed, and according to one police report, in a month all provisions "have doubled or even tripled in price."[4]

Only bread remained available and abundant and grew increasingly important in the diet of the poorest. Workers and indigents were reduced to a diet of bread and cheese. On 17 Ventôse (7 March), a woman of the Faubourg Saint-Antoine complained, "For more than eight days she had eaten and given to her husband, a worker, a soup made with oil. The evening before she had supped on an onion, with which she had eaten more than a pound of bread. Thus she suffered from horrible stomach troubles, and her husband no longer had the strength to work."[5] People also protested against the poor quality of wine or eau-de-vie, "poison" that did not even permit one "to sustain oneself." "It is no longer possible to drink them. Every time my man drinks to supplement the lack of food and give him the strength to work, he has felt sharp pains in his guts," asserted a woman on 16 Ventôse (6 March).[6] The government's promotion of a "civic fast" did not succeed. Many women would agree to go without meat only if they could find eggs, butter, and vegetables at reasonable prices.

The crisis was accompanied by terrorist words. Merchants of butter and eggs were accused, often with good reason, of not displaying all their merchandise on the floor of la Halle, as was prescribed, but of keeping back part that they sold on the sly to restaurant owners and customers who paid more money. This infraction was doubly discriminatory: on the one hand, the "rich" did not have to stand in line, and on the other hand, commodities destined for the entire populace were withdrawn from the market. To stop these abuses, searches were demanded and often carried out.

Police spies wrote that "rumors seize the women" and "complaints are the order of the day." They also asserted that the situation caused some women, especially merchants and cooks of the bourgeois, to utter remarks that did not befit revolutionaries. At worst these women praised the Old Regime; at best they weighed liberty and government promises against scarcity. On 12 Ventôse, counterrevolutionaries distributed a series of handwritten "pamphlets" addressed to female merchants that emphasized

4. A.N., F[11] 201 a, report of Grivel on 9 Ventôse.
5. A.N., W 112, 17 Ventôse.
6. Ibid., 16 Ventôse.

the food shortage and asked for the dissolution of the Convention. Their effort had no results.[7]

Indeed, in spite of being the most affected by the shortages, women of the people retained an undeniable awareness of the effort required by the Revolution. The informer Bacon, who liked to do his work among "women of the lower classes" and, unlike his colleagues, privileged all testimonies to their civic spirit, reported several examples of awareness. On 5 Ventôse in a cabaret of the Faubourg Saint-Antoine, he heard these "women of the lower classes" assert that "there is no going back for we have come too far to give up. If it is necessary to eat only bread, we must get used to this." In Parisian cabarets from the Faubourg Saint-Germain to the Faubourg Saint-Martin, women applauded when a female customer affirmed that "we must take good care of ourselves, for we are at a period when the people must watch and suffer a little if they wish to wring the neck of tyrants." And women who complained too much while claiming to miss the Old Regime were reproached for their lack of patriotism by other female citizens, who mocked at this fuss by women with beautiful white bonnets and well-rounded bellies and asserted that everything would end well and it was not necessary to "throw in one's hand."[8]

Nonetheless, times were hard for women of the people. Chasing after food during most of the day, they did not have time to work. Moreover, just as with bread, lines at butchers' doors began in the middle of the night and cost housewives their sleep, an especially precious commodity for workers. Therefore, many women preferred to help themselves directly and attacked the carts bringing agricultural products to the capital from the country early in the morning. These "lootings," or more precisely forced sales, angered the populace because they prevented the merchants from providing Paris with fresh supplies and sometimes took place under frightening conditions. For example, on 17 Ventôse (7 March):

> At the gate and small market of Saint-Jacques, at six in the morning, several carts arrived with provisions. Women stopped the carts and seized butter, which they held back. One woman had been overturned by a movement of a cart and received a very large wound near her eye. The flowing blood did not frighten the other women. Some of them had been knocked down, crushed underfoot, and carried away half-dead. Part of the butter was sold at the legal

7. See "At the Margins of the Revolution," this volume.
8. A.N., W 112, reports of Bacon on 5, 6, 8, 9, and 10 Ventôse.

maximum price and the rest was not paid for. . . . Eggs were sold publicly at three sous each. Some men had mixed with the women and had been served first.[9]

As violent as it was, this was not an isolated example. These seizures followed an unchanging scenario—interception of carts at dawn, distribution of their cargo at the legal maximum price—and multiplied during the month of Ventôse at gates and faubourgs first crossed by carts. Within the city, section authorities encouraged forced distributions on their "territory" by complying indulgently with the demands of crowds gathered around carts or by going in person before the carts arrived in order to seize them and force the distribution of commodities in their sections. The population and even the municipalities of the outlying areas sometimes intercepted carts that provided the city with fresh supplies under the pretext that "since Paris keeps its sugar and its soap, they indeed must also keep what they find necessary."[10] Even if the carts succeeded in crossing without incident the suburbs, the gates, the faubourgs, and the sections that had commissioners who were particularly zealous toward monopolizers, the country merchants were not yet through with their troubles. Scarcely had they arrived at la Halle or any other Parisian market than, in spite of the guard, they were surrounded by a crowd of women and stripped of their wares in less time than it takes to write about this (see figure 3).

Lines before grocers' and butchers' doors were scarcely less turbulent. On 9 Ventôse (27 February), the police spy Hanriot described a line that had truly frightened him on Rue Montorgueil the evening before:

These were not cries but howls, or more accurately, an atrocious roar of rage. Paris in counterrevolution presented nothing more horrible. The women fought among themselves for the right to reach the place of distribution. Several women before me had been struck by kicks and punches, thrown out of lines, and dragged in the gutter. Others cried loudly for revolt, which perhaps would have occurred if the volunteers and the police on horseback had not arrived to repress all these seditious movements.

His colleagues' reports and the statements of interrogations by police commissioners show that Hanriot scarcely exaggerated. One or several

9. Ibid., report of Boucheseiche, 17 Ventôse.
10. The quote is from A.N., W 77 d. 5 f. 291. The residents of the suburbs were in the habit of buying certain products in the capital, but it was now forbidden to take any merchandise from Paris, which caused considerable inconvenience.

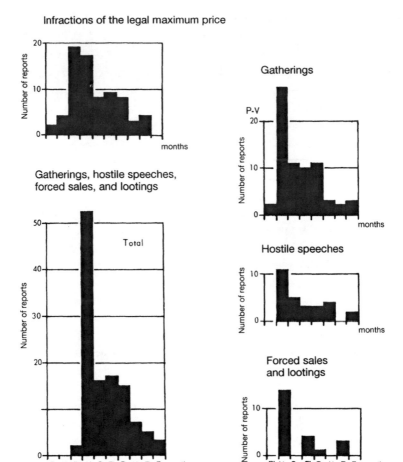

Figure 3. The subsistence crisis during the Year II. Source: Police reports (Archives nationales and Archives de la Prefecture de Police).

hundred women gathered in dawns that were blue with night and frost. The crowds were immense, tempers grew heated, and reactions were prompt and violent. If the elbow of your neighbor struck you in the ribs or her container for carrying food squeezed against your throat, this immediately triggered an angry response. As soon as the doors of a store opened, people rushed forward, and too bad for the weakest, who were thrown rudely to the sides. If an aged woman broke her leg, if another fainted, if a young child was wounded in the arms of her mother, rumors spread about the incident. Children almost perished, women were trampled underfoot and almost crushed, and one woman died following a violent brawl in line. The presence of men, sometimes mentioned in these accounts, increased the tension because, although they arrived last, they made sure they were served first by using their elbows and their physical strength to push aside female citizens who had waited for hours.

In such a charged atmosphere, the least incident could set off a riot and the slightest noise could touch off an explosion. On 12 Ventôse, a woman was accused of having "started a great uproar" by crying that a butcher sold his best cuts to rich women. On 27 Ventôse, two dressmakers spent the night in jail for having imprudently accused a butcher of throwing meat out the window.[11] How can we imagine the emotions unleashed by a dairywoman or a butcher who sold their merchandise above the legal maximum price, or by the announcement that they had nothing more to sell? On 4 Ventôse, a dairywoman was almost strangled by a group of women "under the pretext that she was a monopolizer." We could multiply these examples. Almost every day, police spies or commissioners noted that women had formed a crowd at the door of a butcher and that, insensible to the injunctions of the authorities or to the presence of the guard, they "murmured" and refused to leave before they had obtained meat.

The guard was "despised and scorned, especially by women who tore their weapons from them and made them useless."[12] The women forgot their divisions and joined together against them. If a woman who had cried a little louder than the others was questioned, the line immediately became united. On 9 Ventôse (27 February), a woman "invited her comrades to join with her" to prevent the arrest of a female citizen "who they knew did not mean harm."[13] And this example is not unique. The guard was all the more detested because they often acted brutally and did not hesitate to distribute blows with the butts of their rifles or pike handles. On 23 Ventôse, the rumor flew that a woman had even been crushed by the horse of a gendarme at la Halle.

"There is not a day when we are not obliged to place some women under arrest" noted a police informer on the twenty-second. These women were usually released almost immediately. They referred to their position

---

11. A.N., F⁷ 4648 d. Chomet, F⁷ 4774 d. Raucourt.
12. A.N., W 112, report of Le Harivel, 23 Ventôse.
13. A.N., F7* 2516 p. 9.

as mothers of families, and the authorities frequently recognized that only "bad temper" caused by waiting was responsible for the women's words.

These lootings and gatherings were considered by many to be the cause of the food shortage, which was believed to be artificial and caused only by the women's fear of lacking food. On 25 Ventôse (15 March), the informer Béraud wrote: "It is time that the constituted authorities, or rather, that an express law strike this mass of leeches that devours Paris and that seeks to set off a civil war. They cannot be heard without trembling, and everywhere they pass we see nothing but traces of the sadness they have sowed by crying famine. We can assume that many of these vampires are paid by the [Cordelier] conspiracy."

In a month the tone had changed, and mothers of desperate families were transformed into leeches because Hébert and the other Cordelier leaders had been arrested on 24 Ventôse (14 March). After this date, every woman expressing her anxiety a little too loudly was considered an "agent" or an "instrument" of the supposed "conspiracy" that had tried to starve Paris. This arrest did not concern only women who were housewives. Women had in fact followed the affair attentively since the beginning of the disagreement between the Jacobins and the Cordeliers, and during this crisis some became rather conspicuous in the popular movement.

THE COOKS OF PÈRE DUCHESNE

The incarceration of the "Hébertist" Cordelier leaders on 24 Ventôse Year II (14 March 1794) ended a crisis that began several months before and is known by the name of the "lutte des factions" (the struggle among the factions). The stakes of this struggle involved how far the Revolution should go. On one side, in December 1793, Danton and Desmoulins (the "Indulgent" or "Dantonist" faction) had asked for the release of suspects and questioned the organization of the system of revolutionary government and the Terror. On the other side, Hébert and the Cordeliers (the "Exagéré," Cordelier, or Hébertist faction) had demanded that the Terror be increased and that the controlled economy be strengthened. Robespierre and the Committee of Public Safety tried to maintain an equal balance by denouncing both factions for their weakness, recklessness, "moderatism," and excess. It was difficult to preserve this equilibrium. After the first victories of the Indulgents, the Cordeliers rallied, hardened their position, moved away from the Jacobin club (which was close to the revolutionary government), and attacked Robespierre in veiled terms.

In the first months of the struggle between the factions (December 1793 to January 1794), women did not take a particular position and did not distinguish themselves at all in the popular movement. Some women took the side of the Cordeliers, others were against them, without any major policy becoming apparent. However, at the same time, police reports indicated the propensity of an important part of the female sansculottes movement to support the most radical positions.[14] And those who had been members of the Society of Revolutionary Republican Women certainly did not disapprove of Cordelier motions. The Ventôse subsistence crisis increased this small nucleus to a significant proportion of Parisian women of the strongest popular environments, even if it was still a minority. On 12 and 17 Ventôse Year II (2 and 7 March 1794), the spy Rolin noted that "washerwomen and other female day laborers" preferred "exaggerated" opinions and did not "retain any moderation." The social crisis also affected female laborers. The movements of female workers of the sections, of female sackmakers and spinners in municipal workshops or in the Salpêtrière, all took place within the two months of Pluviôse and Ventôse (February–March). The terrain was ready for a favorable welcome of Cordelier initiatives. Thus, in Ventôse and Germinal (March 1794), "women" appeared to be a specific group in the writings of police informers, albeit a group with less force than in May 1793 or later during the Year III.

During the crisis, the Cordelier galleries were jam-packed with female citizens who did not miss a meeting and supported unconditionally the leaders of the club. It is remarkable that the majority of those who witnessed the trial of the Hébertists at the end of Ventôse did not repudiate even halfheartedly the meetings of 14 and 16 Ventôse (4 and 6 March), during which the Cordelier leaders Carrier, Ronsin, and Hébert preached insurrection and the Declaration of the Rights of Man and the Citizen was veiled with black crepe as a sign of protest. That most women did not declare themselves shocked by these speeches in the accounts of the revolutionary tribunal allows us to suppose that they applauded the talks with enthusiasm. Their applause welcoming the deputation of Jacobins led by Collot d'Herbois who raised the veil covering the Declaration of Rights was much less warm on 17 Ventôse (7 March).

Indeed, the informer Boucheseiche wrote on 19 Ventôse, "The majority of spectators were composed of regulars, all rather discontented with the applause given two days before to the speech of Collot d'Herbois. Be-

14. See "Political Culture and Female Sociability," this volume.

fore the meeting, women had showed their regret at seeing the Declaration of Rights stripped of the veil that had covered it. Such was the spirit of the galleries. Hébert and Vincent especially had expressed the feelings of the women who listened to them." Five days later, another informer also described "these women who applauded [Hébert and his friends] in the Cordelier galleries." If the informers did not exaggerate, we could think that, after having won over a large female public by increasingly virulent attacks against the merchants, Hébert was pushed into the camp opposing the Convention by this same predominantly female "base."

After the announcement of the arrest of the Hébertists, the affair was on all lips and crept into all conversations. Like men, women had occupied both camps, one of which—the "cooks of Père Duchesne"—began to decrease as the repression gradually gained in strength.[15]

Female citizens warmly defended or reviled Hébert, the locus of all the controversy. The source of the passion raised by this affair was the same in both cases: women of popular milieus had placed great confidence in "Père Duchesne," who had known how to touch them by his newspaper campaigns on basic necessities or by his reputation as the "defender of the Rights of Man." We have only to think of the response made by the wife of Janisson, a ringleader of the workers in the Jacobin spinning workshop, who described their difficulties to Hébert on 16 Ventôse and then repeated to her comrades that their affairs were in good hands.[16] "The more they had loved Père Duchesne, the more they regarded him with horror," said women after his arrest. For these women, the Cordelier leaders, and specifically Hébert, had attained the heights of "villainy" because, by their patriotic speeches, they had tricked the people, who were once again "betrayed" by those in whom they had placed their confidence. And the punishment sought should fit the crime—on 27 Ventôse, "it was said in a group of women that the Place of the Revolution is not large enough to contain all those who wish to have the pleasure of seeing Hébert fall. Most of these women were so angry at him that there was no torture that they did not desire to see him undergo."

The furor caused by the supposed treason of those who had been considered until now to be good patriots was accompanied by a feeling of helplessness. The general assemblies and cabarets resounded with sighs, lamentations, and questions: "Who would have suspected it for a minute? Who

15. A.N., W 112, report of Bacon, 29 Ventôse.
16. A.N., F⁷ 4748 d. Janisson.

would have believed it? What is to become of us since we have been so betrayed by men in whom we had confidence?" There was a single response to these sad worries: "We must have the greatest confidence in the Convention in general because, damn it, it spares no one. For us, our true compass is the Convention. We must never lose sight of this for an instant, or else, the Revolution will go to hell!"[17] The confusion was such that the news that Marat had been the first leader of the "conspiracy" or that Robespierre had been arrested spread like wildfire.

However, men and women still refused to believe in the guilt of Hébert and his friends. The wife of Janisson responded to a female comrade in a workshop who had reminded her ironically of her admiration for Hébert, "that he was still not dead." The wife of Lecreps, a regular at the Cordeliers, asserted "that true and good patriots have been arrested and traitors have been left free . . . and that she died of sorrow to see that Père Duchesne was taken."[18] These are not isolated examples. An observer heard women, "the tribune regulars, those who occupied the first rows," say while leaving the Cordelier meeting on the twenty-fourth, "We will have our patriots in spite of the villains who have accused them, and if it is necessary that women become involved, we will."

On 1 Germinal (21 March), the trial began and Parisians rushed in crowds to follow the debates. Female citizens even deserted the doors of butchers as they pushed to get in to the revolutionary tribunal. The public was almost unanimous in hoping for the condemnation of the accused. However, informers remarked that Hébert always had a considerable "party" among the "little people," or the "forty sous,"[19] and especially among women. "I have already said that it was more than likely that Hébert and his associates had many female citizens in their party" wrote one informer after having reported the case of a washerwoman who sought to win her companions over to the accused.[20] Yet we must not exaggerate. The great majority of Parisian women thought the condemnation of the accused

17. A.N., W 112, reports of Bacon, 24, 25, and 27 Ventôse.
18. A.N., F7 4774[16] d. Lecreps.
19. Sansculottes who were the most destitute were given an indemnity of forty sous to attend the general assemblies. The name of "forty sous" thus signified the poorest members of the sansculottes (and is sometimes used as a synonym for workers).
20. A.N., W 174, reports of Bacon, Pourvoyeur, Camuset, and Rolin, on 1, 2, 3, and 4 Germinal, respectively.

who had "betrayed" the people was just. But it is no less certain that others—and an important minority, especially in the strongest popular milieus—disapproved and felt it was a more general condemnation of the sansculottes movement. On 3 Germinal, a police informer heard two women say that "all the good heads were made to perish, and there remained only machines, with only Robespierre left." After the death of Hébert, the wife of Janisson maintained against all dissension that he "had been a good patriot and a good citizen and was executed for the good services he had rendered to the Republic." The wife of Lecreps went further with her reflections: it was "the horror of life" to have killed the best patriots of Paris, who "for a long time . . . hampered the operations of the Committee of Public Safety." Soon it would be other patriots' turn, thus she was going to abandon all political activity and withdraw from the world "because she did not want to go to the guillotine."

The repression began to bear fruit. On 7 Germinal, three days after the execution of the Cordelier leaders, the informer Boucheseiche noted that finally "the spirit of the galleries [of the Cordeliers] is excellent since the regulars have gone to cry on the tomb of Momoro [one of the Cordelier leaders] and other conspirators. These women who made motions before the opening of the meeting no longer return." Nonetheless, we can find in the following months traces of Hébert and the Cordeliers' "party" in the female sansculottes movement. On 14 Floréal (3 May), the revolutionary committee of the Contrat-Social section worried about the Hébertist opinions espoused by the leaders of the popular club of this section and wrote: "This is a smoldering fire that must be constantly watched. The women of the galleries are in the confidence of the leaders of the club, and in the meeting of the twelfth a woman named Millet called the president a traitor because he had said that there were Hébertists, agitators, and intriguers in the club."[21]

Men had supported the Cordeliers and did not pardon their execution, but, if we believe the documents, this position was particularly taken by women from popular milieus. More affected than men by the Ventôse subsistence crisis, both by their responsibility as providers of food and by their economic vulnerability, women had found spokespeople in the Cordeliers. Police informers emphasized that the popular origin of other partisans of Hébert ("the little people," the "forty sous") follows the same pattern. Moreover, this was neither the first nor the last time that these two groups found themselves side by side, as we will see.

21. A.N., F⁷ 4774⁶⁴ d. Paulin.

It is, however, important to remark that although the subsistence crisis influenced women's positions, it was not Hébert the destroyer of merchants whom they spoke of, but "the true patriots," "the good heads of the Revolution." The speeches that they had applauded and even encouraged at the club inveighed against the moderates—violent indictments in which the question of basic necessities did not appear. And who did Hébert attack on 14 Ventôse at the Cordeliers? Chabot, who had denounced the Revolutionary Republican Women on 16 September at the Jacobins; Fabre d'Eglantine, who warned the Convention against "female grenadiers" and "emancipated girls" on 8 Brumaire; and Amar, spokesman for the decree of 9 Brumaire that banned women's clubs. For these militant women of the galleries, among whom very possibly were former Revolutionary Republican Women, these names might have particular resonance.

Whatever their reasons, the "regulars" did not disown the condemned. They no longer returned to the galleries of the purged club, and, perhaps frightened like the wife of Lecreps, withdrew momentarily from political life, while maintaining a strong aversion toward the government.

"THE REVOLUTION IS FROZEN" (APRIL–JULY 1794)

There were few women arrested among the Hébertist section militants because they were largely excluded from structures of the sansculottes movement, from the revolutionary committees to the general assemblies of the sections. Their restricted citizenship placed them outside the framework of the repression. The authorities harassed only the wives of condemned men or those women who had upheld opinions that were too emphatic, often following specific denunciations. On 14 Prairial (2 June), the wife of Janisson was imprisoned, and on 19 Prairial, the wife of Lecreps was jailed one month after her husband.

On 30 Ventôse (20 March) during the hearing phase of the Cordelier trial, the police spy Béraud noted the surprise of many people that the leaders of the former club of Revolutionary Republican Women, suspected of being "part of Hébert's party," had still not been arrested. The arrest occurred fifteen days later. On 13 Germinal (2 April), the Committee of General Security ordered the arrest of Claire Lacombe "for general security measures," and the next day ordered the arrest of the former *enragé* Leclerc and his wife Pauline Léon. During and after the trial of the Cordeliers, the two women had been denounced several times at the revolutionary tribunal by former Revolutionary Republican Women who had disagreed with the oppositional path that they had laid out for the club. However, since the banning of women's clubs five months earlier, the two women were no longer in the limelight. Pauline Léon had married Leclerc on 28 Brumaire Year II (18 November 1793) and resumed the supervision of her mother's chocolate business; according to her own words, she who had fought so that women should no longer be "domestic animals," now "dedicated herself entirely to caring for her household and providing an example of conjugal love and domestic virtues that are the foundation for love of the fatherland."[22] Claire Lacombe had vainly sought work in Paris, then prepared to rejoin a theater troupe at Dunkirk. Although the Leclerc couple spent only four months in prison, Claire Lacombe did not get out of jail until fifteen months later. This may be because the young woman, who signed her name always as "Lacombe, free woman," did not renounce the government of the Year II nor the Robespierrists after their fall and, unlike the majority of sansculotte prisoners, did not attempt to obtain her release by stressing the fact that she had been arrested before 9 Thermidor. But prison broke her: "Her health and her spirits were strangely fatigued" lamented one of her women friends in October 1794. A jail companion wrote about her in February 1795:

> Do you remember the famous Lacombe, the renowned actress and president of the fraternal society of revolutionary amazons? She has become a shopkeeper providing small pleasures to prisoners of the state, her companions in misfortune. . . . Before taking this course of action, she walked with her head high, and she looked so proud, you could imagine her on stage, ready to play her roles; now she is simple, neat as a pin, gracious to the buyers, only a small, modest, bourgeois women who knows how to sell her merchandise at the highest price.

Liberated on 1 Fructidor Year III (18 August 1795), Lacombe left Paris three months later for Nantes. The former head of the women's club, the Revolutionary Republican woman had found an engagement in Nantes to play leading roles, "queens, noble mothers, great coquettes." In spite of pressure from her old Parisian friends, who exhorted her to return to Paris, she abandoned all political activity to devote herself to her work and her loves.[23]

Even if they were not direct victims of the repression of Germinal, Year II, some women clearly saw what was occurring around them—that the relation of forces that gives concrete expression to class struggles in rev-

22. A.N., F⁷ 4774⁹ d. Leclerc.
23. A.N., F⁷ 4756 d. Lacombe; T 1001 (1–3) d. Lacombe. Joachim Vilate, *Les Mystères de la Mère de Dieu dévoilés: 3 volumes des causes secrètes de la révolution du 9 au 10 thermidor* (Paris: n.p., Pluviôse Year III [1795]).

olutionary society worked to the disadvantage of the popular masses. Thus they detached themselves from the revolutionary government, which was increasingly incarnated in the person of Robespierre. The Incorruptible benefited from the trust and even the attachment of a large majority of the Parisian population, but some sincere sansculottes, who had become victims in one way or another of the repression, turned against him through personal or political rancor. Thus the wife of Dubreuil, the former secretary of the Revolutionary Republican Women, who was faithful to the ideas propagated by the club in September 1793, allegedly said "that he was a tyrant and that the government committees wished to assume without right the sovereignty of the people."[24] Other ex-Revolutionary Republican Women or relatives of sansculottes who were affected by the repression spoke similar hostile words. And it is beyond question that, against this background of repression and political disaffection, the subsistence crisis alienated women of popular milieus from the revolutionary government, even if they did not turn specifically against Robespierre.

In the days after the arrest of the Cordeliers, commodities became a little more plentiful, which reinforced the opinion that the famine had been caused by Hébert and his "accomplices." Because the shortage was blamed on the accused, it was hoped that after their sentencing there would once more be abundance. Tempers calmed and housewives patiently put up with lines. On 27 Ventôse (17 March) women of the Faubourg Saint-Antoine remarked that "since Père Duchesne has stopped smoking his pipe, it looks like women are getting along better. For the past two or three days, they have not had fistfights, as they did eight days ago."

During the spring and summer the situation improved. The "gap period" (*soudure*, which in French refers to the difficult period when the grains of the last harvest are almost exhausted and the new harvest has not yet begun) was finished, the supply of provisions was better assured, and city hall had subjected the butchers' shops to municipal control and established a general rationing of meat. Gatherings were less stormy and incidents of insubordination were individual rather than collective. Crowds, still rather considerable, waited peacefully in line. However, difficulties remained and the crisis continued for the most destitute; even though commodities arrived at Parisian markets as well as could be expected, their price still caused the poorest to do without. On 5 Germinal (25 March), a new legal

24. F⁷ 4683 d. Dubreuil. See appendix 3, "Portraits of Militant Women," in this volume.

maximum price was announced, which was judged to be too favorable to the merchants. On 7 Germinal, a woman said in a group of women and workers: "The Convention wishes the happiness of the people, well then! It moves away from this if it does not change the legal maximum price, which is too expensive for the poor sansculotte."

Not only did the Convention not intend to establish a new legal maximum price favorable to the lower classes, but the authorities relaxed the decrees for the controlled economy and surveillance of merchants. Women of the people still thought that if there was a counterrevolution, the merchants would be one of the causes; they were astonished to no longer be supported in their vigilance against these merchants. "The damned commissioners make deals with the butchers and support them against the sansculottes," said the wife of Moquet on 15 Prairial (3 June) after being reprimanded because she had complained about the poor quality of meat.[25] Many female citizens did not understand that silence was now imposed on them or that they would be questioned when they showed their indignation at the greed of merchants a little too violently.

"The Revolution is frozen," wrote Saint Just. The popular masses also were affected profoundly by the social and political malaise, which they expressed in their fashion. Having been asked on 11 Prairial (30 May) to leave the door of a merchant where she was waiting for butter, the wife of Patiense, a dressmaker from the Faubourg Saint-Antoine, said that the people were in a revolution that they would support at risk of their lives, that there was a law (the legal maximum price) one should follow, that "citizens were not behaving correctly," and that she would go to the Convention to see about all this.[26]

9 THERMIDOR

Thus it is not surprising that 9 Thermidor did not represent a rupture for Parisian women of popular backgrounds. Most felt all the import of the trial of the Cordeliers, because for many "Père Duchesne" was, so to speak, physically linked to the problem of finding basic necessities, but the conflict that took place at the Convention appeared to them much more distant. The

25. A.P.P., AA 60 f. 251.
26. A.N., F7 4774[64] d. Patiense.

discovery of the supposed plots was a double-edged sword for the leaders. If the great figures of the Revolution—Hébert, Danton, Desmoulins—had been traitors, then why should Robespierre and his friends be spared?

Let us not make the picture of women who were insensible to the import of 9 Thermidor any gloomier. Part of the female sansculottes movement was affected by the event, and the most conscious militant women clearly perceived its importance for the future of the Revolution. Some women openly showed their sympathy for the insurgents and their worry about their defeat. But even though they only represented a minority of individuals and not a group, their existence enables us to fashion a contrasting image of the female sansculottes.

On 8 Thermidor (26 July), Robespierre threatened his adversaries at the Convention but did not name names. In the night, the frightened deputies met and decided to finish off the Incorruptible. The next day, they prevented the principal Robespierrists from expressing themselves at the Convention and decreed their arrest. Learning what had happened, several women rushed on the ninth to the Jacobins to find out what was going on. The wife of Dubois, Marie Gaillot, a forty-four-year-old espadrillemaker, gives an excellent account of the anxiety provoked by the news: "On 9 Thermidor, while [I was] in citizen Doucet's espadrille workshop. . . female workers returned from outside completely frightened, saying that all was on fire at the Convention. Fear seized me and made me go to the Jacobins with other women workers to learn what had happened. It was eight o'clock."[27]

In the Jacobin galleries, she found many female citizens, "outstanding" militant women (like the wives of Boudray, Lance, and Sergent) and members of the grassroots who were panic-stricken and who for the most part supported the Robespierrists. All that night, female citizens entered or left the galleries in search of or bringing news. Some militant couples shared tasks: while his wife remained at the Jacobins, citizen Burguburu went to his section to follow the developing situation.[28]

The most active or most anxious women also went to the general assemblies of their section. After leaving the Jacobins at nine o'clock in the evening, a half hour later the wife of Dubois urged the general assembly of her section (Brutus) to rally city hall, saying she had "shivered with

27. A.N., F7 4682 d. Dubois. See also F7 3300; arrested, she was freed in Fructidor Year III.
28. A.N., F7 4627 d. Burguburu.

horror" at the announcement of a price on the head of Hanriot, commander of the Parisian national guard.[29] In the Bonnet-Rouge section, the
daughter of the justice of the peace Lebrun applauded the motion to support city hall and even proposed to march on the Convention. As for the
wife of Lance, according to a denunciation of Prairial Year III, "uncertain of
the fate of her dear Robespierre, she left the Jacobins to rush to the general
assembly, where she stayed from one o'clock in the morning until four o'
clock while keeping the most profound silence. All the grief and sorrow that
she felt showed on her face."[30]

The case of the female citizen Dubois who spoke in the general assembly seems unique. Militant women played no active role on 9 Thermidor.
However, some distinguished themselves by unequivocally taking positions. In the Gravilliers section, Geneviève Gauthier and her father violently attacked a lieutenant of the national guard who insulted Robespierre. Her friends, the sisters Barbot, commented on the announcement
of the outlawing of the city government with these words: "Virtue is persecuted, but there are good French people who sacrifice their lives to preserve it." In the Museum section, the wife of Périot allegedly "provoked
the people against the Convention during the night of 9 to 10 Thermidor." When accused in Prairial Year III, she admitted that she had wept
over the fall of Robespierre "because she believed him to be an honest
man." According to later denunciations against her, the wife of Dembreville was with the Jacobins during the night and "went as far as even
dragging canons." And on 10 Thermidor, seeing that the Convention had
prevailed, the wife of Butikere declared "that federalism had triumphed
and we were lost."[31]

However, we cannot pass over in silence the fact that women also supported the Convention. The former secretary of the Society of Revolutionary Republican Women, the female citizen Dubreuil, surprised the citizens of the section of Gravilliers by exhorting them to rally to the
Convention, assuring them that it was necessary for the Robespierrists to

29. City government supported Robespierre and his friends and called the sections to rise to defend them. The call was heard and armed militants gathered before city hall, but nothing was decided and the Convention proclaimed the rebels
outlaws. Little by little, the Place de Grève emptied, and at two o'clock in the morning, city hall was defeated. On 10 and 11 Thermidor (28 and 29 July 1794), approximately one hundred Robespierrists were guillotined without sentencing.

30. A.N., F7 4722 d. Gobo; F7 4586 d. Guillomet, wife of Lance.

31. A.N., F7 4720 d. Gauthier; F7 4586 d. Barbot; W. 546 d. Périot; F7 4669 d.
Dembreville; F7 4627 d. Butikere.

perish and warning them against the risk of setting off "civil war within the Republic."[32]

Many women let events run their course without intervening on one side or the other. The examples we have presented focus on the "outstanding" militant women, who were spearheads of the female sansculottes movement. They mostly went to the Jacobins. The insurgent city hall addressed the Sovereign People, who were represented by armed citizens or citizens deliberating in their general assemblies. Women were specifically excluded from these two foundations of citizenship. In the general assemblies, women remained spectators, except in extraordinary cases, and we know that, even if women could at a pinch carry a personal weapon, they were not part of the companies of gunners who responded to the call of city hall. Just as every other time when the rights inherent to popular sovereignty came into question, women were pushed into the shadows. The experience of 9 Thermidor once again raised the fundamental question of the place of women within the revolutionary movement. Women were members of the people but excluded from sovereignty, female citizens who did not have access to the whole of their citizenship.

It is likely, however, that even if women had possessed the same rights as men, they would not have seemed an important force in the support for the insurgent city hall. Moreover, they could have rushed on their own initiative, as they did on 31 May and 2 June 1793, in order to support city hall and help the gunners assembled on the Place de Grève who waited for directions from the Robespierrists. A rapid glance at police statements shows that nothing like this occurred. There are descriptions of groups of men stamping their feet before city hall, but not once do we find any mention of a group of women. Calls to action, which in May 1793 were one type of intervention by women, had to come from the Robespierrists, a new factor that made 9 Thermidor an almost exclusively male episode.

How distant the summer of the past year seems, when the female sansculottes vigorously expressed themselves. On 9 Thermidor, such expression was almost nonexistent. If female citizens rushed to the Jacobins, if individual figures of militant women emerged, no female movement ever took shape. Most women of the people, who were essentially preoccupied by the cost of living, perceived 9 Thermidor only as a distant event that did not really affect them. Among these women, those who formed the female sansculottes movement adopted different attitudes toward this occurrence. Because of the repression that had struck women, then a larger part of the

32. See note 24.

popular movement, some women turned against the revolutionary government. The political interest and consciousness of others became blunted. A significant number of women rushed to the Jacobins on the ninth and followed the course of events attentively. And the most conscious female militants clearly and immediately perceived the stakes of 9 Thermidor and unequivocally took the side of the Robespierrists. Whatever their response, however, even if they were not all disinterested, women did not play any major role in this occurrence.

3

REVOLUTIONARY DAILY LIFE OF WOMEN OF THE PEOPLE

9 Political Culture and Female Sociability

"Women, whose moral education is almost nonexistent, are less enlightened in principles [than men]. Their presence in popular clubs would thus give an active role in government to people who are more vulnerable to error and seduction," asserted Amar on 9 Brumaire Year II (30 October 1793) before an audience of deputies who were eager to believe him.

"Read the report of Saint Just," advised a woman on 24 Ventôse Year II (14 March 1794) to the customers of a cabaret. "Analyze *Le Vieux Cordelier* of Desmoulins," said another woman in a group of female citizens on 21 Nivôse (10 January). "It is superb! Robespierre has reported on York to the English people!" enthused three friends questioned by their neighbor on the last meeting of the Jacobin club, while elsewhere a militant woman "recited with pleasure" the speeches she had heard there.[1]

A "nonexistent moral education?" Were women permanent minors, deprived of all intelligence and all political sense, so fragile and so frivolous that they were ready to follow the first demagogue who appeared? If we accompany police informers to revolutionary assemblies, cabarets, or the courtyards of popular homes, if we leaf through the statements of commissioners, then Amar's allegation requires serious corrections. Glancing through police reports and registers, we find on the contrary a female Parisian population actively acquiring a true political education. This knowledge was certainly neither uniform nor bookish. Its stages were often modeled on those of militant engagement and came from the simple knowledge of the Declaration of the Rights of Man and the Citizen through the regular reading of living theoreticians of the Revolution such as

1. A.N., W 112, W 191, F⁷ 4774⁹⁵ d. Robin D., F⁷* 2524, p. 135, F⁷* 2523, p. 58.

*pol edu: → practical applications
in & sociability*

Robespierre, and even in certain exceptional cases the theories of Enlightenment philosophers. This education was not limited to theoretical knowledge. A popular and political female sociability also played an intrinsic part in it. Militant women combined a desire to participate in the Revolution with a desire to go beyond the secondary place assigned to women in the Sovereign People. The roads that they took to accomplish this were often crooked and even more frequently full of pitfalls.

GENERAL ASSEMBLIES AND "HERMAPHRODITE" CLUBS

& attend galleries

In revolutionary Paris, there were many opportunities for all men and women who wished to perfect their political knowledge. Since 1789, women had pursued their political apprenticeship in the galleries of various revolutionary assemblies. Their strong presence was remarked in the galleries of the general assemblies of the sections and the meetings of section societies or popular clubs, the most representative expressions of the sansculottes movement.

Almost all sections reserved a gallery for their female residents who wished to attend the general assemblies. Like any other member of the social body, female citizens could present themselves to a general assembly in order to expedite workaday matters such as requests for passports, certificates of public spiritedness, and so on. Like many Parisians, they had the habit of discussing their private and public affairs there, in the spirit of fraternity, solidarity, and "publicity" (in the sense of making public) characteristic of the sansculottes movement. But female citizens crowded into the galleries in order to follow the proceedings about the political life of the nation and the sections. According to the informer Bacon, who specialized in section life and who repeatedly indicated the importance of the female public in general assemblies, many women attended. (Given the lack of statistics on the number of those present, we must content ourselves with his assessments.)

participate in crises

Normally, women had neither the right to vote nor the right to deliberate in these assemblies and were separated from male citizens of the section. But in hours of crisis, such as the spring or summer of 1793, they left their galleries and joined the men to participate in the verbal or physical fight. In some sections, or under exceptional circumstances, women were allowed to speak. They also intervened during the assembly by their comments and their signs of approval or disapproval, especially at decisive moments.

Bacon often described the cries and applause that came from the galleries of women. On 15 Ventôse Year II (5 March 1794), he was obliged to leave the gallery where he attended the Bon-Conseil assembly, because the women's mutterings prevented him from hearing. This didn't matter, he thought; he would go do his work in a neighboring section assembly. But he was scarcely more successful in the Amis-de-la-Patrie assembly, which was stormy because a male citizen had just been denounced. "Noise . . . Noise . . . As the women make a great uproar new sentries have been stationed." The "uproar," "hubbub," and invectives were not signs of women's frivolity or lack of discipline. They were the only way these women, who were denied the rights to deliberate and vote, had to make their opinion known. It is certainly more disciplined to speak after asking permission, but for that it is necessary that permission be granted! The conduct of the wife of Barbaut in the Indivisibilité section shows clearly what the atmosphere could be like in women's galleries. The wife of Barbaut, an adversary of the president of the assembly, called him an intriguer, and scarcely had he opened his mouth when she grumbled loudly enough to be heard: "Here is the Vendée speaking." Her neighbor, the female citizen Berjot, grew indignant in turn: "Why won't you shut up? Do you have to talk all the time? This is none of your business, you; go hold your aristocratic confabs in the Rue du Pont-au-Chou."[2]

This unkind response ended the altercation only temporarily, for the female citizens Barbaut and Berjot were militants who attended the general assemblies assiduously. Other women who were less committed only went to the assemblies when they had the time. And women who disapproved of Montagnard politics did not go to the general assemblies; they expressed their support of the moderates elsewhere. The relatively regular presence of a woman at section assemblies was a sign of "Jacobinism."

The general assembly was not the only place where Parisian women could keep up to date on political life. Many women attended the proceedings of popular societies. Dating sometimes from the first years of the Revolution, these clubs dedicated themselves to educating the people and overseeing the course of the Revolution. They multiplied in the sections during the summer and especially during the autumn of 1793 in order to circumvent the decree passed on 9 September that limited the number of general assemblies to two per week. Thus each section soon had its club which met on days when the general assembly did not take place. Only its

2. A.N., F⁷ 4585 d. 5, pp. 64–75, F⁷ 4694 d. Dupont, wife of Barbaux (Barbaut).

members could deliberate, but in the public galleries men and women attended the debates and listened to the reading of patriotic newspapers or to speeches delivered to the Convention and to the Jacobins. Thus, on 28 Pluviôse Year II (16 February 1794), the Faubourg-Montmartre popular society opened its meeting with the reading of political articles from the *Journal de la Montagne:* "Women listened with great interest for they themselves imposed silence." The female spectators praised popular clubs that lived up to their expectations. On 9 Pluviôse Year II (28 January 1794), young female citizens who were "electrified" by the republican teachings that had been read in the Lazowski club (Finistère section) said, "We would be very aggravated if we had to miss the popular assembly even just once. At least there we improve our knowledge." "By coming here, we become educated and we learn news," asserted women from the galleries of the Maison-Commune popular club.[3]

From their galleries, female spectators remarked on the political situation or the progress of the meeting. If they asked to speak, they were permitted to do so more easily than in the general assemblies. And most important, some sexually mixed popular clubs admitted female citizens as full-fledged members. It is difficult to say how often this happened because we do not possess all the regulations for these clubs, which were usually silent on the subject of women. Early fraternal clubs, which were frequently open to women, disappeared or merged in 1793 with new section clubs and lost their mixture of both sexes as members; these included the Fraternal Society of les Halles, Nomophiles, Minimes, and perhaps that of the Fontaine-de-Grenelle section. What became of the Fraternal Society of the Women Citizens of Unité section that contributed significantly both to the Assembly of Republican Women on 24 February 1793 and the "war of the cockades"? Its case is unique because it appears that this club was not really sexually mixed but composed of two parts, one male, the other female, each possessing its own officers and members. Did it merge in the autumn of 1793 into the new Popular and Republican Society of Unité section, which was not sexually mixed? Was it dissolved as a women's club after the decree of 9 Brumaire? Or did it assume again the old name of the Society of the Indigent, which in the winter of Year II included women?[4]

Several clues indicate strongly without absolutely confirming the sexual mixture of popular clubs in the sections of la Cité, l'Observatoire,

---

3. A.N., F⁷ 3688³, W 191.
4. B.N., Mss., N.A.F. 2705 f. 56, f. 167, Lb(40) in 8° 2463; A.N., F⁷* 2507, p. 160.

Sans-Culottes, Bon-Conseil, Arcis, and l'Homme-Armé.[5] Finally, there is no doubt about the sexual mixture of the clubs in the sections of Luxembourg, Panthéon-Français, Finistère, Pont-Neuf/Révolutionnaire, l'Arsenal, and Amis-de-la-Patrie. Thus there existed during the Year II six to twelve sexually mixed popular clubs in forty-eight sections—from 12.5 percent to 25 percent of the popular clubs of the sections. And if we take into account only the thirty-one sections for which we have information, we arrive at 19.3 percent to 38.7 percent. Thus from around an eighth to more than a third of popular clubs in Parisian sections were composed of men and women. The left-bank clubs were particularly apt to be sexually mixed. If we add to these the clubs of the island sections of Pont-Neuf and la Cité, and even those of Arcis and l'Arsenal that bordered the Seine on the right bank, a compact block emerges. Besides their geographic position, two characteristics link these different sections. On the one hand, most of them had a particularly large female population, and on the other hand, their female inhabitants had trades, such as washerwomen and artisans, which were independent from their husbands' trades. Unlike the female citizens of the Faubourg Saint-Antoine, who worked most often in the workshops or stores of their artisan husbands, these women worked outside of their homes, in contact with colleagues, and consequently enjoyed a richer and more autonomous social life. Not that these workers composed the majority of female members of popular clubs; but their presence gave a particular character to those districts, where women knew how to make their social presence recognized and assertive (see map 4).

Sexually mixed popular clubs were not characteristic only of Paris. According to a sample taken from the addresses sent from the provinces to the Convention between February 1793 to February 1794, in fourteen provincial clubs women placed their signatures next to men's signatures: at Chartres, Frévent (Pas-de-Calais), Cambrai, Saint-Quentin, Laon, Meaux, Beaugency, Orléans, Cosne-sur-Loire, Châteaumeillan (Cher), La Souterraine, Guéret, Saint-Yrieix, and Saint-Barthélémy (Lot-et-Garonne) (see map 3). The addresses of Pau and of Culan (Cher) even stated that female citizens belonged to the club.[6]

5. These clues are found in information about a "fraternal" club, frequently a sign of sexual mixing, and police reports of 27 Nivôse, 11 Pluviôse, and 13 Ventôse Year II.

6. Series C of the A.N.; C. Bloch, "Les Femmes d'Orléans pendant la Révolution," *La Révolution française* 43 (July–December 1902): 49–67.

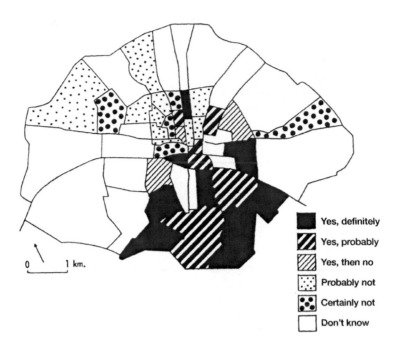

Map 4.   Were women members of the popular society of this section?

Among the sexually mixed Parisian clubs, only the Social Harmony club in the Arsenal section, which dedicated itself primarily to education, admitted women as a matter of principle: "Article II: the principles of social Equality should be solemnly established and practiced, the right to acquire and spread instruction and enlightenment useful to the Public Good belongs equally to both sexes, female citizens will be admitted equally and without distinction from male citizens, to share the patriotic works of the club."[7]

The Luxembourg Society set a quota of one fifth for its female members; in addition, although male citizens were admitted from the age of seventeen years, female citizens had to wait for their twenty-first birthday before they could become members. On 17 August 1793, the Hommes-Libres Society (Pont-Neuf) decided to admit female citizens. Would they pay the same dues as men? the club asked, thinking those dues excessive for women.

7. B.N., Lb(40) 2393 microfiche 9480. See also Lb(40) 3398 (Rules of the Amis-de-la-Patrie popular and fraternal club of both sexes), Mss., N.A.F. 2713 (rules and minutes of the Hommes-Libres popular club, Pont-Neuf section), Mss., N.A.F. 2704 f. 142–162 and N.A.F. 2705 (rules and minutes of the Luxembourg club).

Female members could be assigned to fulfill different duties than men. In the Luxembourg section, they did not hold office but were eligible for three seats on the committee composed of fifteen commissioners. In the Hommes-Libres Society, four female citizens formed one third of the purification committee (which reviewed the political conduct of members). Women also were part of the purification committee in the Fraternal Society of Panthéon-Français, where they could be elected secretaries in office.[8] In addition, all the sexually mixed clubs made it a rule to always include a certain number of women in their deputations, in proportions that varied from a fifth to a third, and even close to a half for the Panthéon section. (In contrast, in all the ceremonies of the cult of the martyrs Marat and Lepeletier, the delegations were predominantly female). In spite of this unequal representation, female commissioners were not tokens. They were not figureheads who had to limit themselves to listening to the men speak. On the contrary, they were frequently designated by the entire deputation to "act as spokesperson" even in the most important circumstances. Thus, during the struggle over section power during the summer of 1793, it was the female speaker of a deputation of the Social Harmony club who caused the Fédérés section, up until then held by the moderates, to tip over to the side of the sansculottes.[9]

From twenty to thirty women were enrolled in each of these clubs. In the Hommes-Libres Society (for which we have the most documents), they represented about one fourth of the members. But only some of the women who were registered attended all the meetings of popular clubs. According to different statements of the Hommes-Libres Society, only about a dozen women met, and these were given various assignments or acted as officers or served on committees.

Popular clubs, wrote Albert Soboul, "constituted from the autumn of 1793 to the spring of Year II, the framework of the popular movement."[10] In fact, in many sections these clubs replaced the general assemblies, which followed their orders. They censured section officials, distributed certificates of public spiritedness, and controlled and directed local political life.[11]

8. *Guerre aux intrigants—Réponse de la Société fraternelle du Panthéon aux inculpations qui lui ont été faites,* 1 Ventôse Year II; A.P.P., AA 201.

9. Albert Soboul, *Les Sans-culottes parisiens en l'an II. Mouvement populaire et gouvernement révolutionnaire, 2 juin 1793–9 thermidor an II* (1958; reprint, Paris: Flammarion, 1973), p. 34.

10. Ibid., p. 614.

11. The certificate of public spiritedness, which was usually issued by general assemblies, testified to the patriotic conduct of its holder. Those who were refused one were, according to the law, considered suspect.

This created an astonishing situation in which female citizens, who were excluded from all political rights, were able to participate in the power of the sections. Contemporaries were perfectly aware of this paradox. The Fraternal Society of Both Sexes of Panthéon-Français section came the closest to an egalitarian sexual mix. It also attracted the most criticism when popular clubs were attacked as organizations that were too independent of the most radical sansculottes. The difficulties it experienced illustrate the problems created by women's activity in sexually mixed popular clubs.

During the winter of the Year II, contemporaries protested loudly over the eminent role that women held in the Panthéon club. They were initially angry that female citizens had the right to deliberate and to vote there and that they took advantage of this right to pass extreme measures. On 1 Nivôse Year II (21 December 1793), two police informers reported that a "deputation of both sexes" of the club had presented itself to the general assembly of the section to inform them of a decree it had passed against "former priests, nobles, and lawyers." The female speaker of the deputation "expanded on the decree by a more than revolutionary speech, claiming that it was necessary to expel all of them from assemblies." Women were thus accused of preaching dissension or of seeking "to make all those who had places lose them."[12] Like many other sections, the Panthéon section was riven during the winter by quarrels between the "patriots of '89" and the "patriots of '93." The conflict opposed militant revolutionaries of 1789, former active citizens, to revolutionaries of more modest birth who appeared in section organizations after 10 August 1792. Justice of the Peace Hû became the spokesperson for the first group and fought with the club, which he accused of dividing citizens and of fostering "hatreds and calumnies against patriots who since 1789 have served the cause of the people."[13] To this conflict between militant revolutionaries of different social origins was added the conflict that divided the partisans and adversaries of political participation by women. Foremost among Hû's recriminations were those against the club's sexual mix. On 17 Pluviôse (5 February), he declared that he had "merited the honor of persecution and that he owed this to the hermaphrodite club of Panthéon [section]," where "intriguers tyrannized their brothers and were themselves enslaved by libertine women who shared with them the honors of office." Not a single attack against the club spared its female members. The occasion was too good an opportunity, given that a large proportion of the population opposed all political activity by women.

12. Police reports of 1, 3, and 19 Nivôse and of 18 Pluviôse Year II.
13. A.N., F⁷ 4745 d. Hû (the quotations from Hû are all taken from this dossier).

& on admission committees

But the flights of oratory against "libertine women" were not a mere tactic. Wounded in his pride and his male ego, Hû was sincere when he said "that he had seen the dignity of men offended by undergoing the censure of some women in order to be admitted as members of this club." These women questioned "educated citizens who needed certificates of public spiritedness on political and dogmatic matters" and refused them "according to whim." His double grievance is obvious: people without enlightenment had power over educated people! Worse, women, who were by definition without enlightenment or reason, had power over educated men!

After the banning of women's clubs on 9 Brumaire (30 October), many had believed that women were now excluded as members from all clubs. On 30 Brumaire Year II (20 November 1793), when a deputation of the Fraternal Society of Panthéon section led by a woman presented itself to the general assembly of this section, "citizens claimed that a woman did not have the right to speak, to deliberate in assemblies, according to the law." And on 26 Pluviôse (14 February), the general assembly of the Panthéon section was thrown into tumult. A deputation of the Amis-de-la-République club, interpreting the decree of 9 Brumaire, was astonished that the section of Panthéon "had maintained up to this day" the rights granted to women in its Fraternal Society when the Convention had forbidden women to meet. The speech of the spokesman for the deputation was interrupted by applause several times, and only when Paris, a club member and elected municipal official, intervened to defend the contrary opinion was the situation restored in favor of the club.[14]

Not all members of the club were themselves persuaded of the validity of its sexual mixture, but its leaders, among whom were women, defended the policy fiercely. Members had their membership cards revoked, one "for having made a motion aimed at expelling female citizens," another for having asserted that women "should not be allowed to deliberate on section affairs, nor should they be permitted to purge section members." "How do you feel about female members?" asked the (sexually mixed) committee of purification when it wished to ascertain the revolutionary opinions of a member, and a hostile response to this question led to expulsion.[15] Replying to the accusations of Justice of the Peace Hû, the officers of the club wrote:[16] "Why do some individuals show so much bad temper against

14. Police reports of 1 Nivôse and of 26 Pluviôse Year II.
15. Police report of 14 Pluviôse Year II and A.P.P., AA 201 f. 121–139.
16. See note 8.

hermaphrodite clubs, whereas city hall, composed of patriots, welcomes them? It is because women can size people up with an accuracy of judgment that frightens intriguers."[17]

This last phrase illustrates perfectly the imbrication existing between membership of women within the club, which shocked some, and the difficult positions that women defended there. There was no question for women of making themselves forgotten in order to be accepted. The most frequently expressed grievance against women of the club was that they only sparingly awarded certificates of public spiritedness. On 8 Pluviôse, the female citizen Ducor, "intriguing and jealous that good citizens had positions without being censured," forcefully supported a proposal to increase to twelve, instead of the two required by law, the number of citizens who must attest to the political conduct of people requesting a certificate of public spiritedness.[18]

Though in other sexually mixed clubs the stir provoked by women's participation did not attain these heights, it existed nevertheless. At the time women's clubs were banned, the Hommes-Libres Society in the Pont-Neuf/Révolutionnaire section asked if female citizens who were not wives of male members should be excluded. During the winter, a female resident of this section rebelled against the vote of four female citizens sitting on the purification committee. She wrote that she found the vote to be illegal because the law forbade women to express their views. And the crucial question of certificates of public spiritedness, a revealing stumbling block in the ties between radical and nonradical members of popular clubs, continued to raise concern. A report of 3 Nivôse (22 December), is instructive on this matter. "There are complaints that the citizens wearing red caps gather in clubs and take names worthy of them, such as 'hard hitter,' 'terrible brother,' and similar ones. It is greatly feared that these clubs are more counterrevolutionary than revolutionary. It has been asserted that they initiate female citizens in their clubs, who have the right to speak in their deliberations."

Wishing to argue that these men were too "extreme" to be revolutionaries, the observer wrote that women participated in their clubs, linking successfully by this absence of transition the militant women and the avant-garde of the sansculottes movement. In general assemblies and in

17. It is doubtful that city hall welcomed mixed clubs, but the assertion recalls the positions in favor of the fraternal club taken by one of its members, the municipal officer Paris.

18. Police report of Mercier on 8 Pluviôse. See also Rolin's report on 5 Pluviôse and Béraud's report on 8 Pluviôse.

popular clubs that were not sexually mixed, women were often conspicuous by their support for the most radical causes.

How can we explain this female extremism? Was Amar correct when he asserted that women were more vulnerable to error and seduction (meaning the seduction of revolutionary individuals)? Should we subscribe to the idea that women are prone to follow extremists on any side because they are not guided by their reason but by a sort of exaltation that is "natural" to them? It is necessary to take our sources into account: these documents were written by men and probably exaggerate this attraction to extreme positions by focusing on it in order to emphasize its scandalous aspect. The opportunity to denigrate groups by insisting on their shocking behavior is too tempting to pass up. This phenomenon is emphasized even more by an almost total inability to see the female sex other than globally. Extremists among the women were mentioned in reports under the generic title "women," even if they were far from representing the majority of female citizens in a section or a popular club. All French women have red hair; all women are extremists. But these exaggerations derive from a reality. It was the politically engaged female sansculottes who attended revolutionary assemblies. It is not surprising that when, as in the winter of the Year II, part of the sansculottes movement grew more radical, some of the women also became more radical. In addition, former Revolutionary Republican Women, whose past tied them to the most radical sansculottes, became members of sexually mixed popular clubs. The issue of basic necessities, often put forward by historians when they remark on the uncompromising attitude of women, played only an indirect part here: during the winter of the Year II, there was no difficulty in finding food. Yet radical sansculottes and militant women shared the same hatred of merchants. And it was among the radical sansculottes that we find the most supporters, perhaps not so much of a theory of equality between the sexes as of the political participation of women. Thus militant women turned toward and supported the people whose ideas they shared and who welcomed them (relatively) favorably.

The offensive against popular societies and clubs, which were often accused of Hébertism, redoubled in the spring of the Year II (1794) during the repression following the Cordelier trial. Even the Fraternal Society of Patriots of Both Sexes, which since 1790 had welcomed women, was affected by the disrepute that fell on popular clubs, particularly those that were sexually mixed. Up until then the club had escaped the attacks against clubs open to women. In autumn of 1793, it had prudently distinguished itself from the Society of Revolutionary Republican Women. Without being established in a section, and thus without local power, it had not suffered much from the oppositions during winter. However, it was undermined by uncertainty, and in the spring it split into proponents and opponents of sexual mixing. Did the law that forbade women to deliberate apply also to the club? Should it thus revise its statutes? Each time the questions were raised, the proponents of sexual mixing won, but the dissension was such that on 21 Germinal (10 April) its purification commission asked the legislation committee for an interpretation of the law.[19] The club began to split apart. In addition, like other popular clubs, it purged itself to excess in order to return to the Jacobins' good graces. For example, on 10 Prairial Year II (19 May 1794), the female citizen Loeillet and the male citizen Dussot were expelled. Dussot had anticipated this action for a month and had thrown his membership card into the fire. As for Loeillet, disillusioned, she had not even renewed her membership; she asserted to the purification committee that they needed intriguers and that she "had done too much for the Revolution"—to which they responded "that one never did too much."[20]

Thus, six months after the banning of women's clubs, popular clubs that had sometimes welcomed women were in turn attacked as organs of the sansculottes movement, an attack that emphasized the place that they gave to women. Yet in most cases, women had only one place—not as actors but as active spectators, just like in section general assemblies. As in the spring, summer, or autumn of 1793, militant women were conspicuous both for their sex and for the extreme positions that they often took. The popular Parisian clubs almost all ended by dissolving themselves in Prairial Year II (May 1794), leaving the stage clear for the Jacobins.

THE FEMALE REGULARS OF THE GALLERIES

The membership of the Jacobin club was exclusively male and of a higher social level than the membership of popular clubs. However, a large public attended their meetings from the galleries. One gallery was particularly filled with female citizens. Woe to those women who "did not have a good reputation," who were suspected of being aristocrats, or who had made

19. A.N., D III 240–242 f. 21.
20. A.N., F7 4698 d. Dussot.

"feeble jokes" about men of color: they were driven out without consideration, unless indeed a hand that was a little too quick struck their cheeks. The female spectators had the right to request permission to speak by writing to the president. They more frequently burst out with exclamations. However, impressed and less at ease than in section assemblies, their behavior was for the most part more reserved. The Jacobins paid attention to the women's attendance. On 15 October 1793, they distributed to all members of the club as well as male or female citizens in the galleries a calendar of meetings, and they never forgot to invite them to their demonstrations.[21]

Most women present were habitual attendees, and it was not without reason that during the Year III they were described as "regulars of the Jacobin galleries." Claire Lacombe was one of the regulars, as were many obscure female militants: the female citizen Maubuisson, the widow Salignac, the wife of Villarmée, the widow Sergent, the female citizen Dubouy, and the wives of Huzard, Fragère, and Lance acknowledged in the Year III that they had attended almost every day. The wife of Boudray, one of the oldest and most faithful spectators, attended all the meetings and even had a "reserved" place "in the gallery to the right of the president, in front of the speaker," where she did not lose a word of the debates.[22] The reputations of revolutionary female zealots began in these galleries, and political friendships formed there. In Ventôse Year II, during the Cordelier affair, a citizen declared to his neighbor in the galleries, "Ah! you are the one coming to my side. I am delighted." Familiar with her as "a warm patriot and a good republican since 1789," a member of the Fraternal Society of Patriots of Both Sexes, he asked her "what she thought of this faction and what was the opinion of the galleries about it."[23]

Women did not go to Jacobin meetings in order to deliberate. There was no question of their having a voice. Rather, the female public was attracted by the desire to "become instructed" and a "curiosity to hear the various opinions" of important leaders.[24]

In the other great Parisian club, the Cordeliers, women did not have a deliberative voice either. But it is probable that this club gave them greater respect, for several female citizens declared that they belonged to it, which no woman ever asserted about the Jacobin club. Thus we have the female citizen Bébiant, "a member of the Cordelier Society since it was founded

21. A.N., D XVI 73.
22. A.N., F⁷ 4610 d. Boudray. See appendix 3, "Portraits of Militant Women," in this volume.
23. A.N., F⁷* 2507, p. 191.
24. A.N., F⁷ 4736 d. Guillomet, wife of Lance, and F⁷ 4774⁶⁸ d. Perrée.

and through esteem nicknamed [by them] their aunt," as well as the wife of Metrasse, who "just like a member of the Cordelier Society . . . has constantly attended their meetings."[25] Unlike the Jacobin club, the Cordelier club drew a female attendance that was primarily local. Several times, different police informers remarked that women were more numerous than men. They also mentioned the presence of "women who were regularly in the galleries, those who always occupied the front row" and made "motions before the meeting opened."[26] We have seen that, during the crisis between Cordeliers and Jacobins in Ventôse Year II, these female regulars constituted the most solid support for Hébert. But not all female spectators approved of the Cordelier leaders, and during the greatest intensity of the crisis of Ventôse, female regulars were overwhelmed by the flood of curious onlookers. There are several examples of altercations between female citizens in the galleries and the Hébertist leaders. Thus at the end of Ventôse Year II, after a female citizen "questioned the conduct of Hébert, . . . Vincent cried out that it was necessary to purge the women because there were women in their midst who had been paid to insult Père Duchesne. . . . This same woman responded to Vincent: 'Yes, rascal, [profiteer?] I am paid by you to applaud you.'" She added "that the scoundrels who were present sought to seduce them and trick them, . . . that she saw more clearly than them." The citizen Ancard then proposed to drive out these "crazy crones," and the female citizen in question had to leave the room under the victorious applause of the "women of Hébert's party."[27]

Female Parisians could also "educate themselves," listen to great speakers, and keep up to date on the sudden shifts in politics from the galleries of the Convention, city hall, and the revolutionary tribunal. These revolutionary bodies deliberated under the eyes of the public, the people. Occupying the Convention's galleries constituted one form of women's actions in times of crisis. When the situation grew calmer, women went to these meetings occasionally, when they knew "there would be something good." The deliberations of the General Council of city hall attracted a large public. The police spy Rolin remarked on this subject on 8 Pluviôse Year II (27 January 1794): "There are many more women than men at the meetings of the General Council. Does patriotism bring them? Do they come out of

25. A.N., F⁷ 4765 d. Larboust, W. 78 pl. 2 no. 121.
26. Police reports of Bacon on 26 Pluviôse and of Boucheseiche on 19 and 26 Ventôse and 7 Germinal.
27. A.N., W 77 pl. 6 no. 363 and pl. 4 no. 267.

simple curiosity? God knows." However, these women were not welcomed with open arms by Chaumette, the chief spokesman for Paris city government, who never lost an opportunity to fulminate against them. A municipal official proposed that they give an indemnity of one hundred livres to a "female gallery regular" who had been burglarized while she was at the council, because her misfortune was caused only by her public spiritedness. After Chaumette's intervention, the General Council moved on to the expected order of the day, given that "the female citizen would be perhaps more useful in her household than in the galleries of the General Council" that she troubled everyday by her chatter.[28] On the first of Nivôse (21 December), the police spy Pourvoyeur wrote that "most of the galleries are filled only with women." On 21 Nivôse, Monic took up the refrain, writing that "most citizens [who go to the revolutionary tribunal] are workers and many women."

Though the meetings of the clubs and popular societies took place in the evening, the Convention, the city government, and the tribunal deliberated during the day. Contemporaries were surprised that many women, who should have been occupied with their household or their work, attended these meetings. But keeping up the bedroom or two rooms of a lower-class family was not really a burden. And work conditions help to explain these crowds of women on the benches of public galleries. Women who earned their living through sewing could work while attending the debates. In addition, rampant unemployment often drove female workers without work to the meeting rooms. This was the answer given on 21 Nivôse (16 January) to the police informer Monic, who was astonished at the number of female workers who "wasted their time" at the revolutionary tribunal and was surprised that they did not have enough work to be busy every day. Likewise, a female seamstress working for the government attended the judgment of Carrier in Frimaire Year III (November 1794), because "work was rare and [she] had nothing urgent to do."[29] And it was common for a peddler, a seamstress, or a washerwoman returning with work to go around to the public galleries if she passed them on her way.

The sansculottes did not consider attendance in the galleries of various governmental authorities to be a passive act but an active way to exercise popular control over elected officials, who were agents of the Sovereign People. Thus a mailman was proud that his wife attended the meetings of the revolutionary tribunal every other day, for "it is necessary that there are

28. Police reports of Latour Lamontagne and of Rolin on 5 Pluviôse Year II.
29. A.P.P., AA 128 f. 180.

always good patriots at the tribunal to impress the judges."[30] In this sense, the substantial presence of women in the galleries, which constituted one of the particularities of their political practice, rose from a desire to exercise concretely a part of sovereignty, even if by a roundabout path. Indeed, women shared with their companions a consciousness of forming part of the Sovereign People, as well as an active conception of sovereignty. However, unlike men, they could not express this directly. Because these women were not able to control elected officials through the right to vote and could not sit as jurors, they attempted to ensure the fidelity of the peoples' representatives from their gallery benches. Militant women developed this practice. The organization of work made this possible and the organization of politics made this necessary, and thus women could compensate for their exclusion from certain rights. In a way, they had been pushed into these galleries by their desire to participate in popular sovereignty.

In the galleries was formed the portrait of militant women as knitters who often left the Convention for the revolutionary tribunal and the revolutionary tribunal for city hall before going in the evening to the Jacobin club or to the popular assemblies. Did these women truly knit? While they listened to the debates, female citizens in the galleries sometimes did handwork—not so much knitting as sewing, or shredding linen to dress soldiers' wounds. The wives of Lance and Despavaux, both linenworkers, took their work with them to the Jacobin club. And two neighbors of the female citizen Marie, who was arrested in Prairial Year III as a Jacobin, stated in her favor that they could not deny that she "often attended Jacobin meetings," but, evil be to him who evil thinks, "she went there primarily for the sake of economy so that she could work without burning wood and light at home."[31]

Though they did not balk at work, were these revolutionary militant women in other respects bad mothers, insensitive to the dangers run by their children abandoned in a home that the women had deserted in order to become intoxicated on speech? This was how they were represented by their detractors from the beginning to the end of the Revolution. But whereas the sansculotte militant was a father of a family, about forty years old, the militant woman was not just a mother of a family.[32] The average age (thirty-nine years old) of women encountered in revolutionary assem-

30. Police report of Rolin on 7 Ventôse Year II.

31. A.N., F⁷ 4774³⁶ d. Marie.

32. Michel Vovelle, *La Mentalité révolutionnaire: Société et mentalités sous la Révolution française* (Paris: Messidor, 1985), p. 117.

blies should not mislead us.[33] Most of the women either had passed their fiftieth year or were not yet thirty (an age distribution that characterized the Revolutionary Republican Women as well). The militant woman was thus a young or a fairly old woman, who did not have to busy herself with many children. The maternal role allotted to women influenced heavily their revolutionary commitment. Mothers of families, however, were not markedly absent from political life and revolutionary assemblies. Though their tasks prevented them from becoming absorbed in militancy, it was not rare to pass in the galleries a woman carrying her unweaned infant in her arms and holding by the hand his older brothers and sisters. On 3 Frimaire Year II (23 November 1793), the wife of Marescot (a linenworker whose husband was in the army) left the Jacobin club with her three children. The oldest was twelve years and the two others were younger; her oldest daughter (a seamstress) who accompanied her, had preferred to dance to the sound of the violin at the ball in a neighboring hall rather than listen to revolutionary speakers.[34] And spectators frequently complained of the cries of children, who kept them from listening quietly to the debates.

No female trade appears to have been a breeding ground for militancy. If seamstresses and washerwomen predominated among the female militants, it is because they predominated in society. After them follow domestics and merchants, and closely after in no particular order come all female trades: workers in the craft industries, bookmakers, embroiderers, spinners, not to mention teachers, midwives and even the landladies of prostitutes. Many women belonged to revolutionary families who had a father, a son, or a husband in the general assembly or the popular club. The female relatives of section officials studded the audience of general assemblies, and, to a lesser degree, the Jacobin club. In Cordelier galleries, wives of employees of the War Office, lead by the Hébertist Vincent, outnumbered the relatives of section officials.

The presence of militant couples was a given of the Parisian popular movement. However, it was uncommon for women to go to the assemblies in their husbands' company. Then did women go there alone? Oh no! This would ignore the richness of women's social life; arm in arm with their irreplaceable neighbors, women of the people went to listen to the debates. In the Montreuil section, the wife of Lance and the wife of Pampelun were

---

33. This average has been calculated from forty-one women (six "regulars" of general assemblies, six "regulars" of popular clubs, sixteen "regulars" of the Jacobin club, and thirteen "regulars" of the Cordelier club).

34. A.P.P., AA 93, 3 Frimaire Year II.

"inseparable acolytes when they went on their pilgrimages to the caves" (of the Jacobins), according to a denunciation of the Year III. Since they had met in the galleries of their section's popular club, they went together to the Jacobin club and took with them several women from their neighborhoods. The men's absence during war encouraged female political conviviality. Those who remained behind pledged revolutionary commitment in words that sometimes reveal a certain female pride: they should not leave to their husbands the glory of defending the Revolution. Arrested in Prairial Year III, the wife of Saint Prix thus wrote in her defense, "I believed that by giving myself to their lying insinuations [going to the Jacobin club and supporting them] I served my country like my husband and my children serve it in the armies."[35]

But the war only exaggerated a situation for which it was not entirely responsible. The formation within the popular movement of separate groups of men and women was rooted in a conception of the relation between the sexes. The lines of sexual division that sometimes cut across the popular movement were the repercussion of a social and cultural distinction between a world of men and a world of women, which were "parallel" and which respected each other. Men would never dream of interfering in a brawl between two neighbor women because that "was none of their business"—and if they had, they would have been poorly received. Not that they turned away while observing an amused neutrality, but they let women settle their own affairs, even if they later testified against one or the other. In the same way, men with prestige or authority acted only as arbiters in political brawls between groups of women, as when Marat intervened on 15 May 1793 between the Revolutionary Republican Women and Théroigne de Méricourt. "Battle[s] of women existed at once inside and outside the Revolution of men," wrote Michel Vovelle.[36] Indeed, this was how women appeared in the descriptions that, we must remember, emerged from pens held by men who were quick to indulge in mockery. If we look at police reports about the confrontations of September 1793 between the women who demanded compulsory wearing of cockades and those who refused, this episode was set "outside the Revolution of men," but the interest that it provoked in the section assemblies reinscribed it within the Revolution. The Revolution indeed belonged to both men and women, even though in general women concerned themselves with political affairs

---

35. See appendix 3 in this volume.
36. Vovelle, *La Mentalité révolutionnaire*, p. 241.

among women and men among men. Thus a male citizen proposed in December 1792 "to assassinate all the nobles and the priests [and] to arm the wives of patriots so that in their turn they could cut the throats of the wives of aristocrats."[37]

This sexual demarcation resulted partially in a male disdain of "women's quarrels." When reprimanded for counterrevolutionary opinions by their servants or their spouses, male citizens responded that "women's quarrels did not concern them" and that they paid "little attention to what a woman could say in these affairs." Individuals who had been accused asked for their freedom by arguing that their accusations rested only on the "chatter of women." But these "borders" between male and female actions were not based only on male scorn. They were also the direct consequence of an affirmation of independence by women within couples. The groups of female citizens who attended club meetings together make this clear. Likewise, in order to avoid using a public scribe who would "cost money," the wife of Despavaux asked her husband to make copies for her of a denunciation that she intended to make, but which she prevented him from signing because, in her own words, "this was not his concern." This was her business. Her husband could help her save several sous but should not get involved. He worried about his action, which risked putting his wife "in a quagmire," but did not argue.[38] Even if they shared the same ideas, both spouses led their own revolutionary life.

Whether militant or not, female citizens who crowded on the benches of the galleries were driven by a concern for independence within marriage, a hunger for education, a desire to keep up to date and to understand the Revolution, and a wish to participate in political life. They had "a mania for running to assemblies," affirmed contemporaries who did not always appreciate this activity.[39] Despite the limitations that stemmed from their place in the Sovereign People and were imposed on them in these various assemblies, women of the people followed with interest the reading of revolutionary leaders' speeches and the debates raised by important questions. Here women got their political education.

For women who did not have the time, or who preferred to relax after their work day on their door step or in a cabaret rather than attend general assemblies or clubs and popular societies, opportunities to "become educated" while amusing themselves were not lacking.

37. A.N., F⁷ 4774³² d. Mallais.
38. See appendix 3 in this volume.
39. A.N., DXLII n° 8, report of Latour-Lamontagne on 17 Pluviôse Year II.

"TALKING POLITICS" AT THE CABARET

Newspapers provided an important opportunity to keep abreast of events and the diverse trends of political life. They were read everywhere, even in the most modest milieus. When searches were conducted through the papers of a female citizen or a lower-class family, commissioners often found at least one or two copies of various newspapers or pamphlets—not to mention patriotic songs. Thus the female citizen Lafrête—a secondhand clothes dealer and the wife of a day laborer, who lived with her husband and their child in a small room and supported the Cordeliers during the Year II—kept at home in the Year III an issue of the *Journal universel,* sixteen issues of Lebois's *L'Ami du Peuple,* two issues of another *Ami du Peuple,* two issues of Fréron's *L'Orateur du Peuple,* and a pamphlet entitled *Leurs têtes branlent, à votre tour après Carrier.* It was the same in most of the sansculottes households: the married couple Gaspard Charvat, a laundress and a section office assistant, owned "almost all of the newspapers of Audoin and some others of Marat." In 1791, Constance Evrard, a cook and a future Revolutionary Republican Woman, subscribed to the *Révolutions de Paris,* read Marat, Audoin, Desmoulins, and "very often" *L'Orateur du Peuple.*[40]

Those who did not know how to read, or whose budget was too strained by the daily purchase of a newspaper, met with tenants of the same house. All the residents, including a former cook living on her pension, a female confectioner, a female worker, and a water carrier, of 255 Rue des Fossés-l'Auxerrois (Gardes-Françaises) gathered each evening in 1793 in the porter's lodge to listen to the reading of the newspaper. In a private house of the Faubourg-Montmartre, another porter welcomed into his home the other patriotic servants of his master in order to read the newspapers.[41] But these groups did not last long because of the political quarrels that often arose among their different members.

The female citizen Goureau de Servigny, a female newspaper and cockade peddler, had an extremely ingenious idea that let her read the *Bulletins de la Convention nationale* tranquilly in her room without spending a cent. She merely removed them in the evening from the walls where they were posted, and after having read them, kept those that seemed to her particularly interesting and used the others as lanterns. Where was the harm since

40. A.N., F⁷ 4758 d. Lafrette (Lafrête). A.P.P., AA 77 f. 192, AA 148 f. 30. See appendix 3 in this volume.

41. A.N., F⁷ 4769 d. Lavigne, F⁷ 4774³⁸ d. Bredin, wife of Masson, F⁷* 2482.

"once the night fell they were useless and the next day others were pasted over them?"[42]

And what evening could be more agreeable for an ardent female patriot than one spent in the company of "good women friends" in a cabaret around a bottle of wine while listening and commenting on a reading of Robespierre's latest speech? At least there the "bellowers" of the general assembly did not threaten to expel them from the meeting each time the women forcefully expressed their feelings. These cabarets were true schools of public spiritedness and patriotism, where enthusiastic hurrahs often rang out and whose lower-class customers were at least half women whom, whatever their district, the informer Bacon called on 25 Ventôse "women of the lower classes, I mean to say of the true sansculottes." All the problems of daily life were discussed, from basic necessities to the Cordelier trial. Wine helped these discussions, and the atmosphere was cordial. Thus, on 6 Ventôse (24 February), Bacon heard in a cabaret on the Rue Dominique "women of the lower classes," a little drunk, speak of the scarcity of meat and assert: "Hell, we too are Republicans! . . . As long as the Seine flows and we have bread, we will be Republicans and we are screwed for being so." While saying this, "they struck the table and cried 'Long live the Republic!'" In this place of political sociability, the newspaper, read in common, disseminated information, propaganda, and reflection. Washerwomen whose husbands were at the front and who, late in the evening, gathered in the cabarets of the Faubourg Saint-Marcel, were among the most faithful readers of the *Créole Patriote* written by the Montagnard Louis Bourdon. For example, on 21 Nivôse Year II (11 January 1794) in a tavern of la Montagne Sainte-Geneviève, they reread twice the article on the Jacobin club and approved strongly of Robespierre. "When the reading was finished, the female citizens cried, 'Long live the Convention! Long live the Jacobins!'" On 15 Nivôse (4 January) in a cabaret of Chaillot, a female merchant of toiletries had read *Père Duchesne* to the other customers "of the lower classes," and a discussion followed between proponents and adversaries of Hébert.

Patriotic spectacles, concerts of revolutionary songs, and free theater for the people were other opportunities for enjoyment and education, along with countless political discussions that occurred between neighbors or in groups in the street.

42. A.N., F⁷ 4730 d. Goureau de Servigny.

These different examples are astonishing if we separate them from their revolutionary context. It is difficult today to imagine a female street merchant after her day of work immersed in reading the National Assembly's deliberations. During the Revolution, this was just one example among many, and the fact that it is not exceptional highlights the importance of female, popular, and political culture.

Reading and writing took on increasing importance at the end of the eighteenth century. "Papers" supposed to account for the social existence of an individual appeared: certificates of baptism, marriage, divorce, and death of parents, bread cards, membership cards in popular clubs, and proof of citizenship for men, were enclosed in a chest at home or carried in pockets. Letters exchanged with relatives who had remained in the provinces or with sweethearts, even if they were written by a public scribe and read by an educated acquaintance, familiarized people with the practice of writing. Literacy was necessary in many occupations. "Laundry books" and "conditions of linen" testify to the commercial relations between a washerwoman and her customers. The retailers of la Halle had to keep a book containing the names and addresses of their suppliers. Landladies had to have their registers. It began to be dangerous to be illiterate. A female fruit merchant who wrapped her cherries in sheets of paper on which was printed a royalist appeal suffered unpleasant consequences.[43] It was also common to read at the workplace. As we have seen, female workers in municipal spinning workshops asked to receive the *Bulletins de la Convention nationale* in the factory, and a female worker distributed "pamphlets" at the exit to the workshops of her trade.[44]

The Revolution accentuated this familiarity with reading and writing. Individual and collective petitions were written documents. The circulation of printed material among the Parisian people, noted by historians of the eighteenth century,[45] confirms the rapid development of reading and writing during the Revolution—a development that was reinforced by an abundant and easily accessible press and that affected a large working-class public that wished to "educate itself." Papers that specialized in political analysis and commentary were predominant. The newspapers read in

<hr />

43. A.N., F⁷ 4711 d. Fournier and F⁷ 4775⁹ d. Ruel.
44. A.N., F¹⁵ 3575–3576; F 1c III Seine 15, 1 Ventôse Year III.
45. Daniel Roche, *The People of Paris: An Essay in Popular Culture in the Eighteenth Century,* trans. Marie Evans in association with Gwynne Lewis (Berkeley: University of California Press, 1987); Roger Chartier, ed., *Pratiques de la lecture* (Paris-Marseille: Rivages, 1985); Roger Chartier, "Les Pratiques de l'écrit," in *Histoire de la vie privée,* vol. 3 (Paris: Seuil, 1986).

cabarets or elsewhere primarily carried political analyses by journalists such as Marat, Hébert, and Desmoulins or reported speeches of revolutionary orators. Here men and women of the people studied the theoretical principles that allowed them to comprehend the Revolution and to clarify ideas that they could defend with the help of solid arguments. In a society where education existed without yet being acquired by all, reading of both the press and posters was not an individual and private act but created political sociability and became integrated into a culture where orality remained privileged. The political ideas of various leaders were read together and out loud, and attempts to comprehend, to analyze, and even to criticize them were made collectively. Passersby read together and out loud a political poster around which a group would form, which might become threatening. For women of the people, who were less literate than men, this mediated access to writing was often necessary. It occurred naturally in public places, such as streets, cabarets, and workshops—spaces of female sociability, which given the interest in the revolutionary common good, became spaces of reading and political practice.

But solitary reading in private and as far as possible from city noise and the presence of others also occurred in the homes of women of the people. This sort of reading created other, more personal ties between a reader and the text (even if the reader was still obliged to read in a faltering manner out loud). The example of the female cockade merchant Goureau de Servigny testifies "to the plurality of uses of printed matter" in popular milieus and shows the progress of literacy.[46]

Moreover, men and women of the people expected the Revolution to accelerate this progress and place education within the reach of all. "In 1789, the people regained their rights because they wished to educate themselves," asserted washerwomen who listened to the reading of the newspaper in a cabaret.[47] The sansculottes were perfectly aware of the power of knowledge, and one of their most cherished demands was that education be accessible to everyone. In the society that was to be born from the Revolution, education, "necessary for all" (Declaration of Rights of 1793), should no longer be a privilege reserved for the wealthy. "The true patriot does not know how to speak well, but fifteen years from now, our children will be well educated" asserted the female spectators of a popular club.[48] And most of the women who addressed the Convention asked in

46. Chartier, "Les Pratiques," p. 155.
47. Police report of 22 Pluviôse Year II.
48. Police report of 3 Pluviôse Year II.

their petitions that it "concern itself immediately" with the organization of national education.

While waiting for this future that they hoped was close but that remained always too distant, female citizens remembered speeches, slogans, and important principles from assemblies and the reading of newspapers. Thus they had knowledge, even if at times vague, of the problems posed by the Revolution as they were presented by great speakers or journalists. Even though they did not always have a high level of education, they were capable of analyzing these problems or at least reflecting on them and were not the political minors described by Fabre d'Eglantine and Amar on 8 and 9 Brumaire Year II. Perhaps they were "less enlightened in principles" than a Convention member or a revolutionary commissioner, but they were emphatically not "less enlightened in principles" than the average grassroots sansculottes. Some women, whose testimonies should be read with caution because their statements were sent from prison in order to ask for their freedom, indeed claimed that "political affairs are above [their] heads," that they were too "simpleminded" to talk about politics because they did not know how to read or write.[49] We find these same arguments of defense in the dossiers of men who were incarcerated. As a whole, glutted with speeches, capable of conceptualization, and conscious of the stakes of the Revolution, women of the people were no more politically ignorant than the men of their milieu and certainly were not manipulated masses blindly obeying the slogans of counterrevolutionaries or extremists, as they have too often been portrayed. In order to understand the politicization of the Parisian female popular class and their political awareness, which might at times seem astonishing and appear exaggerated by the historian, one must consider the political culture acquired by female citizens. Historians tend to perceive the speeches, the articles, and the political texts of a revolutionary leader in themselves, as parts of the political and philosophical thought of a man such as Robespierre, Marat, or Saint Just, or of a group such as the Girondins and the Montagnards. This absolutely necessary process must not make us forget that all these texts that historians study and dissect were listened to daily during the Revolution and were studied and dissected by washerwomen, dressmakers, and so on who were sometimes illiterate but, let us repeat, perfectly capable of perceiving the texts' meanings and scope.

And their reading enabled these women to clarify and shape their aspirations, which were identical to those of men.

49. A.N., F⁷ 4655 d. R. Couppe, F⁷ 4757 d. Lafocarde, F⁷ 4725 d. Gilbert.

10 Political *Mentalité* and Behavior of Women of the People

EGALITARIANISM AND POPULAR SOVEREIGNTY

"There Are No More Kings and We Cut off the Heads of Those Who Wish to Create Them"

Women of the people shared with men a "fundamental egalitarianism" that was characteristic of the popular *mentalité*.[1] Like all sansculottes, their egalitarian spirit, mixed in many cases with a lively sense of dignity, was concerned above all with the necessities of life. Equality first had to show itself concretely at this level, and money should not permit one table to be better supplied than another. "People talk about equality," said women who were indignant at how butchers preferred to wait on cooks, "and yet the money of poor unhappy ones like us can buy only the leftovers of the rich?"[2] The female sansculottes did not demand only "equality of the necessities of life" but also equality of pleasure. Women of popular milieus, like men, were offended that some people possessed more than others. One person could afford to light up his windows while a female dressmaker had to sleep in darkness. Men and women who differed from others by their fine and shimmering fabrics, their luxurious and well cut clothes, provoked bitterness that turned rapidly to anger.

Albert Soboul can thus present the Parisian sansculotte as someone who wanted to share all goods and wealth, whose "irrational and so to speak basic reaction is ... to covet what he does not have."[3] All ostentatious luxury,

---

1. Albert Soboul, *Les Sans-culottes parisiens en l'an II. Mouvement populaire et gouvernement révolutionnaire, 2 juin 1793–9 thermidor an II* (1958; reprint, Paris: Flammarion, 1973), p. 457.
2. Police report of Bacon on 16 Pluviôse Year II.
3. Soboul, *Les Sans-culottes parisiens*, p. 461.

all signs of economic and social superiority, offended and caused resentment and a desire for social leveling and redistribution of goods. Clothing, appearance par excellence, to which women were particularly sensitive, was one of the privileged targets of these abrupt explosions of fury spurred by inequality in a country that wished to define itself through equality. On 9 Brumaire Year II (30 October 1793), "a woman calling herself a Jacobin" shouted at another woman, "You have a beautiful negligée there, but wait, before long, if you have two, you will give me one, that is how we understand it; it will be the same with every other thing."[4] On 5 Germinal Year II (25 March 1794), the informer Mercier saw a woman pursued by a female fish merchant who wanted to take one of her petticoats and who assured her that "those who have two petticoats must give one to those who don't have any."

Egalitarianism did not only inspire a spirit of covetousness. Those who believed they possessed more than necessary were ready to give their belongings up, as the many gifts sent by women to the Convention demonstrate. In one example among others, the female "French Republican," Ducimetière from Vesency, "regarding it a duty of the citizen to donate his superfluity to those who have need of it," offered her present and future savings to the Convention on 25 August 1793.[5]

Many sansculottes thought that the nation's possessions were the people's property and belonged to each of its members. National goods should not be sold to the richest but divided among all, affirmed a militant woman, the wife of Chalandon, who "hoped indeed to receive her share."[6] Even more women, whether they were militant or not, considered all national property to be collective property, to which they believed they had a personal right. Ordered by the guard to leave a line outside a bakery or to break up a gathering, these women combined the "right to national property," equality, and liberty and retorted that they were on "the pavement of the Republic," "the pavement of the nation," and thus that no one had the right to drive them away and they were free to stay there just like the national guards.[7] Workers in spinning workshops who felt that the workshops, which were first municipal and then national properties, belonged to them, also illustrate this belief.

4. A.N., DXLII no. 11.
5. A.N., C 271 d. 667, p. 3.
6. A.N., F7 4637 d. Chalandon. See appendix 3, "Portraits of Militant Women," in this volume.
7. A.N., F7* 2517 f. 265, F7 4771 d. Reine Leblanc, F7 4733 d. Grimont.

All privilege, whether from money or social position, was intolerable to these women. The preferential treatment enjoyed by some prisoners was particularly resented, especially in periods of food shortages, and played a significant part in the frequent threats of massacre in the prisons. "The sansculotte lacks meat, while rich prisoners have it delivered to them in prison" grumbled women in the galleries of a popular club on 8 Ventôse Year II (26 February 1794). "Where is equality? Would as much be done for a simple female merchant?" muttered women when the Brissot family, who were authorized to walk through Paris under the escort of a guard, passed by. It was "not only contrary to regulations but also to equality," complained the director's wife, when a countess imprisoned at the Salpêtrière had a woman servant and an individual room with a fire, while the guards slept in a small unheated dormitory.[8]

The "bad temper" felt by women toward the commissioners responsible for overseeing the sale of commodities arose partially from the fact that commissioners were waited on first. In Nivôse Year III (January 1795), the female helmetmaker Gabrièle Normand said to the daughter of one of these commissioners, who had gone impertinently ahead of all the others, "You should not have more privileges than others, you will sample the line," and replied to the father of the young lady who reprimanded her, "At present there are no more kings, and we cut off the heads of those who wish to create them. We are all equal and your daughter is not more important than I am."[9]

Women's understanding of social oppositions often seemed confused. Nevertheless their antagonism against the aristocracy was always expressed very clearly. For example, a female citizen asserted about the men accused of having wanted to help Marie Antoinette escape: "I wish that all these knaves were skinned alive, for these villains who are of the people like us, who should seek to kill all conspirators, are a thousand times more guilty than the nobles who are guillotined because they fight for their cause that they believe is good, just as we must fight for ours." Many times we find this idea that it was "quite natural for the nobles to support a [political] body

8. Police reports of 8 Ventôse Year II and of 27 September 1793; A.N., F7* 2517, p. 189.
9. A.N. F7 2524, p. 80.

and its system."[10] Conversely, the Revolution was associated with the people, at once its beneficiary and its privileged actor, and nearly invincible.

But who was this "people" who rose up against the aristocracy? They were no longer the Third Estate of 1789 but the "unhappy ones," the "poor," the "small ones," who rebelled against the "fat ones," the "rich." The terms were rarely more precise than this. However, the most proletarian individual had a confused consciousness of an opposition that arose through the world of work. Thus Madeleine Devaux, a young worker in the Jacobin spinning workshop, was dismissed for having said that "the heads [of the workshop] should be guillotined," and the female citizens Decloux, the wife and daughter of a mason who worked by the day, said they "were no more Jacobin than all the other wives of workers."[11]

If the class consciousness of the women of the people remained vague, their class hostility against the wealthy bourgeoisie was acute. Men and women often grouped the bourgeoisie with the aristocracy. After having partially eliminated "the noble aristocracy," it was necessary to eliminate the "bourgeois aristocracy." "He was rich, that was enough," said a woman about a guillotined man when the crowd did not know the reason for his condemnation.[12] In all periods of political and economic crisis, this hostility was pushed to its extreme point.

First noble aristocracy, then bourgeois aristocracy, and lastly mercantile aristocracy: the principal enemy of women of the people remained above all the merchant. His person symbolized all the evils, fears, and resentments of popular revolutionaries. He was counterrevolutionary, a monopolizer, scornful toward the poor and servile toward the rich. This familiar figure concentrated hatreds inspired by all opponents of equality. Often the sansculottes reacted as consumers. Because the sexual division of labor made women responsible for feeding their families, they confronted daily these "leeches of the people," and often the most violent remarks about merchants fell from women's mouths. Women considered merchants to be the successors of nobles. "When we are finished with the former nobles, we will have to deal with the merchant class, and so on and so forth," asserted the wife of Fargeaire.[13] They were rogues and monsters, whom it was necessary to "coerce by force" because their patriotism was "devilishly suspicious." It was even necessary "to purge ourselves of them," for the people "will not

10. Police reports of 27 Nivôse Year II and of 26 September 1793.
11. See "Women at Work" in this volume, and A.N., F⁷ 4665 d. Decloux.
12. Police report of 22 Nivôse Year II.
13. A.N., F⁷ 4702 d. Fargeaire, F⁷ 4711 d. Fragère.

be happy until they go to the guillotine" and the people's safety "depends on their punishment."

To overcome the lack of goodwill of the nobles, the rich, or the merchants, who were opposed to the fundamental egalitarianism of the popular masses, women and men of the sansculottes emphasized the natural rights of the people, which were guaranteed by the Declaration of Rights. These rights included the right to work and to assistance, for "society owed the necessities of life to unfortunate citizens," and the nation should not abandon its most deprived members. They also included the right to education, a means to achieve the real equality rejected by many of the wealthy and to partially reduce social inequalities based on fortune.

Some women aspired to improve the political and social status of women, but this was far from being a characteristic demand of the female popular masses. The acute sense of equality by women of the people did not appear to be affected by their place in society. Some women asserted that they no longer wished to be the "slaves" of men and demanded more rights for women, but they did not preach total equality between men and women. Feminism as we know it did not motivate the female popular masses. It was not part of their *mentalité* and was absent from the aspirations expressed by most women. Should we then conclude that it played no part in their egalitarianism? As we have seen throughout the year 1793, these issues were more complex. Female militants integrated a rethinking of male-female relationships into the framework of politics, which—when they applied to themselves revolutionary principles such as those inscribed in the Declaration of Rights—led them finally to imagine an equality between men and women.[14]

"We Are Sovereign"

An attachment to the notion of popular sovereignty constituted the second characteristic of the *mentalité* of women of the people. For them, the people were the sole and true Sovereign. Public deputies and officials were only its subordinate agents, as a female sackmaker said, or its assistants, as Robespierre would have said. The rights inherent to sovereignty, as they were understood by the sansculottes, took shape when the people deliberated in their general assemblies and when they bore arms. Possessing neither of these rights, women were partially rejected from the Sovereign People. This creates the fundamental ambiguity that underlies all their

14. See "Sexual Difference and Equal Rights" in this volume.

participation in the revolutionary movement: as members of the social body but theoretically excluded from the constituent political body, female citizens were not entitled to complete citizenship. They tried on several occasions to overcome this contradiction and to restore rights inherent in popular sovereignty. Thus in July of 1793, when their acceptance of the Constitution made them part of the Convention, women attempted to reappropriate the right possessed by the Sovereign People of sanctioning laws. This also explains the essential and constant demand up to autumn of 1793 for the arming of women. Women's rights and popular sovereignty appeared tightly linked.

Sharing with men an attachment to popular sovereignty, women came to the same conclusions: control and dismissal of elected officials, and supervision of public officials. The Revolutionary Republican Women became famous in particular for their fierce demands on this subject. But these ideas did not belong only to a conscious minority, and if the Revolutionary Republican Women, a political club, used them to establish a political program, they were strongly rooted in the entire female sansculottes movement—and even, in a perhaps more confused fashion, in the entire female popular masses. Let us recall the example of the female citizen Auxerre, a sackmaker in the municipal store of basic goods, who affirmed in Pluviôse Year II "that the employees and the administrators having been appointed by them, appointed [by the] Sovereign People," they "were only their agents, and that it was rather astonishing that the Sovereign People lacked wood, when its agents were abundantly provided with it." This very concrete conception of popular sovereignty reinforced here the egalitarian tendencies of this worker and serve to explain her demands about working conditions. The notion of the sovereignty of the people was applied to all areas of political *and* social life. A founding principle of the Republic, affirmed in the Declarations of Rights, it was an active principle for female citizens, at once cause and effect of their different demands. For this reason, even though they were excluded from the political rights inherent in sovereignty, women were profoundly attached to these rights and referred to them.

Pushed to its limit, the popular conception of sovereignty ended naturally in an affirmation of the right to revolt, "the ultimate recourse of the Sovereign People" if they were betrayed by disloyal representatives.[15] When the people rose, they represented the law, and deputies should yield. During the insurrections of the Year III, several women insisted to the au-

15. Soboul, *Les Sans-culottes parisiens*, p. 542.

thorities, "We are the Sovereign People." The contradiction we have already evoked assumes all its strength here. During the insurrection, women were part of the Sovereign People, but once it regained its rights, women were denied participation in the Sovereign People. In addition, as soon as the rebellion entered the framework of sansculottes organizations and the revolutionary crowd became the Sovereign People deliberating in general assemblies or taking up arms, women were again pushed to the margins, such as in August 1792, May 1793, and 2 Prairial Year III.

Some women claimed that a dictator was necessary, a leader to save the fatherland. It is impossible to know if these affirmations, uttered by a very small minority, resulted from a reading of Marat or, more likely, from a regret for royalty. But in general women stood out by their hatred of small or great "tyrants." Royalty had been abolished, and a republican woman could not endure the reappearance of "tyranny" at any level. In the final period of the revolutionary government, Robespierre was accused by certain sansculottes women of acting like a tyrant. The same accusation was often made against the commissioners in charge of overseeing distributions. On 22 Germinal Year II (11 April 1794), the wife of Filhastre, who complained bitterly of the shortage of basic necessities, was admonished by a commissioner and responded "that he was just an imbecile and that he wanted to be a tyrant, and that no one had the right to do this." Arbitrariness and contempt were just as insupportable to women, because these qualities should no longer exist. Arrested and led to the revolutionary committee, the wife of Filhastre insisted that she "preferred death to being treated with ignominy." On 29 March 1793, a woman asked the guards the reason for an arrest. When they told her that this was none of her business, "she said that it was not a period when arrests like this could take place."[16]

Every sign that recalled the supposedly outmoded Old Regime was shocking, whether it concerned the arbitrary "despotism" of authorities or the attitude and appearance of the former nobles. For example, Marie Bourdon lodged a complaint against a citizen who, during a dispute, responded "impertinently and with an air like those of the Old Regime."[17] Here we see the egalitarianism of the sansculottes who did not allow any sign of superiority, and in particular any sign of contempt, in social relations. Any reminder of royalty was to be banished, even in the small events of daily life, as a momento of an epoch when inequality was the rule and when the people were deprived of their sovereignty and their rights. In January 1794,

16. A.N., F⁷ 4707 d. Filhastre. A.P.P., AA 90, 29 March 1793.
17. A.N., F⁷ 4774³⁰.

male and female citizens who had the happiness of finding the bean in their piece of cake (a French custom on Epiphany) called themselves the best patriots or sansculottes of the group rather than kings.

During the Year II, the Montagnards' plan for society founded on natural right corresponded to these aspirations of the popular masses—aspirations of women as well as men, who were not only attached viscerally to their rights, but whose very thought rested on the notion of right. On the one hand, this double movement confirmed the Montagnard legislator in his wish to establish natural rights in society. On the other hand, it strengthened the aspirations and demands of women and men of the people who, during the Year II, relied on the Declaration of Rights and on the law. As living principles in popular milieus, they had to be both effective and applicable, as much as possible in the present society, and not remain a dead letter in the present to be applied only to a more or less distant future. This caused the impatience of the popular masses and their irritation at the conduct of authorities or leaders that they sometimes thought was tyrannical. Things were not supposed to be the same as before.

From this feeling, which mixed social and political aspirations, arose the behavior of female citizens. Everyone who rejected the new state of things, regretted the Old Regime, or opposed equality by their political or commercial practice was a harmful enemy who must be eliminated in order to ensure the common happiness. This attitude created firm support for the Terror, distinguished by the cult of the guillotine and frequent denunciations. It also brought about the ardent patriotism of most female citizens and their revolutionary behavior, as they aspired to destroy the opponents of a new world and, at the same time, construct it with their personal conduct, their words, and their belief.

PUNISH ONE'S ENEMIES AND DEFEND THE REVOLUTION
"Saint Guillotine"

Women of popular milieus were fervent supporters of the Terror, which they considered a way to combat the escalating prices of daily life. Housewives ceaselessly demanded "terrorist" measures against the merchants, such as home searches and the enforcement of the maximum. They placed great confidence in the guillotine, like the woman whom Bacon heard say on 26 Nivôse (15 January): "The merchants of Paris are not worth two sous. But they should beware! Saint Guillotine is here!" On 5 Ventôse Year II

(23 February 1794), the police spy Grivel wrote, "The least educated part of the people believe only the merchants and the butchers are responsible for their wrongs; they say that if a good number were guillotined, this example of severity would bring back abundance."

Female citizens did not reserve the guillotine for the exclusive use of merchants. It would also enable them to get rid of all the enemies of the sansculottes. On 11 Nivôse Year II (31 December 1793), women wondered, "What? Won't a time arrive when we can guillotine all the kings?" A female linenworker wished to lead "the last of the so-called gentlemen" to the guillotine.[18] The population, especially women, placed an almost mystical confidence in the guillotine, which became the protective "saint" of the Revolution. The informer Pourvoyeur noted that on 13 Pluviôse Year II (1 February 1794), "the people" said that "the guillotine has acted and performs more miracles than Saint Geneviève has ever done and has even performed more miracles than all the saints in the calendar, without including those still to come."[19] On 26 Ventôse, he wrote, "There is good reason to say that only this saint can save us." Contemporaries noticed that this "cult" was predominantly female: the informer Pourvoyeur commented on 26 Pluviôse (14 February) that people were generally tired of the guillotine, but "it is surprising, it is said, the extent to which women have become ferocious. Every day they attend the executions."

Women's relation to the guillotine has been the subject of much discussion. An entire counterrevolutionary historiography has emphasized it and made this "ferocity" into the very essence of the Revolution. Rejecting this coupling of revolution and the ferocious woman as mirror-image monsters, historians have preferred to see in the parallel that contemporaries drew between women and the guillotine a reflection of masculine *mentalités* that associated women and softness, reserving violent death to the "warrior," to the "combative sex," and were thus shocked by the violence of women. In addition, this association made it possible "not to reject barbarism as something exterior to the human being, but to confine it to the female," to "the other," the "foreign woman."[20] These explanations are not groundless and we can only agree with them. But these analyses concern the representa-

18. Police report of Bacon on 11 Nivôse Year II and A.N., F⁷ 4774⁸⁶ d. M. Raimbaut.

19. Saint Geneviève prevented enemies from entering Paris, just as the guillotine eliminated the enemy from the revolutionary body.

20. Arlette Farge, *La Vie fragile: Violence, pouvoirs et solidarités à Paris au XVIIe siècle* (Paris: Hachette, 1986), pp. 218–223 (on female spectators of executions in the eighteenth century). L. Devance, "Le Féminisme pendant la Révolution," *Annales historiques de la Révolution française* 229 (July–September 1977): 341–376.

tion of a fact. The archives remind us that this fact was a reality: a large number of women were present in front of the scaffold. We cannot study only male discourse, as convincing as it may be, and thus dismiss a question considered troubling by the standards of twentieth-century *mentalités*. What is interesting here is not whether women were more or less "ferocious" than men but why the cult of the guillotine seems to have been predominantly female—even if as we read the documents we remember that these are representations by men.

Parisian women valued the executions, not always as the death of men, but for what the executions represented: the annihilation of the enemy. We cannot deny that the guillotine was itself a spectacle. But let us not forget that this machine was a novelty that performed for the first time in 1792 and was adopted by humanity. Unlike the executions of the Old Regime, which were long, painful, and differed according to the social rank or the crime, the guillotine shortened the sufferings of the condemned and marked the equality of citizens before the law.[21]

The freedom of movement of women of the people is one explanation for their presence at the foot of the scaffold, as it is for their attendance in the galleries of the revolutionary tribunal, city hall, or the Convention. The executions were almost inseparably part of "other street events" that women, the privileged occupants and passersby of the street, encountered on their routes. Studying the executions of the eighteenth century, Arlette Farge put forward the hypothesis "that one did not 'attend' an execution, but that one achieved there a normal, existential gesture, that of experiencing given events with others, in the very places where social reality was constructed and created."[22] The wife of Périot confirms this when, accused in Prairial Year III of having rejoiced at the sight of the condemned, she responded that "when people were led to their execution, she, like many others, had gone there to see, but had never shown either joy or sorrow."[23]

However, this interpretation does not enable us to understand the why of "terrorist" words or attitudes. During the Year III, many militant women, who were called "the furies of the guillotine," were reproached for "complaining often during the reign of Terror about the small number of people guillotined" and of asserting to whoever would listen to them "that all will not go well until there are permanent guillotines at all the cross-

21. Daniel Arasse, *La Guillotine et l'imaginaire de la Terreur* (Paris: Flammarion, 1987).

22. Farge, *La Vie fragile*, p. 213.

23. See appendix 3 in this volume.

roads of Paris." The case of the wife of Lance is interesting; she acknowledged that she was delighted "because she had been a true believer" when the carts of the condemned passed by her home. According to her denouncers in the Year III, she watched them with the help of a spyglass as long as possible and applauded when there were many—"There's a good crop today"—and grumbled when there were few: "That's all there is; it's not worth going." She allegedly even offered her services to pull the rope of the guillotine.[24] We could produce many examples of "bloody" words like these. There were many in the dossiers of people arrested in the Year III (1795). In fact, the anti-Jacobin denouncers of the general assemblies of Prairial Year III emphasized these kinds of attitudes and remarks, exaggerating them or inventing them if necessary to give life to the figure of the "drinker of blood."[25] But we cannot deny that they corresponded to reality, for even in the Year II women were accused by their opponents of "delighting that the guillotine went at a swift pace."

We should not consider these words with our twentieth-century *mentalité*. We must recall the habitual violence at the close of the eighteenth century and the violence present in the living conditions of lower-class women. The entire populace's sensitivity was different then, and if some women perceived executions as repulsive and terrifying spectacles that they preferred to avoid, they were isolated examples. Not that others were bloodthirsty, as the denouncers of the Year III wished to prove. But the majority of the population, whether from popular milieus or not, even men or women who disapproved of the condemnations for political reasons, did not feel this type of physical revulsion—which does not mean, as Farge has emphasized, that the daily spectacle of death only caused indifference.

The informer Perrière expressed personal reflections on this subject in his reports.[26] He indicated that women fainted at the sight of the guillotine or the carts of the condemned. Only women had this response: here is the bipolarization of women-violence versus women-softness-kindness, women monsters versus women angels. One of the fainters was a young girl, whose mother explained her reaction by the fact that she had involuntarily attended an execution one day when she had her period. Since that day, she could not see the scaffold without fainting. Thus her mother felt it

24. Ibid.

25. Dominique Godineau, "Buveur de sang, sang, sanguinaire (an III)," *Dictionnaire des usages socio-politiques (1770–1815)*, fascimile 1, ed. P. Goujard (Paris: Klincksieck, 1985).

26. See in particular the reports of 8 and 17 Ventôse Year II.

necessary to explain her sensitivity by referring to a physiological state in which women are considered more sensitive and subject to extreme reactions, and when, more than at any other moment, they represent "the other," those beings that are foreign to the domain of reason.

These women, Perrière noted, were suspected by witnesses of being aristocrats or relatives of *émigrés,* and no one thought "that this was the natural effect of the sensitivity of certain temperaments." Then he asked that this not be held against the people, whose long string of misfortunes made them see aristocrats everywhere. In addition, he continued, "not everyone is susceptible to this exquisite sensitivity that faints at the sight of pain, whatever the object, nor to the philosophy that, throwing a general regard on men, pity them equally for all the wrong that they have done to themselves so wantonly because it is so easy for them to avoid this. If there is on earth such a people, they would be the victims of other nations, unless all nations resembled them."

Perrière put his finger on an essential aspect of the problem. The country undergoing revolution is at war with almost all of Europe, and during civil war it is surrounded and even populated in part with enemies—and we know well all the importance of the concept "enemy" in the revolutionary *mentalité.* Let us recall here that, in August 1793, the development of the slogan "put the Terror on the agenda"—a Terror that did not limit itself to executions, which were only one of its features—was part of the desire to turn the terror of the enemy against itself. All those accused of rejoicing at executions only did so because these were the executions of traitors, of conspirators—or so they believed—the enemies of the people's rights, who sought to destroy the Revolution in which the people had placed all their hopes for a better existence. The female citizen Boudray gives a perfect account of this attitude. In two letters addressed in the Year II to the Jacobins, she asserts, "It is now or never that the Terror should be the order of the day. If you weaken for an instant the public good will be lost. Patriots will soon have their throats cut and those men whom we are supposed to pity will not tire of shedding the purest blood of the Republic. . . . We can . . . enjoy perfectly [the happiness of all] only when our enemies are all crushed."[27]

This desire for preservation, accompanied by a fear of plots and a wish for vengeance, drove some female citizens to demand more executions.

27. See appendix 3 in this volume.

Although it does not come from a woman of the people and does not concern the guillotine directly, the opinion of the wife of the Montagnard deputy Jullien de la Drôme on the massacres of September 1792 is interesting. This woman, whose sensitivity was profoundly shocked and horrified by what had just occurred in Paris, nonetheless accepted massacres and wrote on 2 and 3 September to her husband: "No barbarous humanity. The people have risen, the people, terrible in their fury, to avenge the crimes of three years of the most cowardly betrayals. . . . I weep, but I cry 'France is saved.' . . . The Prussians and the kings [who have forced the people to act atrociously] would have indeed done a thousand times worse. . . . This bloody day has saved patriots from a new Saint Bartholomew."[28]

The aforementioned reports by the informer Perrière, which demonstrate sentiments similar to those of Jullien de la Drôme's wife, let us understand how the population regarded the guillotine. Perrière placed himself in the group endowed with "exquisite sensitivity," and yet he approved the executions. His attention was not focused, as ours would tend to be, on the execution as a spectacle of a person's death, which he did not enjoy. He introduced another dimension he felt was necessary, a political dimension: the defense of the Revolution. This attitude was not limited to Perrière, a police informer and a committed journalist. It was not so much the pleasure of seeing human blood flow that drove a predominantly female crowd to the foot of the scaffold (indeed, the majority of spectators could not actually see the execution)[29] but the desire and the need to make sure concretely and visually that their enemies were defeated and punished, that the "people" remained the strongest. Ultimately, it was not the blood of a man or a woman that the spectators saw, but the blood of the counterrevolutionary enemy. The historian Daniel Arasse has noted that only the "political guillotine" attracted the crowd, whereas the "ordinary guillotine" did not have the same success.

This political meaning that the spectators inserted between themselves and the guillotine was particularly important for women. Here we can see one reason for their attachment to the guillotine. Men organized in the national guard had a hold over politics thanks to their arms. When they searched merchants' homes or arrested suspects, they could verify—or at least believe they verified—that measures of the controlled economy were

28. *Journal d'une bourgeoise pendant la Révolution, 1791–1793, publié par son petit-fils Edouard Lockroy* (Paris: C. Lévy, 1881), pp. 287–308.

29. Arasse, *La Guillotine*. On alleged acts of cruelty, this author notes that when a clumsy executioner inflicted suffering on the condemned, the crowd grew angry.

enforced and that plots had been foiled. Thus, when Jacques Roux asked on 25 June 1793 for the prohibition of speculation on exchange and the death penalty against monopolizers, measures that female citizens had long demanded, he assured the Convention members that "the sansculottes with their pikes will execute your decrees." The male sansculottes exalted in Saint Pike, symbol of popular strength. But, even if at times women were armed with odds and ends, the pike remained a masculine attribute, and female citizens never had the possibility of making sure by this means that revolutionary laws were being enforced. The guillotine was their substitute for the pike—a passive verification, certainly, but the only possible replacement for a weapon that they were denied. If men divided their veneration between Saint Pike and Saint Guillotine as symbols of popular strength, women privileged the cult of the second.

But this is not the whole story. Studying the political imaginary revolving around the guillotine, Arasse has linked the machine for decapitation to the concept of the people's sovereignty. The guillotine gave the people gathered behind the scaffold "access to the existence" of the body, the political body, the body of the Sovereign People. It was "the performance of the birth of the Sovereign People" and "visually confirmed the terrible omnipotence of universal suffrage."[30] Its political use transformed the crowd into the Sovereign People. Thus the large number of women at executions is not surprising given women's desire to affirm their sovereignty, to become part of the Sovereign People—even if only symbolically, especially if only symbolically, for lack of more concrete possibilities. Prohibited from the legal space of sovereignty, as defined by the rights to vote and bear arms, women placed their trust in all symbolic or imaginary routes that turned scattered individuals or a group into female citizens who were the bearers of sovereignty. For women who were part of the people but who did not possess political rights, being among the political People in whose name justice was rendered at the foot of the guillotine was similar to influencing elected representatives from the galleries.[31] More than the vision of a macabre spectacle, what attracted them was the desire to share sovereignty, to be the Sovereign People. And behind the reproaches that men addressed to women for "wasting their time" at the revolutionary tribunal or for showing "ferocity" before the guillotine was perhaps hidden a reproach for their

30. Ibid., pp. 101, 102, 107.
31. It was "the People who, from below, gave [the executioner] the power to execute," wrote Arasse, ibid., p. 162.

desire to become political beings, female citizens, to participate in the popular sovereignty that men had intended to keep legally for themselves.

Thus, their exclusion from the attributes of sovereignty, and not their "ferocity," drove women in greater numbers than men to the guillotine, just as it led them to the galleries of the revolutionary tribunal. As Arasse puts it, they had at the guillotine the role of "spectator-actors." These women who could not participate in the legal violence wielded by men that was meant to ensure the defense of the Revolution had to account to a masculine society for their "fixed looks" as "furies of the guillotine."[32]

"A Good Female Citizen Must Always Denounce What She Knows"

From 1789 on, denunciations were justified.[33] If silence "is virtuous under despotism, it is a crime . . . under the empire of liberty," wrote a member of the Parisian city government on 21 October 1789. In 1793 and in the Year II, the Republic was threatened on all sides. Denunciation became "the safeguard of liberty," and informers were "the vigilant sentinels of the fatherland."[34] The virtuous denunciation prompts today the same feeling of uneasiness and repugnance as when the guillotine is described as "saint." Men and women of our epoch cannot forget that zealous informers contributed greatly to the mass graves of Nazism. Thus it would be easier to avoid the question of denunciations. However, it is the historian's task to present this aspect of women's political practice without condemnation or glorification, attempting to understand the how and the why of it. Above all, it is important to keep in mind that this act, as questionable as it may appear to us, was considered part of the defense of the rights of citizens against their enemies during the Revolution.

Women were particularly vigilant sentinels. For women who could not bear arms, denunciations were a way to participate in the welfare of the homeland and help their companions who fought against the enemies on

32. Farge, *La Vie fragile*, p. 220.

33. The quotation used as a section heading is from A.N., F[7] 4774[60] d. Roberod.

34. Agier, cited by A. Schmidt, *Tableaux...*, vol. 1, p. 29. Etienne Barry, *Essai sur la dénonciation politique*, 25 July 1793, cited by Soboul, *Les Sans-culottes parisiens*, p. 559. Rules of the popular club of the Bonne-Nouvelle section: British Museum, F.R. 346, 23.

the borders or in the Vendée. Let us recall that the Revolutionary Republican Women originally reserved for women the task of "guarding the interior" by pursuing suspects. In addition, their professional or homemaking activities in the streets of the city enabled women to notice even the most slightly suspicious act.

The archives provide us with 170 denunciations by women from 1793 to Prairial Year III (May to June 1795) but do not include the denunciations lodged by moderate women against the sansculottes in the Year III, nor, of course, those lodged by "professional women," informers who were employed by the police in the greatest secrecy, who slipped into bands of counterfeiters and aristocratic milieus, or prisoners spying on fellow prisoners in the hope of gaining a quick release. More than half of the denunciations (56.47 percent) have political motives. More than a third (37.64 percent) concern basic necessities—contraventions against the legal maximum price, bad quality of products sold, irregularity of weight, refusal to sell to sansculottes, and monopolizing. Denunciations were particularly prevalent during periods of crisis such as the summer of 1793 and spring of the Year II. They disappeared during the Year III, to recur solely about basic necessities during the shortage of Floréal Year III. They often took the form of a complaint lodged against a merchant guilty of fraud or a simple declaration about disturbing facts rather than about individuals. Forty-seven percent of political denunciations did not implicate particular individuals.

The great majority of female informers were not "stool pigeons" acting in the shadows. Only seven remained anonymous, and one of them even proposed to lodge a complaint publicly if necessary. These women usually did not hide their intentions. Before making their deposition, they fought with the person denounced and warned him or her that they would take this step. Their conduct was dictated by immediate anger, or, when it concerned acquaintances, by fatigue over daily repeated counter-revolutionary remarks. Not only was their action overt, but it was prompted by a spirit of publicity that inspired the sansculottes. In their century, the common people had inherited the habit of living together under the eyes of all in broad daylight.[35] Social secrets were not the rule. On the contrary, social facts and acts were characterized by the seal of transparency in popular milieus. Someone who hid in order to act frequently seemed the bearer of a guilty secret because he or she tried to escape from

35. Arlette Farge, *Vivre dans la rue à Paris au XVIIIe siècle* (Paris: Gallimard, 1979); *La Vie fragile*.

Number of denunciations

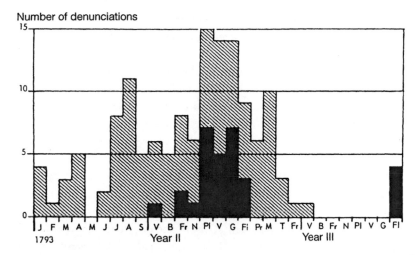

Figure 4.   Dates of 141 denunciations by women; denunciations about basic necessities (black) and political denunciations (shaded) from January 1793 to Floréal Year III.

the gaze of others, a perception that shaped the common people's lifestyle. During the Revolution, when an obsessive fear of counterrevolutionary plots weighed heavily, all secret intrigues, already perceived as abnormal by the popular *mentalité*, took on additional political menace. Thus every female patriotic citizen who worried about the health of the Revolution would report publicly to the authorities anything that others seemed to wish to keep in the shadows: well-dressed citizens who gathered discreetly every evening in a neighboring house, this could indeed be an "aristocratic society"; carts that left by night from a house filled with cloth belonging to the nation; a box that had been hidden under a load of manure; and so on. The police commissioner, the regulator of social life, a familiar character to whom it was customary to disclose private anxieties, served as a conduit at this time for political fears.[36] A female citizen quite naturally took the commissioner even her smallest concern about facts that seemed suspicious (see figure 4).

The archives do not shed light on all the motivations of female informers, but only nine appeared to act out of private vengeance, and only four demanded payment for their denunciation. These statistics should

36. Ibid., both texts.

probably be adjusted upwards, but they nonetheless tend to show that the revolutionary female informer acted more for the common interest than for her own interest.

Female militants, who were more vigilant and completely assured of the validity of civic denunciations, almost provoked them, stringing along suspicious people in order to push them to reveal themselves or catch them red-handed. The militants often had several denunciations to their credit. Thus three female citizens were responsible for at least two denunciations, three women for three denunciations, and one woman for four denunciations. The wife of Boudray, a café owner at the Bains-Chinois, complained in Brumaire Year II of anti-Jacobin remarks made by the customers in her café. In Prairial Year II, she warned the revolutionary committee of her section that "the lives of the representatives of the people were not safe at the Bains-Chinois." In Messidor Year II, she informed on the nocturnal gatherings at a neighboring house. Having heard about a money transaction, the wife of Barbaut pretended to be interested and went with suspects, who were arrested in flagrante delicto. On 19 Brumaire (9 November), a woman whose aristocratic conduct the wife of Barbaut had pointed out two days previously was questioned. Shortly before, having received in error a letter that "announced a conspiracy," the wife of Barbaut had taken it to the revolutionary committee of her section. On 16 Prairial Year II (4 June 1794), she wrote to the Jacobins and drew their attention to the behavior of nuns in charge of the Hospitalières hospital where she had stayed when she was sick. Pretending to be a woman who missed the Old Regime, she had several conversations with the nuns, whom she later accused of making royalist remarks.[37]

When a citizen who had been denounced complained in Prairial Year III, the police commissioner of the Bonne-Nouvelle section opened an inquiry that lets us trace the (not exemplary) mechanics of a denunciation. A member of the Revolutionary Republican Women, Despavaux, learned at the beginning of August 1793 from the citizen Julien and the wife of Charvat, both of whom she had known in the Jacobin galleries, that Auger, Julien's employer, was a monopolizer who hid absolutely essential merchandise and had laid hands on all the hosiery made in Beauce. Julien wrote a rough draft of the denunciation, which the wife of Despavaux had her husband copy. He hesitated at first, fearing trouble,

37. See appendix 3 in this volume.

but after he heard Julien's accusations, he decided to make the copies. Supported by the wife of Despavaux, Julien made his denunciation in a meeting of the Society of Revolutionary Republican Women. There it was pointed out to him "that this was not how such denunciations should be handled." The two denouncers had to sign their declaration on the register of the club. Then it was taken to city hall and to the revolutionary committee of the denounced man's section. A search of his home found nothing. Called to the revolutionary committee, the wife of Despavaux explained that she had made this denunciation because Julien had persuaded her of the truth of his facts. She was released. The wife of Despavaux did not know Auger, and she had no personal reason to have a grudge against him. Believing Julien, whom she thought to be a patriot, she denounced Auger because, she said later, she found it "odious" that in a time "when the people lack everything," he concealed all kinds of merchandise in his store.[38]

The numerous denunciations and their justification by the sansculottes as an act of revolutionary vigilance should not mislead us. All the Parisian population was not composed of sansculottes, and female informers ran the risk, even in the Year II, of harassment, threats, or blows. The role of a "sneak," even a revolutionary one, was not always appreciated, especially by the acquaintances of the denounced person, who would quickly trace the informer. In addition, the authorities, through negligence, incredulity, or repugnance, did not necessarily welcome female informers with open arms, and these women, convinced of the virtue of their action, had to be pugnacious to carry it through to a conclusion.

It is important to recall that arbitrariness was not the rule. One could not denounce here, there, and everywhere, and everyone. If the denunciation appeared serious, it was followed by an inquiry of the section authorities and then, if there was cause, by a judgment, and slanderers were severely punished by the law. The Bonne-Nouvelle club, which considered female informers to be "the vigilant sentinels of the fatherland," had carefully taken measures to avoid "false denunciations, or denunciations based on too flimsy evidence."[39] And when the female informer was an adolescent or a servant lodging a complaint against her master, the authorities increased their scrutiny of the testimony. Denunciations were not always followed by

38. Ibid.
39. See note 34.

arrests, and they were preceded by searches and questioning that could demonstrate the innocence of the denounced person. When a denunciation turned out to be groundless, the female informer was severely questioned by the section authorities in order to determine if she had acted maliciously, thoughtlessly, or overzealously. On 28 Floréal Year II (17 May 1794), the wife of Mouilleron publicly accused a fruit merchant of selling above the maximum price allowed by law. The crowd drawn by the dispute believed her at first, then, persuaded of the falsity of her allegations, turned against her. They demanded loudly that she be led before a police commissioner and "arrested as a slanderer." The commissioner concluded from his questioning "that she was as eager to accuse as she was little concerned to give proof of her accusations." After having heard several testimonies for and against her, the assembled civil committee declared that her "excess . . . appeared to be the result of hatred and a specific revenge or of mental disturbance," a crime under the jurisdiction of the police. She owed her liberty, under the guarantee of two citizens, to her acquaintances who presented her as a model of patriotism.[40] The revoltionary tribunal also took account of the possible personal spirit of vengeance of denouncers. It could even happen that at the conclusion of a trial, the accused who had been washed clean of all suspicion left free, while the denouncers were harassed as "slanderers."

The revolutionary authorities held that denunciation was a civic virtue, a way of defending the Revolution against its enemies. For this reason, patriotic women who wished to behave as good citizens made frequent denunciations. The obsessive fear of plots was often at the origin of their preeminently political act. "Terrorist" attitudes and female informers were only the repressive side of a conduct dictated by love of the Republic and hope placed in the Revolution, which was threatened by enemies opposed to the people's victory. This victory was synonymous with common happiness, which female citizens worked toward through their patriotism.

The Widow's Penny and the Unknown Women of the Battalion

Patriotism—understood in a large sense as love of the homeland and the Revolution—did not only engender civic denunciations. It also expressed itself by a desire to persuade and to contribute to the defense of the country in revolution by oral propaganda, by gifts, or even by physically enlisting in the army.

40. A.P.P., AA 136 f. 90.

Before denouncing someone, female citizens often tried to prove to the accused that he or she was mistaken, and only when that person persisted did an inexpressible indignation drive them to call the guard. Counter-revolutionary statements or behavior completely overwhelmed these women. The wife of a revolutionary commissioner, trembling and stammering because she was so agitated by defeatist remarks, warned her interlocutor that, if he did not hold his tongue, she would denounce him.[41] The wife of Mouilleron, the author of a false public denunciation, is a perfect example of those women then called "ardent patriots" or "exalted patriots." She ceaselessly praised the Republic and did not hesitate when necessary to tussle with those who denigrated it or to have them arrested. Her acquaintances described this wife of a day laborer as "capable of inspiring patriotism in the soul of the coldest men if they could have witnessed . . . the joy with which she made sacrifices for the Republic, or if they had heard her" preach the enforcement of republican laws. Those who were better educated showed their feelings by composing patriotic hymns or by copying them to distribute to their neighbors. These patriotic women adorned themselves with republican attire during holidays, treated their friends to the news of a victory of the troops of the Republic, and so on.

Patriotic female citizens distinguished themselves through numerous gifts poured forth in support of the war effort. The sansculottes often insisted on this aspect of popular patriotism and grew indignant when the most deprived homes bled themselves white for the section collection while richer people only gave ridiculously small sums. Women, who did not fight, made it a point of honor to contribute to the defense of the nation. Although they were sometimes very modest, the gifts regularly received by the Convention represented a real sacrifice for the female donors: several livres, saved from housekeeping expenses or put by to replace a worn-out piece of clothing, but which they preferred to give to the nation who "receives the penny of the widow like the gold of the rich" or to the soldier who knew how to show humanity and bravery. Women always felt this desire to prove themselves as devoted to the Revolution as men were. On 9 July 1793, a porter gave twenty livres per year until the end of the war to the Convention. His wife, "richer in patriotism than in financial means . . . but not wishing to be outdone in patriotism by her husband" sent on her behalf five livres to the Convention.[42] Others gave gifts in kind: shredded linen for dressing wounds, clothing, jewelry, even a portrait of Lepeletier de

41. A.N., F⁷ 4774⁶⁰ d. Osmont.
42. A.N., C 261 d. 561 p. 18 ("Le denier de la veuve"), C 274 d. 696 p. 12.

Saint Fargeau offered by the wife of Allais, a known painter and engraver. These offerings could be anonymous or collective. Although they were poor, the female workers of the sections and the municipal spinning workshops distinguished themselves by their collections. On 18 May 1792, spinners sent 949 livres to the Assembly. Shortly after, the female workers of the Jacobins workshop rushed to participate in a new collection of 297 livres on behalf of the widows of 10 August, each deducting several sous from her weekly salary.

Women's clubs held frequent collections. Dual-purpose evenings of political and civic work took place among knitters in the provinces. While they listened to and commented on the reading of revolutionary texts and discussed local conflicts, they worked to equip soldiers. By March 1793, the Society of Republican Women of Besançon had given 434 shirts, 336 pairs of shoes, 239 pairs of gaiters, 137 pairs of stockings, 30 outfits, not counting jackets, trousers, handkerchiefs, collars, hats, bags, gloves, and several rifles, to different battalions. The female citizens of the Nancy club, after having sent to the army eight boxes of shredded linen, compresses, and bandages, "offered to continue their work until the peace." Worried by the decree of 9 Brumaire Year II that prohibited women's clubs, they asked at the Convention that they still be permitted to meet with this aim and expected as a prize for their zeal an interpretation of the decree permitting them to continue to be part of the Nancy popular society.[43]

We can see in these various gifts from women a spirit of solidarity and a desire to contribute with their poor means to the victory of the Revolution by denying themselves small pleasures, as well as a desire not to be outdone by the men.

Female donors often expressed their regret that they were only able to offer these poor sums and could not, like their male companions, give their lives to the homeland, which they swore however to defend at the risk of their lives if necessary. These were not idle words; they were truly bitter that they could not serve the Republic with arms in hand. The repeated requests of militant women to bear arms is part and parcel of their requests for their political rights. Although their action did not have the same significance as men's military service, women fought at the front, sabers or rifles in hand.

43. A.N. C 252 d. 435 p. 10, C 281 d. 772 p. 14.

A petition entitled *The Departure of 900 Female Citizens from Paris, Who Enlisted, Disguised as Men, to Leave for the Front to Combat the Tyrants of the Nations,* signed by Manette Dupont, demanded from the Convention a decree permitting women to "form a new corps of defenders of the French Republic composed of female citizens."[44] It contained a plan for setting up this corps, which was to be called the Fernig Corps in honor of two famous sisters who were aides-de-camp of Dumouriez and was to be made up of ten thousand female citizens aged eighteen to forty years, organized in one hundred companies of combatants grouped in twenty battalions and five legions. "To the tyrants, to their slaves" would be engraved on the arrows shot by the combatants of the corps of archers, who would each possess in addition a saber and two pistols. The soldiers of the second legion would each be armed with three javelins. Pikewomen, light infantry armed with muskets, and trench workers equipped with two pistols, a hatchet and a saber made up the other legions. In the face of the enemy would fly the mottoes inscribed on the flag of each legion, reminding them that in the country of liberty, women did not fear to fight like men: "In our country, all are equal to defeat the tyrants," "Free Women," "Live free or die," "The Republic or death," "Everything will go well." The uniforms were described in an incredible precision of details. These female combatants would have their hair cut short so that they would lose no time fixing their hair. Their heads would be covered with a helmet of bronze that had "a brim and visor of chamois, plume, and panache tricolored at its end." The petition was not limited to these demands from women warriors. It also asked that the rich be taxed for a fourth of their income, that the clerks of former prosecutors be forced to join the army, and that merchants employ only women as assistants so that these latter, without jobs, would enlist. A little song that followed the petition and was signed by the citizen Poirier asserted:

> Long live the sansculottes,
> And you will wear them;
> Abandon your hearths
> Dressed as lads. Let us march. . . .
> We wear pants
> That's the way women are now.

It is difficult to assess the authenticity of this text, a curious mixture of references to amazons armed with bows, sansculottes armed with pikes, and

---

44. Published in *Les Femmes dans la Révolution*, EDHIS, without reference (beginning of 1793).

"free women" wearing pants. It seems that, even if nine hundred enlisted Parisian women did not stand behind this petition, it is still not a male pastiche but indeed written by a woman and indicative of women's feelings as they had developed in 1793.

Needless to say, Manette Dupont was not listened to. On the contrary, taking as pretext the cohort of women such as spouses and prostitutes who, sometimes accompanied by their children, followed the army and hampered the course of operations, the Convention decreed on 30 April 1793 that all women, combatants or not, would be dismissed, with the exception of washerwomen and cooks necessary for military service. Whatever the petition of Manette Dupont may say, there were surely not nine hundred Parisian women fighting in the Republic's armies. How many were there, then? One or several hundred French women? We can find forty-four, but any real breakdown is impossible, because they were not listed in a census and it is often the chance of the archives that permits the discovery of one here or there.[45] We can only say that the female soldier in the revolutionary armies is neither a myth nor an exceptional character.

Their testimonies did not describe either the female warriors with gleaming uniforms of Manette Dupont or beautiful amazons with hair flying in the wind, but recounted simple stories where heroism became part of daily life. Adolescent girls barely out of childhood, sometimes without family ties, hoped to find a refuge and fulfill their desire for adventure while defending the Revolution, or women departed with a relative, husband, father, or brother. Most were not yet twenty years old. They were called Rose or Marianne, Queen or Liberty, and nicknamed Carefree or Goes with a Good Heart. They were often obliged to hide their gender at their enlistment and served as gendarmes, gunners, grenadiers, riflemen, chasseurs, or mule-drivers. Rose Bouillon, the wife of the volunteer Henry, fought in the sixth battalion of Haute-Saône. "Applauding the patriotism of her husband and wishing to also contribute to strengthening the Republic, she left two children . . . in her mother's care, changed her women's clothing for men's clothing, and went to join her husband at the above mentioned battalion where she enlisted as a volunteer." The wife of Favre, the captain of the gun-

45. The list of forty-four is based partially on my own research in the archives, completed by J. P. Bertaud, *La Vie quotidienne des soldats de la Révolution* (Paris: Hachette, 1983); F. Gerbaux, "Les Femmes soldats pendant la Révolution," *La Révolution française* 47 (July 1904): 47–61; Raoul Brice, *La Femme et les armées de la Révolution et de l'Empire* (Paris: Ambert, no date).

ners in the Contrat-Social section, first joined the army to fulfill her role of nurturer. Having learned that the soldiers lacked everything, she sold her belongings to bring aid to her husband and joined him at Liège on 11 February 1793. There, "love of [her] country put arms in her hands," and the gunners of Contrat-Social named her second in command. In the vibrant declaration of young Marie Morelle, the idea of a world turned upside down is pervasive: "I leave my distaff and my spindles to the one who will be cowardly enough to stay at home, and I'll make sure to take his rifle and his saber in order to fill his place."[46]

These women fought bravely, shared the fate of the troops, bivouacked in the snow, and were present at all the sieges and battles. At Limbach, when her husband died at her side, Rose Bouillon remained at her post and continued to fire until the battalion retreated. The wife of Communeau made three "bandits" from the Vendée bite the dust at Saint-Pierre Chemillé. At Antwerp, the female citizen Marthès seized an Austrian imperial eagle, and at Hondschoote, young Anne Quatresols, fifteen years old, had two horses killed under her.[47] Respected by their superiors and their companions in arms who considered them to be valorous soldiers, these women were sometimes elected officers or noncommissioned officers, such as Lieutenant Ursule Aby, or the noncommissioned officers Pélagie Dulière; Angélique Duchemin, to whom Napoléon III gave the Legion of Honor as a reward for her service record; Marie Schellinck, a young Belgian, who enlisted in 1792 and died in the army in 1802; and Catherine Pochetat, a young Parisian artist who took part in the attack on the Bastille in 1789 and the Tuileries on 10 August 1792. Some were taken prisoner. When the identity of Favre's wife was revealed by chance at the last moment, she was not executed but sent to the enemy headquarters, where they tried in vain to extract information from her about the French army. Having pretended that she did not understand German, she could upon returning to France report the different conversations she had heard among the enemy. Many women were wounded. The female citizen Degressain who returned from the front at the end of the Year II inspired pity in those who met her. She was disfigured, having only one ear, a long

46. *Archives parlementaires* 73, p. 86 (R. Bouillon); A.N., F⁷ 4704 d. Favre, *Journal des débats et de la correspondance des Jacobins*, no. 412; *Moniteur*, XVI, 539.
47. A.N., F⁷ 4652 d. J. Heurtet, wife of Communeau; *Moniteur*, XVII, 169 (Marthès), XIX, 590 (Quatresols). On A. Quatresols, see also the police report of Dugas on 8 Ventôse Year II and B.N., N.A.F. 2662 f. 140.

scar on her cheek, another in the corner of her eye, and scars covering her thighs.

After the decree of 30 April 1793, most of these female soldiers continued to serve for a while as if nothing had happened. We have found only a single woman who immediately yielded to the decree, possibly because, having enlisted under a male first name, she had been "recognized as a woman." Several women asked the deputies for permission to continue their military service. Applauding their bravery, the deputies gave them pensions but denied their requests. In the field, their superiors who appreciated their action—and were usually relatives—did not judge it necessary to dismiss them in accordance with the decree. The captain of Fartier's wife, a gunner in the tenth battalion of the national *fédérés* of Paris, even authorized her in writing on 8 June 1793 to continue her service in his company.[48] Women even fought again in Napoleon's army. Those who returned to their homes did so for completely different reasons than the decree, and at much later dates than April 1793. And when they arrived in Paris, the sansculottes and the Jacobins received these women warmly. On 24 February 1793, the female citizen Ledague, a young girl of twenty years who had served the Republic for six months and won fame at the siege of Lille, stated before the general assembly of the Amis-de-la-Patrie section that she wished to resume military service in the next campaign. Not wishing to set off again without the approval of Parisian "true republicans," she asked them to grant her the "glory" of returning to the front. After showering her speech with applause, the general assembly enlisted her as a volunteer in the section battalion.[49] Even after the decree of 30 April, the Jacobins bowed before the courage of these women and did not hesitate to give them assistance. On 8 Ventôse Year II (26 February 1794), almost one year after the decree, Anne Quatresols, who had enlisted in the cavalry when she was thireen years old and who distinguished herself by brilliant deeds in the battles of Hondschoote, Lille, Aix-la-Chapelle [Aachen], Namur, Maëstricht, and Dunkirk, was welcomed by the applause of the Jacobins, who organized a collection in her honor.

These female soldiers were certainly a minority, and their contribution to the strength of the army was insignificant. Those who fought were young girls or hot-headed women, who often had a relative who was a soldier. Whatever the circumstances that led them to enlist, their motivations

48. A.N., F⁷ 4702 d. Fartier.
49. A.P.P., AA 266 f. 285; *Les Révolutions de Paris* 183.

were the same as those that drove all patriotic women, who were when necessary capable of identical courage. Specific opportunities allowed them to demonstrate their courage, but many women of Parisian popular milieus participated in the same patriotic spirit. When they claimed that they were ready to shed their last drop of blood for the Republic, they should be taken seriously.

The same feeling was behind, on the one hand, their cult of the guillotine and their denunciations, and on the other hand, their gifts and their enlistment in the army. This sentiment was love of the Revolution, the bearer of hopes, which must be defended as much against its external enemies, the "coalition of tyrants" against the Republic, as against its internal enemies, the counterrevolutionaries, aristocrats, plotters, and all the social groups, "the rich," and merchants, who were opposed to that equality without which the Republic was but a vain word.

love of republic

11 At the Margins of the Revolution

COUNTERREVOLUTIONARY WOMEN

At the beginning of the Revolution, royalist brochures appeared in the form of dialogues between Père Duchesne and his wife, who represented "traditional sense," defended nonjuring priests and the king, and considered the Revolution to be the work of Satan.[1] That counterrevolutionary propaganda could have taken this form indicates that part of the population hoped or even accepted as fact that most women would eventually join the camp opposed to the Revolution.

Historians have often adopted this idea. Thus Jules Michelet, although he maintained that "women were in the avant-garde of our Revolution," considered them above all as the first counterrevolutionaries. With their passionate temperament and their greater closeness to nature ("daughters of the sidereal world"), they were, he wrote, "dangerous in politics" and caused revolutions to abort.[2] Public opinion and historiography still clings to this idea that women, or "woman" we should say, is a conservative and a potential reactionary because of her "nature" or because of sociological, cultural, and religious conditions. Counterrevolutionaries were certainly not knitters, but it seems important to evaluate the extent to which this idea about women's nature is justified for the revolutionary period.

The archives show that most Parisian women of the people were, to varying degrees, in favor of the Revolution and that they did not constitute

1. B.N., Lc(2) 584 in 8°, *Grande conversation du Père Duchesne;* Lc(2) 585 in 8°, *Grande colère de la Mère Duchesne;* Lc(2) 586 in 8°, *Grand jugement de la Mère Duchesne.* "Mère Duchesne" was an imaginary character who was used by both the revolutionaries and their opponents.
2. Jules Michelet, *Le Femmes de la Révolution* (Paris: 1854), pp. 20, 180, 236.

a rebellious group. However, there will be no attempt here at quantification or exhaustiveness because the problem posed is not whether there were more revolutionary women or counterrevolutionary women. Instead, we are interested in examining the counterrevolutionaries' dossiers for evidence that women were more susceptible to counterrevolution than men.[3]

For this purpose, we will not dwell on the examples of the former nobles, women of the Old Regime bourgeoisie, relatives of *émigrés,* or those who enjoyed great affluence and chose the counterrevolutionary camp for reasons of class. Likewise, we will not take account of those women who hoped that their royalist statements would take them to the guillotine where they would find a death that they did not have the strength to inflict on themselves. "Misfortune, when it is excessive, does not leave any place for reflection. All means are good for liberating oneself from a life whose weight one can no longer support," asserted one of these "suicides."[4]

Counterrevolutionary opinions were also not necessarily responsible every time a woman sent the Revolution "to hell" and cursed the nation when she found herself on the margins of a society that hounded her for social reasons. Antirepublican incantations by (frequently drunk) prostitutes or female thieves arose more from defiance and anger against society than from a profound hostility against its political system. The same type of "bad temper" was responsible for the counterrevolutionary remarks made by some women during subsistence crises.

Drunkenness, indignation, despair, and "dementia" often occurred together in the same person, whether she was a candidate for suicide, a prostitute, a thief, or a tramp. Authorities and witnesses agreed in recognizing that an interrogated woman who made seditious remarks was in a state of crisis and had lost her reason. Such actions usually referred to a state of psychological instability that resulted largely from deplorable living conditions rather than real counterrevolutionary sentiments. All these women from popular milieus—we will even say marginal backgrounds in order not to use the anachronistic term *lumpenproletariat*—were probably not fervent followers of the Revolution. Without a developed political consciousness, they did not belong to the female sansculottes movement. However, they were not hostile to the Revolution in "normal times." It was in times

3. I have studied 177 dossiers of counterrevolutionaries, found primarily in A.N., series F[7] and W, and in A.P.P.

4. A.N., F[7] 4774[78] d. Poirier called Ribourg.

of political or social crisis that they might increase the popular rank and file of counterrevolutionaries.[5]

The situation was different for those women who, having all their reason at their disposal, regularly flaunted counterrevolutionary opinions. Some women felt both a sentimental and symbolic attachment to the king and his family. The king, in spite of the Revolution and beyond his death, remained sacred to these women. They had wept for the death of the innocent individual and considered him a martyr, whose bits of clothes or locks of hair they kept carefully like holy relics. The less fortunate collected coins bearing his effigy, which they covered with kisses and tears. Most of these women were among the poorest of the counterrevolutionaries; many worked in trades or were paid domestics. Those who were better off added political discourse to their sentiment and sacred devotion. They thought that the government should be a monarchy and refused to acknowledge the legitimacy of the Republic. The deputies were usurpers, and the nation, which they did not recognize, had stolen the late king's goods.

Without supporting royalism openly, women asserted that they detested the Revolution. Hostile to Jacobins and to Montagnards whom they reproached for banning the Girondin deputies, loving blood, and provoking the massacres of September 1792, these women were part of what was then called the "moderates." With unveiled social disdain, they claimed that they were on the side of "decent people," or landowners, and against the "rabble," the "mob," "riffraff," "beggars"—in short, the "sansculottes dogs." These women, who belonged mostly to the middle classes, rejected the popular revolution and the disruption of values that drove the poorest to demand their share of dignity and to occupy the social space that these women wished to reserve for "well-born" people. "There is an order to kill decent people and elevate the mob," asserted one of them, and a female shopkeeper, offended that "at present one saw only the rabble and riffraff," wished for the return of the *émigrés*. The economic question arose when a person with a private income claimed to dislike the Revolution because "one must respect property," and another woman maintained that, as a good "aristocrat," "she would not wrong anyone living on his income."[6]

5. The study of the royalist uprising of Vendémiaire Year IV (5 October 1795) would probably provide interesting data on this subject.

6. A.N., F⁷ 4754 d. Laborderie Rose; F⁷ 4680 d. G. Doublet; F⁷* 2482, 29 Pluviôse and 23 Messidor Year II; F⁷ 4735 d. M. S. Guérin.

At this stage of the Revolution, just as the sansculottes sometimes associated the bourgeoisie with the aristocracy, these women connected the wealthy with aristocrats and rejected the Republic in favor of Old Regime society.

These "female moderates," who were especially expressive during the spring and summer of 1793, applauded Marat's death, boasted that his assassin was a woman, and mourned the failure of assassination attempts against Robespierre and Collot d'Herbois in Prairial Year II. They rejected all revolutionary symbols, from the cockade to the tricolored flag, which were "rags good for wiping one's bottom."[7] They rarely attended section assemblies, but supported moderate offensives and protested conscription or the Left side of the Assembly. On 20 September 1793, at the height of the war of the cockades, the police spy Béraud saw pass on the Boulevard Poissonnière "a large cohort of women . . . vomiting abominable songs against the Jacobins [with the] refrain 'Long live the *muscadins* [youthful opponents of the Jacobins who dressed like dandies].' They wanted, they said, to tear out the eyes of people who approached them." At the end of Frimaire, these women supported the Dantonist Indulgent campaign. On 22 Frimaire (12 December), several women asked, individually or as part of a deputation supposed to represent "the female citizens of all sections," that the Convention release their husbands who were imprisoned as suspects. On 30 Frimaire (20 December), they demanded a commission responsible for examining the motives behind the arrests.[8]

An equally significant number of men shared these ideas and made similar remarks. The opponents of the Revolution, men and women, tried several times to touch the entire female population by sounding chords that were supposed to move them: sensitivity and, in particular, the issue of basic necessities. These attempts were not successful everywhere and never led to a movement of the entire group, but the problems of getting fresh supplies of food could have created a real ferment of popular and female counterrevolution. Women of the lower classes could be driven to counterrevolution by their social responsibilities as housewives. The reports of informers mentioned female "moderatism" in September 1793 and at the end of Pluviôse and beginning of Ventôse Year II (mid-February 1794), two periods when a food crisis intensified a political crisis. The remarks heard by informers linked economic difficul-

---

7. A.N., F⁷ 4644 and F⁷ 4774⁹⁰ d. Chavignot, wife of Rentais.
8. A.N., C 286 d. 840 pp. 12, 16, 20, 21, 22, 25 and d. 843 p. 16.

ties and displeasure with the government. Thus on 20 September 1793, while complaining about the price of commodities, a woman asserted, "If our husbands have made the revolution, we should indeed make a counterrevolution if it is necessary." This is an extreme example. More frequently, consumers' grumbling was less radical, closer to complaints than to threats. "Why didn't they leave us as we were? At least then, we could find all that we wished with money," lamented a woman about the Maubert market on 2 Ventôse Year II (20 February 1794). Her neighbor added, "Ah! Hell! if I did not restrain myself, I would damn the new regime." And women for the most part restrained themselves, through affection for the Revolution. But if housewives were disappointed, if the Revolution could not fulfill the great hopes placed in it, even if it was not, for the time being, synonymous with equality or common happiness, these women, prey to fatigue and weariness, blamed the Revolution for their wrongs but did not really reject it. Women arrested in lines for desiring a king to remedy present difficulties were in a minorty compared to those women who accused merchants of monopolizing and demanded searches of the merchants' homes.

Faced with the public spiritedness of most female citizens, moderates turned to the female merchants of la Halle, who were politically volatile and doubly affected by the problems of the time, as consumers and as workers with nothing to sell. On 29 September 1793, the police spy Latour Lamontagne wrote: "Worry over basic necessities grows each day. Malicious people increase their attempts to incite demonstrations in Paris. The women of la Halle in particular appear overwrought, and if it is necessary to judge by their uncivic and audacious remarks, they are preparing new scenes where they are manipulated into playing the chief roles. A horde of aristocrats' valets even insolently applaud these bold women and provoke them by their remarks." In Ventôse Year II, in the middle of the subsistence crisis, when vegetables, butter, and eggs had disappeared from the markets, the counterrevolutionaries started a campaign aimed at these merchants. On the morning of 12 Ventôse, la Halle was strewn with handwritten leaflets intended for "female citizen merchants." The author, who claimed to work in an administration, emphasized the scarcity of food and asserted that "if the counterrevolution happens, it will come about through women." He invited them to go in the number of twelve hundred to the Convention to demand its dissolution in order "that a head be named instead of seven hundred thieves." This demagogic maneuver failed completely. Even the spy Latour Lamontagne, who was always ready to see behind each woman a potential counterrevolutionary or at best an instrument of the "malevolent people," acknowledged on 15 Ventôse the failure of this activity.[9]

Thirty-six women out of one hundred counterrevolutionaries who were questioned belonged to merchant professions.[10] In their statements, they frequently claim that "they [the nobles, the masters, the rich] were the ones who enabled us to live." Whether there was an abundance of food or the markets were empty, those who owned stores and belonged to a higher level of the mercantile hierarchy openly displayed counterrevolutionary sentiments, but the behavior of small merchants, whose speech and thought did not always coincide, was much more complex.

On the one hand, there was a well-supplied fruitseller whose posh clientele had deserted the small shop for a prison cell. She campaigned among the other shopkeepers for "the party of the masters because they enable us to live" and asserted "that she would rather sell to the rich than to the sansculottes because the rich paid better and the sansculottes did not have the means to pay and were all beggars."[11] This woman truly fought for the cause of her customers and shared their social scorn of men and women of the people. On the other hand, there were six female flower and fish merchants, "fishmongers" from the Place Maubert. On 25 Prairial Year II (13 June 1794), they went to the home of a former noble who had taken refuge at Châtillon, invited him to drink, embraced him effusively while complimenting him on the upcoming return of the ex-nobles to Paris "given that they were the ones who enabled them to live," and added that as good republicans they had made a speech thanking the Supreme Being for having saved Robespierre from an assassination attempt. Then they knocked at the door of patriots from Châtillon, announcing their intention of organizing a holiday in honor of the Supreme Being. Nobles and patriots gave them assignats to get rid of them. We might conclude that this was a trick, bordering on begging, to extort a little money—which was as good to receive from the hand of a noble as from a patriot. But the story does not end here. If we check the collection of representative texts from the sansculottes movement published by Albert Soboul and W. Markov, we will be surprised to note that it includes an address sent in homage to the Convention by these five women in the name

---

9. A.N., W 77 no. 11, 343; reports of Bacon on 14 Ventôse and of Latour-Lamontagne on 15 Ventôse.

10. These one hundred counterrevolutionaries include those whose professions are known and exclude nobles and women in states of crisis.

11. A.N., F⁷ 4680 d. G. Doublet.

of all their colleagues from the Place Maubert. This address repeats all the aspirations of the Parisian sansculottes—the right to work, to assistance, to education, and so on—and asserts that the entire nation will perish "rather than return to the chains it has broken." These female merchants who did not know how to sign their names had certainly neither written, nor dictated this petition with its bombastic style, but they had paid someone to do it, paid for its printing. Are these fishmongers like a two-faced Janus? No, like most of the women from the markets, they were conscious of belonging to the "People," by whom and for whom the Revolution was made, but they were also connected to the privileged classes through business relations. They tried as well as could be expected (apparently rather well in regard to their conscience, and rather poorly according to the revolutionary authorities') to reconcile these two aspects of their existence.[12]

The female merchants of la Halle—the heroines of 5 and 6 October 1789, as they liked to recall, but also the privileged targets of the moderate sirens—occupied a place that was separate from the revolutionary movement. If we believe police informers, these women made uncivic remarks during the period of the food crisis, but their complaints, examples of their legendary outspokenness, were manifestations of acute feeling against the present situation rather than real counterrevolutionary sentiments. Although these women were largely exploited by the counterrevolutionaries, they never entered into any action. These female workers did not place themselves in the forefront of the revolutionary movement. We find few among the female militants, and in the autumn of 1793 they were the fiercest opponents to the wearing of cockades and the Revolutionary Republican Women. But behind their violent physical and verbal demonstrations, which were part of their image as undisciplined rebels, we can discern a certain legalism, tinted even with conservatism. Each year under the Old Regime, they carried their best wishes to the monarch. During the Revolution, although revolutionary extremism frightened them, they were respectful toward the National Assembly. In spite of their virulence during the war of the cockades, they asserted that they would wear the cockade if the Convention decreed it. And the speech of the female merchants of the

---

12. A.N., F⁷ 4632 d. M. Hubert, wife of Camus, F⁷ 4704 d. Ferlen, F⁷ 4722 d. G. H. Girault, wife of Geoffroy, W 46 no. 3073. Arrested shortly thereafter, the women were released on 10 Fructidor Year II. Their petition was published by Walter M. Markov and Albert Soboul in *Die Sansculotten von Paris: Dokumente zur Geschichte der Volksbewegung 1793–1794* (Berlin: Akademie-Verlag, 1957), p. 409.

Place Maubert was filled with sincere respect toward the Convention and its efforts.

Other female occupations were dependent on customers who were hostile to the Revolution. Thus women who created works of luxury directly for noble or ecclesiastical customers had rather marked counter-revolutionary tendencies. Female milliners, embroiderers, lacemakers, or master dressmakers appear in high proportion on the list of counter-revolutionaries (12 percent). In contrast, the female workers of the skilled craft industries, whose occupations also suffered because of emigration, cannot be found among our sample. In these kinds of work, production was organized differently. Female workers did not own their own businesses. Paid by master artisans or dependent on large merchants, they did not have direct contact with privileged customers and thus did not feel that they were on the side of "decent people."

"Like master, like servant" it is said, and the archives do not contradict the proverb. Among our one hundred counterrevolutionaries, we find eleven servants, of whom nine worked for nobles or priests. Finally, we cannot forget the female employees of municipal or national administrations, who make up 5 percent of our sample. We know that most of the managerial staff in municipal spinning workshops was moderate or royalist. The female employees of hospitals, most of whom were former nuns, often displayed their militant royalism shamelessly. For example, the Salpêtrière seems to have been a veritable center of counterrevolutionaries. The "female officials" there subscribed to the newspaper *L'Ami du Roy*, went to the masses given by nonjuring priests, made uncivic remarks, and blamed the patriots. Manon Blanchard, who was a paying boarder at the Salpêtrière, complained on 16 Prairial Year III (4 June 1795) that, as a good republican, she had inspired hatred and was "treated like a criminal" and made an "object of scorn and ridicule." She had been forced to walk completely naked in the courtyard, and the others had hastened to strike her while calling her "a wicked republican," so that she was "within an inch of death."[13]

Although incomplete, this survey from the archives does not let us claim that women of Parisian popular milieus were more attracted than men to counterrevolution. However, several times an image appears that associates men with revolution and women with counterrevolution—just as we have seen another image that associates women with radical patriots. The

13. A.N., F⁷ 4776, Finistère.

apparent contradiction between these two images stems from an idea about and a representation of the two sexes but also illustrates the impasses caused by perceiving women as a whole.[14] When revolutionaries used the generic *women*, they did not mean by this term the groups of women that they associated with counterrevolutionaries or with sansculottes extremists. When a moderate wrote that "if the counterrevolution occurs, it will come about through women," he did not address the entire female population but a very specific group, "female citizen merchants." Our sample does not show that women were counterrevolutionary because of their "female nature." It demonstrates that the counterrevolutionary positions of some women, just as of some men, originated in their given socioprofessional categories.

There remains another motive, which until now we have deliberately passed over in silence, that has often been put forward to justify a possible privileged link between women and counterrevolution: women's devotion to religion. In our search of the records, women's attraction to counterrevolution did not appear with the force habitually given to it: does this mean that during the Revolution, women did not have a special attitude toward religion and the Church?

FANATICS AND "STUPID DEVOUT WOMEN"

The Poor Priests and the Little Statues of the Virgin

Michel Vovelle has emphasized that during the eighteenth century, "dimorphism according to sex" increased in religious practice, with women showing a greater attachment to religion than men. More recently, Timothy Tackett has insisted on the role women played, most often alongside nonjuring priests, in incidents provoked in the provinces by the Civil Constitution of the Clergy.[15] What do the Paris archives have to say on this subject?

We find in the dossiers women who show an attachment to Catholicism.[16] The majority of them (58.3 percent) were arrested for their "fanatical" behavior. They hid nonjuring priests, concealed liturgical ornaments that had become national property, and went to mass or had it said at their

---

14. See "Sexual Difference and Equal Rights" in this volume.

15. Michel Vovelle, *La Mentalité révolutionnaire: Société et mentalités sous la Révolution française* (Paris: Messidor, 1985), pp. 42–44; Timothy Tackett, *La Révolution, l'Eglise, la France: le Serment de 1791* (Paris: Cerf, 1986).

16. Without searching systematically for these women, I have found sixty (not including nuns, who form a particular case).

homes by nonjuring priests. In brief, they only recognized the Church as it had existed before the Civil Constitution of the Clergy of 1791. Young girls raised by nuns, servants of parish priests, devout old maids, and female members of the Paris working classes marked by the influence of convents in their neighborhoods: these women were frequently close to the former clergy. Some missed all of the Old Regime, the king as well as the priests: a rosary and an engraving of the royal couple could both be found in the pocket of a young female linenworker who had been raised by a priest. The wife of Hébert, fifty years old, strongly and publicly condemned Convention deputies because they had voted for the king's death, had "destroyed the poor priests," and wished "to remove God and put rascals [the martyrs for liberty] in His place."[17] Without being this virulent, other women renounced the Revolution because of dechristianization. Religion as they had known it was one of the pillars of their society, and those who wanted to change it, those who set the "sansculotte Jesus" against the priests, were troublemakers without morals or law.

And yet there is no trace of counterrevolutionary sentiments in 15 percent of the dossiers, which sometimes describe excellent patriots who held religious beliefs or practices. In Floréal Year II (May 1794), the wife of Lecreps, a militant regular of the Cordeliers, kept crucifixes, a portrait of Christ, and little statues of the Virgin in her home. "She had never been inspired to fanaticism, she explained, but . . . she had always followed the education that her father and mother had given her, and she would respect and keep forever the little statues of the Virgin because she could not destroy them, given that she had no other God than Liberty of whom these objects reminded her." Likewise, for many women who did not reject the Revolution at all, praying to God remained a daily and important act. And in the galleries of women in the club of Lombards section, it was certain that "God would punish" the moderates.[18]

Because they reveal a variety of religious attitudes, the dossiers do not permit hasty schematization. We must seek traces elsewhere of dimorphism according to sex—for example, in a very beautiful text by the Montagnard deputy Lequinio.[19] Taking an interest in the fate of women in or-

17. A.N., F⁷ 4775²⁸ d. M. U. Thierry de Vienne, F⁷ 4739 d. Hébert.
18. A.N., F⁷ 4774¹⁰ d. Lecreps and report of Bacon on 8 Ventôse Year II.
19. Joseph-Marie Lequinio, *Les Préjugés détruits*, 2d. ed. (Paris: 1793), chapter 14, "Women." I thank Françoise Brunel and Jacques Guilhaumou for pointing out to me the existence of this text.

der to question it and advocate a "civic and moral equality" between the two sexes, Lequinio dedicated two pages out of twelve to religion. Women's religiosity was for Lequinio a given of social life—and of the enslavement of women—and devotion was a female characteristic. He gave as a reason the "sensitivity" and the "need to love" of the "weak sex," for whom it was an "inexpressible consolation . . . to love at least one ideal being." Women "were devout, because they had a great need to love, and this was remarkable especially when their careers faded," when time had spoiled the charms of their sex. He concluded that "[if you wish] to break your chains, . . . above all, learn to escape from the empire of religious prejudices."

Without entering into these considerations, police reports show the same tendency. Although they fail to report a particular attraction of women for counterrevolution, their reading makes forcefully apparent this "dimorphism according to sex." On 24 December 1792, women demanded the celebration of midnight mass. On the Thursdays of 30 May (on the very eve of the anti-Girondin revolt!) and 6 June 1793, ladies of la Halle and "wives of the sansculottes" asked permission for the customary Corpus Christi processions. During the Year II, female merchants of la Halle and elderly women who missed the exterior signs of religion complained about the lack of masses or the closing of churches, and preferred Sundays to "Decadis" (the tenth day of the Republican "week," or *décade*). In Nivôse, women were again at the origin of a petition "based on the Rights of Man" to obtain the freedom to practice their religion.[20] But police informers did not indicate that these attitudes led to counterrevolutionary positions—on the contrary. Hymns to Saint Geneviève, carried by the voice of the song merchant, slipped through alleys and through open windows, and the female merchant abandoned her stall for a moment, the seamstress put off her work until later, the female passerby made a detour, and all crowded around the singer, happy to hear and to hum with him "the tunes of times past." However, if the thoughtless singer started to sing "Geneviève, a countess of great nobility," his audience fled, "as if insulted by an improper expression." When Robespierre fell sick, women prayed for him, convinced that "only God could guarantee the days of this incorruptible patriot."[21]

20. A.P.P., AA 220 f. 227, 30 May, 6 June 1793; AA 173, 30 May 1793; AA 163 f. 19 and 20. Police reports of Dutard on 30 May and 7 June 1793, and of Le Harivel on 2 Nivôse Year II.

21. Reports of Dutard on 17 June 1793, and Bacon on 1 Ventôse Year II.

Police reports make especially apparent the need some women had for religiosity, a need only partially fulfilled by the cult of the Supreme Being, which they welcomed with pleasure to the extent that it permitted them to rediscover elements of their religion while remaining patriots. Speeches in favor of the Supreme Being and against the villainy and hypocrisy of priests were especially appreciated by women. On 30 Nivôse Year II (19 January 1794), the speaker of the day at the former Petits-Pères, who had glorified public spiritedness, religion, and the Supreme Being, received much applause. "We are extremely happy to have come to church to hear the preacher say that it is necessary to recognize the Supreme Being. With such truths one will never stop doing good for his country," rejoiced old women when they left. For many, the churches rebaptized as Temples of Reason remained churches where they went on "Decadi" to listen to secular preachers speak of the Supreme Being. "In the past, one saw in the churches many more women than men. It is the same in these temples of Reason: few men and many women," remarked a police informer on 30 Ventôse Year II (20 February 1794). The most striking example of how some women combined their religious feelings and their patriotism is given by Catherine Théot and her faithful followers.

The Poor Will Triumph

We know how Vadier, a member of the Committee of General Security, used the "Théot affair." On 22 Prairial Year II (10 June 1794), he made the Convention laugh with a spirited report that blew out of all proportion a meeting between inoffensive female mystics and an old woman who took herself for "The Mother of God" (Vadier, by word play, transformed her name Théot into Théos), which he presented as a counterrevolutionary plot by fanatics. On 9 Thermidor, he reported on a probably fabricated letter by Catherine Théot to Robespierre, in which she identified him as the Messiah she expected.[22] Vadier is not what interests us here, but Catherine Théot and her public, those "few stupid devout women" as Robespierre called them on 9 Thermidor Year II.

22. Albert Mathiez, *Contribution à l'histoire religieuse de la Révolution française* (Paris: F. Alcan, 1907); Albert Mathiez, "Les Divisions dans les comités de gouvernement à la veille du 9 thermidor d'après quelques documents inédits," *Revue historique* 118 (1915). G. Lenotre, *Le Mysticisme révolutionnaire: Robespierre et la Mère de Dieu*, 2d ed. (Paris: 1926).

Born in 1706—or 1725—of day laborers in Baranton, near Avranches, Catherine Théot went to work in Paris as a servant.[23] Ever since childhood, she had been fascinated by mystic readings on the lives of Catherine of Sienna and Theresa of Avila. Convinced that she was herself "inspired by God," she practiced various mortifications, such as a belt, garters, and a bed of iron spiked with nails. As a new Eve who would redeem the faults of the first, she had been chosen by God, who spoke to her, to save the world. In the final years of the Old Regime, she gathered around her a small number of followers, most of whom were relatively old people recruited from the milieu of lesser artisans or small shopkeepers from the popular neighborhoods where she lived. Later her neighbors remembered her as a poor old woman who repeated to anyone who listened "that the great and the king would fall, the churches close, priests be destroyed, confessionals burn or be changed into sentry boxes and that the people would prevail over all." She endeavored to convert the priests of several Parisian parishes to her ideas, assuring them that if they did not confess their errors publicly, they would be punished with iron rods. The result was not long in coming. She was imprisoned in the Bastille in December 1779. She remained there for five weeks before being moved to a hospital, which she left in 1782. She was then welcomed into the Rue des Rosiers home of the widow Godefroy, a worker in trimmings for clothes, where she lived until 1793.

She resumed her "lectures," as she called them, and gained a larger audience that included those who were impressed that her past predictions of drastic societal change had been "fulfilled" by revolutionary events. Dom Gerle in particular, a former Carthusian monk and former member of the Constituent Assembly who had been attached in 1779 to another prophetess, Suzette Labrousse, joined the small group of the faithful.[24] The police who searched her home in January and then June of 1793 at the order of city hall described Catherine Théot as "a peaceful old maid" who inspired pity. Catherine Théot and the widow Godefroy moved to the Rue Con-

23. Most information concerning Catherine Théot and her prophecies has been taken from A.N., F[7] 4775[27] d. Théot. I also used the depositions of fifty-nine people who went at least once to see Catherine Théot, which I have found in the archives.
24. Suzette Labrousse, who also heard God order her to reform the Church and pull down the great of this world, left at the beginning of the Revolution to persuade the Pope in Rome, where she was imprisoned as mad in the Castle Saint Angelo. Dom Gerle asserted to the Constituent Assembly that the Civil Constitution of the Clergy was indeed the work of God because Suzette Labrousse had predicted its existence eleven years before. When he was refused a certificate of public spiritedness, he went to his former colleague Robespierre, an act exploited by believers in "the Théot business," who presented it as proof of Robespierre's ties to this group.

trescarpe (Observatoire) where in Floréal Year II she was kept under surveillance by the Committee of General Security, then arrested on the
twenty-eighth (17 May 1794).

Albert Mathiez wrote that reading her religious "doctrine," probably
shaped by Dom Gerle, throws one back "to the heart of the Middle Ages,
during the time of millenarian heresies." Catherine Théot was the mother
of the human race—"the New Eve," the wife of the Holy Spirit, "the
daughter of God, the mother of God, she has the Word of God and pro-
duces God." God had chosen her for the salvation of the human race. She
alone knows His secrets and she will save the world by spreading the
Truth. This depended on the reading of the Holy Gospels in the future and
not in the past. She wrote in March 1793 to Chaumette, whom she wanted
to convert to her ideas, "Rely on this truth that the past is only the figure of the future. In consequence, believe that there has really never been
a Moses, or a Solomon, or a Mary, or any visions, or a Savior, or any Apos-
tle, or a gospel, or a reign of God." All these were only parables announcing what is actually happening or will happen soon. If it is written
in Genesis that on the sixth day God created man in His image, this is not
in the past, for "a thousand years are only one day in the eyes of the
Lord," man is not yet really complete, we arrive only now at the end of
the sixth day and God will finally "give to man the degree of perfection
for which He destines him, both spiritually and corporally." Catherine
Théot was the Virgin who would give birth to the Savior, who is none
other than the Word, the word of God who speaks through her mouth.
This was the "parable of the Virgin": The Virgin had spiritually conceived
Jesus Christ, and Catherine Théot produced "the Word of God," "which
is the same thing."

Thanks to her, God had already lifted five of seven seals that weighed on
the Gospel. When the last was lifted—a "Great Event" that the faithful believed was imminent—the Apocalypse would occur, "restoring . . . the
earth to its original state of beauty and happiness in which Adam had lived
before his fall." Contrary to what the "impious and blasphemous" clergy
pretended, God was not spiteful and vindictive but acted out of "sentiments
of peace." Thus the world would be regenerated in its original beauty, and
all men would be saved and live in great brotherhood.

This Savior who would soon appear prepared the path "by the destruction of all powers and principalities on the earth, by lowering the moun-
tains and raising the valleys (the people), by making the stars (the great)
fall from the sky, by shaking the powers of the skies (the tottering thrones);
and the great Babylon (Rome) who had intoxicated all the Kings of the

earth with the wine of its prostitution (its idolatries, its cruelty and its superstitions) would be treated as it has treated us."

Théot explained these "theories" in meetings of about fifteen people, which were held at the home of the widow Godefroy. At the start there was no ceremonial. People came to hear her, the widow Godefroy, or Dom Gerle read and interpret the Holy Gospels, particularly Saint John, or the homilies of Saint Augustine "to prove that up until then all the doctors of the Sorbonne and all other men had discussed the Gospel in vain." Then hymns were sung. The followers called themselves brothers and sisters, and Catherine Théot "our mother." Near the end of Germinal (mid-April 1794), in anticipation of the imminent "Great Event," Catherine Théot, inspired by God, kissed each newcomer on both eyes, both cheeks, the chin, the forehead where she traced a sign of the cross, and then on the mouth. These were the marks of seven seals of God's light, made to renew God's seven gifts and which conferred "immortality of the body and the soul" to all who received them, assuring them of being among the first to be saved during the "Great Event."

Servants, merchants of both sexes, artisans, their wives or their workers, but also those who had private means, and a doctor, thus received kisses that gave them salvation. Given the fact that three-fourths of the audience were women, there was a great risk that the earth would be populated primarily with women on the day after the Great Event. If these women were no longer in their first youth, they were still not "elderly overly devout women." The male public was distinctly older.[25]

"Those who had been at [Catherine Théot's] home formed two distinct classes: the feebleminded and the curious," a citizen wrote.[26] Except for a small number of female regulars who were absolutely convinced that Catherine Théot gave immortality, women who were questioned about the gatherings said they had gone primarily out of amused or favorable curiosity. With an aura of sacredness from the "fulfillment" of her previous predictions and her stay in the Bastille, Catherine Théot attracted women who had heard of this "phenomenon," whose characteristics were exaggerated by rumor: she was 120 years old; she had been imprisoned for twenty years; priests had tried to poison her; and so on. The rumor that she conferred immortality gave her a public that was not firmly convinced but said to themselves that one never knows, so why deny oneself this protection? Thus sol-

25. The average age for sixteen women was forty-nine and a half years. For three men, the average age was sixty-six years.

26. A.N., W 164 d. Bouteloce.

diers on the eve of leaving for the front went there on their own initiative or were brought by their mothers. Women went there in the hope of protecting relatives who were in the army. And besides, "it must indeed be true that she is more powerful than others, since people ask her for protection."

The announcement that the "Great Event" was close at hand impelled her followers to bring their acquaintances to Catherine Théot. Girault's wife was brought by a female neighbor who assured her "that there was no time to lose, that the moment of general happiness approached, that those who had confidence in it need not die." For many people, curiosity combined with credulousness. And women who were curious, impressed by Catherine Théot and the "good advice" that she lavished on them, occasionally returned. The old woman seemed to possess a comforting and persuasive power. Jeanne Renard had gone to hear her because of the rumor "that this woman greatly comforted people when they were in pain." After going to see Théot, the armsmaking husband of Blasié, who sold leftovers at la Halle, ceased to be an idler who would not leave his bed before six o'clock in the evening and did nothing except fight with his wife; he became a good spouse and worker, and harmony reigned between the couple. These attributes made Catherine Théot loved by her former neighbors, who remembered her with emotion. The seventy-year-old café owner Garin went to see her occasionally to make sure that she had everything she needed, taking her coffee and sugar "because he had heard her say such beautiful words of consolation when speaking to him of God that he had wept."[27]

The "good principles" and "good advice" that Catherine Théot dispensed did not apply only to religious life and private conduct. All those who confessed ingenuously to have gone to Catherine to hear her speak of God, whether they were convinced believers or simply curious, added that they did not think they did wrong, for she urged them to practice patriotic behavior. The relatives and friends of the participants, who were sometimes convinced revolutionaries, did not worry about this credulous curiosity and regarded it with amused indulgence. Thus the widow Duchargé, one of the old country women who went often to Catherine Théot, was the sister-in-law of the carpenter Duplay (Robespierre's landlord), the sister of the Jacobin mayor of Choisy, and the aunt by marriage of the Montagnard Convention member Lebas and of a Quinze-Vingts section commissioner.[28]

27. A.N., F⁷ 4774⁸⁹ d. Renard; W 60 no. 3356 and F⁷ 4720 d. Gautherot, wife of Blasié; F⁷ 4715 d. Garin.

28. A.N., W 79 no. 9 and W 80 no. 13.

Those women and men who were present at her lectures recollected that Catherine Théot was perhaps inspired by God and capable of conferring immortality, but also that she had assured them that France was protected by Providence, that it would win the war because God was at the head of its armies, that "all the children of the homeland were brothers [who] fought at the front [and] would return victorious and covered with laurels," and that the poor would triumph. The nonregulars who heard Catherine Théot announce the victory of the army (of God), followed by the regeneration of men and the universal happiness of equality, linked her predictions to the present situation and to revolutionary speeches on regeneration and common happiness and understood that Catherine Théot announced the triumph of the Revolution, for such was the will of God.

These connections became all the more compelling since Théot repeated that "God had permitted the year 1789" and that it was necessary to submit to revolutionary laws because "men made them through God's inspiration." Since He was the direct inspirer of the Convention, the committees, and the courts, to disobey them was to disobey Him. When the authorities examined the faithful for possible counterrevolutionary sentiments, they came up against a wall of incomprehension. The Revolution fit into the divine plan, and it was unthinkable that God wished to destroy His work or punish the revolutionaries. The merely curious took comfort in their opinion that the Revolution should triumph and that this victory would ensure an era of happiness, fraternity, and equality. The convinced followers believed that this would bring on the reign of God and that Catherine Théot would govern the earth. We do not know how others envisioned this triumph of a society without classes.

It remains that Catherine Théot, convinced by God himself of the Revolutionary government's place in the divine plans, invited her public to pray for the conservation of the Convention and the victory of the revolutionary armies, to submit to the will of the Supreme Being, and "to fulfill their duties as citizens and to celebrate the days of the *décade*." During the food crisis in the spring of the Year II, she urged them not to "wait in line for commodities, [but] to content themselves with eating bread as they would eat a good stew."

Thus there was nothing subversive in these meetings where submission to the laws was preached. The gatherings were far from the plots that some wanted to see in them. There was also nothing revolutionary in this doctrine, which considered the Revolution, right into its democratic phase, a divine intervention that aimed at reestablishing an earthly paradise where "God alone would reign." The idea of submission to a God, even a good and "prorevolutionary" God, is very different from the theory developed by the sansculottes on the sovereignty of the people who had risen to recover their natural rights. This was only an inspired, and, in a sense, patriotic, old woman who had during the Year II gained the sympathy of a lower-class and largely female public who had the pleasure (or the need?) to hear about a God (or Supreme Being) who supported the Revolution and would confirm its victory, who detested and crushed the enemies of the Republic, whether they be kings, priests, or the aristocracy, and who extolled equality and brotherhood. This audience mixed credulity, superstition before a "woman inspired by God" who would protect their children and their soldier husbands from death, satisfaction at hearing comforting words on a personal and reassuring level about the future of the Revolution, and the need not for a religion—for a large part of them did not come to seek that—but for the expression of religious feelings that were not opposed to patriotic sentiments. This accounts for the relative success of Catherine Théot.

It is equally possible that in the spring of the Year II a small number of women, bewildered by the struggle between factions, the Cordeliers' elimination, and the consequent political void, were attracted by this mysticism. Before having been "weak enough to let herself be carried away by this fanatic gathering," the wife of Lhomme was, according to her neighbors, "an *enragé* democrat." And two female Cordelier regulars, who were nicknamed the "sansculottes sisters," were also arrested, then released, as disciples of the Mother of God.[29]

Besides the female audience of Catherine Théot and the female public of the Temples of Reason, dimorphism according to sex continued under other forms during the Revolution. There was no decisive break; the revolutionary episode did not affect an evolution that had been in progress for several decades. "Molière's devout character was a man, but it was female devouts who the mocking sansculottes would spank in 1792," remarked Vovelle. Indeed, our survey shows that, although devout men were not totally absent in revolutionary Paris, *devout* most often meant "female." In addition, the privileged ties between women and religion cannot be reduced to the image of a devout woman who is a little ridiculous in her excess. The archives reveal women who were good Christians attached to specific aspects of their

29. A.N., F⁷ 4774²³ d. Lhomme and F⁷ 2482, 4 Prairial Year II; F⁷ 4775²¹ d. Soutierre.

religion, without fuss but with a steadiness that seemed all the more un-
shakable in its tranquillity. Their faith, as part of private life, did not clash
with the Revolution and was not the belief of "fanatics" who simultaneously defended the religion of the Old Regime and rejected the Revolution.
The behavior of these revolutionary believers brings out, not in the most
striking but ultimately in the most concrete fashion, "the intensification of
dimorphism according to sex." It was not men who prayed for the health of
Robespierre and the conservation of the Convention or went to hear
Catherine Théot. Also indicative of this dimorphism is that fact that reference to social class is essential in a study of women's counterrevolutionary
opinions but is unnecessary here. We may discuss a particular social group
(female merchants of la Halle, old women, and so on), but membership in
a particular social class did not visibly influence the religious opinions of a
Parisian woman.

Although this dimorphism was flagrant during the Revolution and continued to become even more pronounced, we still cannot justify, at least
within Paris, the image inherited from the nineteenth century of men discussing politics at the cabaret while women listened to the instructions of
a reactionary parish priest. As we have seen, Parisian cabarets were not frequented only by men, and the political discussions overheard there by police informers usually had women as protagonists. And these women were
not, all things being equal in other respects, more sensitive than men to
counterrevolutionary opinions. There was a clear dimorphism as far as religious attitudes, but it was not yet equivalent to a political dimorphism.
The varying religious attachments of a large part of the female popular
masses did not have as a corollary the weighty influence of a counterrevolutionary clergy, which was not in a dominant position in revolutionary Paris. Can we then imagine a relation between the ideological movement that tended to exclude female citizens from public life and the
movement that made women, led by their parish priest, potential counterrevolutionaries? When the cabaret and all other public places were forbidden to women, the church offered rare possibilities for social contacts
among those expected to pass their lives in "their interior." Thus the clergy
were able to influence strongly the political commitments of their faithful,
which was not the case when women had other social outlets.

This being said, during the Revolution in Paris, sexual dimorphism of
religious attitudes existed, although it did not lead to a more marked
counterrevolutionary tendency in women of the people. If, because of the

very nature of its source, "fanatic women" were indeed a majority in the dossiers of arrests, we still cannot claim that they were in the majority in the female population. And many other women did not seem to have suffered or be troubled by the new givens of religious life, which, let us repeat, did not change in general the support Parisian women felt for the Revolution.

12   Sexual Difference and Equal Rights

A specific concept of sexual difference predominated during the Revolution, and we can trace the portrait of the ideal woman in the revolutionary imagination. Militant women disagreed with these notions and developed another concept of women as created by the Revolution. This issue is important because the discourse of exclusion was based on an opposition between male and female roles. Various concepts of the difference between the sexes were central to questions such as the political existence of women, their place in society, their civic rights, and thus the complete enforcement or infringement of the principles of 1789.

THE LIMITS OF NATURE

The Ideal Woman

As represented in the speech of several leaders or the thoughts of the populace, this ideal woman resembled a sister to that Sophie imagined by Jean Jacques Rousseau for his Emile. The philosopher believed that "the primary and most important quality in a woman was gentleness," an opinion shared by many revolutionaries.[1] Gentleness, reserve, and timidity were women's natural and essential characteristics. According to the deputy Amar, gentleness formed one of her virtues, her charm.[2] It was "sweet" to hear women begin to sing La Marseillaise, but when men joined in, the song became "noble and glorious."[3]

---

1. Jean Jacques Rousseau, Emile ou l'éducation (1762; Paris: Garnier-Flammarion, 1966), p. 482.
2. Moniteur, XVIII, 299–300, report by Amar on the prohibition of women's clubs and meeting of the Convention on 9 Brumaire Year II.
3. Report by Perrière on 17 June 1793 (A.N., F lc III Seine 27).

As a consequence of this gentleness, women were weak. Physiologically they were the opposite of man, who was "strong, robust, born with great energy, audacity, and courage" and who "stood up to dangers and inclement weather through his constitution"[4]—everyone knew that women hibernated at the first sign of wintry weather! Women's inferiority was not only physical. It was also the reason why they were "more stubborn in their prejudices" and lacked "unlimited application and dedication, strict impassivity, and self-abnegation," or, in brief, "the moral and physical force required by the exercise of political rights."[5] They also lacked energy and courage. And if the leaders recognized that in certain exceptional cases— notably female soldiers—firmness and courage prevailed over this natural weakness, this was caused by the "miracles of Liberty," love of the homeland, and hatred of tyrants. It was no longer human beings who fought, but Liberty herself who assumed the terrestrial appearance of these women. Certain words made sense only in the masculine: *energy* ("manly"), *courage, firmness, intrepidness.* In describing the young fighter Anne Quatresols, Collot d'Herbois assured the Jacobins that "I do even include her among women, but I declare that this girl is a man because she has confronted death on all perilous occasions like the most intrepid warriors."[6]

Female soldiers' exclusion from the army illustrates with particular eloquence these revolutionaries' concept of sexual difference and the roles of men and women. The Republic could have turned these female combatants into heroines and placed them center stage to exalt devotion to the homeland. Even without going so far, there was no reason to deprive itself of good soldiers. The decree of 30 April 1793 was intended to rid the army of numerous prostitutes and soldiers' wives. Why take advantage of this legislation by adding to these categories female combatants, who were not very numerous, and whose brothers in arms recognized their propriety? But, as Collot d'Herbois expressed clearly, these female soldiers confused the habitual representation of sexual difference. The qualities that could have made them heroes were "masculine" characteristics. The role of women in the army was to be nurturers not female warriors. The decree allowed only canteen women and washerwomen there. And women could not attain the status of heroines except through the role meant for them. *Les Révolutions de Paris* stated this directly. After expressing their opposition to the exis-

---

4. *Moniteur,* XVIII, 299–300, report by Amar on the prohibition of women's clubs and meeting of the Convention on 9 Brumaire Year II.

5. *Ibid;* A.N., F⁷ 4611 d. Bouin.

6. Jacobin meeting on 8 Ventôse Year II (*Moniteur,* XIX, 590).

tence of female soldiers, the journalist addressed women: "For you, heroism consists in bearing the responsibility of the household and domestic pains."[7] The *Recueil des actions héroïques et civiques* gave as an example a young girl who "was unsparing in her care for a mother struck by a repellent illness and devoted herself totally to her duties as a home nurse."[8] A female soldier was recorded in the honor roll of the *Recueil,* but she appeared there as a devoted wife not as a female combatant. When her husband fell next to her, Reine Liberté Barreau seized his cartridges and continued to fire at the enemy; only after victory was certain did she go to care for her husband. We read in the *Receuil* that she abandoned fighting to take care of the wounded, proving thus "that she had not renounced the virtues of her sex." And the engraving that accompanies the text is still more explicit, for it has her say: "Let them bite the dust; I owe you all my care."[9]

Rousseau asked if women were "capable of solid reasoning."[10] Amar responded to this question in his report: "In general," women were "not very capable of lofty meditations and of serious conceptions." Thus they could not serve the Revolution with their intelligence. Moreover, on 5 Nivôse Year II (25 February 1794), a police informer reproached women for occupying the galleries in place of a citizen "who could be useful to the Republic through his reflections."

From these "natural" attributes followed duties that were just as "natural": the responsibilities of mothers and wives. Women were most useful to the Revolution within their homes, comforting their patriotic husbands with their gentleness and raising their children with republican principles. However, two conceptions of women emerged. The first, held by the majority and supported by Amar, gave women the right to attend debates in the assemblies as spectators because "it is necessary that women educate themselves in the principles of liberty in order to make their children cherish them." The second, a conception clearly held by the minority, had as a spokesman the editor of the *Révolutions de Paris,* Prudhomme. He stated

7. *Les Révolutions de Paris* 183, 5–12 January 1793.
8. Cited by P. Goujard, "Une Notion-concept en construction: l'héroïsme révolutionnaire," *Dictionnaire des usages socio-politiques, 1770–1815,* facsimile 2 (Paris: INALF-Klincksieck, 1985). On heroes and heroism, see Michel Vovelle, *La Mentalité révolutionnaire: Société et mentalités sous la Révolution française* (Paris: Messidor, 1985); Mona Ozouf, "Le Panthéon," in *Les Lieux de mémoire,* vol. 1 (Paris: Gallimard, 1984).
9. P. Goujard, "Une Notion-concept"; J. P. Bertaud, *La Vie quotidienne des soldats de la Révolution française* (Paris: Hachette, 1983), p. 152; B.N., Estampes, Qb 1.
10. Rousseau, *Emile,* p. 501.

that "women should not seek news outside their home at all: it is sufficient that they wait and receive it solely from their fathers or their children, from their brothers or their husbands."[11]

Thus a sexual distribution of space (public male and private female) based on "natural" and physiological features of each sex was advanced to justify the exclusion of women from political life. By giving women and not men "breasts for nursing," "nature" had assigned them uniquely to domestic tasks, declared Chaumette, the prosecutor of the Paris city government.[12] According to Amar, women, who were "made to soften men's mores," could not take "an active part in heated discussions that are incompatible with the gentleness and moderation that constitutes the charm of their sex."

"Women Should Not Concern Themselves With Politics"

Behind this discourse on nature, we can easily discover the motivations for expelling women from the political world. First of all was the fear of a possible challenge to masculine superiority. For example, a soldier grew indignant over the existence of a female officer and added: "Every day soldiers experience the shame of receiving her orders, which infinitely displeases them."[13] In September 1793, when the question over whether women could and should wear cockades was posed, many thought that this would be humiliating for men.

Women shared these ideas and affirmed that they would not get involved in politics. The ladies of la Halle refused to wear the cockade because "women should not concern themselves with current events." Some female citizens returning from a popular society were reminded of their duties as nurturers and mothers by their female neighbors: "Ah! Here are some female Jacobins, they would do better to go make their soup and wash their [baby's] swaddling cloth."[14] The behavior of the women who made these remarks was often inconsistent with their words. The widow Boulliand said that she "had never written about politics," having always thought "that it was not at all a woman's responsibility," yet she knew very well Rousseau's writings, was a Jacobin regular, and sent a "plan for arms" to the Committee of Public Safety. The female citizen Flint, the divorced wife of Rivarol, thought that "women should limit themselves to domestic virtues, retreat

11. *Les Révolutions de Paris* 17, p. 150.
12. Speech at city hall on 27 Brumaire Year II: *Moniteur*, XVIII, 450.
13. *Moniteur*, XVII, 739.
14. Police report of 25 September; A.P.P., AA 70 f. 44, Berjot.

into their duties, and should never mix in state affairs," yet she had translated *The Rights of Man* by Thomas Paine.[15] And the ladies of la Halle were not the last to state vigorously their opinion of political problems.

The simple idea that women could acquire the same rights as men terrified certain people because such an upheaval would create an era of folly and desolation. On 8 Brumaire Year II (29 October 1793), men spoke in a cabaret about the red cap and the Revolutionary Republican Women, whom they claimed were armed with pikes and daggers. This alleged arming, believed to be "humiliating" for their sex, provoked a totally irrational fear in these men. Women were going to cut the throats of their companions at a moment when they did not expect it, then "they would abandon everything and . . . and let a Catherine de Medici reign among the women, who would enslave men."[16]

This apocalyptic vision of women arming themselves to assassinate men during a sexual Saint Bartholomew's night reappears several times during the Revolution. It stemmed from the image of the female, a malefic creature and a force of destruction. The myths of Pandora and Eve, sources of miseries for humankind in Greek and Judeo-Christian civilizations, resurfaced again during the Revolution, and reasons offered for eliminating women from political life arose directly from these myths. Thus a sansculotte explained that "Marie Antoinette, the wife of the last tyrant, was the ruin of France, that Corday had assassinated the Friend of the People, and that many other things were women's responsibility, and thus he wanted to say that women should not be allowed to deliberate on section affairs." Some female citizens assumed the responsibility for this new "original sin." Those women who asked the Convention on 8 Brumaire Year II to ban the Society of Revolutionary Republican Women gave as a reason the fact that "the misfortune of France was introduced only through a woman."[17] The Revolutionary Republican Women refused this imaginary representation and stuck to the facts. They rejected their supposed simultaneous links to Catherine de Medici, Elizabeth of England, Marie Antoinette, and Charlotte Corday, remarking that Charlotte Corday did not belong to their society and that their sex had only produced one "monster,"

15. A.N., F⁷ 4611 and F⁷ 4729 d. Goud, widow Boulliand; F⁷ 4774⁹³ d. Flint, wife of Rivarol.
16. Report of Prévost on 8 Brumaire Year II.
17. A.P.P., AA 201 f. 121–139; A.N., C280 d. 761 p. 28.

whereas for four years the country had been betrayed by "countless monsters produced by the male sex."[18]

Drawing on the same image of the destructive woman, arguments that were somewhat more rational also contributed to the negative judgment of militant women. The discourses of leaders and police reports reveal the political fear of a struggle between the sexes, a fear that was based on this vision of women generating chaos. When added to the existing class struggle, the struggle between the sexes would destroy the unity of the Republic, disrupt society, and lead straight to anarchy and the failure of the Revolution. According to a police informer, the demands by women and women's clubs could thus only be "an apple of discord" that the counterrevolutionaries had thrown among the populace.[19] Amar became a spokesperson for this concern: the aristocracy "wished to establish" popular societies of women "to make them battle men." He added a political reason to the "natural" reason for prohibiting women's clubs: women "whose moral education is almost nonexistent" could be attracted by the enemies of the Revolution. And on 6 Pluviôse Year II (25 January 1794), the Convention recalled that women's societies had been forbidden because "it is easy to lead them astray and into error." According to the circumstance and the speaker, women were thus "instruments," whether of the moderates or of the more radical patriots, but were almost always the instruments of the speaker's "enemy." These different connections are not surprising to the extent that the female population was composed of diverse people, who belonged to different social levels and had divergent political opinions. But these witnesses tended to group "women" as a homogeneous whole. In addition, the bipolarization between moderate and radical sansculottes always involved the extremes of the political spectrum. The image of a destructive woman, whether an ally or the instrument of "the enemy," combined with the image of an excessive, exaggerated, hot-headed woman. Amar, who in his report insisted on women's gentleness, added that they "were constitutionally disposed to an exaltation that would be disastrous in public affairs."

Thus *mentalités* (the contradictory images of a gentle and weak or hotheaded and harmful woman) and political reasons (the fear of division, of women's lack of political education, and of women's violence) combined to

18. A.N., C 275 d. 710 p. 44.
19. Report of Latour Lamontagne on 21 September 1793.

result in a desire to exclude women from the political field. This desire was presented as determined by nature, which had made the two sexes different. Therefore, militant women who did not obey nature could only be monsters if they departed from the ideal of gentle and weak mothers and wives.

The "Men-Women"

"Each sex is ascribed an occupation that is proper to it; its action is circumscribed in this circle, which should not be overstepped because nature, which has posed these limits to man, commands imperiously and does not accept any law" (Amar report). This idea that nature poses limits, bounds that should not be crossed, reappears frequently. One woman "had dared to drag cannons" and had "left the bounds of her sex"; another urged her companions not to overstep the "limits prescribed by nature."[20] Women who did not follow this good advice were the opposite of the ideal woman. They were inevitably bad mothers: on 17 Pluviôse Year II (5 February 1794), rebelling against "the rage" of some women to "run to the assemblies," the informer Latour Lamontagne reported an anecdote. "The other day, a woman who never missed a meeting of the Jacobins found her child burned when she returned home. [Her] poor [husband] has left her, wishing to live no longer with someone who believes that, for a woman to be a good Jacobin, it is necessary to be a bad mother."

Politics and beauty did not go along together either. The informer Dutard thought that militant revolutionary women were all "fearfully ugly," and the Girondin Gorsas called them "Medusa's heads whose appearance petrifies." Another observer wrote that they were astonishingly dirty, and a fourth that, through shouting, their lips had turned black! Battling on 1 Prairial Year III with young rebellious washerwomen, the section authorities were astonished "that despite their face of candor, their character was so atrocious, their youth and their beauty showing little harmony with their language."[21]

Though we do not frequently find the combination of militant woman and loose woman in the official discourse, it often appeared in the pamphlets and remarks of the populace. In 1793, the Girondin Lanjuinais called

20. A.N., F⁷ 4669 d. Dembreville; F lc III Seine 27, speech given by Joséphine Fontanier on 24 Frimaire Year II, Unité section.

21. Police reports by Dutard on 31 May 1793, by Charmont on 1 Nivôse Year II, and by anonymous on 4 May 1793. Gorsas, *Courrier des Départements* of 29 May 1793. A.N., W 547 no. 52.

the Revolutionary Republican Women the "remains of debauchery." A journalist wrote that Claire Lacombe was a "bacchante" who thought only of wine, food, and men.[22] The men of the people were still more direct: militant women were "whores." They had "intimate liaisons" and indulged in "pleasure parties" with the sansculottes who defended them. In September 1793, a female servant even described the latter as "procurers and pimps of Jacobin women." The female citizens of the Panthéon-Français fraternal society, which during the winter of the Year II shared section power, provoked the fantasies of their opponents: they were "libertines without morals or virtue," "single women," and "nymphs" who danced around prisoners before retiring with revolutionary commissioners to abandon themselves to another kind of frolicking.[23]

These "female grenadiers," these "emancipated girls," these "bold women who no longer blush" were not only ugly women, slatterns, bad mothers, and "whores," but they sometimes even became hybrid monsters, "mixed beings" as they were called in 1789 in a pamphlet signed "Women of the Third Estate."[24] And in the sexually mixed "hermaphrodite clubs" only "men-women" could sit, those who, "shamelessly, put on the virile tunic and made the disgusting exchange of the charms given by nature for a pipe and trousers."[25] But the "men-women" should beware! Olympe de Gouges, the "man-woman" par excellence, who "wished to be a statesman," was punished by the law for "having forgotten the virtues that belong to her sex." The wife of Roland, "a monster in every respect . . . has sacrificed nature, by wanting to rise above it. The desire to be learned has caused her to forget the virtues of her sex, and this forgetting, always dangerous, ends with her death on the scaffold."[26]

There was no place for women who left the "bounds of their sex," who "reversed the order of nature," and "confused the sexes indecently"—in brief, who no longer obeyed a rigid conception of sexual difference.[27] The

22. Lanjuinais, *Dernier crime de Lanjuinais aux assemblées primaires, sur la constitution proposée en 1793*, B.N., 8° Lb(41) 723. *La Feuille du Salut public* of 23 September 1793.

23. A.N., F⁷ 4613 d. Bourguignon, F⁷ 4774²⁰ d. Lesage and Laudry. A.P.P., AA 201 f. 121–139.

24. Fabre d'Eglantine, 8 Brumaire Year II, *Archives parlementaires* 78, p. 21. Chaumette, 27 Brumaire Year II; see note 12. *Pétition des Femmes du Tiers-Etat au Roi*, B.N., Lb(39) 920.

25. Chaumette, 27 Brumaire Year II; see note 12.

26. "Aux Républicaines," *Moniteur*, XVIII, 450, 29 Brumaire Year II.

27. Dehaussy Robecourt responding as president of the Legislative Assembly to the women's petition asking for the right to bear arms, 6 March 1792: *Archives parlementaires* 39, p. 424. *Les Révolutions de Paris* 213.

subsequent success of the word *knitter* demonstrates this belief, as does Catherine de Medici's rise to the Pantheon of female monsters beside Marie Antoinette and Charlotte Corday. This character, made fashionable by the success of Chénier's *Charles IX* (1789), united the different negative images of women: a being of the shadows, endowed with public power; the cunning poisoner; the domineering mother using the influence exercised over weak sons for deadly purposes; and, like Marie Antoinette, a foreigner.

Two opposing images of women during the Revolution emerge: the positive one of a mother devoted to her family, whose activity takes place in the private circle of the home, and its negative counterpart, the militant woman who transgressed this idealized vision by participating in public life.

Revolutionaries' conception of political participation by women could not be separated from the political context, however, and these two fundamental representations gain more or less prominence according to the course of events. Militant women were denied their female attributes when they questioned the established power. Most of our examples occur around three historic moments. In May 1793, the Girondins called the women who struggled against them "bacchantes" and described them as "frightfully ugly." In the autumn of 1793, the Revolutionary Republican Women took an oppositional course at a time when the female sansculottes protest movement was at its height yet already revealing signs of weakness. At this same time, the image of woman as wife and mother confined to the private sphere was emphasized. And during the Year III the image of the monster, of the renegade, reappeared forcefully. In contrast, positions taken in favor of political participation by women occurred primarily in the summer of 1793, a unifying period that experienced the consequences of the female upsurge in the Parisian sansculottes movement. But these discourses were only partially dependent on the political situation, which allowed hostile *mentalités* to express themselves with full scope.

The image of the gentle woman, dedicated only to her family, did not arise with the Revolution. The revolutionary period was inscribed in a movement that tried to make this image a reality. The extremist and excessive discourse of Prudhomme or of Chaumette, or the more "measured" and more representative discourse of Amar, followed the same direction: exclude women from public and thus from politics. However, even in the long run, the Revolution preserved its own features. We cannot, for fear of a limited understanding, disregard the existence of an important popular female movement, which frightened numerous contemporaries because it was female or because it was popular. This fear drove them to destroy it and send these female revolutionaries or these rioters back to their homes while insisting on the fact that they were women. Thus the decrees destined to exclude female citizens from the public and political field (9 Brumaire Year II, 1–4 Prairial Year III), which corresponded to a general evolution and reinforced it, cannot really be understood without reference to the action of popular militant women. Both Revolutionary, event-oriented history and change over the long term are brilliantly articulated here.

However, not everyone shared this vision. The revolutionaries of both sexes affirmed that the Revolution must break with the past on the social and political status of women, as it had to break with the past in all other things.

WHAT ARE THE NATURAL RIGHTS
FOR THE WOMEN OF A FREE PEOPLE?

Two Theoretical Texts

On 3 July 1790, in the fifth issue of the *Journal de la Société de 1789*, an article by Condorcet appeared: "Sur l'Admission des femmes au droit de cité" (On the admission of women to citizenship). In September 1791, Olympe de Gouges published her *Déclaration des droits de la femme et de la citoyenne* (Declaration of the Rights of Women and the Female Citizen). In spite of their differences (if only in the personality of their authors), these two texts share essential points and clearly dominate the (abundant) writings of the years 1789–1791.

Faithful to Enlightenment philosophy, Condorcet and Olympe de Gouges characterized humans as sensitive beings endowed with reason. Women, who possessed these qualities, thus belong to the human community and are born with the same rights as men, even if they are not conscious of having lost these rights in society. The physical, cultural, or social differences that exist between men and women cannot be invoked to justify women's exclusion from political rights, because it is not physical ability or social role that determines the rights of each individual but the capacity to reason. "Why can't beings who risk pregnancy and passing indispositions exercise the same rights that it would be unimaginable to take away from people who have the gout every winter and who catch cold easily?" asked Condorcet. And he continued: "Can a natural difference between men and women that can legitimately justify the exclusion of a right be demonstrated?" "What do [men and women] have in common? Everything," Olympe de Gouges asserted. The emphasis was not placed on the difference between the sexes but on what they had in common: reason, and consequently, rights.

From the moment when women were excluded from their natural rights by the prohibition against their "working towards the law," the "principle of the equality of rights" was violated and "a tyrannical act" occurred (Condorcet). As long their rights were not restored to each member of the social body (and thus to women), the government will remain vitiated. For Condorcet: "Either no individual of the human species has real rights, or all have the same rights; and anyone who votes against the right of another, whatever his religion, his color, or his sex, has henceforth renounced his own." As for Olympe de Gouges, she argued in her article XVI that "the Constitution is nothing, if the majority of individuals who compose the nation [defined in her article III as the union of women and men] has not cooperated in drafting it."

Both Condorcet and Olympe de Gouges reach the same essential conclusion: there is "tyranny" because there is no Constitution. Thus, for these two authors, women's exclusion from political rights is the source of despotism and oppression (to be despoiled of rights is an oppression, and there is oppression of the social body as soon as a single one of its members is oppressed). The society that ratifies this exclusion cannot claim to be free, nor can its lawful government.

Olympe de Gouges insisted twice on an equal distribution between the sexes of "positions, employments, responsibilities, dignities, and industry." The two authors emphasized that women were by the sides of men when men rose to regain their rights.

Olympe de Gouges and Condorcet claimed to be theorists of natural rights, and these two texts have an undeniable significance. However, at the end of his essay, while again recalling that the right to vote is a "right of nature" common to all human beings, Condorcet proposed to extend the right possessed in the Old Regime by women who were owners of fiefs (the "right of fief") to women who owned properties (the right of property). This singular restriction, which completely contradicts the rest of his text, appears to be a compromise, staking out an evolution from the "right of fief" to the "right of nature" by means of right of property. Condorcet certainly violates his own principles here, but we cannot affirm that Condorcet claims that only female owners can possess the right of suffrage. The fact remains that in the project of the Declaration of Rights, in which Condorcet participated (adopted on 29 May 1793, but rendered null and void by the insurrection of 31 May to 2 June), the question of the "admission of women to the right of the city" was not raised, even indirectly.

It is often argued that demands for women's rights were specific to the beginnings of the Revolution. But we have seen that the female upsurge in the sansculottes movement in the summer of 1793 let loose a stream of questions and demands on this subject. Militant women tried at this time to become integrated members of the Sovereign People (in protests for the right to bear arms and to vote for the Constitution, and in the war of the cockades). Without going so far as to defend the vote for women, some sansculottes imagined a different place for them in revolutionary society. Like Condorcet and Olympe de Gouge several years earlier, the supporters of political participation by women—at least of a minimal participation by women—based their claims on the universality of natural right.

"The Declaration of Rights Is Common to Both Sexes"

If women are part of the human community, they should be able to enjoy the natural rights of each member. Unless we question whether they belong to the "human race" and establish "like Mahomet . . . as a general thesis that they are exclusively destined" for male pleasures, how can they be denied the right to assemble, "a right common to every thinking being"? asked the deputy Charlier of Amar on 9 Brumaire Year II.

Women belonged not only to the human race but also to the social body. In a response to Prudhomme on 10 February 1793, the female citizen Blandin Demoulin, president of the Dijon women's club, presented this argument: "Because in [a republican] government each individual is an integral part of the whole, he must cooperate in the good of the republic. It follows necessarily that women, who are part of society, must contribute, as much as they can, to the good of all" and "make themselves useful to the public good."[28] And how could they make themselves more useful than by uniting, which proved the necessity of women's clubs?

Six months later, the female citizens of the Paris section of Droits-de-l'Homme used the same reasoning before the Revolutionary Republican Women: women "endowed with the power of feeling and expressing their thoughts" had the right and even the duty of "taking their place in the social order" and of "working towards the common good."[29] They remarked that the club "was one of the elements of the social body and [that] it was not the least essential element." They became more specific and concluded with the assertion that women, like men, are social beings: "the Declaration of Rights is common to both sexes." However, they did not elaborate on the nature of these rights and in particular did not say a single word about the

28. *Les Révolutions de Paris* 189.
29. *Discours prononcé à la Société des Citoyennes Républicaines Révolutionnaires . . .*, B.N., Lb(40) 2411.

right to vote. They demanded in fact the right to participate in political life as members of the social community, and not the right to become part of the electoral body. Perhaps they thought, as several passages of the discourse lead us to believe, that the latter could not occur until after a long evolution and that it was better to limit themselves for the moment, in spite of their impatience. In this perspective, they were grateful to the Revolutionary Republican Women for having "broken one of the links of the chain of prejudices" and invited them to "persevere" with courage, in spite of "the clamor of small spirits whom the news astonishes."

Others who were less timid developed the same argument, pushed it to its conclusion, and demanded the right to vote in the name of the Declaration of Rights. "The rights of man are also ours," asserted the female Republicans of Beaumont when they assured the Convention that they also had the right to vote for the acceptance of the Constitution. One Parisian woman was even more explicit on 4 July 1793, when she asked the deputies to enforce the Declaration of Rights, the foundation of the Constitution, and thus to give the vote to women.[30] These female citizens did not have to construct a particular discourse on their rights. It was sufficient to recall the Declaration, the guarantor of natural rights for everyone. To admit that the Declaration also concerned women resulted in the recognition of equal rights between the two sexes.

These women who wished to be recognized on the political scene did not advocate a confusion of the sexes. They did not reject the traditional roles of the two sexes, but they refused to accept an inequality of rights. For example, the female citizens of the Droits-de-l'Homme section distinguished between (common) rights and (different) duties. Because nature had made men stronger, their duties were public: "Reason and propriety wished that they occupy jobs first. . . . It is necessary to yield to this," they sighed. But this division between private and public was not insurmountable: once they had accomplished their "first obligations" as mothers and wives, women could very well dedicate the rest of their time to public and political life. Others did not resign themselves so easily and asserted that, in the name of equality, women must not only possess civic rights but even attain political office and share power with men. These women did not reject their domestic tasks but saw them as compatible with the possession of their rights.[31]

30. A.N., C 267 d. 631 p. 19; Archives parlementaires 68, p. 254.
31. See the reports of Latour Lamontagne on 21 and 22 September 1793, Olympe de Gouges, Déclaration des droits de la femme et de la citoyenne, Cahiers

Natural right, proclaimed by the Declarations of 1789 and 1793, was indeed central to this protest movement. However, the debate was not taken up in these terms at the Convention. Natural right is of universal application: each human being possesses at birth the same imprescriptible and inalienable rights that society must guarantee each of its members. At a time when revolutionaries did not dream of renouncing the universality of this philosophy it was thus impossible for adversaries of women's political rights to justify their position. Its mere evocation was an argument in itself, and an unanswerable argument. Therefore those who were opposed to the rights of women approached the question in another way. They insisted on the difference between the sexes and posed as an initial postulate that nature, by creating women physically and intellectually inferior to men, had partially excluded them from the social body. This postulate served as a conclusion and allowed them to avoid the question of natural right. Thus, during the century of Enlightenment, the old question was asked once again, albeit in a secular form: did women have a soul (reason), and did they belong fully to the society of human beings?

It is one thing to support the thesis that women, with their domestic vocation, were excluded from society by nature. It is another thing to confront this thesis with a radically different social reality, which could only generate contradictions. Thus certain individuals did not risk entering this terrain, but nonetheless refused to become involved in the debate on the question of natural right, brushing it aside with a sweeping gesture: "Don't speak to me anymore of principles," cried the deputy Bazire on 9 Brumaire Year II at the Convention, in response to Charlier.[32]

FEMALE CITIZENS OR HELOTS?

It goes without saying that, in spite of the desires of some, women were part of the nation and of the people. Their presence at each unifying demonstration and at revolutionary festivals was indispensable[33]; thus the fact that they belonged to the social body was admitted, at least symbolically. But the refusal to recognize all of their rights bestowed on them a very

---

de doléances des femmes et autres textes, ed. P. H. Duhet (Paris: Editions des femmes, 1981), or the speech given by the female citizen Monic to the Revolutionary Republican Women's club, in Proussinale, *Le Château des Tuileries . . .*

32. See note 2.

33. Mona Ozouf, *La Fête révolutionnaire* (Paris: Gallimard, 1976); Ozuf, "Le Panthéon."

complex citizenship. This is illustrated by the word *citoyenne* (female citizen). What indeed is a female citizen if she does not have political rights?

In April 1791, during the debate over the voting system based on the poll tax, Robespierre called the expression "passive citizen" an "insidious and barbarous phrase," where the adjective completely contradicted the word that it qualified. This "new expression" represented "the obvious violation of the rights of man."[34] Passive citizens and female citizens, both deprived of their rights, were in similar situations, the former because of their lack of fortune and the latter because of their sex. But the man who could not achieve the necessary contribution to vote and serve in the national guard was clearly designated, a particular adjective marking his exclusion from the political body. This adjective expressed the "obvious" violation of the rights of man. After 10 August 1792, when the entire male population could exercise its rights, the two adjectives (*passive* and *active*) disappeared and only the word *citizen* remained in its integral sense. It was not the same for the term *female citizen*. Women formed one of the categories of "passive citizens." However, the expression *passive female citizen* was never used. For many, the restriction was implicit. The feminine declension of *citizen* (*citoyenne*) was sufficient; an adjective was unnecessary. But it was never said that the Declaration of Rights of Man and the Citizen concerned only men. Compared to the term *passive citizen*, the violation of principles contained in the term *female citizen* was certainly less manifest, but this absence of clear definition was at the same time ambiguous. It even allowed the possible reversal of the situation in favor of women by giving a political dimension to a word that did not actually possess it.

In the spring of 1793, during the discussion of the project of the Constitution, some deputies clearly perceived the ambiguity of the term *female citizen* and the contradiction existing between a Declaration of Rights that guaranteed the natural rights of all individuals and a Constitution that gave political rights to only half the population. The deputy Pierre Guyomar (who was close to the Girondins) published a pamphlet in which he defended political equality between the sexes.[35] He asserted that he saw no difference between man and woman "in the characteristic

34. Speech by Robespierre, "Sur la nécessité de révoquer les décrets qui attachent l'exercice des droits du citoyen à la contribution du marc d'argent, ou d'un nombre déterminé de journées d'ouvriers," in Robespierre, *Textes choisis*, vol. 1 (Paris: Les Editions Sociales, 1956).

35. Pierre Guyomar, *Le Partisan de l'égalité politique entre les individus, ou problème très important de l'égalité en droits et de l'inégalité en fait*, April 1793 in *Archives parlementaires* 63, pp. 591–599.

feature" of the human species, reason. The two sexes were not alike of course but, he wrote, "I do not see how a sexual [biological] difference ranks as a difference in the equality of rights." Certainly, "custom" established that woman "be concerned with inner affairs, while the man handles outer affairs," but "sedentary life is not sedentary to the extent that it leads to the exclusion from [electoral] primary assemblies." Then he demonstrated how, by not giving political rights to women, revolutionaries showed a "monstrous inconsistency," a "political heresy capable of overthrowing everything" and undermining the very foundations of the democracy that they sought to build. "*Either liberty and equality belong to both sexes*" he wrote, "*or indeed the immortal Declaration of Rights contains a fatal exclusion.*" Thus although the nation was composed of men and of women, the first, who were the sole possessors of sovereignty, "formed a body against the spirit of article" III of the Declaration: that "the principle of all sovereignty resides essentially in the nation; no body, no individual could exercise an authority that does not expressly derive from it." And even though it was stated that each individual had the right to contribute by means of the vote toward forming the law (article VI), half of the community decided laws for the other half. There was thus "usurpation of power," an act "detrimental to sovereignty." As Guyomar observed, if the sovereign nation is composed only of men, "the term *female citizen* is ridiculous and should be removed from our language." Women will be the "helots" of the Republic, the helots, rather than slaves: those who, although they live in the city, do not have a place there. Therefore Guyomar rejected Rousseau's distinction between the subject ("subject to the laws of the state") and the citizen ("participating in sovereign authority").[36]

Romme, another deputy (a Montagnard) who also defended the vote for women, similarly refused this distinction. On 17 April 1793, he defined for the Convention the links existing between the social body, the political body, and the citizen. The social body was composed of all individuals who lived under the same law. As soon as they were adults, these individuals, men and women, entered the political body. Sovereignty resided in them, and all possessed the right to vote "without distinction of position or sex." On 29 April, the Girondin Lanjuinais rejected Romme's proposal and contested this absence of distinction between the adult "subject" and the "citizen." For Lanjuinais, all "subjects" in a society could not be citizens, even if

36. Jean Jacques Rousseau, *Du Contrat social* (1762; Paris: Garnier-Flammarion, 1966), p. 52.

they are called citizens: this is the case for women. To "clarify [the] constitutional language," he proposed that one return to the designation of "active citizen." By openly naming the person who possessed political rights, this term made it possible to close up the breach opened by the very existence of the term *female citizen*.[37]

"The female citizen: a woman who should be restricted to the interior? a social being?" stammered some, stumbling on the contradictions they had raised. "The female citizen, a social being and thus a political being," responded women and men who knew how to take advantage of the conceptual vagueness surrounding this term. If in 1791 Olympe de Gouges wrote the *Déclaration des droits de la femme et de la citoyenne* to show that the rights of women had been passed over in silence, in 1793 militant women refused to consider this omission as such and assured the legislators: "You yourselves have declared our rights." Not possessing the rights of the citizen, they could affirm nonetheless that, inasmuch as they were members of the human and social community, the Declaration applied to them also, and consequently, they could demand its full enforcement and thus their political rights. The term *female citizen* was the pivot of this continuous interplay between the social body and the political body.

The "Free Woman"

"A congenial female citizen is delighted to be able to embellish herself through her hair and her face; this is her first and foremost happiness," wrote a citizen hostile to the wearing of the cockade by women in 1793. "It is as reasonable for a woman to concern herself with the charms of her face as it was for Demosthenes to pay attention to his voice and his gestures," Condorcet asserted in 1790, meaning that it was not lack of reason that guided women's conduct, but that they used their reason for goals that differed from men's aims "through the fault of laws" and the difference in sexual roles.[38]

During the Revolution, women asserted that it was necessary to change this. They rejected the limiting image of futile, brainless women, preoccupied only by their clothes and motivated solely by the desire to please men. Women associated this image with the condition of an "enslaved people" and countered it with the image of the women of a "free people," who

37. *Archives parlementaires* 62, p. 263 (Romme); 63, p. 561 (Lanjuinais). Dominique Godineau, "Autour du mot citoyenne," *Mots* 16 (March 1988): 91–110.
38. A.N., F7 4774[8] d. Lebreton; Condorcet, "Sur l'Admission des femmes au droit de cité," *Journal de la Société de 1789* (3 July 1790).

responded with dignity to frivolity, with energy to weakness, with activity to passivity, and who were worthy emulators of mythic Greek and Roman women.

A woman's attempts to appear more beautiful revealed clearly a people's degree of enslavement. Women of a "free" nation were not coquettes; they did not seek to fascinate men with their exterior appearance, through the pleasure of the eyes. But if women had to renounce the artifices of physical seduction, men should also show themselves to be equal to republican liberty and learn to appreciate and love their companions for their moral qualities and not for their surface appearance. To the devil with finery and diamonds and long live virtues and children for a modest young girl, the cockade for the Revolutionary Republican Women, and the "laurels of glory" for a female soldier.

Thus on 24 Frimaire Year II (14 December 1793), the adolescent Joséphine Fontanier declared before the sansculottes of her section:

> It is now no longer the time when a woman, debased and degraded by the false and frivolous cult that one paid to her and with which one claimed to honor her, was at most regarded as a second-rate being destined only to crown her husband with flowers and to ornament society like roses decorate gardens. Ah! citizens, how can you aspire to the name of republicans, if you still think that beauty is the chief quality of a woman. . . ? No, no, citizens, leave to the court of despots and to corrupt cities that keep their stupefied slaves this false manner appreciating half of the human race. . . . Let us view with scorn, or rather with compassion, these frivolous women, these ephemeral beings who only know and only wish to dazzle. . . . No more frivolous ideas for us; indifferent henceforth to the color of a ribbon, to the fineness of a gauze, to the shape or the price of our earrings, our virtues will be all our finery and our children will be our jewels.[39]

Six months before, Parisian authorities had written about the Revolutionary Republican Women: "Female republicans, women prefer the esteem of free men to the insipid homage of degraded and servile beings, to the pleasures of slaves, to storybook ghosts, to the languor of knights, to the sighs of the eternal seraglio where sex stagnates in the land of enslaved peoples. They scorn finery, and their diamonds are cockades."[40]

At the same time, in her plan for the organization of female soldiers, Manette Dupont swore to "renounce [until the end of the war] the seductions of love" and to wear short hair in order to lose no time "over a cos-

39. See note 20.
40. *Manuel des autorités constituées de tous les fonctionnaires, agens et employés politiques, civils et militaires de la République* (Paris: Déroy, an IX [1801]).

tume that only serves to fascinate eyes and that becomes entirely useless to female citizens whose goal is to be invincible."[41] All considered themselves to be "free women," an expression that Claire Lacombe added to her signature ("Lacombe, free woman") and that Manette Dupont gave as a slogan to one of her "legions" of female soldiers.

Energy is characteristic of "free women," as opposed to the women of an enslaved people. The description given of these latter irresistibly evokes the modern image of a "woman-object" meant only for the pleasures of men—who were themselves slaves—and that perpetuated their own slavery and even that of men. In contrast can be found the "free woman," acting in the general interest and no longer dependent on her particular interest, who participated in the defense of the Revolution. These texts presented a new image of women in a vocabulary usually reserved for men: zeal, tirelessness, surveillance, activity, audacity, courage, sacrifice, glory, and so on. These properties were not presented by authors as male attributes whose extraordinary presence in a woman was miraculous, but as the natural qualities of republican women.

The creation of a "free" people allowed the powers of each individual to blossom. Thus the "free woman" could be born. The negative hypertrophied characteristics of an "enslaved" people yield before the development of positive qualities that accompany membership in a "free" people. The "free woman" has the ambition to avoid restricting herself to domestic responsibilities; she wants to work actively toward the common good and toward the conquest of freedom for all of humanity. She refuses a rigid definition of the difference between the sexes and the stereotyped distribution of qualities that accompanies this definition. However, she does not seek to become a "man-woman," a "mixed being," to "reverse the order of nature." In this conception, the human being is not condemned to evolve only in a strictly limited sphere: on the contrary, he or she is able, according to that individual's own specificity—sexual or other—to develop the range of human qualities and to realize fully his or her humanity. The richness of this image stems from the fact that it does not express itself in terms of reversal—the exchange of one sex for the other—but in terms of additions and development.

This optimistic vision of the world, of the evolution of humanity in which the Revolution permits the creation of a new man (and, in this case, of a new woman) who is no longer degraded by the Old Regime, is charac-

41. *Départ de neuf cent citoyennes de Paris* . . . (Paris: Guilhemat, no date).

teristic of a form of revolutionary thought. But although these women advocated this image of the "free woman," they also felt that at least two conditions were necessary for a woman to be free: she must be part of a free people *and* she must possess her natural rights. In reminding people that the first condition was fulfilled, they implicitly raised questions over the nonenforcement of the second condition.

The human being is free only when not subjugated to the power of any other human being. The familial and social status of women scarcely agreed with this definition. The qualification of a "free woman" enabled one to play on this fundamental paradox: women were members of a "free" people but subject to masculine "despotism." The issue of slavery (oppression by a tyrant) was also juxtaposed to the condition of women.

Slavery of Women, Slavery of Men

In many texts the idea reappears that in the Old Regime women were doubly "slaves" because they were subjected to the despotism of the "tyrant" like the entire population, plus subjected to a specific oppression against their sex. Thus women raised the question of the evolution, in a free and egalitarian society, of individual relations between men and women, which had been distinguished up until then by the mark of the male yoke.

The Montagnard deputy Lequinio was one of those who emphasized male oppression the most.[42] His essential focus was the relations between men and women. He was not interested in these relations in terms of the more general theme of social organization like Condorcet, Olympe de Gouges, or the popular militant women in 1793, but in terms of private relations. Therefore he did not say much about the political rights of women; this was not the principal subject of his reflections. He certainly raised the question with identical references and the same system of thought as those already evoked: women had received from nature the same rights as men, which were recognized in the Declaration of Rights. But, unlike other "feminists" who, without erasing the specificities of the two sexes, considered women members of the human community, Lequinio privileged sexual differentiation. What others asserted insistently, he did not deny, but his intentions were different. His thought was dominated by relations of strength, the antagonisms or contradictions that exist between men and women. He did not think in terms of human beings but in terms of men-women. He stated repeatedly that the "strong sex" oppressed the "weak

42. Joseph-Marie Lequinio, *Les Préjugés détruits,* 2d ed. (Paris: 1793).

sex," which should gain its liberty and escape from this oppression. Curiously, we must turn to this Montagnard deputy in order to find a vision of male-female relations seen in terms of the struggle between the sexes. He is very close to Olympe de Gouges on this point.

In addition, Lequinio believed that, even in a just society, an individual can achieve full liberty only by working to get rid of the prejudices that shackle her. Evoking the image of an enslaved woman, he saw her as the slave of men and her own errors, which contributed to her slavery and indeed even increased the domination that men exercised over her because of her moral "weaknesses" (devotion, vanity, triviality): "As long as this amiable sex is the slave of her passions, she will be, in spite of all, the slave of the unjust sex, which profits from her very weakness to keep her perpetually subjugated."

Interested in describing male domination, he did not examine the collective dimension of liberty (free women of a free people). The female slave did not fall by the wayside when a people gained its liberty; restoring her rights did not suffice to make her a "free woman." Public liberty and the "establishment of the rights of man" were doubtless necessary for the emancipation of women, but even the most equitable laws would procure them only "an appearance of liberty" as long as they were bound by their prejudices, which supported men in their domination, giving them a "scepter." For Lequinio, ribbons, pearls, and diamonds were signs, not of the enslavement of an entire people, but of the slavery in which man kept woman. This "free woman" released from her prejudices, whom militant men and women of 1793 considered to be a reality of revolutionary society, Lequinio wished for with all his heart. Like Condorcet, he recalled the force of habit; like Olympe de Gouges, he called for a new consciousness on the part of women. But whereas these two authors referred to the civic rights of women, Lequinio privileged only the issue of masculine domination. If women wished to be truly free, they must "break their chains" themselves, for never would men consent to lose "an authority that was so old, so universal, and so convenient." It was thus for women, and for them alone, to win their liberty from men, and to do this, they must first abandon their failings (attachment to finery, to jewels, and to religion).

As we see, Lequinio holds a completely separate place in the current of thought that, from Condorcet and Olympe de Gouges to the militant women of 1793, took an interest in the status and the rights of women. Imagining the question primarily from the point of view of the oppression of one sex by the other and of the individual, interior, and private struggle against "prejudices," he did not take into consideration public relations between the individual and society and did not represent "feminist" thought as it expressed itself during the Revolution.

In spite of his unique approach, Lequinio remains a man of his time. Occasionally taking different directions, his reflections did not disagree with those already presented. His thoughts even joined these other reflections sometimes, notably in September 1791, when, during the debate on divorce, he wrote: "In all nations until now, women have always lived dependent on their spouses, or rather in a true state of slavery, always gauged by the degree of despotism in the political system of government."[43]

Indeed, other texts often draw the parallel between male oppression and royal despotism, between the power exercised by one sex over another and that which, in the Old Regime, a man (the king) or a social group (the aristocracy) exercised over the populace. Their origin was the same: the law of force. In both cases, the oppressive group seized the rights of the oppressed group, robbed them of their dignity, degraded them, and corrupted them. It was abnormal that a "free" society still harbored "degraded" female slaves. Thus Guyomar spoke "of the feudally ridiculous error," of "barbarously feudal" customs, of a "formal aristocracy of men." Thus a member of the Revolutionary Republican Women wrote in the autumn of 1793: "Men . . . perceive that to the degree women become enlightened their marital despotism will disappear, like that of the former king, and they will be obliged to renounce their despotism that they shamelessly want to keep under the republican regime. They have tried in vain; women are beginning to see that they are not created to be more debased than men."[44]

But it was the president of the Dijon women's club who best developed this thesis.[45] The desire of some men to keep women in a state of inferiority was a "system as despotic towards women as the system of aristocracy towards the people. It is time to carry out a revolution in the customs of women. . . . It is time to reestablish them in their natural dignity. Indeed! What virtue could be expected from a slave?" On the contrary, by becoming free, women will become "more perfect." Emphasizing the influence of women over men, she concluded: "Everywhere that women are slaves, men will bow under despotism."

43. *Moniteur*, XI, 398.
44. Guyomar, *Le Partisan;* letter of the wife of Dubreuil in the *Journal des débats de la Société des Jacobins* of 3 October 1793.
45. See note 28.

Condorcet and Olympe de Gouges had already asserted this: as soon as a member of the social body is oppressed (and to be deprived of their natural rights and to be subordinate to another is oppression), all other members are equally oppressed. A woman was free only if she belonged to a free people, and conversely, a people could not be free unless their women were free, collectively and individually. The notion of reciprocity was central to this conception: reciprocity of exchanges between men and women, between individuals in the heart of a community; reciprocity between the dependency, the dispossession of their rights, "the slavery" of an individual in the community and "the slavery" of the entire community.

We must not be misled by these different examples. These ideas were very much in the minority, and the question of women's social and political condition did not agitate either women of the people or women of the bourgeoisie. These conceptions were first expressed in the enthusiasm of the Revolution's early stages by women of the well-to-do milieu who published pamphlets defending the rights of their sex. Then in 1793, when the female sansculottes asserted their strength within the revolutionary movement, the problem was raised again by women of more modest origins. Their texts, which were not great theoretical writings, rarely circulated in the form of pamphlets and are harder to find in the archives. The prohibition against women's clubs and the publication of the Amar report, a true indictment against all participation by women in political—and even public—life, ended these thoughts. But we still cannot claim that, in the radical phase of the Revolution, the question of women was not raised. The men and women who posed it, in 1789–1790 as in 1793, did not form a structured movement. The authors of the texts rarely knew each other and did not have contact with each other.

A few political leaders also defended the rights of women. They were isolated, and none, with the exception of Romme, posed the problem within the Assembly itself. Nor did they form a group. Their positions were primarily personal, coming from open-minded men who applied revolutionary principles to the entire population. We can find Girondins and Montagnards among them—just as we find, in much greater number, representatives of these two positions among the opponents of political equality between the sexes. For the overwhelming majority of deputies, the question did not even exist—except in the autumn of 1793, when the strength of the female sansculottes compelled them to raise it at the Convention. Though they sought to change relations between men, they did not ever consider challenging the relations that existed between women and men (except on the crucial question of marriage and divorce), perhaps because, as Lequinio wrote with an astonishing lucidity, their authority was "so convenient." Everyone subscribed to a vision of sexual difference that excluded women from politics.

The partisans of equal rights privileged what men and women shared in common, what made both human beings. They brought forth a new image of woman in their project for a new society and thus raised the question of (civil, social, and political) equality between the sexes, equality here taken as "reciprocal to liberty."[46] They imagined the rights of women within a general concept of social organization. In this approach, women were always considered in the context of a larger whole: the community of thinking human beings, the social body, the Sovereign People. Thought of in terms of reciprocity, the question of masculine oppression was linked to the idea of progress, the liberty of all humanity. Giving women back their rights was seen as a necessary condition for reaching a truly free, democratic society. In order for the human species to achieve its goal of liberty and happiness, the relations between the two sexes should no longer be tainted with "despotism" and women should consequently be able to enjoy all of their rights.

46. Florence Gauthier, "Triomphe et mort du droit naturel en Révolution," appears in a collective work by the seminar "Les langages de la Révolution française" (Collège International de Philosophie, 1984–1985).

4

A MASS WOMEN'S MOVEMENT

13 From the Militant Woman to Crowds of Women, November 1794–March 1795

The respite and lull after the fall of Robespierre's followers were brief. Housewives' fears, which had calmed a little during the summer, rose again in the autumn of 1794. There was a coal shortage and it was necessary to fight to get any. The price of candles and soap was exorbitant because merchants no longer observed the legal maximum price, which was officially suppressed on 4 Nivôse Year III (24 December 1794). Angry murmurs over the price of commodities increased while hostility toward merchants grew. The coming winter added to the fear. A political reaction ✓ began to set in.

THE RISE OF ANGER AMONG WORKERS AND WOMEN (WINTER 1795)
The Revolution on Trial

Women did not have a privileged place in police reports, but they were part of the political scene. The Jacobin gallery regulars supported the campaigns of this club in the streets, and from the beginning of autumn, these women were the most active of the groups who sought to "influence public opinion." During the attacks on the premises of the Jacobins on 19, 20, and 21 Brumaire Year III (9, 10, and 11 November 1794), which led to the prohibition of the club on 22 Brumaire, female citizens in the galleries were insulted, struck, and whipped by the *muscadins*. A female usher tried prevent the *muscadins* from entering the hall. She was slapped, beaten, and wounded in the eye when hit with a stick.[1]

---

1. A.P.P., AA 95 f. 459.

Women who defended anything that recalled the regime of the Year II met in the galleries of the Convention, which was becoming a veritable home for popular resistance, as the incident which took place on 14 Brumaire (4 November) shows. At a gallery entry, two women were reprimanded in a threatening manner by one of the regulars, the widow Béliard, a fifty-year-old stockingmaker: "Are you of Tallien's and of Fréron's [leaders of the anti-Robespierre reaction] party? If you are Girondins, you will be guillotined." "We are patriots of 31 May, and we do not mention 9 Thermidor. We will speak of it when the time comes," she added, complaining that "[female] patriots like her were horribly oppressed." A citizen tried to intervene, but he was addressed sharply by a young girl, who told him, "You indeed have the look of an aristocrat." Scarcely had he time to turn around when another woman punched him: "Aristocrat! It would be better for you to go to the front like our husbands." The widow Béliard then spoke to the female citizens in two other galleries: "Today it's the people's turn, and hell, we will bring them into line!" A voice objected from the back of the Convention: "But indeed, you have aristocrats in your gallery!" The name of Carrier was uttered—a deputy responsible for the "drownings of Nantes," who was being judged for his "terrorist" excess. The widow Béliard replied, "You accuse us of being of Carrier's party. Yes, I am and I take pride in it. He is a republican and a brave patriot and two million heads will fall before his." The guard arrived and the widow Béliard called for help from friendly tribunes: "Help! Help! I am oppressed, I am being arrested!"[2]

The trial of Carrier had a powerful effect and symbolic value. For popular militants it became synonymous with reaction and defined the existence of two "parties." "Some feared that impunity would be assured to crimes inseparable from great revolutions. . . . Others saw an unequivocal intention to put the errors of the revolution on trial as a pretext to put the revolution itself on trial," wrote a police informer on 20 Brumaire (10 November).

Thus from autumn on, militant men and women were aware of a political confrontation and placed the Convention in the opposing "party." This realization was in essence purely political; the issue of finding basic necessities was not really part of it. The widow Béliard and her female friends in the galleries did not mention it on 14 Brumaire. On 1 Frimaire (21 November), two washerwomen who sought to stir up public opinion invoked the issue of basic necessities only after having noticed that the theme of

2. A.N., F⁷ 4704 d. Ferrin, widow Béliard, F⁷ 4658 d. Crosne Pierre.

Carrier had no effect.[3] What was immediately at stake was the "trial" that some wished to hold for the Revolution, in other words, political reaction. As the police report of 20 Brumaire indicates, the opponents "relied on the shortage of basic necessities" to spread their ideas, but this was not their chief concern. Women did not appear as a specific force, but they intervened as much as men. Once again, the archives refute the common opinion that "women" (and all women) were moved only by supply problems. It was not because women overwhelmingly occupied the foreground during particularly acute subsistence crises that they were absent from the scene when more clearly political questions were raised. Though the popular female masses had little direct impact at the beginning of the Year III, we must remember the fact that the most conscious militant women saw clearly the stakes of the political situation barely several months after 9 Thermidor and strove to thwart the progress of the reaction.

A Deadly Winter   During the winter, newspapers like Babeuf's *Le Tribun du Peuple* or *L'Ami du Peuple* by Lebois and Châles helped to spread the idea among a growing number of men and women that a violent confrontation or "civil war" existed between two antagonistic groups. These journalists based their statements on facts that shocked the sansculottes: the return of the Girondin deputies (a repudiation of the days of 31 May to 2 June 1793), the repression of former section officers, and the renunciation of the values of the Year II. The reign of respectable people, "decent people," succeeded the reign of the People, who must be returned to the position that they should never have left. It was a question, as Babeuf remarked, of "marking the distance."

At the beginning of winter, "young people" (or *muscadins*) paraded and took center stage, wearing combs in their bouffant hair and completely different outfits from the sansculottes. They carried sticks and bragged that they would strike the head of the first "blood drinker" that they should meet. In the evening, they crowded into the shows, accompanied by women of the bourgeoisie or by courtesans of the Palais-Royal, who had replaced the republican cockade with green ribbons in homage to Charlotte Corday. Prostitution, which had been prosecuted during the Year II, spread and now was flaunted. And while luxuries flourished again that had been morally forbidden during the Year II, the social crisis got worse, marking a growing split between a wealthy minority who could again spend without fear and

3. A.N. F⁷ 4607 d. Bollée.

did not hesitate to do so and the popular social strata that experienced horrible conditions of existence. While the restaurant owners of the Palais-Royal rejoiced, the commissioners of charity panicked as the number of destitute people continued to grow.

Not since the beginning of the Revolution did the popular Parisian masses have to confront such a grave crisis. Following the abandonment of maximum legal prices, the assignat collapsed and fell to 20 percent of its nominal value in Frimaire (December). Under the double influence of inflation and a shortage of goods, all commodities reached vertiginous prices, reducing the poorest to chronic malnutrition. The weather aggravated this situation. The winter of the Year III was one of the most severe in the eighteenth century. The thermometer descended to −10°C at the beginning of Nivôse (the end of December) and reached −16°C on 4 Pluviôse (23 January 1795). The icing up of the Seine made it difficult to supply the capital with necessities, especially with grains and fuel (wood and coal).

Many occupations were reduced to unemployment because of the lack of raw materials. The numbers of workers in arms workshops were cut ruthlessly, falling from 5,400 to 1,146. The crisis of the Year III was also a work crisis. Informers remarked on many "workers," groups of wheelwright journeymen, carpenters, and locksmiths, who asserted that, without employment and given the "increase in the cost of commodities," they found it "impossible to exist." The washerwomen could get neither soap nor wood for laundering, the sections distributed almost no work, and the spinning workshops slowed down. Unemployed men and women joined the increasingly imposing army of the indigent. The weakest among them died. The sick and the elderly succumbed to hunger and cold. And, a terrible novelty, bread also was in scarce supply from the beginning of winter. Lacking sufficient flour, bakers could not provide for all of their customers, who often left with empty hands. The situation deteriorated with frightening speed. An initial reduction to a pound and a half of bread per day per adult (two pounds per worker and one quarter pound per child) decreed by the government on 7 Ventôse (25 February) did not improve the situation. Several days later, on 25 Ventôse, another decree reduced the rations to one pound per person and one and a half pounds for manual workers. If we recall that during times of food shortage, bread represented almost the sole food for lower-class people, we can fully understand the significance of these successive reductions.

The "Furies of the Guillotine"   In the lines for commodities, women "expressed their discontent . . . in not very moderate terms" and hounded

the commissioners in charge of distribution with their imprecations: they
were dogs, scoundrels, brigands, intriguers, and enemies of the public good.
They lacked nothing, whereas the people who paid them lacked everything.
"They were present-day kings, but patience, patience, their turn would
come and the guillotine would do its job" prophesied a young female
worker. The same fate was promised to merchants who made "the people
perish of hunger." "If the increase in the cost of commodities continues,
we will have to put the pikes to use in the bellies of merchants," workers
threatened on 3 Nivôse (23 December). "Civil war is inevitable," they
concluded.[4]

The idea, which had begun to take shape in autumn, that the Convention did nothing to guarantee the happiness of the people, thus gained
ground in the popular social strata. At the end of winter, their misery caused
them to reject the Convention, but this was not just a desperate and apolitical reaction by the poverty-stricken who were dying of hunger, the response of "blind anger";[5] on the contrary, it corresponded to the political
mentalité of the sansculottes. The goal of the Revolution was the happiness
of the people with all of their rights. The essence of the representatives' task
was to work to realize and preserve this happiness and these rights. From
the moment that the representatives deviated from this goal, out of inability or unwillingness, they were traitors to their mandate and became
"tyrants" who caused oppression, and therefore the Sovereign People declared themselves in revolt. These ideas were a result of the theory of natural right and were part of the Declaration of Rights of 1793. Women and
men of the sansculottes included the right to existence as one of their natural rights, and they did not see the principles of the Declaration as moot.
Thus it was in the name of these principles that the Convention was chal-
lenged during the winter of the Year III. People grumbled in the streets of
the capital, in its cafés, and even within the galleries of the Convention that
"the representatives did not work for the general interest," "are not at all
concerned with making us happy," and only think of ruining the people.
"The Convention has pulled down a tyrant in order to become a tyrant itself, . . . [it] censors the people." "This is the reign of tyranny, all the good
patriots have been put in prison." But "we will know how to make the sovereignty of the people clear when the time comes and how to take revenge
on those who are responsible for providing for our needs." "There will come

---

4. A.N., F7* 2524, 80, and police report of 3 Nivôse.
5. K. D. Tønnesson, *La Défaite des sans-culottes: Mouvement populaire et réaction bougeoise en l'an III* (Oslo: Oslo University Press, 1959), p. 134.

a time when we will brand the deputies on the forehead with a red iron," when "we will go to the Convention to put a gun at their throat and to dismiss them."[6]

The recognition that some wanted to end the Revolution spread as a result of the militancy of those men and women who first came to this realization during Carrier's trial—or even earlier, on 9 Thermidor. On 18 Nivôse (7 January 1795), police informers reported that women had gone through the corridors of the Convention the day before saying "that people wanted to put the Revolution on trial, that the aristocrats lifted their heads, but this will not last long." However, at the beginning of winter the insurrection was still not really the order of the day, and so it was postponed to a later date.

Robespierre and his friends were restored to public favor. The comparison between their epoch and the present situation was clearly to their advantage. On 18 Nivôse (7 January), the female baker Pommier was denounced by her customers for having said that "since Robespierre, recognized by all good patriots as a good republican, had been assassinated, the counterrevolution had taken place. . . . It was not surprising that the seventy-one [recalled Girondin deputies] had assassinated Robespierre in order to do as they pleased, that they had thirty-six francs a day [an allusion to the doubling of their salary], that even if they did not have their hands steeped in blood, they did have their hands in the till." On 13 Pluviôse (1 February), a woman questioned for having incited the pillaging of a soap cart provoked the fury of the police commissioner "by comparing justice to Robespierre." Bold militant women asserted that Robespierre should not have been killed without being heard and that he had "been sacrificed as a victim who had no other intention but to bring happiness to France and to deliver it from the tyrants who govern it today." In the groups of female citizens from the Tuileries garden, it was asserted that it was "impossible that a single man could have oppressed seven hundred [deputies]."[7]

Needless to say, remarks like this were also made by men, and in police reports "women" did not yet appear as a specific force. The group entitled "women of the galleries" emerges clearly, however. Statements of arrests confirm the importance of women's action in the Convention galleries, where, along with "workers" (unemployed journeymen or day workers),

6. Police reports of 10, 12, 18, and 22 Nivôse and A.N., F[7] 4766 d. Marguerite Laroche.

7. A.N., F[7] 4774[78] d. Pommier; A.P.P., AA 163 f. 354; A.N., F[7] 4753 d. Klipsis; police report of 20 Ventôse Year III.

female citizens opposed *muscadin* spectators. "The galleries of the Convention were filled with bricklayers and women who went regularly to the Jacobins, who referred to themselves as Montagnard," the report of 27 Nivôse (16 January) states. The opponents of these women called them "furies of the guillotine," the most widespread expression then, or "knitters," the nickname passed on by posterity. From the galleries, the women stirred up a constant opposition and supported the Montagnard deputies. Among many other examples: on 27 Nivôse, two women made "vile remarks" against several Convention members; on 19 Pluviôse (7 February), the "female regulars" interrupted the applause of the moderate galleries with mocking cries. On 21 Pluviôse, they tried to prevent the removal of busts and paintings of Lepeletier and Marat, and then brought down the house with applause for two Montagnards who affirmed that they were ready to fight to defend the rights of man and the democratic cause.[8]

Women were also present in groups hostile to the government that formed in the street and around the Convention. "Malevolent people seek to profit from circumstances and unleash within the groups some of these women, whose morality knows no principle, and who still support terrorism, of which they were the mainstay, exacerbating by their yapping the weak heads who listen to them," wrote informers on 17 Ventôse (7 March).

On 24 Nivôse (13 January), after burning the newspaper of Châles, a group of youths decided to go whip the "Jacobin women who frequent the galleries of the Convention." One month later they repeated this proposal without having, it seems, the courage to actually confront them. But it was not safe for a knitter to find herself alone before a band of "young people." She would be beaten and whipped under the sarcastic remarks of these bullies because she disapproved of their anti-Jacobin masquerades, because she wore around her neck a medallion showing a man coifed with a red cap, because she had been seen dancing at the Jacobins(!), or because she made "inflammatory motions." These attacks, which were frequent in Pluviôse and Ventôse (January to March), confirm women's importance in the popular reaction against the government. They also reveal the open arrogance and scorn felt by the sons of the bourgeoisie for women of the people. The violence exercised by the gilded youth against their female political opponents assumed a sexual character. The youngest women were whipped "with much indecency," their bonnets were torn off, and their corsets were ripped. On 20 Pluviôse (8 February), when the women left a Convention gallery, the widow Dupertois and her daughter were surrounded by a dozen

8. Police reports of 28 Nivôse and 20 Pluviôse; *Moniteur*, XXIII, 419, 421.

muscadins who called the mother "shrew, fury, and Jacobin" while kicking and punching her and running their hands over the blouse and skirts of her daughter. However, the mother stopped them and took out her knife to "avenge the honor of her daughter."[9]

In the autumn, militant women had supported the sansculottes against the moderates who attempted to regain control over the section general assemblies. Thus on 30 Brumaire Year III (20 November 1794), when the moderates finally prevailed in the Fontaine-de-Grenelle section during the conclusion of a tumultuous meeting, they decided to exclude female citizens from the galleries because "for a long time, unfortunately for too long a time, women had attended meetings and sometimes troubled the assembly." During the winter, most sections were taken over by the moderates, but sansculottes who tried to reverse the balance of power in their favor could still count on the active support of women. On 10 Ventôse (28 February) the assembly of the République section was turbulent and the sansculottes were close to gaining victory. Their "party was reinforced by a large number of women who were concealed behind them but who uttered cries of rage according to cues given to them and who raised their hands during votes. . . . These women made the worst remarks while leaving the assembly. One of them promised to have crushed glass in her pocket to throw in the eyes of the royalists for next *décadi*."[10]

During the winter, women could also be found in clandestine gatherings held by patriots against the ruling power. In Brumaire (November) and Germinal (March), the widow Salignac, a former Jacobin regular, was suspected because of the "rather large gatherings of men and women who remained at her home [every night] until eleven o'clock and sometimes midnight." Another militant woman, the wife of Huzard, was arrested for "having had gatherings at her home." On 27 Nivôse (6 January), a neighbor of the couple Monic informed the Committee of General Security that a "gathering of Jacobins . . . took place at the home of the female citizen Monic, where they deliberated clandestinely." On 20 Ventôse (10 March), the sansculotte Vacret was arrested for holding at his home "meetings of men and women declaring themselves Jacobins for life and proposing ways

9. A.P.P., AA 251, 20 Pluviôse Year III, widow Dupertois; AA 95 f. 758. A.N., F7 477412 and F7 4774[85] d. Lefevre, wife of Quillet; police reports of 25 and 26 Nivôse, 3, 4, and 25 Pluviôse, 17 and 25 Ventôse, and 19 Germinal Year III.

10. A.N., F7* 2509, 30 Brumaire Year III; F7* 2476, 10 and 11 Ventôse Year III, F7 4774[86] d. Racine.

to reestablish the reign of Terror." An employee of the North spinning workshop had allegedly organized gatherings on the premises of the factory, reuniting former revolutionary commissioners and two militant women of the section, "both women Jacobin regulars." In Prairial Year III, the couple Portail was questioned for, among other things, "having been found at the home of the female citizen Bernier . . . at secret meetings against the public good."[11]

The most important and the best known of these gatherings was the one that had been held since the beginning of Pluviôse (mid-January) at the home of the wine merchant François, the stovemaker Langrelet, or the concierge of the "Maison Carnavalet." Begun with the goal to help the families of imprisoned sansculottes, these meetings were allegedly transformed into a veritable conspiracy to prepare an insurrection, to free the incarcerated patriots, and to preach sedition in the Faubourg Saint-Antoine. Among the eighteen names listed in a denunciation dated 10 Germinal (30 March), seven belonged to women: three wives of former revolutionary commissioners, a militant woman (the wife of Barbant), the concierge of the "Maison Carnavalet," and the wife of François, "a rabid Jacobin woman" who probably influenced her husband. This conspiracy was broken up at the end of Germinal: six women were implicated along with nineteen men.[12]

Women and Workers

Thus during the winter, all places of popular resistance were marked by a strong female presence. "You make war against us because we have nothing. . . . Our knitters, our armsmakers, our heads of families are not worth your shopkeepers, your financiers, your *émigrés*, your peacemakers, your Vendéens, and so on," wrote Lebois in *L'Ami du Peuple* of 28 Nivôse (17 January).

A year before, would he have used the knitters as an example? We do not think that he placed them at the front of the list out of simple gallantry. Even though it was occasional, the presence of female citizens in the as-

11. A.N., F⁷ 4775¹² d. Salignac, F⁷ 4746 d. Huzard, F⁷ 4774⁴⁸ d. Monic, F⁷ 4775³⁷ d. Vacret, F⁷ 4648 d. Christophe, F⁷ 4774⁷⁹ d. Portail.

12. A.N., F⁷ 4748 d. Jabel, F⁷ 4758 d. Lagrelet, F⁷ 4712 d. François, F⁷ 4748 d. Janson, F⁷ 4775²⁷ d. Thiboust, F⁷ 4775⁴⁴ d. Vernaury, F⁷ 4604 d. Bodson, F⁷ 4649 d. Claudel, F⁷ 4775⁴⁴ d. Véron, F⁷ 4649 d. Cladène, AF II* 299, 2 Floréal Year III; A.P.P., AA 158, 3 Floréal Year III; *Moniteur*, XXIV, 326. On this conspiracy see Tønnesson, *La Défaite des sans-culottes*, p. 154 and chapter 5.

semblies of the Year II had left traces that the crisis brought into daylight. Women of the people were doubly affected by the crisis, as housewives exposed for hours to the cold and workers who were vulnerable economically. It would be vain to try to decide whether it was the social reasons or the more strictly political reasons that led militant women to the front ranks of the opponents. It is necessary, however, to emphasize that, most of the time, their discontent took a political form. Lebois's reference to the knitters rather than to mothers reflects this fact. Women who were conspicuous during the winter of the Year III were former militant women, or gallery regulars.

In the autumn of the Year III, militant women rose against the new course given the Revolution. They were only individuals, and thus we cannot speak of the emergence of a group of women. But in the winter, the presence of the female sansculottes, the knitters, and the female gallery regulars is striking. The economic crisis affected the popular female masses, but it was the female sansculottes movement that mobilized under its effect, and its interventions thus have an explicitly political meaning.

In keeping with their incomplete citizenship, militant women had developed during previous years a political practice with a looser structure than that of their companions. This practice proves particularly interesting in the Year III. The imprisonment of the sansculottes and the domination of moderates in the Parisian general assemblies put that political practice at the forefront by making partially obsolete the accustomed forms of political sociability of the Parisian sansculottes, those of 1793 and the Year II. From the moment when the sansculottes no longer controlled the constitutive elements of their sovereignty, when the political life of the popular masses no longer occurred through the section system, action by men and women took place on an equal footing and the importance of women increased. Accused of putting himself at the head of a gathering and of having excited the people to revolt, a citizen pleaded: "Never have I been seen in the cabarets or in the cafés, never have I been found in public places, or in groups of the people's assembling, rarely could I even be seen on public esplanades."[13] Cabarets, public places, groups, were the exact places, at least as much as in the general assemblies, where a good part of women's political life had taken place since the beginning of the Revolution. This shift in practice is also one of the reasons for the role assumed by women in the popular movement during the winter of the Year III.

13. A.N., F⁷ 4665 d. Guillaume Defavanne.

After the knitters and before the fathers of families in Lebois's list of the typical sansculottes during the Year II, armsmakers appear—a reference to those workers without employment who, according to police reports, were the most seditious elements of the population, even more so than women. The unemployed, whether they were armsmakers or wheelwright journeymen, locksmiths, blacksmiths, carpenters, pit sawyers, joiners, or masons, were by their very situation gravely affected by the economic crisis, and because they had by force of circumstance the most free time, it is scarcely surprising to find them in the galleries or in groups alongside female citizens. Because they were not hired when they presented themselves at the Place de Grève in the morning, these unemployed workers discussed the economic and political crisis in the Convention galleries during the day.

This was not the only reason for the importance of the wage-earning group during the winter of the Year III. We might be fooled by a switch in vocabulary, because the word *worker* henceforth replaced the term *sans-culotte* in police reports. This substitution certainly had an effect: the "sansculotte" is no longer a subject of official discussion in the Year III. Still, these *"workers,"* who would probably have been called "sansculottes" in the Year II, were indeed wage-workers. All the statements of arrest for men in the galleries or in groups referred to journeymen or day laborers. We know that the militant sansculottes of the Year II were mostly recruited from the independent craft industries: 41.6 percent were artisans among those analyzed in Paris by Albert Soboul, as opposed to only 12.4 percent of journeymen, workers, apprentices, and day laborers.[14] Thus there would seem to have been a shift of the sansculottes toward the wage-earners and away from the artisans. However, Soboul has defined as militant sansculotte in the Year II "every citizen who had an active political role, whether in a popular assembly or in the general assembly."[15] "Workers" were arrested in the Year III for being conspicuous in the galleries of the Convention or in groups, and not for their presence in section assemblies. Just as for women, the new rules of political life in the Year III, when the section system no longer represented the only opportunity for popular intervention, reveals the engagement of the wage-earning group, which had

14. Albert Soboul, *Les Sans-culottes parisiens en l'an II. Mouvement populaire et gouvernement révolutionnaire, 2 juin 1793–9 thermidor an II* (1958; reprint, Paris: Flammarion, 1973), pp. 448–450.
15. Ibid.

been hidden in previous years by the sansculottes organization. Interventions of "workers" during the winter of the year III, like the interventions of women, had a political meaning even though they took place outside the frame of organizations extant in the Year II. The crisis of the Year III played a large role in this breakthrough. The social confrontation between the classes was exposed with a new acuteness. And the revolutionary bourgeoisie, represented by the Robespierrists who worked for the common happiness, gave way to a bourgeoisie avid for riches and pleasures—which emphasized social and political antagonisms.

This was not the first time that these women and workers had found themselves side by side. The same association was present in the Year II. In gatherings, in cabarets, and at the revolutionary tribunal, police informers had listened to "women and workers." In the galleries of popular clubs, it was again female citizens and workers, "men in aprons," and water carriers who were remarked on by informers. And in the month of Germinal, informers noted among women and the "forty sous" the survival of an Hébertist "party."

Women and workers resembled each other in many ways. According to the viewpoint of others (men, bourgeois), their alleged absence of enlightenment and common ignorance united them and caused the two groups to be minors in political life, or, as it was written, they were "easy to lead astray because of their weakness."[16] There is no need to expand on the significance of this slip of the pen. This "weakness" was one of the principal reasons given by Amar against women's political participation on 9 Brumaire Year II; it was also offered by moderates against the sansculottes in the Year III, and several discourses by the bourgeois on popular militants bear a strange resemblance to speeches given in the autumn of the Year II against militant women.[17]

Moreover, a significant proportion of women were wage earners. Besides the designations that united them ("the women and the workers"), we can also find fusions that eliminated the distinction between the two groups (women = workers). And in the Year III, women and workers were the first to be affected by the work crisis that accompanied the subsistence crisis.

16. A.N., F⁷ 4774¹⁴ d. Louis Jean.
17. In his article "Sur l'admission des femmes au droit de cité," *Journal de la Société de 1789* (3 July 1790), Condorcet had made this connection for an opposite aim: "If one admits such reasons against women, it is also necessary to take away the right of citizenship from the group of people who, destined to work without rest, can neither acquire enlightenment nor use their reason."

But not all women were wage earners. Another analogy links these two groups: they are both "marginal," not in the Revolution but within its structure, women being excluded by a restricted citizenship and urban wage earners participating only in a secondary manner for reasons that do not concern us here. Women and workers could be found in places of great popular political sociability, but not as a constituted, formal group. These places were indeed in the margins of the sansculottes movement but are not uninteresting and are even important in the Year III. It is thus not surprising that it was exactly at this time, when section assemblies did not play the same role in the popular movement, that women and workers appeared forcefully on the Parisian political scene.

THE TROUBLES OF VENTÔSE AND GERMINAL (END OF MARCH 1795)

Tall Nanette and Similar Women

At the end of Ventôse, public notices calling enthusiastically for an uprising were placarded on the walls of the capital: *Peuple, réveille-toi, il est temps* (People, it is time to awaken) on 22 Ventôse (12 March); and on 23 Ventôse, *Au Peuple, des vérités terribles mais indispensables* (To the people, terrible but indispensable truths). The first demanded the application of the Constitution of 1793; to achieve this, the sansculottes and their wives were to regularly occupy the galleries of the Convention and reconquer the sections. The author asked the people to prevent "its enemies from going in its name... to fawn upon the Convention (or rather the government) for its glorious works and assure it that they were happy and that all goes well." Everywhere they were displayed, these posters attracted many passersby who commented favorably on them.[18] In contrast to previous years, they no longer criticized the executive responsible for enforcing revolutionary laws passed by the legislators, but the legislators themselves to the extent that they betrayed natural rights. Admittedly, they did not specifically refer to natural rights, but the members of the Convention were indeed called into question because they were estranged from the rights of the people and its happiness. The reference to the Constitution of 1793 was in this sense significant.

18. *Peuple, réveille toi, il est temps,* B.N., 8° Lb(41) 1708, cited by K. D. Tønnesson, *La Défaite des sans-culottes,* p. 157. On the gatherings provoked by these public notices, see A. N., F7* 2526, p. 99 (the widow Babin), F7 4774⁴⁴ d. Magnier; A.P.P., AA 50 f. 109; police report of 23 Ventôse.

In the days that followed, other public notices covered the walls. One of these satirical tracts, written as a song, was the work of a woman: *Le Réveil républicain par une Démocrate.* The author, the female citizen Dubois, called on Parisians to awaken in order to save liberty and asked for the "democratic Constitution of 1793." She emphasized the food shortage, the price of commodities, the lines, and the reduction of bread and attacked the "big newly rich merchants," the "young people," and the "governors and rulers." She took up all the themes already evoked: because the rights of the people had been confiscated, the Convention should bring about the happiness of the nation under pain of betraying its oath, and the people should rise up and demand the Constitution because by fighting for liberty they are sure to always triumph, and so on.[19]

Was it these placards that inspired the washerwoman of the Faubourg Saint-Marcel nicknamed Tall Nanette to put into practice on 25 Ventôse (15 March) one of the instructions of *Peuple, réveille-toi?* When a deputation of the former Sans-Culottes section went to the Convention to announce that henceforth it would take its former name of Jardin-des-Plantes, Tall Nanette, accompanied "by a great number of women of her sort," burst into the departure place and insulted the commissioners and the Convention, saying with irony: "The section of dead-with-hunger is going to ask for bread from rogues and villains, it is necessary to speak firmly to them." These women commanded that the deputation not congratulate the Convention, but on the contrary demand bread from them. The women accompanied the deputation to the Convention, and others joined their procession, spoiling the good progress of the day expected by the section moderates. Once they arrived, Tall Nanette and one of her female comrades entered after the deputation in order to make sure that it did not "toady to" the Convention members.[20]

The same day, bread rations were again reduced to one pound per person per day. A spirit of rebellion rose in all the lines. The commissioners in charge of bread distribution were obliged to flee in order to escape the women's fury. The women proposed to visit the homes of merchants and to overthrow the Convention. On 27 Ventôse (17 March), a young female day laborer cried at a baker's door that "if all women resembled her the Convention would soon be ruined,"[21] and Tall Nanette made herself conspicuous again by saying "that it was necessary to fall on the Convention to ask

19. In *Les Femmes dans la Révolution* (Paris: Edhis, 1982).
20. A.N., F7* 2524 p. 100 and F7 4774⁵⁶ d. Nanette.
21. A.N., F7 4770 d. Marie Louise Lavoye.

it for bread [and] if it refused, it was necessary to set on the merchants to pillage them." "A coup was anticipated," wrote a police informer.

The Faubourg Saint-Marcel was again the site of serious troubles on 27 Ventôse (17 March). In the morning at the Finistère section, "women enlisted workers to gather and go to the Convention" to ask for bread. They led them to the police commissioner's home to get his bell or a drum in order to assemble the people. He refused, but approximately eight hundred rioters forced two civil commissioners to go with them to the Convention, where they read a petition written in the name of the Finistère and Observatoire sections. The deputies remarked that the women, who were very numerous, urged the men to revolt. Two days later, outside a bakery in the République section, women who supported the petitioners threatened to rise as a group to go to the Convention and inquire what had become of the last harvest, "that they would indeed now see if they will be called bloodthirsty."[22] Women were responsible for the day of 27 Ventôse; women supported it; women again tried to prevent the arrest of a citizen of the Finistère section on 29 Ventôse. But there were limits to action by women: "the time for distribution of bread and meat having arrived, each woman left to go shopping" and the man was arrested, the cautious policemen having him go through a hidden door.[23]

On 1 Germinal (21 March), the three sections of the Faubourg Saint-Antoine, preceded by a company of gunners, went together to the Convention to ask for the enforcement of the Constitution and to complain about the food shortage. At the Tuileries, some "young people" were thrown in the water by workers. Among the groups supporting the petitioners of the faubourg, police informers noted "many women, instigators, who incited citizens to revolt." During the vote for "greater enforcement of law and order" that followed the faubourg petition at the Convention, a woman's voice rose from the galleries, crying that the royalists assassinated the patriots. Article XI of this repressive law, by which Convention members meant to protect themselves from a popular insurrection, stated that those guilty of "seditious cries" or of "threatening movements" within the Convention risked deportation. Women of the galleries were among the first to be affected.[24]

In the following days, while the government prepared for a test of strength, tension did not subside, stirred up by women and workers who

---

22. Police reports of 27, 28, and 29 Ventôse; *Moniteur*, XXIII, 717, XXIV, 3.
23. Ibid., all sources.
24. *Moniteur*, XXIV, 36; Tønnesson, *La Défaite des sans-culottes*, chapter 8.

met in groups at the Palais-Royal or at the Porte Saint-Denis. Some "young people" tried to "fraternize" with the workers but did not receive a warm welcome, "particularly at the Arsenal workshop where several women called them *muscadins* and threatened to throw them in the water."[25]

Women on the Move

There was not enough bread. Everyday, in different districts, several hundred people went without. Despairing women claimed to prefer a rapid death to this slow agony. Anger often followed discouragement: on 5 Germinal (25 March), "several pregnant women had seemed to want to give birth at that very moment in order to destroy their children, and others had asked for knives to stab themselves; tears and signs of despair followed threats."[26]

Thus on 7 Germinal (27 March) the uprising of the Gravilliers section began. The day before, in this lower-class central district, women had called men cowards for not "showing up," insisting that it was impossible to live with such a small quantity of bad bread. Female sackmakers at the Sainte-Elisabeth workshop in the nearby section of the Temple had gone through the workshops, trying to force their comrades to join them in order to go to the Convention.[27] On the morning of 7 Germinal, indignant at only receiving a half pound of bread after they had spent the night at the baker's door, women refused it and assembled. A procession of approximately six hundred women accompanied by several men made its way toward the Convention. At the head of the demonstration, they brandished the "Table of the Rights of Man." Inviting all those women whose path they crossed to accompany them, the stream of people grew, and they arrived at the Convention in impressive numbers. In spite of their insistence, only around twenty of them from a variety of sections were allowed to enter the meeting hall, where, encouraged by the galleries, they demanded that at least the legal pound of bread be distributed to them. The refusal to receive them as a complete group and the president's responses spurred their discontent. Those women who could not enter the meeting hall exhorted the crowd in front of the Convention to join them. Cockades were torn from bonnets in the greatest of confusion, some rejecting them as a sign of protest, others as a symbol of Jacobinism. Several women were arrested for saying, "Be pa-

march on Convention

25. Police report of 4 Germinal.
26. Police report of 5 Germinal.
27. Police report of 7 Germinal.

tient, there will come a time when we will fuck them in the ass with their half pound of bread at the end of a cannon," but they were freed by their female companions. During this time, the rioters formed an illegal general assembly in the Gravilliers section to deliberate over basic necessities. Returning from the Convention, female citizens crowded into this general assembly and stopped female passersby to force them to attend it.

The next morning, the troubles recommenced. At 9:30 A.M., the Rue du Temple was traversed by "a crowd of people" calling "good male and female citizens" to join them to seek bread. All day in the Gravilliers section, women and workers formed groups. The demonstrators of the previous day reproached men for their cowardice in not going to free the five people arrested on 7 Germinal. After new questioning, female citizens murmured that freedom only existed for saying "Down with the Jacobins." They spoke of opening the general assembly and of seizing cannons and expressed "fear that the big merchants would not share the same opinion." In the evening, groups dispersed after having "postponed the party" until *décadi* (10 Germinal), and men invited women to meet with them on that day.[28]

In the general assemblies of 10 Germinal, whose tumultuous character was shaped more than a little by the presence of female citizens, the subject under discussion was the food shortage. In these hours of crisis, women descended from their galleries to deliberate and sometimes even to vote with the citizens. This seems to have been particularly the case in the Quinze-Vingts section, where a petition was drafted asking for the reopening of popular clubs and the enforcement of the Constitution of 1793. On 11 Germinal, supported by female spectators in the galleries, this section read its petition at the Convention, reminding it that rebellion is sometimes a sacred duty.[29] The same day, when sacks of flour meant for bakers in the Droits-de-l'Homme section had not arrived by seven in the morning, men and women asked the president of the section to open the general assembly in order to deliberate over basic necessities. During this time, a citizen went through the streets of the section with bell in hand and invited the residents to go to the assembly: his call was drowned out by the applause of groups of women waiting before the bakeries. Six hundred people gathered in the premises of the general assembly, but the movement did not really have an

28. Police reports of 8 and 9 Germinal. *Moniteur*, XXIV, 85–87. A.N., F7 4771 d. Leblanc, F7 4774[14] d. Legros, F7 4774[63] d. Parisel, F7 4693 d. Duney, F7 4775[29] d. Marguerite Thomas, F7 4678 d. Doderay, F7 4586 d. Barbot. A.P.P., AA 241 f. 27, 90, and following, AA 96 f. 356. Tønnesson, *La Défaite des sans-culottes*, chapter 8.
29. *Moniteur*, XXIV, 106.

insurrectionary character and the section authorities easily managed to prevent it from being transformed into a structured general assembly.[30]

On 12 Germinal, only a fourth of a pound of bread per person was distributed in some sections. In the Cité section at nine in the morning, women gathered together and, accompanied by two young drummers beating their drums, with two gunners at their head, drove those whom they met to go first to the illegal general assembly taking place at the Temple de la Raison (Notre-Dame) and then on to the Convention. Neighboring sections (Pont-Neuf, Fraternité) supported these appeals. Several women seized a drum and wanted to force the civil commissioners to march with them. In the northern districts, while workers entered the workshops and led their comrades to the Convention, women, under the approving eye of the guard, liberated flour and potatoes at a price they thought reasonable. In several sections (Bondy, Nord, Finistère), women used violence against the civil commissioners.

Finally, a crowd of men and women gathered outside the Convention. The witnesses agreed that there were at least as many and perhaps even more women than men among the insurgents. The women were not just housewives concerned only about the food shortage. Forcefully joining the deputations of sections who had come to present, without any aim of insurrection, their complaint about basic necessities, these women hurled hostile cries against the Girondin deputies and the *muscadins,* demanded the liberation of "patriots incarcerated since 9 Thermidor," and thus gave a political meaning to these steps. The insurrection ended in failure. In the evening, when the crowd had left the hall, the Convention decreed the immediate deportation of "four great culprits" (the Montagnards Billaud Varenne, Collot d'Herbois, Barère, and Vadier), the arrest of eight other Montagnard deputies, and a state of siege in the capital.[31]

The next day was nevertheless politically stormy, though confused. In the evening, "around a hundred women gathered at the Place des Victoires nationales, claiming that the Representatives of the People were sending a regiment of cavalry to Paris to prevent the sections from going all the way to the Convention when they had complaints . . . to present, but that they

30. A.P.P., AA 136 f. 193. A.N., F⁷ 4771 d. Leblanc.

31. Police reports of 13 and 14 Germinal. A.N., F⁷ 4775 d. Tarreau, F⁷ 4699 d. Duval, F⁷ 4584 d. Baillet, F⁷ 4776, F⁷* 2492 f. 42, W 547 no. 52, F⁷ 4429. A.D.S., VD* register 987, p. 38. *Moniteur,* XXIV, 111–114. *Le Messager du Soir* of 14 Germinal. *Procès-verbaux de la Convention nationale imprimés par son ordre,* vol. 58, p. 108.

did not give a damn, that they had decided to fight to the death." Everywhere in the lines, women murmured that "Paris was going to be besieged and bombarded," for "the Convention wanted to make war on the people because it wanted to bring the people to account."[32]

These days marked an important turning point. The divorce between the Convention and the popular masses was confirmed. The acuteness of the class struggle was clearly perceived: the Convention had not only failed at its mandate but even wanted to make "war on the people" who would not accept death from hunger. Proud of their rights and of their sovereignty, the rioters wanted to know what had become of *their* basic necessities (the right to existence) and wanted the Convention to be accountable to them (control of elected officials). They reminded Convention members that they had been elected to ensure happiness for all. The gesture of female citizens of the Gravilliers section who on 7 Germinal marched on the Convention preceded by the Table of the Rights of Man was particularly eloquent: they placed themselves on the side of the law, whereas in their eyes the Convention deputies who violated the Declaration of Rights were acting illegally. Equally meaningful was the female rioter who, on 12 Germinal, asserted that the people's home was in the Convention.[33]

These ideas, reiterated since the winter by the most politically aware people, were henceforth shared by the majority. Though popular demands did not separate politics (the Constitution of 1793, liberty for imprisoned patriots) from famine, it was the latter that nevertheless brought about this new situation. During the autumn, female citizens rose up individually against the Convention for political reasons, and then during the winter a group of militant women appeared. At the beginning of spring, the group of "women" appear with a surprising strength and violence in all the archives. To the extent that all women of the people were now affected, demands by women had, in contrast to previous months, a socioeconomic rather than a strictly political coloring. Though militant women, always present in these movements, claimed to be part of a political group, most female crowds, moved by the economic situation, acted like members of a social class, which did not always distinguish clearly among the Convention deputies.

32. Police report of 14 Germinal.
33. *Moniteur,* XXIV, 111–114.

These women were often at the origin of different movements, present in semivoluntary groups that were transformed into gatherings of rioters (7 Germinal at Gravilliers)[34] or in voluntary gatherings that they most often initiated (25 and 27 Ventôse at the Faubourg Saint-Marcel; 12 Germinal at Cité). When a movement needed to be large, women incited men by calling them cowards. Once the riot was launched, women accompanied men, and in the heat of action they were frequently the most virulent. During the repression that followed these successive defeats, women were again concerned with preventing arrests. Militant men and women—sexual difference was unimportant in this case—who were conscious of the strength of these female groups, their extreme sensitivity to the problem of finding basic necessities, and their readiness to revolt more rapidly than men, thus turned toward them. We can already detect in the popular movement an internal development that would continue to prevail: militant men and women addressed the popular female masses, who in turn addressed the popular male masses.

However, women were not manipulated. They acted spontaneously from the beginning—and later on as well—driven by anger and despair. Even police informers, who had been inclined to consider women mere "instruments" manipulated by "intriguers," no longer expressed this opinion. Hunger, the obstacles that prevented them from fulfilling their responsibility as nurturers, as well as new forms of political sociability, were the fundamental causes of this massive irruption by women of the people on the social and political scene. Less affected by the political reaction in the sections that brought the moderates to power, women perhaps also felt less fear and, because they had been forbidden to act in most sections, were less tired, less worn-out, and so could provide relief for the sansculottes movement.

In a context at once defensive and insurrectionary, in which the people no longer possessed all of their rights, women, by their strength, got themselves included in the Sovereign People, both in its general assemblies and when, invading the Convention, the people made its wishes known.

As in the winter, women shared the limelight with the workers. The groups mentioned in police reports and statements were usually composed of women and workers. The sudden jump in the popular movement at the beginning of Germinal was in large part caused by the "workers," those wage earners whose importance grew during the winter. However, the emo-

34. Georges Lefebvre, "Foules révolutionnaires," *Annales historiques de la Révolution française* 11 (1934): 1–26; George Rudé, *The Crowd in the French Revolution* (Oxford: Clarendon Press, 1959).

tions of Ventôse and Germinal concealed a shift in the privileged link between women and workers. Before these days, the latter were more present in police reports. During the riots, the two groups are cited equally in the archives. From mid-Germinal to Prairial, the equilibrium would be reversed, leaving the stage open solely for women in Floréal. Not that the male "worker" opposition was weakened, but women assumed such importance at this time that they overshadowed others.

14 Firebrands,
     April–May 1795

DESPERATE MOTHERS

There was no longer just a food shortage but a real famine throughout Paris. Bread rations had shrunk with lightning speed. From mid-Germinal (the beginning of April 1795), a quarter of a pound per day and per person had become the norm in almost all sections. A month later, the residents of neighborhoods that were less well supplied with food had to be content with two ounces of bread; and in the last *décade* of Floréal (9–19 May) this sad situation was common to all sections. On 25 Floréal (14 May), on the Rue de la Tixeranderie, only one ounce of bread was distributed to each individual. Despite these dizzying limitations, a significant part of the population got no bread at all: 250 people on 27 Germinal (16 April) in the single section of the Champs-Elysées, 162 people on 1 Floréal (20 April) in the Guillaume-Tell section, 300 people the next day in the Indivisibilité section, and so on.[1]

Given the fall of the assignat to 8 percent of its nominal value in Germinal and the runaway inflation, police informers worried on 3 Floréal (22 April) about the "high prices increasing daily, from one hour to the next, of all commodities and essential merchandise," which kept the popular masses from access to the free market. They were reduced to a frightening state, made even more cruel in contrast to the splendid life of some of the bourgeoisie. At a time when rationed bread cost three sous per pound (1 livres = 20 sous), the bourgeoisie were able to spend ten livres for one pound of (unsubsidized) white bread and therefore did not suffer from the

---

1. See the police reports, the statements of police commissioners (A.P.P.), and the committees of arrondissements (A.N., F⁷ 4776) or the registers of civil committees (A.D.S., VD*).

food shortage. On the contrary, they stuffed themselves with pâtés and brioches. Everyone became indignant at this: "This insults the destitute who only have one piece of bread."[2]

"One must become a thief in order to live," the husband of a female day worker despaired on 13 Floréal (2 May).[3] One either stole or deprived oneself of the little one had so that one could eat and cling to life. Police commissioners recorded the petty thefts committed by the famished, and the employees of Mont-de-Piété (pawn shop) did not know which way to turn.[4] Lodgings became barren and empty. In the Faubourg Saint-Antoine, the Tinel family lived in one room; the father was a journeyman locksmith, and the mother and two daughters were hatmakers. "They owned nothing; they lived between four walls and the little that they had in the room was not enough to pay the rent twice" (forty-four livres!) wrote the police commissioner.[5] There were no words to describe the sorry state of the common people, without employment, without strength to work, and spending all their time in lines. Old people went to the poorhouse and newborns to the Enfants de la Patrie, formerly the Enfants Trouvés (foundling hospital). After having decreased at the beginning of spring, the number of deaths grew alarmingly in Floréal (May). People died of hunger in the streets of the capital.[6] The sight of women and men fainting from need became a familiar part of the Parisian landscape. Every day from mid-Floréal (the beginning of May), police informers mentioned with particular monotony that "in the streets one sees many people who collapse from weakness and hunger." For lack of more solid food, they were given a glass of wine and a piece of bread.

The despair was proportionate to this situation: "Suicide has never been as common," wrote a police informer on 26 Floréal (15 May). Corpses floated in the Seine: from 22 Germinal to 1 Floréal (9–20 April), at least seventeen people were dragged out of the water, all dead. Every day, starving women and men hurled themselves into the river, and their numbers grew with time. Women threw themselves into the water with children in their arms.

The fate of these children without bread or milk, whose undernourished mothers could give no more, affected public opinion the most. In all streets and squares, one passed mothers who cried because they could not get bread

---

2. Police reports of 12, 20, 23, 24, and 29 Germinal, 12 and 20 Floréal.
3. A.P.P., AA 50 f. 277.
4. A.P.P., AA 188 f. 243.
5. A.P.P., AA 219 f. 120 and A.N., F⁷ 4775³⁰ d. Tinel.
6. See the Archives de l'Assistance Publique; police reports of 29 Germinal and 10 Floréal; A.P.P., AA 163, 4 Floréal.

for their families and called on death to deliver them and their offspring, whose cries of hunger they could not bear. On 26 Germinal (15 April), a police informer heard a woman say to her little daughter in front of the Tuileries: "My child, your father shed his blood here on 10 August. Very well! I will break your head on this same cobblestone rather than watch you die of hunger." "The sight of weeping women and mothers excited . . . compassion impossible to suppress in sensitive souls," wrote police informers on 25 Floréal (14 May). But they did not fail to remark regularly that these mothers were the most dangerous to public order. Their very responsibility as nurturers was the foundation of their anger and was inseparable from their tears. On 11 Floréal (30 April), a female seamstress provoked a revolt at a baker's door because, she said "as a mother, it is indeed hard to hear requests for bread every minute and be unable to give it."[7] Tears and anger led to a call for action. In police reports, desperate and insurrectional remarks made by mothers occurred together or one after another.

FROM REFUSING BREAD TO RIOTING

As always in an acute subsistence crisis, women intercepted carts loaded with provisions and proceeded to popular price fixing. This practice, which was not new, became an almost daily occurrence from mid-Germinal.[8] In addition to the principal grievance expressed, the lack of bread and the expense of other commodities, was added all the usual complaints in periods of food shortage: lines began the evening before, women lost sleep and part of their work time; the crowd was such that some people were wounded; men who were present roughly pushed female citizens out of the way; and so on. Often, especially in the central sections, the bakers' doors were forced open. The commissioners and the guard, which did not distinguish itself by excessive zeal, were obliged to flee, and women remained in control. For example, Robillard, a baker in the very poorly supplied neighborhood of the

---

7. A.P.P., AA 71 f. 92–94.

8. Carts loaded with potatoes or flour were stopped in this way by women on 22 Germinal (Mont-Blanc section), 25 and 27 Germinal (Poissonnière section), 28 Germinal (Finistère and Observatoire sections), 30 Germinal (Temple, Arsenal, and Panthéon sections), 1 Floréal (Nord and Faubourg-Montmartre sections), 2 Floréal (Halle section), 6 Floréal (Lombards section), 7 Floréal (Bonnet-de-la-Liberté, Droits-de-l'Homme, and Observatoire sections), 9 Floréal (Arcis section), 10 Floréal (Lombards section), 12 Floréal (Butte-des-Moulins section), 21 Floréal (Nord section), 23 Floréal (Amis-de-la-Patrie, Butte-des-Moulins, and Arcis sections), 24 Floréal (Gravilliers section), and so on. See the police reports: A.P.P.: A.D.S., VD*; A.N., F7*.

Sainte-Catherine market (Indivisibilité), did not know how to protect himself from the anger of his customers, who were seamstresses and washerwomen. On 21 Germinal (10 April), he fled, and his store was partially looted. The following day, fights occurred at his door. On 26 Germinal, disturbances again took place. And on 28 Germinal, the guard was forced to abandon its post, the baker's window panes were broken, and the receipts were plundered. The next day and on 14 Floréal (3 May), the same scenario was repeated.[9]

Feeling mocked, women refused the paltry quarter of a pound of bread and threatened those who were weaker and ready to receive it without complaint. On 21 Germinal (10 April) in the Bonnet-de-la-Liberté section, there was complete chaos; threats to drag in the gutter "the first beggar-woman" who took her quarter pound of bread rose alongside the cries of those who, having ignored these warnings, were pushed and punched.[10] On 26 Germinal (15 April), the distribution of bread was interrupted in the Temple section, and the commissioners in charge of distribution "were forced to abandon their posts because of the fury of some women who forbade others to take their portion of bread, with the threat of being whipped and dragged by the hair."[11]

After opposing the distribution, women went as a group to the civil committee to demand an increase in the amount of bread and often forced the authorities to accompany them to the Subsistence Office for this reason. The commissioners sometimes managed to curb the demonstration and limit the number of women who accompanied them as a deputation. But more often, they were dragged along by the women and resembled hostages more than leaders of the deputation. The office was thus continually assailed by troops of angry women. However, events seldom went further than this. In themselves, these demonstrations were not really serious threats to the government, but their frequency could only increase a spirit of revolt (see figure 5).

It did not take long for urgent but legal requests for additional rations to become antigovernment riots. In several of these stormy gatherings, housewives threatened to go to the Convention and even to seize cannons (Bonnet-de-la-Liberté, 21 Germinal). Sometimes, the demonstrations increased, swelled, and overflowed the narrow perimeters of the section to fill

9. For all these disturbances, ibid.

10. Report of 22 Germinal and A.N. F⁷ 4774²² d. Denis Levêque.

11. A.P.P., AA 241 f. 108–112. From 25 Germinal, these refusals to accept bread were noted every day in many sections.

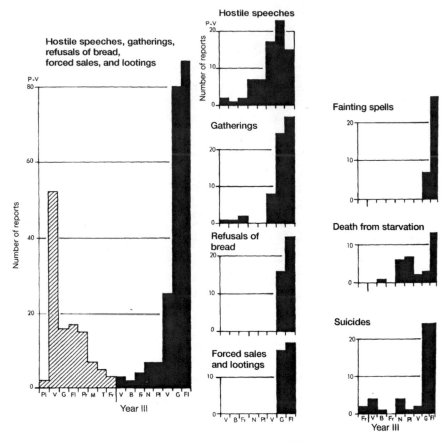

Figure 5. The subsistence crisis during the Year III. Source: Police reports (Archives Nationales and Archives de la Préfecture de Police).

the streets of the city. Women from different neighborhoods met at a crossroads, where they decided to go to either the Committee of Public Safety or the Subsistence Office. They threatened "people who seemed willing to receive their modest portion of bread," proposed to enter homes to force the indifferent to accompany them, and made the commissioners in charge of bread distribution lead them. Beginning spontaneously, these processions were quickly augmented by militant men and women. People spoke of "going to the revolution," of attacking the government committees. "I am only a woman, but it is necessary that we beat the hell out of the Convention. They are all rascals. At least the Jacobins gave us bread," asserted a woman demonstrator on 2 Floréal (21 April). Another woman advised her companions to "throw out" the Convention, convinced "that if the women began first, the men would support them."[12]

Though the Convention was threatened, it was the civil commissioners in particular who had to confront the women's rage. They were detested by the common people, who accused them of privileging some, beginning with themselves, and of plotting with merchants and the government to create the food shortage in order make people die of hunger. A significant number of the exasperated commissioners responded to insults and threats with physical or verbal brutality, which only inflamed the situation. We can easily imagine the indignation provoked by commissioners laughing in the face of starving women who cared nevertheless for their own dignity: the women could just eat hay, planks, or even "wipe their behinds and lick their fingers."[13] Hanging would be too good for the commissioners.

In the Finistère section, in spite of the presence of the guard, the commissioners were forced to run away on several occasions because of the sarcastic comments, threats, or objects that women threw at them. Since 12 Germinal (1 April), the civil committee of that section was assailed daily by female citizens who came "constantly to insult and threaten them in their refuge" and to accuse them of "squandering their basic necessities" and of "plotting" to reduce the women to famine. In the same street, women who passed off-duty commissioners insulted them and provoked passersby against them. At the end of Floréal, women gathered three or four times a day before the doors of the committee, hoping to make the commissioners come out to accompany the women to the Subsistence Office or to the Convention. An eighteen-year-old ironer, Joséphine Rouillére, distinguished herself by leading them. Humiliated and frightened, the commissioners tried to cajole her by complimenting her on her youth and her beauty, but because compliments did not transform into bread, they had no effect.[14]

"IN THE NAME OF THE SOVEREIGN PEOPLE AND THE LAW"

On 11 Floréal (30 April) in the Bonnet-de-la-Liberté section, a "troop of furies" invaded the civil and charity committees. The disturbances that shook this section, reported in great detail by the commissioners, show different

12. These demonstrations took place on 1, 2, 3, 6, and 7 Floréal. See the police reports and A.N., F⁷ 4774⁴⁶ d. Vilambre.
13. A.P.P., AA 251 5 Floréal, AA 50 f. 202; police report of 6 Floréal.
14. A.N., W 547 no. 52.

kinds of action taken by women in Germinal and Floréal. Going even further, they took a sufficiently serious turn that, at a call to order, the Convention gathered in an extraordinary meeting at eleven o'clock in the evening.[15]

According to a scenario that soon became classic, everything began in the morning. Around six o'clock in the morning, housewives stopped the flour cart meant for the bakers of the section under the pretext that the women only received three ounces of bread, whereas in the neighboring section the ration amounted to ten ounces. They opened the sacks of flour, judged angrily that it was "unfit for human consumption," forbade the distribution to take place, forced all the merchants to close their shops, and promenaded this cart through the streets, while the armed guard refused to intervene. Growing more and more numerous, the women besieged the hall where the civil and charity committees were meeting. Far from reestablishing calm, the threat that the Convention would send troops if the women did not release the cart was greeted with boos and a commissioner was wounded by "these wild women." One of the few men present proposed to raise the alarm and to declare the crowd in revolt. While the mob thus made threats in the section, a group of women went to the Subsistence Office, where they were assured that a sack of flour destined for "nursing mothers" had been sent to the civil committee. Not having seen this flour, these women returned "like furies" to the section and accused the commissioners of having stolen this sack from them. The commissioners tried to explain that it had been mixed in with the others. Their explanations were to no avail. "However much they spoke to the women, the women did not wish to hear anything, although they understood very well for the most part what was said to them."

Finally, the crowd forced the doors of the hall, and "toward five o'clock in the evening these women and some men dared to put the committee under arrest in the name of the Sovereign People and the law. They entered as a group, inflicting the greatest humiliations on the commissioners, calling them thieves and claiming that they ate white bread while the people ate

---

15. *Moniteur* XXIV, 356. For an account of these disturbances, see the detailed statement of the civil committee on 11 Floréal (B.N., Lb (40) 1747, published by W. Markov and Albert Soboul, *Die Sansculotten von Paris: Dokumente zur Geschichte der Volksbewegung 1793–1794* (Berlin: 1957), doc. no. 107), the statements of the police commissioner (A.P.P., AA 78 f. 6) and from the surveillance committee (A.N., F7* 2476 f. 126), and the statement of a witness (A.N., F7 4775[45] d. Viget). On the arrested ringleaders, see A.N., AF II* 299, F7 4684 d. Duclos and F7 4774[86] d. Rabasse.

black bread." Then a man said that "if the people were in revolt, if they had disloyal representatives, it was necessary to accuse them, judge them, and punish them on the spot." Several hours passed in "vague (and stormy) discussions that did not reach any conclusions." The commissioners unsuccessfully tried to vindicate themselves, "but the crowd did not want any excuses." In the greatest confusion, new commissioners charged with representing the insurgent people were elected. But at the announcement that troops marched on the section, the rioters left the hall little by little, and soon only a "small number of women" remained, keeping "a silence all the more remarkable in that it followed the most boisterous and insulting complaints." When four deputies accompanied by a very large armed force arrived around midnight, they found that the committee had been freed. However, they immediately took measures to arrest the ringleaders, four men and five women who were identified by the commissioners.

We can draw several lessons from the account of this day given by the civil committee. The dominant note is the local and confused character of the demonstration. Several times male and female rioters declared themselves in revolt, several times they proposed to place the committee under arrest, but still they could not prevent it from communicating with the Convention. Not once was a call raised for revolt against the government or a proposal made to form a general assembly. The Sovereign People who, wishing to punish their "disloyal representatives," had declared themselves in revolt only represented the residents of this section who intended to investigate the conduct of the section commissioners and even to dismiss them. The statement insists on the spirit of revolution, but this spirit was directed against the commissioners. The distribution of flour that day had only set fire to powder. The commissioners defended themselves without difficulty on this point, but the women "did not wish to hear anything, although they understood very well for the most part what the commissioners said," "they did not want any excuses." The crowd wanted to take advantage of this misunderstanding to "settle scores" with the hated commissioners. For this reason, the scope of the demonstration was limited.

The day of 11 Floréal was also characterized by the involvement of many women; the statement of the besieged committee and the witnesses agree that women made up the vast majority of the crowd. At the convention, the riot was described as being the work of a "very large group of women, supported by men who, appearing at their orders, were ready to aid them." The terms employed by the civil commissioners suggest a shift in the relation between men and women. Women were doubtless alone at the beginning of the demonstration, and then several men joined them. Men became more and more numerous once the women had forced the doors of the committee, although clearly women remained in the majority and were the last to leave the hall. Many women intervened in the discussion, and the commissioners remarked several times that women were "the most aggravated." They also noted that "these women and some men" had arrested them.

However, the rebels appointed five commissioners who were men. And the vocabulary used to describe one of the most important moments of the day is even more disturbing: "the men responsible for appointing the commissioners." This was the only time in the very long statement that the phrase "the men" is used alone. We know that women were in the majority in this crowd. Does this mean that, in spite of this majority, women did not participate in the choice of "these citizens who represented the people"? If this is so, we have a new, particularly illuminating example of the complex relations between women and popular sovereignty. It was indeed women who placed the civil committee under arrest "in the name of the Sovereign People and the law" and thus acted in the name of popular sovereignty. But once this was accomplished, only the men present held sovereignty through the right to vote, and women no longer formed part of the Sovereign People. Whatever the case, this statement overturns the description of this day given at the Convention. According to this description, men only appeared "by order of the women," but they were overrepresented among the ringleaders according to their numerical importance in the crowd.

The choice of section committees as the privileged target, which shows the limits of this reaction, resulted partly from the fact that the crowd was made up mostly of women. Only a question of degree distinguished this movement from the daily demonstrations in which women insulted the commissioners at bakers' doors or besieged them in their "refuge." There were few militant women in the Bonnet-de-la-Liberté section who could have influenced the direction of the movement. The day of 11 Floréal was not the work of the sansculottes but of the female popular masses. Knitters were not at the origin of this local revolt and did not direct it; instead, housewives and mothers, exasperated by the food situation, turned against the commissioners whom they knew and who served as scapegoats. Thus we must be careful not to generalize and claim that the riot's limited nature, probably the result of the overwhelming presence of women, was necessarily the conclusion of every female demonstration.

In addition, this episode shows the strong potential for mobilization by the female masses, and their function as detonator. Once again we must recognize not just the limitations but also the political consciousness of women of the people. In this local movement, without real outlet, the discontent nevertheless expressed the political ideas of the Revolution. In the eyes of the rioters, the civil commissioners were disloyal: they had "stolen" the flour that belonged to the populace; they had violated the peoples' rights by scorning their right to existence. Thus the commissioners were arrested in the name of the law and dismissed by the Sovereign People in revolt.

Moreover, the limited character of the revolt did not keep it from being dangerous. On 11 Floréal, the Committee of General Security passed a decree aimed directly at the women. The Military Committee was required to take all necessary steps to promptly arrest and judge the ringleaders of the seditious mob and gatherings that led to pillage and insults to the civil commissioners and other public government officials. Women saw through this decree and they were the first to protest it.

"MEN ARE COWARDS"

Women were just as conspicuous by their vehemence in groups as by the anger they expressed at the doors of bakers or civil committees. They always occupied the galleries of the Convention and were often arrested there for having excited trouble or brandished their quarter pound of bread with rage. Women also gathered around the Convention and formed groups inspired by the "furies of the guillotine." A report shows that even a "club of knitters" gathered every day in front of the Convention. "After having made contact with each other [the women] spread in groups and protested against the Convention, in which, they said, there was too much confidence."[16] Since the winter, militant women had formed such groups to emphasize the legislators' "treason." In the spring, they continued their activity, and henceforth were supported by all the female popular masses. The "regulars" were no longer the only ones who filled the galleries at the Convention, and nor were the knitters the only ones who formed angry groups.

The Convention and the merchants were the women's specific targets, but in their anger, some women had come to curse the Republic and to wish for a king who would give them bread. The ladies of la Halle were in complete agreement with these sentiments, and on 6 Floréal (25 April) they even proposed to go to the Convention to demand a king. But the historian K. D. Tønnesson rightly noted that we "must not exaggerate the importance of these royalist remarks, which rather than expressing true counter-revolutionary sentiments often resulted from a need to find particularly

16. A.N., F⁷ 4775⁴⁶ d. Vilambre.

bold statements in order to express hatred of the existing regime."[17] Moreover, these sentiments frequently occurred during crises of acute despair. As always during serious subsistence crises, many women shared the sentiments that motivated Parisian women who marched to Versailles on 5 October 1789: "Bread, but not at the price of liberty." The idea even arose that Convention deputies organized the famine to drive the people—headed by women—to demand a king. When women exclaimed that it "mattered little to them if they had a king as long as they had bread," other women responded, "Don't you see that they seek to make us die of hunger to force us to ask for the Old Regime? . . . All right then, screw it, we don't want any of it!"[18] These examples of royalist women of the people increased and were not isolated, but they remain an example of a minority of individuals and did not constitute a characteristic of the entire female popular masses. Popular royalism, which was predominantly female, existed during the famine of the Year III, but the presence in police statements of women (or men) who asked for a king is negligible in comparison to women who turned for inspiration to the Year II rather than to the Old Regime.

Women contrasted conditions during the Terror to the present period and its negative qualities: "In Robespierre's time we had bread and . . . now we die of hunger." They perceived the famine as a violation of the right to existence. From this grew the feeling, already evoked, of the legislators' betrayal and a return to tyranny and to slavery, because the people's right to existence and other rights that were inseparable were not respected. "It is eight months since we have had bread. Today we no longer have any. We are in slavery," asserted a citizen on 30 Germinal (19 April). "Yes," responded a female citizen, "the popular clubs have been closed in order to put us back into slavery. We are all idiots."[19]

It has been said that women dominated the groups because they were more numerous there and held the "most incendiary positions." *Women above all* became a frequent expression in police informers' reports. "In the groups . . . women above all" "appeared the most irritated" (25 Germinal), "appeared to play the principal role" (7 Floréal), "pour[ed] forth the most ab-

17. K. D. Tønnesson, *La Défaite des sans-culottes: Mouvement populaire et réaction bourgeoise en l'an III* (Oslo: Oslo University Press, 1959), p. 239.

18. Reports of 27 and 28 Germinal, 7 and 13 Floréal.

19. Report of 1 Floréal.

surd remarks and threats" (8 Floréal), "dared to make the most violent and seditious speeches" (18 Floréal), and "appeared very dissatisfied" (30 Floréal).

Not content with expressing their anger in the most lively terms, women called upon men to act. Almost every day police reports described, with remarkable consistency, the same scene.[20]

"Women say that men are jackasses to behave like this" (24 Germinal)

Women call men "jackasses for not going to the Convention to ask them why there is no grain" (25 Germinal)

"Women say that men show no heart when they accept such a modest ration" and add that they would rather that there was no more bread "because then [their] cowardly husbands would be forced to demand it" (26 Germinal)

Two women were questioned at the door of a baker for having cried that "all men were idiots for not gathering to march on the Convention" (28 Germinal)

"Women . . . poured out the most incendiary remarks, tried to provoke men to insurrection . . . called them cowards" (5 Floréal)

"Women . . . scoff at men, call them cowards. . . . A great number of them wish to go so far as to revolt" (7 Floréal)

"Women call men cowards if they do not appear" (8 Floréal)

"Women say to men that they are all cowards to behave in such a manner, given that there is an attempt to make the people die of hunger" (19 Floréal)

"Women provoke men to rebellion and pillage by uttering insults" (22 Floréal)

"Women cry against the Convention, saying that men are damned idiots for enduring hunger" (30 Floréal)

And several dossiers of militant women confirm that it was indeed women who played the role of "spokespeople for the revolution."

As a sign of antigovernment opposition, female citizens enjoined men to forsake guard duty. In characteristically extreme language, women threatened to gouge out their husbands' eyes or knife their husbands in the belly

---

20. Police report and A.N., F⁷ 4597 d. Bertrand (28 Germinal).

if they persisted in obeying the summons. Their remarks could be accompanied with expressive gestures, meant to ridicule the government: women lifted their skirts and, in the middle of the street, "wiped their behind with a summons to stand guard" or tore it up mockingly under the nose of the commander while saying to him, "No bread, no guard."[21]

These incessant appeals had to be stopped. Police reports and dossiers of female citizens who were questioned show clearly that these demonstrations cannot be attributed solely to the activity of militant women. We do not have, as in the spring and summer of 1793, a drive by women within the framework of the sansculottes, who by now were largely disorganized, but a true preponderance of women in the popular movement. The importance of women in the resistance of winter, and even more in the spring of the Year III, is one of the essential characteristics of this period. The repression against the sansculottes who stood out in the Year II made possible in turn the development of action by women, and its strength only grew.

The constant energy deployed by women to drive men to revolt was remarkable. "It is necessary that men march on the Convention," said a woman on 17 Floréal (6 May).[22] Did she mean that it was the responsibility of men to take charge of the revolt? These appeals show that women considered incomplete the revolt of a female crowd accompanied by some militant men—and the riot of 11 Floréal in the Bonnet-de-la-Liberté section is perhaps an example of this. By their desperately repeated insults, women sought to rebuild a popular movement, rich in all its components. Let us not forget this fundamental given in the case of uprising: only men possessed arms, and in particular the cannons, required to overthrow the government.

Thus women dedicated themselves to shaking up male apathy. They consciously assumed the role of detonator, of "firebrands." "If they began the dance, men would join them." "We will be followed by many other sections who are counting on us, and not just women, but also men who support us," asserted women on 2 and 17 Floréal.[23] But who helped whom? We find here the same structure as in the insurrection of Germinal (and which will be the same in Prairial): women rose, men followed them (with their weapons!), and in their turn women supported the men. The characteristic

---

21. A.N., F⁷ 4737 and W 546 d. Humbert, wife of Guyot, F⁷ 4743 d. Hervain: A.P.P., AA 188 f. 203; reports of 1, 2, and 21 Floréal.

22. Police report of 18 Floréal.

23. A.N., F⁷ 4774⁴⁶ d. Vilambre; A.D.S., VD* register 794, p. 32.

relations between men and women are present in the riots. Sexual roles existed at the heart of the crowd. Even if women ended by withdrawing to the background (but not by disappearing), the reciprocity of the two sexes was fundamental.

"Men are cowards": already in May of 1793 militant women pronounced the same phrase and played the same role of inciting action. Certainly, in May 1793, women did not set off the anti-Girondin insurrection. However, before it exploded, contemporaries presented this development as a possibility: women "hoped that they would be assisted by men," wrote a police informer on 13 May. "Women began the movement . . . men came in support of the women," wrote a deputy at the Convention on 18 May.[24] And without wanting to make excessive generalizations, it is necessary to acknowledge that the days of 5 and 6 October of 1789 followed the same pattern of a demonstration by women, followed by men organized in the national guard who had come "to support them" (as stated in *Les Révolutions de Paris*), and behind whom the women ended by withdrawing.[25] Men "supported" women, then women "supported" men in a pendular movement: this nonegalitarian complementarity of the sexes, which emerged forcefully during the Year III, is not unique to it. Incitements to action were indeed a constant of women's behavior in the revolutionary movement. And even when women were in the minority in a crowd, they still assumed this role. To take just two famous examples, on 14 July 1789, Pauline Léon "led the citizens against the partisans of tyranny and . . . roused cowards to leave their homes"; and on 10 August 1792, Claire Lacombe "not only fought the satellites of a treacherous court," but also "rallied the citizens that a continuous fire put to flight"—while elsewhere a young woman "harangued the throng."[26]

Behind the spontaneity of the crowd and its apparent disorder, male and female roles thus took shape in the riot. The revolutionary insurrections did not all submit to these "rules," but during certain periods of crisis, collective *mentalités* expected women to be the ones to summon to revolt, to generate action, to start the movement, and to bring men along with them. In their studies of the revolutionary crowd, Georges Lefebvre and after him George Rudé, who were not very sensitive to the relations between men

24. See "Birth of the Female Sansculottes Movement, 1789–1793" and "Women as Guardians of the Nation," this volume.

25. Ibid.

26. A.N., F⁷ 4774⁹ d. Leclerc, T 1001¹⁻³ d. Lacombe; Moniteur, XIII, 538.

and women, have ignored these sexual roles.[27] But these roles were thought of as a given by the popular movement, were recognized by the population, and were assumed by women.

Frequently (but never in the Year III), contemporaries wrote that women were "put forward by men" because they feared repression less. These are reflections by men (deputies, police informers, journalists) who could not conceive of an intervention by women that was not initiated by men. It is true that, in explosive situations, a militant (man or woman) sometimes tried to light the match by turning to female citizens. In thus giving the initiatory role to women, the militant could both act out of concern for his or her own protection and respond to this conception of the roles of men and women expressed in collective representations. In these cases, women were the inevitable mediators between the militant and the masses. It was expected that the revolution would be born from their acts and from their voices.

[margin annotation: P= initiators]

The efforts by women in the Year III were not in vain. At the end of the Floréal (mid-May), the idea of an imminent day of insurrection had taken shape in the entire Parisian populace. If one is to believe their opponents, militant women had shown in the last *décade* of Floréal a "suspicious" agitation, satisfaction, and self-confidence. "Patience, the brigands will not always have the upper hand. The Montagnards will recover. The moment is not distant," repeated the wife of Périot.[28] The report of 26 Floréal (19 May) emphasized a relative period of calm, but, it continued, "this heralded tranquillity, as real as it is at this moment, can also be seen as the calm of death." In the final days of the month, police informers drew increasingly sinister pictures of streets in the capital, where "one will soon see only walking cadavers occupied in paying their final respects to those who have preceded them to the tomb."

But among these "walking cadavers" spread the rumor "that if the distribution of bread is not more abundant, the Faubourg Saint-Antoine will, on the first of Prairial, rise as a group and encourage the rest of Paris to follow its example."[29]

27. Georges Lefebvre, "Foules révolutionnaires, *Annales historiques de la Révolution française* 11 (1934): 1–26; George Rudé, *The Crowd in the French Revolution* (Oxford: Clarendon Press, 1959).

28. See appendix 3, "Portraits of Militant Women," in this volume.

29. Police reports of 28 and 30 Floréal.

15 "Bread and the Constitution"

On 30 Floréal (19 May) the section assemblies were especially turbulent. In the Bon-Conseil section, women entered the general assembly in force, asked for bread, and, according to their adversaries, provoked a "real riot." At the entry to the Popincourt general assembly, a female citizen supposedly distributed a printed petition that was none other than the appeal *Insurrection of the People, to Obtain Bread and Reconquer Its Rights,* which presented the outlines of a plan for revolution and served to rally the insurgents.

The uprising of the Faubourg Saint-Antoine was expected the next day, and preparations were made for it. In the Droits-de-l'Homme section, the female citizen Leblanc gathered several people around the guard corps for this reason. At eleven thirty at night in the Finistère section, the wife of Devaux "provoked the people . . . to open the doors of the general assembly, saying that if the deputations of the Faubourg Saint-Antoine were going to arrive, it was necessary to open the assembly"; supported by other women, she forced the civil committee to give her the keys to the hall, "claiming that the small number of revolters she was part of were sovereign and could violate all the laws."[1]

"YOU WILL MARCH!"
The morning of the first day of Prairial (20 May), unquestionably marked the height of the mass women's movement. Everywhere, women, alone or accompanied by militant men or workers, triggered the insurrection. The

---

1. A.N., F⁷ 4774⁷⁴ d. Pernet (Bon-Conseil), F⁷ 4771 d. Leblanc, W 547 no. 52, wife of Devaux. A.P.P., AA 266 f. 229.

movement differed from previous riots in the Year III not only by its consequences but also because it immediately possessed an insurrectional
character.[2]

The beginning of the revolt was marked by groups of women who traveled in continuous waves to the Convention. In many cases, they went first
to the civil committee, most often with the intention of forcing the commissioners to march with them. In some sections, this step differed little
from the proceedings two months before, although women were now more
determined and had decided at all costs to obtain bread. The commissioners
were mistreated: in the Bon-Conseil section, one who the day before had
sought armed force to chase female citizens from the general assembly was
"assailed by these furies of the guillotine and could not escape their homi-

2. For descriptions of events in the sections see:
Arcis: A.N., F^7 2499 pp. 30–60, W 546 no. 35, F^7 4687 d. Dumont, F^7 4702 d. Fa-
bien, F^{7}4680 d. Doujeval, F^{7}4577 d. Albacq, F^7 4574^{25} d. Longival, F^7 4741 d. Henry,
F^7 4628 d. Cabrol
Arsenal: A.P.P., AA 71 f. 137–140; A.N., W 546 no. 18, F^7 4774^{33} d. Mansienne
Bon-Conseil: A.N., F^7 4774^{67} d. Pernet, F^{7}4775^{50} d. Wabe
Bondy: A.N., F^7 4775^{29} d. Thomas, F^7 4775^{11} d. Saint-Prix, F^7 4775^{32} d. Toupiolle
Champs-Elysées: A.N., F^{7*} 2473 p. 53, F^{7*} 2475 4 Prairial, F^7 4629 d. Bunon;
A.D.S., VD* 794, p. 121
Droits-de-l'Homme: A.N., F^7 4633 d. Cannonkel, F^7 4774^{66} d. Millet
Faubourg-Montmartre: A.N., F^7 4729 d. Gonthier
Fidélité: A.N., AF II 50, d. 350, p. 10
Finistère: A.N., W 547 no. 52
Fraternité: A.N., F^7 4775^{45} d. Vidot
Gravilliers: A.N., F^7 4586 d. Barbot, F^7 4720 d. Gauthier
Jardin-des-Plantes: A.N., W 546 no. 21 Paradis
Halle-au-Blé: B.H.V.P. Ms. 932
Lombards: A.N., F^7 4695 d. Dupré and F^7 4774^{84} d. Provost
Marchés: A.N., F^7 4582 d. Augien
Museum: A.N., F^7 4665 d. Deffaut, F^7 4774^{67} d. Périot, F^7 4774^{39} d. Mauger,
W 546 no 29
Nord: A.N., F^7 4584 d. Baillet, W 546 no. 34
Observatoire: A.N., F^7 4774^{51} d. Moreau, wife of Houssel
Poissonnière: A.P.P., AA 214; A.D.S., VD* register 987, p. 73
Temple: A.N., F^{7*} 2491, F^7 4767 d. Delaunay, F^7 4774^{26} d. Louis
Tuileries: A.N., W 546 no. 23, F^7 4774^{32} d. Mandrillon
Faubourg Saint-Antoine: A.N., F^7 4648 d. Christon, F^7 4741 d. Henry, AF II 50 d.
385, p. 10, F^{7*} 2491, F^7 4615 d. Boyer, wife of Ladroite, F^7 4775^{45} d. Vignot, W 547
no. 46
On the entire city and on the Convention, see police report of 2 Prairial: A.D.S.,
VD* register 794, p. 45; A.N., W 546 no. 38, W 547 no. 43, F^7 4746 d. Huret; B.N.,
N.A.F. 2676, p. 204; *Moniteur*, XXIV, 297–514. For a precise description of the Prairial insurrection, see K. D. Tønnesson, *LaDéfaite des sans-culottes: Mouvement populaire et réaction bourgeoise en l'an III* (Oslo: Oslo University Press, 1959).

cidal hands before suffering several blows. At last his colleagues came to his aid." Elsewhere women invaded the civil committees and affirmed that it was necessary to march to the Convention. Around ten o'clock in the morning in the Finistère section, the same women who had besieged it for several days managed to force the doors, but despite their efforts they could not rout the commissioners. These women then called armed citizens to help them. Faced with their guns and fists, the commissioners were forced to leave their "asylum" and accompany the women to the Convention. "Old fellow, you have a full belly, that is why you do not wish to march with the others. But you will march," asserted young Joséphine Rouillère to one of the commissioners, while male and female citizens promised a not very amusing future to one of his colleagues: "Villain, you do not have long to reign. For the moment it is as if you were nothing, and tomorrow you will be like nothing at all."

In several sections women seized drums. In the Arcis section a little before ten in the morning, a group of female rioters forced their way into the police station of Pont-au-Change and seized two boxes. Improvising drums, they beat time to rouse the residents of the neighborhood to go to the Convention. The chief officer tried to recover his boxes, but with no success! Women threw themselves on him. Pursued by these rebellious women, he fled up to an apartment and shut himself inside, throwing closed the double locks. He thought his last hour had come as women threatened to break down the door, strip him of his epaulettes, and cut him to pieces, until a ruse of the police commissioner delivered him from that unenviable position. In the neighboring Fidélité section (previously Maison-Commune), the commander of the armed force was also "besieged" by several women who demanded the drum with the intention of marching on the Convention. In the afternoon, the streets around the Arsenal were covered by women calling people to arms. Not far from there on the Pont-Marie, "wild" women overcame the resistance of the commander of the guard, swore that the flag of the Fraternité section "would march" at their head, and descended from the parapet to seize it. In the central sections, the officers who refused to accompany the rebels were abused by women, who tore their epaulettes from them. On the Rue Saint-Denis, groups of female merchants of la Halle tried to disarm the faithful national guards at the Convention, calling them "bloody idiots." The patrol, who brandished their bayonets in an attempt to break up these gatherings, was pushed back with cries of "Down with Bayonets!"

Not only did female rioters challenge almost everywhere those who were ready to defend the Convention, but they also compelled, if need be with armed force, all men and women who were in their way to follow them. For example, the female citizen Gonthier from the Faubourg Montmartre followed a group of women, who, she said, repeated to her, "Come, Gonthier, come if you are a good female citizen, come with us." One of them said, "Look, see, my child draws only blood from my breast instead of milk." "Aren't you going with us? Are you afraid?" asked the Museum section women of the female citizen Périot who took time only to close her shop before joining them.

In several sections such as Gravilliers, Arsenal, and Nord, female demonstrators went into shops and workshops and climbed upstairs to force the recalcitrant and the workers to come with them. In the sack-making workshop of Sainte-Elisabeth (Temple), a militant woman sought to rouse her comrades. Along the quais, on the boulevards, in the alleys, and at crossroads, women called for insurrection everywhere. In the Tuileries section, only a few meters from the Convention, after they had opposed with particular violence the distribution of bread while making a tour of the bakers, approximately fifty women threw themselves on another woman who had just taken her ration and tried to force her to go with them by grabbing her skirt and throwing stones at her. "We must support the faubourgs who are going to come down. All these rascals will have to fart," threatened one of the ringleaders, her knife in hand. In the north, in the Bondy section, the female citizen Saint Prix read the *Insurrection of the People* to her male and female neighbors and urged men to write the slogan "bread and the Constitution of 1793" on their hats. To the west, in the Champs-Elysées section, the former member of the Revolutionary Republican Women Solende exclaimed with joy "that she was going to get dressed up and go to Paris to seek women, and if she should find herself in the fight, she would do as the others." In the south, in the Observatoire section, the wife of Houssel asked to join the Faubourg Saint-Antoine, which "marched for the good cause," and proposed to sound the alarm herself in order to gather citizens.

To the east was the Faubourg Saint-Antoine, a site of great interest for several days. There, early in the morning, women forced other women to leave houses, shops, and even passing coaches. Around ten o'clock, an initial gathering of approximately four hundred women went to the Convention, their drum beating double time and the "coalwoman" Louise Catherine Vignot at their head, dressed as a man, wearing a three-cornered hat with a red and blue plume, and holding a saber in her hand.

Thus coming from all points of the city, by the end of the morning one group of women met in front of the Convention.

WOMEN AT THE CONVENTION

The assembly had opened at eleven o'clock, with the indignant reading by a deputy of the plan of the *Insurrection of the People*. The reading was showered with applause by women in the galleries, who broke into "ironic laughter" at the decree passed against the rebels. While a proclamation to the Parisians was being voted on, the first women who had arrived at the Convention filled one of the galleries and, perched on the benches, asked forcefully for bread. Their cries were repeated by other female spectators. The president was obliged to put on his hat (a custom when requesting silence) to reestablish calm. According to the *Moniteur*,

> The cries 'for bread! for bread!' began again. Attempts to calm the women were in vain; some laughed at the state in which they saw the Convention, while others waved their fists at the president and the other representatives of the people. Their example spread; the second gallery on the other side also filled with women who uttered the same cry. The assembly remained in the greatest calm; at the end of a quarter of an hour the tumult quieted a little.

Not for long! The president scarcely had time to pronounce several phrases and remove his hat when he again had to put it on and break off because of women's cries. After fifteen minutes he could make himself heard, but just as he opened his mouth, a woman cried: "We have waited long enough, damnation!" while her female neighbors let out a torrent of abuse and gestured threateningly toward the deputies.

From that moment, it was almost impossible for the deputies to make themselves heard amidst the cries and mocking laughter of women in the galleries who asked for bread and the Constitution of 1793. At the moment when the president ordered the galleries emptied, "very violent blows" were heard at the door of the meeting hall.

A little over an hour had passed, during which time the first groups of female protestors and about ten men had got past the barricades of military police protecting the Convention and were trying now to break down the door of the meeting hall. The female citizen Ladroite of the Faubourg Saint-Antoine boasted the next day: "You should have seen me yesterday . . . with the wife of Lemoine from the Faubourg Saint-Marcel as we broke down the door of the Convention with logs. I have a completely swollen fist. Only my little son who was with me worried me; without him it would have been better." A bench was placed across the door: the female rioters used it as a battering ram after having thrown down the policeman who had climbed on top of it.

As soon as the first noise of blows reverberated in the Convention hall, some women left the galleries to take part in the assault. By order of the president, soldiers and two *muscadins* succeeded in forcibly emptying the galleries of their female occupants. Scarcely had they finished when the door gave way under the blows of male and female rioters, but the women were pushed back by the gendarmes and the national guard, who advanced with bayonets pointed forward and sabers unsheathed. A second assault was soon launched, but without success. Several women were wounded; one of them, "having seized the saber of a gendarme who wished to drive her back, had seriously hurt her hand."

Rumor inflated the incident: the gendarmes had struck women with their sabers, had cut their arms, a deputy had severed the fist of a woman, another had stabbed three women! Spread indignantly, this false news antagonized the population and contributed more than a little in driving men to take up arms against the Convention. "Run, run, go to the Convention, women are being killed there," cried a female citizen to her male neighbor, and elsewhere a militant sansculotte persuaded the citizens "who were already inflamed to march on the Convention by shouting to them that the deputies were attacking their wives and it was necessary to leave immediately."[3]

The men of the Faubourg Saint-Antoine and armed citizens from other sections—"bread and the Constitution of 1793" written in chalk on their hats—finally joined the women at the Convention around three o'clock. The fight began again at the meeting hall door. "At three thirty-three," wrote the *Moniteur* with astonishing precision, "a large crowd of women and men armed with guns, pikes, and sabers entered the Convention," demanded "bread and the Constitution of 1793," and chased the deputies from their benches in order to claim those benches themselves.

The deputy Féraud was killed by the rebels. Although it is not certain who struck the fatal blow, there is no doubt that the crowd, or at least a group of male and female insurgents, attacked this deputy. A little later, a woman who was lightly wounded on her thumb and had blood on her clothes recounted: "We had entered the Convention to demand bread, and these scoundrels said that we were riffraff. I noticed the deputy Féraud and grabbed him by the neck. Several of us got together and dragged him out of the hall by his hair and then we cut off his head."[4]

3. A.N., F⁷ 4741 d. Henry, F⁷ 4774⁴⁵ d. Michel.
4. A.N., W 548 no. 72.

A twenty-three-year-old secondhand dealer, Marie Françoise Carle Migelly, was suspected of having fired the gun that had perhaps killed Féraud. She acknowledged "having struck the deputy Féraud's head with a clog at the moment when he had just been knocked down by a bullet and was still struggling."[5]

The consequences of these events are known. Threatening the Convention deputies, the insurgents read the *Insurrection of the People* at the bar of the Convention. In the middle of an incessant tumult, the crowd demanded bread, the Constitution of 1793, a new Parisian city government, the release of imprisoned patriots, the arrest of hostile deputies, the return of the Montagnards arrested in Germinal, searches of homes for supplies, and the replacement of section authorities. The Montagnard deputies who remained at the Convention rallied to the insurgents and proposed a series of decrees that were favorable to them. Around seven o'clock, the head of Féraud perched at the end of a pike was presented to the imperturbable Boissy d'Anglas, who occupied the chair of president. During the night, the rioters were chased from the meeting hall by the armed forces of sections faithful to the Convention, and the deputies separated at four in the morning after having decreed the arrest of fourteen Montagnard deputies and annulled all the decrees passed under duress during the day.

During the meeting of the first of Prairial, women were constantly present in the crowd. Several times, deputies indicated that women even distinguished themselves by "the ferocity of their speech and their incitements," as they "threatened and incessantly attacked [the deputies]." The *Moniteur* reported that at one point a woman "with bare arms" waved violently at the gallery from the speaker's box, and that a little later another women tried to make herself heard from this same spot. Outside the Convention, women also showed their hostility. They surrounded the deputies who passed and asked them for bread; they strenuously opposed the proclamation and the decrees passed that morning against the insurgents by the Convention.

5. M. F. Carle Migelly was not representative of the women who invaded the Convention. She had been arrested in 1792 for royalism and had then proposed to serve as a prison spy. Freed in the Year III, she formed the project of assassinating the deputy Boissy d'Anglas. According to E. Lairtullier, she was condemned to death on 24 Prairial of the Year IV. A.N., W 180, F⁷ 4633 d. Carlomigellix, F⁷ 4774⁴⁶ d. Migellie (Migelly), F⁷ 4651 d. wife of Collot. There are rather fantastic and romantic passages about her in E. Lairtullier, *Les Femmes célèbres de 1789 à 1795 et leur influence dans la révolution* (Paris, L. Boulanger: 1893), vol. 2; J. Claretie, *Les Derniers Montagnards* (Paris: 1868), pp. 356–361.

The Female Rioters

Male and female rebels demanded "bread and the Constitution of 1793." For many, this slogan signified especially bread and an end to the present situation. Clearly articulated political objectives were expressed frequently only by militant women, for whom these goals predominated over concerns for food. "With all the fervor of a maniac," the wife of Périot exhorted the other "scoundrels" "not to give up until we receive the Constitution of 1793 immediately" and cried: "Courage, today the Montagnards are going to triumph. We must crush the moderate toads. We have with us the army, the brave gendarmes, and the faubourgs. . . . We must ask for Billaud, Collot, Barère, and the Montagnards who are under arrest and besiege the Convention until they are returned to Paris."[6] These militant women made ending the food shortage, which certainly concerned them, subordinate to passing political measures (the enforcement of the Constitution, the return of the Montagnard deputies and the expulsion of Convention moderates, the installing of a new city government, and so on).

And yet there were female rioters without any political consciousness, whose sole motive for revolt was the lack of bread. Several female rebels of Prairial had even been questioned during the Year II for thoughtless counterrevolutionary words. They were not agitators but women without precise political ideas, who may have blamed the regime for their misfortunes in the Year II, and who one year later marched against the Convention because they were hungry.

Between these two extremes—militant women and apolitical paupers—most women saw a connection between their victory and a possible return to the Year II, symbolized by the Constitution of 1793. This was the political twist that the female (and male) sansculottes among the rioters offered to the sometimes more confused aspirations of the female popular masses. In this sense, the slogan "bread and the Constitution of 1793" was indeed the clearly articulated expression of the demands of women of the people, even if most of them privileged the former. As a police observer wrote several days later: "Bread is the foundation of their insurrection physically speaking, but the Constitution is the soul."[7] Similarly, though few women asked specifically for the return of the Montagnard deputies, there were many more women who characterized the success of the insurrection by these words: "If the Jacobins had the upper hand." Such words show that

6. See note 2 (Museum) and appendix 3, "Portraits of Militant Women," in this volume.

7. A.N., F⁷ 4743 d. Hernox.

the Jacobins were identified with the rights of the people. Like the appeal *Insurrection of the People,* most of the female demonstrators linked irrevocably their demand for bread and for "common rights." They expected the movement to end both the shortage and "tyranny."

Above all, they aimed their demands at the Convention and the merchants. Many women added their complaints about section authorities to those about the Convention. When, that afternoon, the Montagnard deputy Romme proposed that "the civil committees of each section be replaced in the name of the People," he received "the liveliest" applause. Fewer women distinguished the Montagnards from the Convention deputies in general.

In contrast, from confirmed militant women to simple female rioters, hardly a single woman forgot merchants in the list of their enemies. A great many men certainly felt the same way, but men were less likely than women to harp on this theme. For many women, the attack on the Convention was inseparable from an inevitable attack on merchants. The wife of Gatrel thus asserted that "the merchants and the Convention are all damned"; the "furies" of the Arsenal section "swore aloud that after having annihilated the Convention, they would pillage merchants and others." Flamand's wife, a tailor who, during the disturbances in the Tuileries section, saw the body of Féraud pass, interspersed her applause with these words: "Bravo, bravo, soon it will be the merchant's turn to get this treatment; it is necessary."[8]

The apolitical female rioters limited themselves to these two principal enemies, whereas female sansculottes added another political adversary. The sisters Barbot wished "to do justice to all aristocrats, moderates, and merchants." "Young men," a symbol of both political reaction and social inequalities, were often threatened: announcing the death of Féraud, a female linenworker asserted "that this is not the end, that soon the heads of those who have their hair puffed up will be carried on pike"; a female porter also demanded that "all the merchants and the *muscadins* be hanged." And the wife of Périot, after blaming the "moderate toads," continued, "The merchants will have their turn later. . . . There are complaints about the guillotine, but the guillotine will be called *muscadin* from now on. . . . Yes, we must have the traitors' blood."[9]

"Yes, we must have the traitors' blood." This phrase illustrates the punitive will of the rebels. If there was a sentiment that these militant

8. A.N., F7* 2524 p. 135, W 546 no. 23.
9. A.N., F7 4774[86] d. Raimbaut, F7 4747 d. Inca, and appendix 3 in this volume.

woman could share with the entire female (and male) popular masses, it was the sense that their mandate had been betrayed by the Convention deputies. Setting aside the hot-headedness typical of this type of rebellion, which favors extreme language, we find among male and female insurgents affirmations of a desire to punish that was inseparable from notions of sovereignty and popular justice, as well as the idea that in order to end the food shortage it was necessary to return to the Terror. Many rioters essentially said that if they were to recover their rights, the people had to deploy violence toward their enemies, whom it was necessary to suppress. Under revolutionary intoxication, these sentiments predominated among the insurgents who were later accused of having spoken bloodthirsty words.

Sound the Alarm, Roll the Cannons

The insurrection continued for three days,[10] but women did not continue to play the dominant role. Although they were present in the crowds' movements, they were missing once the insurrection took shape in the framework of sansculottes organizations.

This was particularly clear on 2 Prairial (21 May). This day was characterized by the holding of (illegal) general assemblies and by the threats of insurgent batallions of the national guard that aimed their cannons at the Convention. Women did not assume a role in the standard accounts of the day. Their activity had not ceased, but they could not play a part in either the general assemblies or in the national guard, from which women were excluded.

That morning, a gathering that was very threatening to the government was held at city hall. It denied legitimacy to the Convention by taking for itself the name of National Convention of the Sovereign People. The Convention deputies feared that different sections would join and create an Insurrectional Central Committee or a new city government to lead the movement. (There was nothing to this.) Female residents of the neighborhood were present during this episode. That morning, they had forced a commissioner to sound the alarm at city hall. In the neighboring section of Arcis, women who had demonstrated the day before, having lost none of their determination, gathered with the aim of going to city hall and urged passersby to attack the Convention. The women again took by force the guard post containing the cannons with which they hoped to dissolve the

10. See Tønnesson, *La Défaite des sans-culottes.*

Convention. And yet, women could not attend the general assembly of the section, where the decision was made to appoint a new city government.[11] Once again we see the myopia that never stopped restricting the place of women at the heart of the popular movement. Women were always present during spontaneous demonstrations. They sounded the alarm at the Convention, tried to seize cannons, and urged others to revolt, but they disappeared from the documents as soon as the Sovereign People organized themselves in assembly.

And so, except for female citizens of the districts close to city hall, women did not play a pivotal role on 2 Prairial. In little menacing groups, they surrounded the Convention but did not try to force the doors, insulted the national guards who were faithful to the Convention, and supported the Faubourg Saint-Antoine. In all of these examples, women's actions were only subordinate.

Other women pursued their commitment of the day in what seemed to them the logical manner. They wished to recover, if necessary by force, the provisions that had been "stolen" from them by Convention deputies and merchants. In the Faubourg Saint-Antoine, the storage warehouse of the Republic was attacked by male and female citizens from every section, who forced the authorities to distribute to them the provisions (biscuits) that were stored there. Beginning at nine o'clock in the morning, the distribution lasted seven hours. Then for three hours the crowd searched the storehouse.[12] In different sections of the city, incidents provoked by women occurred over food supplies.

These different examples indicate that although women did not become apathetic on 2 Prairial, they did not display any interest in the major events of the day, such as the illegal general assemblies and the gunners gathered before the Convention. It may be that female citizens, supportive of action by men, only participated in limited, individual, subordinate actions. It may be that they turned their attention to the supply of food, withdrew into the social realm, and abandoned the political arena to male citizens gathered in general assemblies. Only the female residents of sections that gathered at city hall were part of the main events of 2 Prairial. But their absence from the Arcis general assembly illustrates perfectly the absence of Parisian women from the important events of 2 Prairial. We see here the limits to action by women, limits forced upon them because female citizens were

---

11. *Moniteur*, XXIV, 517, 520–524; A.N., AF II 50 d. 385 p. 10, F^7 4687 d. Dumont, F^7 4702 d. Fabien; A.P.P., AA 61 f. 386.

12. A.P.P., AA 219 f. 119, AA 136 f. 205; A.N., F^7* 2500.

excluded from the rights founding citizenship. However, these limits were also internal: women could have tried to impose themselves upon section assemblies, as they had done already in times of crisis. They preferred to take charge of a redistribution of "monopolized" subsistences.

On 3 Prairial, while the government prepared to attack the Faubourg Saint-Antoine, the insurrection exhausted itself. Then militants of both sexes turned to women again, encouraging them to start a new demonstration, in the hope that men would follow. This schema (militant men and women arousing groups of women who in turn galvanized the men) previously invoked during the Germinal riots, can be seen clearly in police reports as well as in isolated events: two men and two women unsuccessfully urged the female residents of the Faubourg Saint-Antoine to seize drums and sound the alarm because, they said, "then the men will come after."[13] In the evening, women took the initiative to set free the journeyman locksmith Tinel, who was to be executed at the Place de Grève for having paraded the head of the deputy Féraud at the end of a pike on 1 Prairial; the crowd returned him in triumph to his home in the Faubourg Saint-Antoine. The news spread like a trail of gun powder that "the women of the faubourg" had just "returned life to a brother."[14]

The next day, women distinguished themselves again when a troop of more than a thousand armed men, sent by the Convention under the orders of General Kilmaine, entered the Faubourg Saint-Antoine. Surrounded by the residents of the faubourg, it had to make a not very glorious retreat: "We were surrounded by a countless multitude of armed men and by a horde of shrews who were a thousand times more atrocious than the men," wrote Kilmaine.[15] Louise Catherine Vignot was asked later if she was not "among the women who urged the citizens to stop the troop who was in the faubourg from retreating." At ten in the morning, the government committees ordered the faubourg to return Tinel and the cannons of the three sections: if it refused, the faubourg would be considered in a state of rebellion, would no longer be provided with fresh supplies, and would be besieged by the national guard. This proclamation created a disturbance. Some residents of the faubourg wanted to resist to the end, whereas others were discouraged. For the most part, female citizens were on the side of the resistance: "assembled in all the corners," they "created an uproar" and urged the men to persevere, wrote a witness.[16] Thus the wife of

13. A.N., W 548 nos. 71 and 74.
14. A.N., F⁷ 4662 d. Dauphinot, W 547 no. 61, F⁷ 4276 wife of Sergent. See appendix 3 in this volume.
15. Cited by Tønnesson, *La Défaite des sans-culottes,* p. 315.

Ladroite and her eldest daughter were accused of having spent the day in the Grande-Rue of the faubourg, "making the most incendiary and provocative speeches, saying that it was unendurable that the cannons be returned." And the police commissioner asked Louise Catherine Vignot "if she had not agitated for keeping the cannons"; had the young girl decided to fight when she left in the afternoon "to go for a walk," as she claimed, her sword at her side, or did she judge it safer to confide this compromising object to a neighbor?

Outside the faubourg, "women like furies exhorted the men and shouted: 'We must support our brothers of the Faubourg Saint-Antoine, get the best of the deputies, and show no mercy to merchants and *muscadins.*'" In the Poissonnière section, women said that "we must not allow the Faubourg Saint-Antoine to be destroyed; we must help it," and in the Gravilliers section, women wished to seize cannons to go to their aid.[17] Armed men also showed their intention to rejoin the faubourg, but they finally submitted to the ultimatum, and "at eight or nine o'clock everything was over."[18]

The Forbidden Street

The surrender of the faubourg sounded the death knell of the mass women's movement—and of the sansculotte movement in general. The first day of Prairial had been its apogee. During that day and the following days, contemporaries had perceived the beginning of the insurrection. Their accounts, vocabulary, turns of phrase, and even ellipses show that for many, the sense of an "emergency," and then the process of remembering the event, was profoundly marked by the importance of women. This importance was in the first instance numerical: "This is a bad misguided woman, why isn't she the only one?"[19] Participants and witnesses referred constantly to the role of women and, frequently, characterized the day of 1 Prairial through female demonstration: "the day that women had been at the Convention," "when women brought trouble there," "at the moment when women took over the hall," "women worked to save the Republic," "to have been seen on the side of the women," and so on.

The force of this view of women's activity was such that it came to hide reality and was invoked to confuse the issue. In self-defense the insurgents,

---

16. See note 7.

17. Report of 5 Prairial; A.N., F⁷ 4776; A.P.P., AA 266 f. 106.

18. Tønnesson, *La Défaite des sans-culottes,* p. 323.

19. A.N., F⁷ 4635 d. Catille (report of the civil committee of Quinze Vingts on the wife of Provost).

often spontaneous ringleaders, maintained that they had been forcibly dragged by demonstrators or blamed their actions on one or several anonymous women who sometimes appear indeed to have come straight from their imagination, as if the easiest and most credible defense consisted in protecting oneself under the shadow of women's action. Though these specious allegations barely fooled the accusers, they accepted them as fact, as an inevitable and necessary part of every retranscription of the event. In themselves, these allegations give an account of the importance of the group "women" while contributing to its exaggeration.

Another indication of the prominent position held by this group of women at the heart of the popular movement in Prairial and during the Year III were the accusations that a number of militants had spoken in "groups of women" and had driven these women to revolt. For the upholders of order, a man was "that much more dangerous when his duties led him to speak frequently to women."[20]

The authorities emphasized the role played by women during the revolt. "We cannot conceal that in the stormy moments that have troubled this city hall, women have played the role of firebrands," sighed the civil committee of the North section one and a half months after events.[21]

From the evening of 1 Prairial, in the Convention liberated from the rebels, the deputy André Dumont asked that the entry to the assembly galleries be definitely forbidden to women. "It is necessary," he continued, "to exclude them from political assemblies, where women have nothing to do, and where they can only make trouble." These decrees were passed without difficulty. On 1 Prairial, the Convention members forbade women to enter the galleries. On 4 Prairial, fearing that the women would only trouble the general assemblies summoned to pursue the "terrorists," the members deprived women of the right to attend any political assembly.

For female citizens forbidden any political space, there remained the street. But even this space was too much. On 4 Prairial, in a unanimous decision, the Convention decreed:

> Whether misguided or incited by enemies of liberty, women abuse the regards we have for the weakness of the sex, run through the streets, assemble, form up in ranks, and create disorder in all the operations of the police and

20. A.N., F7* 2476, p. 138.
21. A.N., F7 4584 d. Ravinet, wife of Baillet.

the military. [Therefore] we decree that all women withdraw, until otherwise ordered, to their respective homes. Those women who, one hour after the posting of the present decree, are found in the streets, gathered in groups of more than five, will be dispersed by armed force and then arrested.

Finally, on 8 Prairial, judging that the wives of the arrested Montagnard deputies could "in leading astray others, be very dangerous," the Convention ordered them to leave Paris and to remain under the surveillance of their respective municipalities. The day before, arguing that women had been "the principal instigators" of all the insurrectional movements, two deputies had demanded that the ringleaders of Prairial be judged by military commission, or at least be arrested by their sections. The Convention did not take any notice of this intervention for, as it recalled very justly, women like men were included in the measures passed against the insurgents. However, in some sections several days later, the "law concerning women who could have caused men to revolt" was discussed.[22]

There were no less than four proposals for repressive decrees concerning women in eight days! The unprecedented nature of this fierceness gives a good sense of women's role on 1 Prairial and the fear that they provoked among the Convention deputies.

There is often a tendency to link together without more ado the decrees of 1 and 4 Prairial (20 and 23 May) with those of 9 Brumaire, Year II (30 October, 1793) on the prohibition of women's clubs, without taking account of the circumstances in which they had been passed. In this perspective, their only cause was the misogyny of the deputies. In order to show at any cost that the Revolution was "antifeminist," we end up forgetting and hiding the important role that women played. At the origin of the decrees of Prairial Year III lay the energy and the violence of women of the insurgent people against a social and political power: the decrees aimed at women as one of the most active constituents of the popular movement and not at women per se because of their gender. These decrees dovetailed, however, with a movement to enclose women in their homes and make them into "women of the interior." The street, which the Convention wished to forbid them on 4 Prairial, was certainly a site of expression for militant women, but it was also one of the spaces of female sociability, the place where women of the people evolved. In the wish to turn women into cloistered housewives, *mentalités,* the installation of a new dominant ideology, and the fear of a mass women's movement of popular origin were mixed together.

22. *Moniteur,* XXIV, 515, 519, 555, 563; A.P.P. AA 266 f. 235; B.H.V.P., Ms. 932, p. 20.

The decrees of Prairial and other evidence show women as a very specific group, a differentiated part of the popular movement. We can recognize here the lines of sexual division that traversed the popular movement, each sex having its own role to play. And, in the fireworks over the exceptional character of the event, which were only the consequences of the previous months, the role of women was indeed one of "firebrands," detonators of the entire popular masses. This function explains both their importance in the first hours of the insurrection and their relative effacement in the following hours.

We are speaking here of groups and not of individuals. It may have been men who acted as ringleaders, but they were immediately followed (or hoped to be followed) by a group of women, and then by a mass of men "shaken up" by the women. These stages are evident in the words of the police inspector who wrote on 3 Prairial, "It is principally women who are incited, who then pass all their frenzy to the men's spirits, inflaming them with their seditious words and exciting the most violent agitation."

These lines and various episodes of the insurrection clearly show an internal development in the popular movement, which was glimpsed in Germinal and assumed all its force in Prairial. The male (or female) militants addressed themselves primarily to women, who in turn encouraged action by men. It could be said that this schema is convenient and a little simplistic in its linearity, but I do not think so. Nonetheless, although illustrated by several descriptions, it remains a schema and is capable of variations—which do not, however, cause it to lose any of its explanatory force.

Without excluding the possibility that women were pushed forward for reasons of protection, it seems that when an (isolated) militant asked women (in a group) to utter the slogans of the insurrection or to sound the alarm, it was also because, in the collective representation of the riot, it was in some way necessary for women to begin it, with men (in a group) taking over from them later—just as earlier women spoke scornfully to men because it was necessary for men to support the women. These *mentalités* that assigned to women the role of launching the insurrection were common to both sexes. Though the majority of our documents are from male sources, depositions by women also show that 1 Prairial was experienced as a day of women. Even if later, as victims of the repression, accused women had an interest in invalidating their role, they ascribed the blame, like men, to other anonymous women.

As we shall see, in confirmation of their importance, women did not escape the repression that followed the failure of the revolt.

16 Women's Silence

The repression began during the night of 1 Prairial, when the Convention, in two simultaneous decrees, forbade women access to its galleries and ordered its "good citizens" to gather starting from 5 Prairial in general assemblies in order to disarm or arrest "the assassins, the drinkers of blood, the thieves, and the agents of the tyranny who preceded 9 Thermidor." On 4 Prairial, the Military Commission was created, a military court that judged six Montagnard deputies, twenty-three rebel gendarmes, and one hundred twenty-nine insurgents, including fourteen women. Lastly, the Committee of General Security arrested people who were caught red-handed during the insurrection or were denounced in the following days.

THE ARRESTS

The incomplete archives that exist cannot give us an exhaustive list of the men and women imprisoned in Prairial. Nonetheless, we can find traces of one hundred forty-eight Parisian women who were arrested following the insurrection, and we can add nineteen women who were questioned but kept their freedom for various reasons.

More than two thirds of these one hundred forty-eight women (one hundred and one, or 68.2 percent) were prosecuted by section assemblies. One hundred and one women were accused in thirty-four sections from which we have minimal information: the average then would be three women arrested per general assembly. In referring to K. D. Tønnesson's calculations of an average of twenty-five arrests per section, we obtain an even cruder estimation than the one Tønnesson complains about: women constituted 12 percent of section arrests. This represents a minimum. Reasonably, we can assume an average of between 10 and 20 percent. But this data is not really comparable because women did not belong to categories that were particularly affected, such as section employees of the Year II and gunners who were sometimes arrested collectively. In making allowances for this point, it is not uninteresting to relate these statistics to other "crude estimations" concerning the proportion of women in sexually mixed popular clubs, which went from a fifth to a fourth. Even leaving aside all other statistical data, these enable us perhaps to "measure," very approximately, the revolutionary commitment of Parisian women. In addition, if we exclude from the calculations the twenty-three gendarmes and six deputies judged by the Military Commission, we find a proportion of 11.86 percent women passing before the commission, a figure that is identical to the percent of women accused in section assemblies.

The average number of female citizens harassed by the general assemblies is only a vague index of female engagement in revolutionary political activity. In fact, the number of section arrests varied enormously from one section to another. Our data is terribly fragmentary, often discovered by chance: it ranges from zero to eleven women denounced in general assemblies, and no guidelines emerge from it. In contrast, the data concerning the female rioters arrested during the insurrection shows that they tended to live in central districts (from Arcis to Bonne-Nouvelle), the faubourgs of the north, Saint-Antoine, and less frequently Saint-Marcel.

More than half (53.4 percent) of the women of whom we know the reason for their arrest had participated in the insurrection of Prairial. But 42.2 percent of the women were arrested only for their previous activity. In addition, 47 percent of the rebels had distinguished themselves during the Year II or III. A more profitable distinction than the division between the female rioters of Prairial and the others is the distinction between militant women possessing a visible political history (54.5 percent of the total) and female citizens "without a history" (42.3 percent of the total).[1] Scarcely more than a fourth (26 percent) of the insurgent women were militant women. And whereas the Committee of General Security and still more the Military Commission arrested a disproportionate number of female rebels without a political history (80 and 92 percent), the section general assemblies reversed this relation with a proportion of two

1. The 3.2 percent remaining concerns women whose sole reason for indictment was participation in the massacres of prisoners in September 1792.

thirds militant women and close to a third for those women "without a history." This is not surprising: we know that the section repression privileged the leaders and the militants of the Year II. These figures clearly indicate that the repression was the same for women as for men. Moreover, they once again contradict the too commonly held thesis that views all women as housewives responding only to the price of bread. We can thus remark that 28 percent of the women accused by their section whose reason for arrest is known were there *only* because of their history of political action during the Terror.

At least thirteen of the women accused by their section had belonged to clubs that welcomed women: six were members of the Revolutionary Republican Women, five belonged to the sexually mixed popular clubs, and two were members of the Fraternal Society of Patriots of Both Sexes. In contrast, only six women (4.8 percent of the total and 6.4 percent of section arrests) had among the chief accusations against them participation in the massacres of September 1792. This percent was apparently higher among men, which might lead us to believe that women's participation was only secondary in those days.

The chief accusations against 40 percent of the ninety-three women arrested by their sections (35 percent of the total 123) referred to their attitude during the Year III. However, only one woman was prosecuted solely for the violence she had shown in the spring of the Year III.[2] Considering the action by women during this period, this statistic is amazing. Moreover, some civil committees complained bitterly about it. Thus the Finistère section wrote on 19 Prairial (7 June 1795) that although it had denounced in the general assembly of 5 Prairial several female citizens who had ceaselessly "persecuted" it, a large number of women were not named by the police commissioner. "Seeing that impunity made the guilty bold and encouraged the arrogance of some women who hoped to resume their criminal actions at bakers' doors," it firmly denounced them afresh, concluding with three washerwomen sent before the Military Commission.[3] Let us also recall the complaints of their Faubourg-du-Nord and Quinze-Vingts colleagues about "firebrands" and "bad women." Some of the denunciations refer to female action in the spring of the Year III and in Prairial in particular. But these references exist only to permit accusations

2. A.N., F[7] 4774[46] d. Millard (arrested as an example).
3. A.N., W 547 no. 52.

concerning the Year II: the role *of women* during the Year III partly inspired a traditional indulgence and thus allowed the pursuit of *the militant women of the Year II*, the knitters. The general assembly denounced "women" as an anonymous collective, but it knew how to show indulgence toward those women who might have been "misguided" by hunger or the cries of their children and about whom they were not particularly concerned. Wishing to put a definitive end to the popular movement and the Year II, the general assembly's pity was barely shown toward those women who had supported the "system of blood." The militant women of the Year II were arrested in the name of the collective female action of the Year III, in which more than a third did not take part!

THE ACCUSED WOMEN

The average age of the thirty-three women who declared it was thirty-nine years old, an average remarkably identical to that of the average age of regulars of clubs and popular societies in the Year II—and just as little representative as that average. In fact, the accused women form two age brackets of fifteen to thirty-four years, on the one hand, and forty-five to sixty-four years, on the other hand, separated by the chasm of thirty-five to forty-four years—those women who, responsible for children, were rarely seen on the benches of clubs (see figure 6).

Few members of the oldest group (fifty-five to sixty-four years old) are included among the female rioters of Prairial, and none appear among the women without a history of political activity, whose average age drops to thirty-three years. In contrast, the average age of female militants makes a spectacular jump to fifty years. Was the revolutionary militant a grandmother? We must not let ourselves be misled by the supposed precision of figures: our samples are unfortunately very limited. In addition, the female prisoners of an advanced age had every interest in announcing this fact in order to inspire greater indulgence. Other details that are not quantifiable show the existence of young militant women, such as the sisters Barbot and their friend Gauthier, the wife of Barbant, Pauline Léon, Constance Evrard, or Claire Lacombe, to cite only the most notorious. Consequently, if unlike the male "father of a family" the militant woman was usually not the center of a household, for all that she was still not a grandmother but a woman whose continuous engagement was unimpeded by young children. These women were nevertheless no longer adolescents: this group clearly forms part of the "women without a political history" that included almost three fourths of the Prairial rebels. These young women without a political past

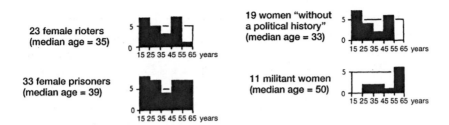

Figure 6. Age of female rioters and prisoners of Prairial Year III

often distinguished themselves in the crowd of female rioters. Think of the three, eighteen-year-old washerwomen who terrorized the civil committee of Finistére, or twenty-two-year-old Louise Catherine Vignot, who led the women of the Faubourg Saint-Antoine on 1 Prairial. Moreover, the same had occurred in previous months. Women arrested during the winter or spring of the Year III for militant actions were on average older than those women questioned during the demonstrations.

Some women indicated their profession, or, for lack of employment, that of their husband. Not surprisingly, we encounter again four large categories: women in trade, artisans, seamstresses-washerwomen, and day laborers. We also find most of the professions for women, from servants to women who maintained or had maintained ties with prostitution. In order to know the "social milieu" (a vague but practical term) of the accused women, these different professions can be arranged under two rubrics: "workshops and shops" and a broadly based class of "wage laborers." The results obtained are in relative agreement with the work on militant sansculottes. The workshop and the shop, "this central pivot of the sansculottes movement,"[4] dominated the group of militant women (53.5 percent). The wage laborers, although represented, were less numerous (37.2 percent). The variations are even more marked for accused women without a visible political history: more than three fourths of them were wage laborers—and not even a tenth worked in a workshop! In the crowd of Prairial, between about one third and two thirds were wage laborers. Here again we see the weak representation of the artisan class (12 percent) in relation to the part that it played in the accusations (22.9 percent).

4. Michel Vovelle, *La Mentalité révolutionnaire: Société et mentalités sous la Révolution française* (Paris: Messidor, 1985), p. 112.

Whether we refer to George Rudé's work on the revolutionary crowd, which presents a very different picture of the male participants in Prairial, or to Albert Soboul's work on the sansculottes of the Year II (only 20 percent of these men were wage laborers),[5] we find that wage laborers represented a far larger proportion of female rioters and militants. Beyond the fact that our category "wage laborers" is very broad and that we are examining here the militant women of the Year II through the prism of the repression of the Year III, this difference corresponds to a greater proportion of women in wage labor occupations, which was globally true for workers in this period. Moreover, if bourgeois men were active within the Revolution during the Year II (15.5 percent of the militant men identified by Soboul came from the liberal professions), their female relatives, even if they shared their ideas, were rarely active militants. Social and sexual memberships intersected here to make revolutionary militant women out of women of the relatively popular milieu. The moderate women of the bourgeoisie did not support their companions in the general assemblies with either their voices or actions.

The relationships between socioprofessional category and degree of revolutionary commitment show that women from the world of shopkeepers and especially from the artisan class were more politicized than those who were wage laborers. Only a fifth of the female shopkeepers and artisans lacked a history of political activity, and this percent decreases to 15.8 percent if we include only the artisan class. The political commitment of female wage laborers, however, was not negligible at 38 percent: among the specifically female activities of sewing and laundering, militant women surpassed even women without a political history. Moreover, the day laborer mason Decloux wrote in defense of his wife and his daughter, accused of being "furious Jacobins," that they "were not Jacobins like all the other wives of workers who had been impregnated with opinions and maxims."[6]

This social composition is evident in the level of education of the accused women of Prairial; more than two thirds knew how to sign their name. This already high percentage—which shows the influence of the capital—

5. George Rudé, *The Crowd in the French Revolution* (Oxford: Clarendon Press, 1959); Albert Soboul, *Les Sans-culottes parisiens en l'an II. Mouvement populaire et gouvernement révolutionnaire, 2 juin 1793–9 thermidor an II* (1958; reprint, Paris: Flammarion, 1973), pp. 433, 455.

6. A.N. F⁷ 4665 d. Decloux.

reached 87 percent for militant women who, in addition, clearly mastered writing better than women without a political history, of whom only 43.5 percent knew how to sign their name.[7]

The arrests of Prairial confirm the existence of militant families: 31 percent of the accused women had a male relative who was arrested or disarmed. In addition, 12.8 percent had a member of their family who exercised an official function in the Year II. If we limit ourselves only to women accused by their sections, these statistics rise respectively to 40 percent and 13.8 percent.

At the conclusion of this study, we can try to draw up a typology of the accused women of Prairial. Let us begin with the case of the most frequent character, that of the knitter of the Year II: a young woman, between twenty and thirty years old, single or married to a soldier or militant; or in contrast, a woman of fifty years or older, free of pressing maternal responsibilities, who could be part of a popular club during the Year II. Relatively well-read, she was often employed in the shop or the artisanal workshop but also could be found holding the beetle of the washerwoman or the needle of the seamstress. The accused woman without a political history appears her reverse image in many ways. Besides the maternal responsibilities that she had not yet or fully assumed, she was younger, whether she had barely reached her twentieth year or had just passed her fiftieth birthday; she did not assiduously attend the political assemblies of the Year II and acted more out of anger than political reflection; and she was an unskilled worker with less education. The female rioter of Prairial evidently formed a composite of these two types of women: young girls without a history of political activity who rose up for bread but became ringleaders, whose declared enemies were indiscriminately civil commissioners, merchants, or Convention members; and older women with explicitly political motivations, who expected the return of the Jacobins and the Montagnard deputies from the success of the insurrection. And, even if she was recruited from an extremely broadly defined group of wage-workers, the female rioter had the preliminary stages of literacy.

7. These percentages are based on the forty-six women (twenty-three militant women and twenty-three "without a political history") for whom we have information on this subject.

PRISON

Two months after their arrest, most of the female prisoners had regained their liberty. The last were released either at the end of Vendémiaire or the beginning of Brumaire of the Year IV (mid-October 1795) after the failure of the royalist insurrection of 13 Vendémiaire (4 October), even before the decree of amnesty of 4 Brumaire (25 October). A dozen women had even avoided prison, having judged it preferable not to wait for the police to knock at their door, or having been left under house arrest for reasons of health. Among arrested couples, the husband was freed at the same time as or after his wife.[8]

The authors of petitions who requested their freedom invoked above all their status as mothers, a status, rather than an active responsibility, for it mattered little if it had been a long time since their adult children had needed their care; what counted was that they had brought children into the world and raised them. Moreover, the authorities were sensitive to this fact, especially if the children or their father had fought for the Republic. Petitions skillfully exploited the image of woman. How could she have "intrigued" in the general assemblies given the fact that women did not deliberate? She had succumbed to error because of the weakness of her sex. Humanity demanded consideration toward the weakness of her sex. She was a woman and consequently never mixed in politics. And so on. Even better, since nature had created woman as weak and sweet, how could she be capable of her supposed crimes? "Nature, which gave me the weakness of my sex, also assigned me the habits and the demeanor," wrote the youngest of the Barbot sisters, who, however, was never known for conspicuous docility. Of one of the denunciations brought against the wife of the revolutionary commissioner Chalandon, it was said, "Doesn't it outrage a man to suppose that a woman could influence" the deliberations of the revolutionary committee?[9] The stereotype of female weakness carried still more weight if it was accompanied by the "thoughtlessness" of extreme youth or, on the contrary, of that "critical moment" that made every woman of a certain age still more morally unstable.

Some women admitted to having been tricked by Jacobin propaganda: "I could not protect myself from the powerful influence that was exercised over my mind by impostors whose apparent patriotism seduced me. I believed that by giving myself to their lying insinuations I served my coun-

---

8. There is a single exception: A.N., F[7] 4774[64] d. Pathie.
9. See appendix 3, "Portraits of Militant Women," in this volume.

try like my husband and my children serve it in the armies," wrote the wife of Saint Prix. Afterward, the authorities showed indulgence toward the authors of these full apologies, especially if the accused women trumped their "natural" weakness as women with social weakness: "These people were without education and consequently easy to misguide, but they could not be dangerous," wrote a civil committee about the Portail couple at the end of Messidor.[10]

Others did not deny their political commitment and, acting as accusers of their accusers, in barely veiled words they showed their affection for the Year II. Accused of having "instilled the infernal spirit of Jacobinism in her husband and her children," the wife of Boudray responded that she had only instilled "the spirit of liberty and equality" in them. Denounced as a "terrorist" and Jacobin, the wife of Villarme replied "that she had sometimes combated royalism in her district." The female citizen Barbot the younger acknowledged having "frequented several times the meetings of the Jacobins, a popular club protected by the law, supported by public opinion, assembling under the eyes of the people and the Convention": she prided herself on having "shared enthusiasm for the good" and doubted that there had been "wrong" done in this club. And the wife of Lenoir railed against "the system of illegal arrests of which she was the victim" and wrote that the accusations made against her could only have been uttered by royalists and enemies of the country displeased by her revolutionary conduct.[11]

More than half of the accused women were only released on bail and were placed under surveillance; in only 12 percent of the cases was it specified that the female prisoner would enjoy liberty without conditions. The militant women protested against these discriminatory measures. The female citizens Barbot the younger (who signed as "female prisoner of the state") and Boudray rejected them in the name of republican honor: "I plead for neither probation nor surveillance. I prefer dungeons or death to these infamous suspicions," wrote the first, and the second thundered that "a half-justice will not suffice for Republicans . . . ! Complete justice is necessary! . . . The order declares that my arrest is a sufficient punishment. A punishment! Only the guilty deserve this."

The female rebels who passed before the Military Commission benefited from a relative indulgence, to the degree that none was condemned to death

---

10. See ibid., and A.N., F⁷ 4774⁷⁹ d. Portail.
11. See appendix 3 in this volume, and A.N., F⁷ 4775⁴⁶ d. Villarme.

(there were thirty-six death sentences, including eighteen gendarmes and six deputies) or imprisonment (seven condemnations). Those who received the heaviest penalties were judged before the Montagnard deputies, whose appearance marked a turn toward greater leniency. Consequently, punishments often had little relation to the accusations. Only one woman was condemned, along with her husband, to deportation (among a total of eleven deportations). The majority of accused women were given punishments of imprisonment ranging from two months to six years. Only three were released, which was relatively few if we remember that a total of 40 percent of the accused men were set free.

AN EMETIC OMELET

Dry statistics do not account for the complete weight of the repression, which was endured not just by accused individuals, nor can they account for all its aspects.

Many cases were tragic, as in the example of the Dunel family. Entering Dunel's home on 16 Prairial (4 June), a police commissioner of the Faubourg Saint-Antoine charged with arresting Dunel, a thirty-two-year-old employee of the Republic's clothing office, found only the bodies of Dunel's wife and children. Dunel was discovered several days later hidden under a false name at the Hospice de l'Humanité. He explained that, after leaving the general assembly of Popincourt and "remembering what his family had suffered during the months when he had been held prisoner," he bought twelve pellets of emetic and asked his wife to please forget him because "sooner or later he was a doomed man." She threw her arms around his neck and said that she wished that they would perish all together. An honest housewife, she paid all their debts, then prepared an omelet out of verdigris and emetic. To be sure that they did not escape death, the Dunels lit several charcoal fires in order to suffocate.[12]

Was this an extreme case? Yes and no: yes, by the emotion and horror that it highlights, and no, because Dunel was not the only one who could not bear the failure of the insurrection. On 4 Messidor (23 June), an unemployed gardener declared to the police commissioner that he had just discovered that his wife, a porter about sixty years of age, had hung herself. She "had shown great anxiety and grief, becoming taciturn and melancholy over the movements that had taken place in Paris several days after the first of Prairial," and ever since had not stopped repeating that they were lost,

12. A.P.P., AA 219 f. 125–131.

without resources, "that nothing would die down, that it would never end." We find at random in the archives other examples of desperate suicidal gestures. When the commissioners of the Faubourg Saint-Antoine informed the wife of Boutry that she was under arrest, her husband, a gendarme, put a gun in his mouth and fired it. And Tinel, who on the first of Prairial had run through the streets of the city with the head of Féraud at the end of a pike, never did carry his own head to the scaffold. After shouting at the commissioners that he would not be guillotined, he slit his throat and threw himself from the roof on which he had taken refuge.[13]

It is impossible to avoid alluding here to the famous "Martyrs of Prairial," those Montagnard deputies who, condemned by the Military Commission, preferred to kill themselves. Françoise Brunel recalls, incidentally, that in eighteenth-century literature there was an obsessive concern with suicide as a symbol of liberty; this shows how, far from signifying a refuge in death, the collective gesture of the "Martyrs of Prairial" was an appeal against an iniquitous judgment and "actively anticipated the future."[14] Our examples do not have this aspect of symbolic and exemplary death. However, beyond despair and horror, they can also reveal the last act of free men who refused to submit to the judgment of their opponents. "Liberty or death" they asserted in the Year II.

If these suicides were paroxysmal gestures, many Parisians, without going so far, were overcome by the uprising's failure, which they felt closed the door to hope; and all the more in that, although arrests rained down on lower-class families, the crisis still did not end. Women felt the weight of the repression on a daily basis. At a point when poverty and scarcity had made housekeeping an extreme struggle, how were they to live and nourish their children when they lost at least half of each work day in proceedings to liberate their husbands? If we describe the situation of lower-class housewives before Prairial as destitute, there is no word to describe the state that followed the arrests. Dozens and dozens of women wrote to the Committee of General Security, stating that, after having sold all their clothes and furniture—even the bed—to nourish their children and the prisoner, they had nothing left and would soon be reduced to begging. Let

13. A.P.P., AA 210, 4 Messidor Year III. A. N., F⁷ 4614 d. Briant, wife of Boutry, F⁷ 4775³⁰ d. Tinel.

14. Françoise Brunel, *Introduction à la publication des écrits de Goujon* (forthcoming).

us paradoxically allow a man to speak, the citizen Pathie, a carpenter and former revolutionary commissioner of the Quinze-Vingts section: liberated before his spouse, he drew up an account of his situation, which corresponded to the plight of all women of the people whose husbands were imprisoned—and the Pathies did not even seem to have children:

> I am unable to work, as every day I must go to the Committee of General Security to request her release, going in the morning, returning in the evening. I have been obliged to sell my possessions in order to live and to make her time in prison more bearable. I have sold everything. For more than four years, I have had nothing at all. I do not know how to recover from my destitution. . . . A great many families have been placed in the most horrible situation by the tyranny exercised in all Paris sections. What will they do this winter, having sold everything? How can they ever hold out, having nothing more, especially if the winter is as harsh as it has been?[15]

The repression of Prairial sought to reduce to nothing all who could remain among the sansculottes and to end definitively the popular movement and the specter of the Year II. It achieved this goal.

THE VOICE OF MARIANNE

Order and silence reigned in Paris. Police observers wrote in the days that followed the insurrection:

7 Prairial: "The arrest and incarceration of terrorists and other suspect individuals occurred without objection. No one refuted it. The men watch. The women are silent."

"Married women regret losing their arrested husbands who are confined according to the law, but they are content to shed tears without complaining."

9 Prairial: "Complete submission to the laws of the Convention, respect of men, silence of women."

10 Prairial: "The calm is perfectly reestablished. . . . The workers have resumed their work. The women have returned to the bosom of their households. They have become mute about political events."

20 Prairial: "One no longer sees in this great city those tumultuous gatherings, and except for some grumbling, the scandalous threats, seditious cries, and frenzied clamor of these furies of the guillotine are no longer heard."

15. See note 8.

Leaden silence, a city as dead as one where women's voices are extinguished. The remarkable insistence by police observers reveals the extent to which women's cries must have been haunting during the Year III, and to which they had permeated the capital. The contrast must have been brutal, perhaps even more revealing of failure than executions or desperate deaths. The historian of the Revolution only possesses written documents, but those who wish to recreate the film of the popular movement of the Year III must not forget this sound track; this overwhelming silence that left such traces in writing must be perceptible on it.

Before coming to grief, these voices of women made the streets of the city ring with anger, despair, and hope. "Vectors of rumor" or supports of incitement to action, these voices ceaselessly haunted the Parisian Revolution and punctuated events from 1789 to 1795.[16]

Along with curiosity, speech is an essential characteristic of women. Women are known for being talkative, garrulous, and longwinded. An entire series of expressions related to speech are associated with women. The French word for a *gossip*, for example, is gendered female (*commère*) not male (*compère*). Retranscription of the amused, even contemptuous, regard cast by a male society on women is rich in comic possibilities. From the gossip's talk, we slide down the social scale to the *voix de poissarde* (voice of the fishwife), which is so insufferable to the ears of the bourgeois: a scornful regard is cast by one social class on another's uncivilized, savage behavior. The political correlative to such expressions is "in the clamoring of the furies of the guillotine," which no longer reveals either amusement or scorn, but spite and hostility.

From the beginning, then, the voice is a characteristically female attribute. As such, it cannot and must not leave the space where the ideal woman evolved: as a faithful disciple of Jean Jacques Rousseau's misogyny, who thought that heaven did "not give [women] such a sweet voice to say insults." The journalist Prudhomme wrote that "their amiable babel would become ruined if it crossed the threshold of their households," running the risk of thus being transformed into "sterile cackling" that troubled the deliberations of assemblies.[17]

16. Jacques Guilhaumou, "Description d'un événement discursif: la mort de Marat à Paris (13 juillet—16 juillet 1793)," *La Mort de Marat,* ed. Jean Claude Bonnet (Paris: Flammarion, 1986).

17. Jean Jacques Rousseau, *Emile ou l'Education* (1762; Paris: Garnier-Flammarion, 1966), p. 483; *Les Révolutions de Paris,* 1–9 Frimaire Year II; police report of Latour Lamontagne of 5 Pluviôse Year II.

Accounts linger over the particular sonority of women's voices. The civil commissioners of the Finistère section dwell at length, not over the insults that the young washerwomen Françoise Galateau may have cast at them, but over her "yelping voice that predominated over all the other women." On 29 Floréal Year II (17 May 1794), the section authorities took care to note in their statement that it was "with a very piercing and very resonant voice" that another washerwomen "put on trial" a pork butcher. And the anti-Girondin "cries" of militant women gathered before the Convention in May 1793 had so resounded in the ears of a police observer (himself Girondin) that he was not content to just emphasize this but directly attributed the darkness of the women's faces and lips to these cries![18]

When women were perceived as a group, they were often associated with noise. "Rumor seized hold of the women," the observer Charmont wrote on 5 Ventôse Year II concerning the subsistence crisis. Rumor, complaints, noise, and uproar were the daily elements of lines of housewives who sometimes became "scolds" in police reports. In periods of crisis, they lingered over the description of their voices, like Hanriot in his picture of la Halle on 9 Ventôse Year II: "It was not really shrieks but howling, or better said, an atrocious vociferation." The authorities called in such circumstances often noted that they found it difficult to make themselves heard and to calm the cries of women. And who then was able to silence them? On 24 Prairial Year III (12 June 1795), a serviceman responded placidly to a citizen who reproached him for letting his female companion break out in insults against the Convention: he claimed that he "could not restrain the tongues of women." And a police commissioner wrote in August 1793 about a female porter who was questioned for having made a disturbance at a baker's door: "The importunate and persistent volubility of her tongue that nothing in our office could stop shows what she is capable of."[19]

Thus women possessed a particular aptitude for using their voices to cause gatherings. However, noise or screams that troubled public order were not necessarily threatening to social and political order. And women's voices were only accused of a potential for danger when they did not limit themselves to expressing nonpolitical anger but became, on the contrary, the privileged vector of political opinions. And this indeed happened during the Revolution. The civil committee of the Quinze-Vingts section was conscious of a real danger when it wrote laconically on the subject of a woman arrested in Prairial Year III: "We do not know if her heart is good,

18. See note 3; A.P.P., AA 136 f. 89; report of Dutard on 4 May 1797.
19. A.P.P., AA 62 f. 419–421 and AA 176, 4 August 1793.

but her tongue is fatal." It had been said of Claire Lacombe in September 1793 that she was "very dangerous because she was very eloquent."[20]

During the Year III and to a lesser degree in 1793, these voices of women became alarming by the calls to action, and more precisely by the insurrectional action, that they expressed. One month after the fall of the Robespierrists, police observers indicated that it was female speech that expressed the opinions of and was amplified by the Jacobin and antigovernmental movement. Women were not merely the principal vectors of rumor, but the vectors of all oral propaganda. Through their voices, militant women carved out a reputation as revolutionaries; at least that was how they were sometimes represented, as in the report on a female citizen that described her as "an extremely dangerous woman . . . one of the most renowned for her vociferations."[21] Significantly, when militant couples were arrested, the wife was always accused of having gone to spread the "good news" in the streets, the groups, and the workshops. Police reports described this propaganda by emphasizing its medium, female voices. "In groups many speakers who sought to influence public opinion were noticed. . . . Women made the most noise," expressing themselves with "excessive vehemence," "a warmth that often had unfortunate consequences"; women "inflamed the weak heads who listened to them by their *yelping*," and so on.[22] This propagandist function of women was largely based on their privileged relations with the street and the groups that formed there.

Carriers of propaganda and of calls to insurrection, the voices of women also masked the speech of the enemy and hindered his action. On 21 Pluviôse Year III (9 February 1795), the female regulars of the Convention galleries "tried to disturb by their vociferations" and their "cries of fury" the removal of Marat's bust from the meeting hall. In general assemblies, militant women "uttered shrieks of rage" to support the sansculottes. On 12 Germinal Year III, the "harpies" who entered the Convention "prevented the representatives from deliberating for four hours by their hideous howling."[23] To their opponents, the voices of these women who were no longer women but furies, harpies, and shrews were just "vociferations," "cries of fury," "howlings," "yelpings," and "barkings." Their voices were associated, particularly during the Year III, with revolutionary resistance. What dish

20. A.N., F⁷ 4635 d. Castille, T 10011–3 d. Lacombe.

21. A.N., F⁷ 4775¹² d. Salignac; A.P.P., AA 229 f. 164.

22. Police reports of 13 Fructidor, first supplementary day Year II, 3 Vendémiaire and 17 Ventôse Year III.

23. *Moniteur*, XXIII, 419–421; A.N., F7* 2476 10 and 11 Ventôse Year III; *Le Messager du soir*, 14 Germinal Year III.

could be more exquisite, more savory for a great counterrevolutionary devil, ready to gobble up in a single meal all of the popular movement, than the scarlet tongue of a knitter? On an engraving entitled *Le Souper du Diable* (The devil's supper), we see the Devil at table while a sansculotte turns the spit and a little devil prepares to skewer a knitter who calls the "Great Saint Marat" for help. The Devil specifies that he wishes the tongue of this knitter for dessert.

Must we conclude that in the popular movement women primarily incited action and men primarily took action? Women spoke (or shouted) and men acted? No, for women also participated physically in this action, and if they called out to men who controlled armed force, it was to give birth to a common action by men and women, the action of the popular movement, rich with all its elements. In addition, we cannot separate the voice from what it expresses. To the lapidary formula "women speak," we must in every case add: "What did they say? And what were the consequences of this speech?" We can then approach the problem under a different angle: female speech, often a prelude to an insurrectional act, the generator of action, finally becomes one of the elements of action. Here lies one of the original features of the participation of women in the revolutionary process and of their place, as a distinct group, in the popular movement.

We could say that order and silence reigned in Paris. Certainly, in Prairial, women were still arrested for having complained about the lack of provisions and basic necessities or for having insulted and threatened the Convention, but these words, the fruits of exasperation rather than political action, were spoken by a small number of individual women and no longer, as in the previous months, by "the women." Though the term *women* appeared in police reports after the insurrection, it referred to a previous situation and did not reflect the present situation. Even distributions of bread, although scarcely more abundant, were made "in the greatest tranquillity"; those women who wished to inspire their comrades to refuse their ration were no longer followed. And in the brawls that sometimes disturbed the lines, housewives fought against each other and no longer formed a common front against the authorities. In Messidor (June to July), when misery was at its height, grumbling began again, but it was no longer accompanied by the diverse movements of women that had marked the spring of the Year III. Women were content henceforth to applaud the increasingly frequent actions of individual women, such as thefts of bread displayed at the Palais-

Royal at twenty francs a pound in the sight of paupers, which was devoured on the spot by the male or female thief.

Even if according to the report of 24 Messidor (12 July) "the situation in Paris is not at all encouraging," the resistance was broken, and for a long time. On 18 Messidor (6 July), police observers heard it said, "If the rich lacked everything like us, the Convention would have ceased to exist long ago and the people would have been pushed to insurrection. . . . They [the people] go where they are led. Is it necessary to suffer? They suffer. Is it necessary to fight? They fight. But seeing now that they were tricked in all that one had them do, they will only rise again when they are forced to and for reasons that are clear to them." These disabused reflections clearly show the end—and the failure—of a popular revolution, characterized by the alliance between the revolutionary bourgeoisie and the popular masses.

The first of Prairial saw the high point of a mass female movement and sounded its knell. Later, Babeuf's plot (winter to spring 1796) did not assign any place to women. They did not exist any longer even as a group with negligible force and were no longer thought of except as minor auxiliaries. The only reference that we find on this subject in Babeuf's papers is that women and children, directed by the conspirators, would help them by hampering the march of troops and by throwing projectiles from windows at them.

We find several women at the sides of the Babouvists, but these were isolated individuals and not part of a larger movement. In addition, like their number, their role was completely secondary. The archives on the Conspiracy of Equals do not show figures of militant women as we find in previous years. Essentially responsible for the distribution of newspapers and pamphlets and for welcoming new recruits, they were part of those named subaltern agents by the bill of indictment. They gathered in cafés, like that of Bains-Chinois owned by a militant woman of the Year II, the wife of Boudray, where the denunciator of the conspiracy saw "a confused gathering of both sexes" discussing and singing patriotic songs.[24]

24. A.N., F^7 4277 4276. The five women judged by the Tribunal of Vendôme were all freed (F^7 4278); none were part of the militant women of the Year II, who were only represented by the female citizens Boudray and Sergent. In contrast, there were many husbands of militant women among the men judged "fit to command." *The Tribun du Peuple* included only 5 percent women among its subscribers.

The Conspiracy of Equals allows us to measure the distance traveled since barely a year before, when women were considered "firebrands" to whom militants appealed. The military character of Babeuf's Conspiracy is not the only explanation. If women had represented the same force as they did during the Year III, it is very likely that the conspirators would have taken them into consideration. If Babeuf and his friends were not interested in a mass movement of women, this was because after the failure of the Prairial insurrection, there was no longer a mass women's movement.

Conclusion

The voices have died, and the book has drawn to a close. Now another story is beginning for the nineteenth century, about its labor revolts, feminist struggles, and the *petroleuses* (female arsonists) who will replace their grandmothers, the knitters. It is the nineteenth century that will witness the imposition of the image of the woman excluded from the public domain, the image of a woman more submissive than ever to "marital despotism." This is the image of the dependent created by the Napoleonic civil codes, fixed in the frozen pages of gender laws founded on inequality. Surely the common woman will remain rebellious for a little while to this process of domestication;[1] she will know how to slide between order and disorder, between rules and liberty. But the fact remains that men will dominate in this century even more than they did during the Revolution or eighteenth century. And, in the shadow of the code, in the shadow of other forms of struggle, in the shadow of collective *mentalités*, the place of women during the Revolution will gradually grow obscure, and the fact will seem to be that 1789 was only a men's revolution.

Thanks to the archives, however, we can still recover traces of the part that common women took; we can resuscitate the women's revolutionary movement and return it to its proper place. Because women, too, have a political past that is often ignored and crushed under the weight of representations inherited from the nineteenth century—our memory is forgetful. Women's history has much to contribute to the political field, just as it did to that of the *mentalités*. The archives await. They still have much to teach

---

1. Compare M. Perrot, "La Femme populaire rebelle," *L'Histoire sans qualités;* or J. Guillais, *La Chair de l'autre: Le Crime passionnel au XIXe siècle* (Paris: Orban, 1986).

us; their consultation just might surprise us and shake up a number of received ideas about women as historical subjects.

For the Revolutionary period, the archives have allowed us to reveal the existence of a women's movement, an element of the popular Parisian movement formed by ordinary women—nurturers and workers. Female involvement in the Revolution took several forms. Explosive and discrete, it had its moments of glory and its moments of crisis. The fall of 1789, the spring of 1793, and 1795 distinguished the "heroines of the fifth and sixth of October," the Revolutionary Republican Women, and the "furies with human faces spewed forth from hell." Either as known militants or as insubstantially documented silhouettes passing quickly through the archives, ordinary women were always present in the Parisian revolutionary movement, in the midst of which they at times developed an original political response that corresponded to the particularities of their social functions or political status.

All of the women of the people were housewives faced with shortages. Yet the question of subsistence is not the only motive for their intervention in the Revolution. In fact, the relations of women to subsistence differ as we follow the degree of their involvement. It is for this reason that the most militant women concerned themselves only secondarily with issues of subsistence. Although the whole of the female sansculottes movement makes itself most evident during periods of food shortage, its positions nonetheless take on political colorations even then (the spring of 1793 and 1794, the winter of 1795). Looking back, it is true that the specific identity of the popular female masses is directly related to the problem of food supply that constitutes its principal focus (October 1789 and the spring of 1795): the demand for bread is the source for the formation of numerous and distinct crowds of women. However, these crowds are never lacking in political awareness, if only because militant women were also always present. Finally, even if in the course of political events women are not distinguishable by their force from the entire body of citizens (17 July 1791, and protests for the abolition of royalty in the spring and summer of 1792), that does not mean that they were absent. They were present, not so much as a differentiated female component but rather as individuals of the female sex.

At the heart of the popular movement, as in the sentimental realm or the working world, men and women follow the same path, intersecting and diverging, rejoining or ignoring one another. Men's disdain or respect, their pride or worry about women's independence, the willingness of some for women to be at the same level along the paths of the Revolution, and for others their insistence on male superiority, indicates the existence of flimsy, thin, and often turbulent ties that united male and female citizens during the Revolution. And the riots reveal the existence of gender roles around which "rules" were partially constructed that the crowd obeyed.

At the core of these relations between women and the Revolution is the question of citizenship. Whether focusing on the female cult for the guillotine, a hunger riot, or a women's club, the historian often ends up beached upon a shore. He or she comes to ask: But isn't studying the female revolutionary movement to finally ask oneself how to be a female citizen, to ask how one can take part in political life without possessing full and complete citizenship? How can one be a part of the Sovereign People and not enjoy a single one of its attributes?

The author of the *Encyclopedia* wrote that the female citizen cannot exist in an autonomous fashion; she can only be the wife of a citizen. For the numerous revolutionaries who shared this view, the female citizen was before anything else a "citizen" under the domestic roof. Many women insisted as well upon the familial tie between male and female citizens, but they did not present it as one-sided. It was not a man who, by a private familial relationship, granted a woman (his wife, his daughter, his sister, or his mother) citizenship, but the whole of the citizen population in relation to the whole of the female population. Once men attained citizenship when they recovered the totality of their rights, the reciprocal ties uniting all individuals of the Republic implied that women, too, be recognized as citizens. Unlike those who conceptualized the female citizen as a woman defined by a private and individual relation at the center of an enclosed, domestic, and familial space like the home, the female texts present her as a woman defined by a social and plural relation conceived at the core of a public and political space; amid the entirety of the family of citizens; within the nation. To borrow the familial language, it was in fact a social tie that made the female citizen, a title that honors women who belonged to a free people who solemnly declared the rights of man and of the citizen.

She never possessed the political rights of a citizen. This exclusion weighed upon the political practice of women and on their participation in events. Revolutionary society thought itself democratic because it was founded upon the natural inalienable rights of each individual. But half of the population was excluded from these rights. The social body and political body were distinct; in Rousseau's terms, the Republic would have "subjects" who were "submissive to the law of the state" and citizens who "participat[ed] in the sovereign authority." Though this principle affirmed the sovereignty of the people, it was nonetheless impossible to name the "subjects" as anything else but *female citizens*. In this way, even though women remained the "helots" of the Republic, the universality of the revolutionary ideas asserted in the Declaration of Rights opened the door to the future. Conformity to principles necessitated that one day the female citizen would acquire full political rights.

Few women claimed them during the Revolution. But they nonetheless demonstrated citizenship. They invested the political space that was opened, and they gave life to the political being of the female citizen. After 1796, the term *female citizen* smacked of vulgarity, and in the posh circles of the directory, it was reserved for servants. Under the Consulate and the Empire, in order to qualify women as members of the nation, the terms *Madame* and *Mademoiselle* were preferred. All references to the social and political body were rubbed out, and women were designated according to their familial and private ties, which, in a society that prepared a patriarchal civil code, was more helpful in officially distinguishing between the property of the father and that of the husband. Yet the emperor and jurists still had much to do. The word did not disappear as they wished, and it has continued to live in the people's memories and exists to the present day, endowed with all of its political meaning.

The militants of the Revolutionary period, the knitters, gave reality to the female citizen, who was still the clandestine passenger of Enlightenment dictionaries. They inscribed this word in history for eternity, and even if they are forgotten, we are indebted to them for this heritage.

Appendix 1:
Chronology of the Revolution

1789

5 May : Opening of the Estates General
14 July : Storming of the Bastille
25 August : Declaration of the Rights of Man and the Citizen
5–6 October : Women's march to Versailles followed by the National Guard. The king is brought back to Paris

1790

2 February : Dansart creates the Fraternal Society of Patriots of Both Sexes
30 May : Creation of spinning workshops of the Jacobins and the Récollets
3 July : Condorcet, *On the Admission of Women to Citizenship*
12 July : Civil Constitution of the Clergy

1790–1791

Creation of women's clubs

1791

23 March : Etta Palm d'Aelders creates the Society of Female Friends of Truth
End of May : Outbreak in the Récollets spinning workshop
20–21 June : Flight and arrest of the king at Varennes
17 July : Massacre at the Champ-de-Mars
September : Olympe de Gouges, *Declaration of the Rights of Woman and the Female Citizen*
3 September : Constitution of 1791 (suffrage by those who pay property tax)
30 September : End of the Constituent Assembly, beginning of the Legislative Assembly

1792

January–February : Price fixing riots in Paris

March: Arrival of Claire Lacombe in Paris

6 March : Pauline Léon reads a petition to the Legislative Assembly signed by 319 Parisian women asking for the right to organize a national guard

26 March : Speech of Théroigne de Méricourt to the Fraternal Society of Minimes section

20 April : Declaration of war on the "king of Bohemia and Hungary"

20 June : Demonstrations at the Tuileries

25 July : First speech of Claire Lacombe to the Legislative Assembly

10 August : Antiroyalist insurrection; storming of the Tuileries

10–11 August : Convocation of a Convention elected by universal masculine suffrage

2–6 September : Massacres in the prisons

20 September : Last meeting of the Legislative Assembly; law on divorce. Battle of Valmy

21 September : First meeting of the Convention; abolition of the monarchy

1793

January–May : Confrontation at the Convention between the Girondins and the Montagnards

1 January : Lequinio, *The Prejudices Destroyed* (2d. edition)

21 January : Execution of Louis XVI

10 February : The president of the Dijon women's club writes to *Révolutions de Paris*

22 February : Assembly of Republican Women

24 February : Petitions to the Convention from the Assembly of Republican Women and from laundrywomen calling for measures against "speculators and monopolizers"

25–26 February : Price fixing riots in Paris

11 March : Beginning of the Vendée revolt

April : Guyomar, *The Partisan of Political Equality between Individuals*

17 April : Romme defends the political rights of women at the Convention

30 April : Women excluded from the army

1 May : The women of Versailles and the Faubourg Saint-Antoine demand price controls

10 May : Creation of the Revolutionary Republican Women club.

15 May : Théroigne de Méricourt is whipped by the Revolutionary Republican Women

31 May–2 June : Parisian revolt; fall of the Girondins

24 June : The Convention votes for the Constitution of 1793

25 June : Jacques Roux reads the "manifesto of *enragés*" to the Convention

25–27 June : Soap shortages in Paris

30 June : Address of Parisian authorities to the Revolutionary Republican Women

Beginning of July : Speech by the female citizens of the Droits-de-l'Homme section to the club of Revolutionary Republican Women

July : Addresses of women who accept the Constitution

13 July : Assassination of Marat by Charlotte Corday

27 July : Robespierre enters the Committee of Public Safety

10 August : Festival of Unity and Indivisibility of the Republic

17 August : The Hommes-Libres Society (Pont Neuf) accepts women members

26 August : The Revolutionary Republican Women read their petition to the Convention

September : Interventions of the Revolutionary Republican Women in the sections

4–5 September : Popular demonstrations in Paris; "Terror is the order of the day." Arrest of Jacques Roux

Beginning of September : War of the Cockades

16 September : Claire Lacombe is accused by the Jacobins

21 September : Cockade required for women

29 September : Controls on prices of foodstuffs and wages

YEAR II

10 October (19 Vendémiaire) : The government is declared revolutionary until peace

28 October (7 Brumaire) : Scuffle between Revolutionary Republican Women and the women of la Halle about the red liberty cap

30 October (9 Brumaire) : Amar report; prohibition of women's clubs

3 November (13 Brumaire) : Execution of Olympe de Gouges

1794

December 1793–March 1794 (Nivôse–Ventôse) : "Struggle among the factions" (offensive of "Dantonist Indulgents," then of "Hébertist Cordeliers")

Beginning of February (Pluviôse) : Agitation of women workers in sections

February–March (Pluviôse-Ventôse) : Agitation in spinning workshops

March (Ventôse) : Food shortage in Paris

14 March (24 Ventôse) : Arrest of the leaders of the Cordeliers

24 March (4 Germinal) : Execution of the leaders of the Cordeliers

30 March (10 Germinal) : Arrest of the "Indulgents"

2–3 April (13–14 Germinal) : Arrest of Claire Lacombe, Pauline Léon, and Leclerc

5 April (16 Germinal) : Execution of the "Indulgents"

17 May (28 Floréal) : Arrest of Catherine Théot

27 July (9 Thermidor) : Arrest of the Robespierrists

28–29 July (10–11 Thermidor) : Execution of the Robespierrists

31 August (4 Fructidor) : Release of Pauline Léon and Leclerc

YEAR III

September–November (Vendémiaire–Brumaire) : Outbreaks in the North
spinning workshop (formerly the Récollets)
November–December (Brumaire–Frimaire) : Trial of Carrier
19 November (22 Brumaire) : Closing of the Jacobin club
24 December (4 Nivôse) : Abolition of price controls

1795

January–March (Pluviôse–Germinal) : "Lagrelet Conspiracy"
February–March (Ventôse–Germinal) : Shortages
25 February (7 Ventôse) : Bread is rationed to one and a half pounds per person
12–13 March (22–23 Ventôse) : Insurrectional posters in Paris
15 March (25 Ventôse) : Bread is rationed to one pound per person
17 March (27 Ventôse) : Outbreaks in the Faubourg Saint-Marcel
27 March (7 Germinal) : Demonstration by women at the Convention; revolt in
the Gravilliers section
1–2 April (12–12 Germinal) : Insurrection throughout Paris
April–May (Germinal–Floréal) : Famine (one eighth to one quarter pound of
bread per person). The women call the men to action; various demonstrations
by women
20–24 May (1–4 Prairial) : Prairial revolt
20 May (1 Prairial) : The Convention prohibits women from entering its galleries
24 May (4 Prairial) : The Convention prohibits women from attending political
assemblies and gathering in groups of more than five in the street
24–29 May (5–10 Prairial) : Arrest of male and female militants
18 August (1 Fructidor) : Release of Claire Lacombe
22 August (5 Fructidor) : Constitution of the Third Year

YEAR IV

26 October (4 Brumaire) : End of the Convention; beginning of the Directory
December 1795–May 1796 (Frimaire–21 Floréal): Conspiracy and arrest of
Equals (Babeuf plot)

Appendix 2:
Sections of Paris

See map 1 on p. 6.

1. Section des Tuileries (1790–Year IV)
2. Section des Champs-Elysées (1790–Year IV)
3. Section du Roule (1790–October 1792); Section de la République (October 1792–30 Prairial Year III); Section du Roule (30 Prairial Year III–Year IV)
4. Section du Palais-Royal (1790–August 1792); Section de la Butté-des-Moulins (August 1792–August 1793); Section de la Montagne (August 1793–21 Frimaire Year III); Section de la Butte-des-Moulins (21 Frimaire Year III–Year IV)
5. Section de la Place-Vendôme (1790–September 1792); Section des Piques (September 1792–5 Prairial Year III); Section de la Place-Vendôme (5 Prairial Year III–Year IV)
6. Section de la Bibliothèque (1790–September 1792); Section de Quatre-Vingt-Douze (September 1792–October 1793); Section Lepeletier (October 1793–Year IV)
7. Section de la Grange-Batelière (1790–August 1792); Section Mirabeau (August–December 1792); Section du Mont-Blanc (December 1792–Year IV)
8. Section du Louvre (1790–6 May 1793); Section du Muséum (6 May 1793–Year IV)
9. Section de l'Oratoire (1790–September 1792); Section des Gardes-Françaises (September 1792–Year IV)
10. Section de la Halle-au-Blé (1790–Year IV)
11. Section des Postes (1790–18 August 1792); Section du Contrat-Social (18 August 1792–Year IV)
12. Section de la Place-Louis XIV (1790–August 1792); Section du Mail (August 1792–September 1793); Section de Guillaume-Tell (September 1793–Messidor Year III); Section du Mail (Messidor Year III–Year IV)
13. Section de la Fontaine-Montmorency (1790–October 1792); Section de Molière-et-Lafontaine (October 1792–12 September 1793); Section de Brutus (12 September 1793–Year IV)
14. Section de Bonne-Nouvelle (1790–Year IV)
15. Section du Ponceau (1790–September 1792); Section des Amis-de-la-Patrie (September 1792–Year IV)

16. Section de Mauconseil (1790–August 1792); Section de Bon-Conseil (August 1792–Year IV)

17. Section du Marché-des-Innocents (1790–September 1792); Section des Halles (September 1792–May 1793); Section des Marchés (May 1793–Year IV)

18. Section des Lombards (1790–Year IV)

19. Section des Arcis (1790–Year IV)

20. Section du Faubourg-Montmartre (1790–Year IV)

21. Section Poissonnière (1790–Year IV)

22. Section de Bondy (1790–Year IV)

23. Section du Temple (1790–Year IV)

24. Section de Popincourt (1790–Year IV)

25. Section de Montreuil (1790–Year IV)

26. Section des Quinze-Vingts (1790–Year IV)

27. Section des Gravilliers (1790–Year IV)

28. Section du Faubourg-Saint-Denis (1790–January 1793); Section du Faubourg-du-Nord (January 1793–Year IV)

29. Section de Beaubourg (1790–September 1792); Section de la Réunion (September 1792–Year IV)

30. Section des Enfants-Rouges (1790–September 1792); Section du Marais (September 1792–June 1793); Section de l'Homme-Armé (June 1793–Year IV)

31. Section du Roi-de-Sicile (1790–August 1792); Section des Droits-de-l'Homme (August 1792–Year IV)

32. Section de l'Hôtel-de-Ville (1790–21 August 1792); Section de la Maison-Commune (21 August 1792–Fructidor Year II); Section de la Fidélité (Fructidor Year II–Year IV)

33. Section de la Place-Royale (1790–August 1792); Section des Fédérés (August 1792–4 July 1793); Section de l'Indivisibilité (4 July 1793–Year IV)

34. Section de l'Arsenal (1790–Year IV)

35. Section de l'Ile-Saint-Louis (1790–November 1792); Section de la Fraternité (November 1792–Year IV)

36. Section Notre-Dame or Section de l'Ile (1790–August 1792); Section de la Cité (August 1792–21 Brumaire Year II); Section de la Raison (21–25 Brumaire Year II); Section de la Cité (25 Brumaire Year II–Year IV)

37. Section Henri-IV (1790–14 August 1792); Section du Pont-Neuf (14 August 1792–7 September 1793); Section Révolutionnaire (7 September 1793–10 Frimaire Year III); Section du Pont-Neuf (10 Frimaire Year III–Year IV)

38. Section des Invalides (1790–Year IV)

39. Section de la Fontaine-de-Grenelle (1790–Year IV)

40. Section des Quatre-Nations (1790–April 1793); Section de l'Unité (April 1793–Year IV)

41. Section du Théâtre-Français (1790–August 1792); Section de Marseille (August 1792–August 1793); Section de Marseille-et-Marat (August 1793–Pluviôse Year II); Section de Marat (Pluviôse Year II–22 Pluviôse Year III); Section du Théâtre-Français (22 Pluviôse Year III–Year IV)

42. Section de la Croix-Rouge (1790–3 October 1793); Section du Bonnet-Rouge (3 October 1793–Germinal Year III); Section du Bonnet-de-la-Liberté (Germinal–Prairial Year III); Section de l'Ouest (Prairial Year III–Year IV)

43. Section du Luxembourg (1790–Brumaire Year II); Section de Mutius-Scoevola (Brumaire Year II–Prairial Year III); Section du Luxembourg (Prairial Year III–Year IV)

44. Section des Thermes-de-Julien (1790–8 September 1792); Section de Beaurepaire (8 September 1792–20 Pluviôse Year II); Section Chalier (20 Pluviôse Year II–Pluviôse Year III); Section des Thermes-de-Julien (Pluviôse Year III–Year IV)

45. Section de Sainte-Geneviève (1790–August 1792); Section du Panthéon-Français (August 1792–Year IV)

46. Section de l'Observatoire (1790–Year IV)

47. Section du Jardin-des-Plantes (1790–August 1792); Section des Sans-Culottes (August 1792–10 Ventôse Year III); Section du Jardin-des-Plantes (10 Ventôse Year III–Year IV)

48. Section des Gobelins (1790–August 1792); Section du Finistère (August 1792–Year IV)

Appendix 3:
Portraits of Militant Women

FRANÇOISE DUPONT, THE WIFE OF BARBANT
(OR BARBAUX, BARBAUT)

Françoise Dupont was born in 1768 and was a washerwoman of fine linen.[1]
She lived on the Rue Couture Sainte-Catherine aux Filles Bleues in the
Indivisibilité section. Her husband had been in the army since 1792.

On 27 September 1783, she denounced to the Arsenal revolutionary
committee speculators who had made counterrevoluationary remarks; she
had been introduced to the speculators without letting them learn of her
patriotism. According to a denunciation of 24 Brumaire Year III, she would
have done "all that was possible" to have them guillotined. On 17 Brumaire
Year II, she denounced the female citizen Aubry, mother of a deputy under
arrest, who lived at the home of an *émigré* and had sold her horses and her
cart to keep them from being requisitioned, hid her silverware, sold suspect
newspapers, and had her son get a place for her aristocratic coachman in the
military transport. On the same day, the wife of Barbant took to the revolutionary committee a letter that "announced a conspiracy" and that she
had been able to read because it had been improperly addressed. On 6 Prairial Year II, she wrote a letter to the Jacobins along with another female citizen, in which she "called their attention" to the counterrevolutionary behavior of the nuns of the Maison des Hospitaliéres; having stayed there
while sick, she had made them believe that she missed the Old Regime and
in this way was able to learn their opinions.

1. A.N. F^7 4585 pl. 5 pp. 64–75, F^7 4694 d. Dupont, wife of Barbaux. Also found
in A.N., F^7 4582 d. Aubry, F^7 4726 d. Giret, F^7 4774^{46} d. Milet.
For more portraits of militant women, see Dominique Godineau, "Les Femmes
des milieux populaires parisiens pendant la Révolution française," (Ph.D. diss., Paris
I, 1986).

She was described in a denunciation of Prairial Year III as a "fury at the guillotine nourished on Hell to destroy the French human species" and as "sister knitter of the Jacobin, city hall, and revolutionary tribunal galleries" and accused of having been "the secret agent and confederate of Laîné," a former revolutionary commissioner who was close to the Cordeliers. According to another denunciation, several days before 9 Thermidor Year II, she spoke of the "splendid motion" made by Robespierre at the Jacobins club. She had added that if he were lost, the Republic would be lost. In the Year III, several people accused her of having made "terrorist" remarks; she bragged of having caused citizens "who were aristocrats according to her" to be arrested, of having had at least thirty-five people guillotined, and of serving as a witness ten times at the revolutionary tribunal (the only ones against whom she seems to have actually testified were the three speculators who were arrested because of her denunciation in September 1793), and claimed that she was ready to have her best friend guillotined "if he did not think as a true Jacobin." She was interested in the life of her section and frequented assiduously the galleries of the general assembly, where she did not hesitate to make herself heard.

In the Year III, she was part of the Lagrelet conspiracy. During the same period, she urged female citizens to "throw their bread in the faces of the commissioners" and to "fall on the new rulers" whom she accused of creating the famine. She compared them to "her poor Robespierre," during whose tenure "at least we ate and the executions were humanely prompt," whereas the new leaders killed the people "with languor." Also, "as long as the selfish merchants, the former nobles, the rich, all who had been and who were priests had not been guillotined or dispatched en masse, nothing would go well." She had likewise promised the guillotine to the "*muscadins* or other people dressed properly." Far from admitting defeat, she said, "Good patriots will regain the upper hand, and if they don't, the Republic is doomed." According to her accuser, in the days that preceded the insurrection of Prairial, she had shown "much agitation," displaying "extraordinary satisfaction" on her "sinister face" and naming "those whom she would guillotine." She took part in the insurrection and according to the same denunciator, "danced while laughing" and wore a red handkerchief, a rallying sign that she called her favorite handkerchief or her "handkerchief of blood." On 5 Prairial, "seeing that the battle was lost," she moved promptly to the Droits-de-l'Homme section. Denounced and ordered under arrest, she escaped the police by moving several times after that. It does not seem that she was ever arrested; her order of release was signed on 29 Vendémiaire Year IV by the Committee of General Security.

MARIE MARGUERITE AND MARIE ELIZABETH BARBOT
(OR BARBEAU)

The Barbot women were notions retailers.[2] They lived at 17 Rue Transnonain in the Gravilliers section with their brother Charles (who was forty-four years old), an archivist during the Year II of the popular club of his section, cited in the arrest records (see Albert Soboul and Raymonde Monnier, *Répertoire du personnel sectionnaire parisien en l'an II* [Paris: Publications de la Sorbonne, 1985]). The women knew how to write.

One of the Barbot sisters, probably the younger Marie Marguerite, signed the petition of 6 March 1792, in which Parisian women asked for the right to form a national guard. The two sisters signed another petition of women on June 1792 demanding the "punishment of conspirators."

Marie Marguerite Barbot was the principal tenant of the house where she had lived since 1781. In 1792, she had disputes with her landlord, who, she said, "had sprung a trap" on her by inserting "by surprise" in her contract a clause meant to make her pay assessments (284 livres) that she did not have the means to pay. Brought before the Châtelet, she was condemned to pay, and then on 21 August 1793 was declared not competent at the Bureau des Conciliations. She complained at the Convention on 5 October 1793 in a written statement followed by a "Petition to the effect of seeking a law against the tyranny of landlords." On 25 Pluviôse Year II, she took her case before the Gravilliers general assembly, to which she wrote: "To warn the brave sansculottes of the tactics that selfish rascals use in order to abuse the confidence of people of good faith, it is useful to denounce and make known these monsters who are unworthy of society." After this act, her landlord lodged a complaint before the police commissioner.

The women frequented the Jacobin club. On 9 Thermidor Year II, Marie Marguerite wrote, "Virtue is persecuted, but there are good French people who sacrifice their lives to preserve it." On 24 Brumaire Year III, like all the women of the Jacobin galleries, Marie Marguerite was whipped by the *muscadins* who had come to attack the club; later, her opponents asserted that pistols had been found beneath her underskirts (which does not seem very likely). During the winter of the year III, the two sisters "exhorted and roused their neighbors to revolt." They were also accused in Prairial of having had secret meetings at their home. On 12 Germinal and 1 Prairial, along

---

2. A.N., F⁷ 4586 d. Barbot, A.N., D III 240–242 d. 4 pp. 118–120 W. (Walter M. Markov and Albert Soboul, *Die Sansculotten von Paris: Dokumente zur Geschichte der Volksbewegung 1793–1794,* [Berlin: 1957], doc. no. 41), C. 152 f. 2, AEII 1252 C190, A.P.P., AA 139 f. 375–377; on their sister, A.N., W 76 d. 2 f. 124.

with their friend Gauthier, they led the section women who demonstrated at the Convention. During the insurrection of Prairial they said, "If the Jacobins had the upper hand, guillotines would be placed at all street corners to do justice to all aristocrats, moderates, and merchants." They were declared under arrest by the general assembly of the Gravilliers section on 3 and 6 Prairial. Marie Elizabeth was put on probation on 30 Thermidor Year III. While still in prison, her sister wrote a document to the Committee of General Security on 9 Fructidor Year III:

> Representatives, I declare false and slanderous all the allegations against me. The national representation will always be my shield and the guide of Republicans. I can be reproached for no actions, and no words, even ones that are inconsequential. Only royalists wish to sacrifice me. Their desire has given birth to fables and procured my arrest. . . . I have frequented several times the meetings of the Jacobins, a popular club protected by the law, supported by public opinion, assembling under the eyes of the people and the Convention. I have shared the enthusiasm for the good, and I take pride in this. Any wrong (if it has occurred) is as foreign to me as it is odious. I have never carried arms, and nature, which gave me the weakness of my sex, also assigned me the habits and the demeanor. . . . I have courageously expressed my opinions. The persecutions far from frightened me but made my humble soul proud. My blood circulated for the Republic, I wanted to shed it for the Republic. . . . Representatives, read and pronounce. I plead for neither probation nor surveillance. I prefer dungeons or death to these infamous suspicions. . . . You return me to my family, to my position, to the forgetting of vengeance, to social harmony, to love of the Republic.
> Barbot the young, or
> female prisoner of the State in the Maison de Pélagie for three months.

She was set free on 25 Vendémiaire Year IV.

There existed a third Barbot sister, Marie Anastasie, a servant in the Sans-Culottes section, of whom a neighbor wrote on 26 Nivôse Year II: "She is a good patriot who has almost died twice since the Revolution: once at the Manège three days before the massacre of patriots at the Champ-de-Mars, and the second time through the spitefulness of one of her female neighbors on 11 August 1792."

ANNE ROSE BERJOT

Anne Rose Berjot was a seamstress who lived at 1 Rue Marché-Sainte-Catherine, in a cramped workshop on the fourth floor, in the Indivisibilité section.[3] She knew how to sign her name.

3. A.P.P., AA 70 f. 44; A.N., F⁷ 4595 d. Berjot, F⁷ 4585 d. Barbant, C 152 f. 2.

She signed the petition by women asking in June 1792 for "the punishment of conspirators." Because the popular club in the Indivisibilité section was not sexually mixed, she was part of the Société de l'Harmonie Sociale (Society of Social Harmony), a sexually mixed popular club in the Arsenal section. During the summer of 1793, she was appointed the spokesperson of a deputation for the club, and it was perhaps she who, as speaker for this society, made the moderate-led Indivisibilité section swing over to the side of the sansculottes. On 25 July 1793, when she returned to the club in the company of female friends at 9:30 P.M., she was insulted as a "female Jacobin" and a woman who was mixed up in politics; a brawl ensued. She also attended the general assemblies of her section. According to one of her letters dated 12 Prairial Year III, "of the one and indivisible and democratic Republic," she had grown indignant over how the trial of Lucille Desmoulins and Danton progressed. In Floréal Year III, she was taken to task by women who accused her of being a Jacobin because she still wore the cockade. She was declared under arrest by her section general assembly after the Prairial insurrection. However, she denied having participated in it, asserting that "curiosity" had driven her to the Rue Sainte-Honoré on the evening of 3 Prairial.

WIFE OF BOUDRAY (OR BAUDRAIS)

The wife of Boudray was approximated fifty years old, the owner of the Bains-Chinois café on the Boulevard des Italiens in the Lepeletier section.[4] She was the "mother of 27 children" (miscarriages? grandchildren?). According to Soboul and Monnier's *Répertoire,* her husband was Jean-Baptiste Baudrais, a man of letters, a member of the municipal General Council, a Jacobin who was arrested several times, subscribed to the *Tribune du Peuple* in the Year III, was deported to Cayenne from 1802 to 1817, and died in Paris in 1832. She had a son who was a gunner in the Revolutionary Army.

She signed the petition at the Champ-de-Mars on 17 July 1791. The secretary of the Fraternal Society of Patriots of Both Sexes, on 25 September 1793 she wrote a letter to the *Moniteur* (to which she subscribed) asking it to stop confusing her club with the Revolutionary Republican Women. She went to all the meetings of the Jacobins and had a "reserved" place in the galleries where she could closely follow the debates.

4. A.N., F[7] 4610 d. Boudray; F[7]* 2479, 15 Prairial Year II; F[7] 4278; *Moniteur,* XVII, 755.

We have three denunciations by her. The first, sent on 26 Brumaire Year II to the Jacobins, asked them to remain strong because "it is now or never that the Terror should be the order of the day" if all the patriots were not to have their throats slit, and reported that the clients of her café spoke ill of the club and threatened her as a Jacobin. On 15 Prairial Year II, she declared to the revolutionary committee of her section that the male employees of the Bains-Chinois (Chinese baths), all aristocrats and suspects who lacked money but spent much, jeopardized the lives of deputies—in particular Robespierre—who frequented this establishment. Finally, on 2 Messidor Year II, she wrote to the Jacobins that very suspicious gatherings took place in a house next to hers, and she complained that "the revolutionary government could never work well as long as public officials were aristocrats and counterrevolutionary."

She did not participate in the insurrection of Prairial Year III because of sickness, but was denounced in the general assembly of her section on 8 Prairial Year III. A bath employee accused her of being a terrorist and of having raised her children according to bloody principles; the children were "heard to speak of cutting and slicing heads, and that blood did not flow enough." He reproached her with having made at least fifteen pounds of shredded linen to dress wounds for the soldiers! Other members of the general assembly accused her "of having said that she wished to eat the hearts of those opposed to the sansculottes," of being a "member of the fraternal society of the furies of the guillotine," of having been present at the Jacobins on 9 Thermidor Year II, of having held in her café "secret meetings of murderers" whose slogan was "patriot" (!), and finally, of having "applauded and encouraged the rebels [of Prairial] who passed by on the boulevard." In response to these accusations, she asserted that she had not "instilled the infernal spirit of Jacobinism in her husband and her children," but indeed the spirit "of liberty and of equality," and that she regretted not having made more shredded linen for wounds; she called the other denunciations slander. Released on probation on 29 Thermidor Year III, she wrote to the committee of general security that a "half-justice will not suffice for Republicans."

She was one of the only militant women of these years who later participated in the Babeuf conspiracy, her café serving as a gathering place for Babeuvists. A police report of 18 Floréal Year IV says, "The woman of the café especially poured forth insults and abuse and appeared to wish to inflame people."

MARTHE PINGOT, WIFE OF CHALANDON

Marthe Pingot was born in Paris in 1760.[5] She lived at 5 Rue du Paradis in the Homme-Armé section. Her husband, a shoemaker born in 1750, was a revolutionary commissioner in the Year II, was arrested in Thermidor Year II and in Prairial Year III, was retained as "fit for command" by the Babeuvists, subscribed to the *Tribun du Peuple,* and was arrested several times under the Directory, the Consulate, and the Empire (see Soboul and Monnier, Répertoire, p. 353).

She signed the petition of 6 March 1792 by Parisian women asking for the right to arm. Shortly after 10 Thermidor Year II, the news flew that, like her husband, she had been arrested; it was said that "she deserved it at least as much as he." The fact was false, but she was declared under arrest by the general assembly of her section on 8 Prairial Year III. She was accused of having influenced the deliberations of the revolutionary committee and of having told certain citizens that she would "veto" their certificates of public spiritedness. She became indignant when a sentry was placed at the door of the general assembly with orders to prevent women from entering the hall and to direct them toward the galleries, a measure that, according to her, "could only have been given by the aristocrats who did not wish her to recognize them when they spoke." The second charge against her was that she said, "it was necessary to cut off the heads of all priests, nobles, merchants, and at least sixty members of the Convention" and that she supported "the system of terror" by saying "that nothing would go well until there were permanent guillotines in all the crossroads of Paris." Her egalitarianism was the cause of the fourth reason for her arrest: she had asserted that national goods should not be sold but should be given to the people and that she hoped indeed to receive her share. She was released on 25 Vendémiaire Year IV.

ANNE FÉLICITÉ COLOMBE

The owner of the Henri IV printshop located in an apartment on the Place Dauphine, Anne Félicité Colombe printed *L'Ami du Peuple* and *l'Orateur du Peuple* of Marat.[6] On 4 December 1790, the authorities searched her printshop and seized newspapers being printed. She assured them that

---

5. A.N., F⁷ 4637 d. Chalandon, F⁷ 4774⁹² d. Richebraque, AE II 1252 C I 90.
6. A.N., F⁷ 4624 pl. 1, pp. 25–69; B.N., Lb⁴⁰ 2260, *Discours de Monsieur Le Clerc.*

she was proud of printing these "sheets" rather than royalists newspapers, protested the search "as illegal and detrimental to the rights of citizens," and refused to tell them where to find Marat. Etienne, attacked by Marat in his newspaper, brought suit for defamation against Colombe, and she was condemned to pay him twenty thousand livres of damages and interest for having undermined his reputation by the "calumnies" that she had printed, and was forced to print and post six thousand copies of the sentence. On 1 January 1791, she started proceedings to have the previous judgment declared null and void, which she won. Etienne was condemned to pay her twenty thousand livres, which she gave to the poor of her neighborhood. A speech by Leclerc, the future *enragé*, given on 1 April 1791 to the Jacobins, had also been printed by her shop. After the fusillade of the Champ-de-Mars on 17 July 1791, she was arrested as the owner of the shop that printed *L'Ami du Peuple*. In 1793, she was a member of the Society of Revolutionary Republican Women; according to M. Cerati, *Le Club des Citoyennes Républicaines Révolutionnaires* (Paris: Editions Sociales, 1966), she was one of the club's most assiduous members. In the autumn of 1793, when the women's club was attacked, Jacques Roux, who defended it, cited her in issue 268 of his newspaper beside Claire Lacombe as a well-known revolutionary woman.

MARIE MARTIN, WIFE OF DESPAVAUX (OR DESPAVEAU)

Marie Martin was born in 1736 and was a linenworker who worked for a notions dealer.[7] She lived at 205 Rue de Grenelle in the Fontaine-de-Grenelle section. Her husband guarded an *émigré*'s home that had been taken over by the revolutionary government. She could sign her name but did not know how to write.

She brought her work with her when she went to the Jacobin club everyday and was known there in the galleries as "a good patriot." She joined the Revolutionary Republican Women's club. She was admitted to it on 6 August, but we find her name at the bottom of a "republican poem" in honor of Marat on 17 July. At the beginning of August 1793, she organized a denunciation against a notions dealer of the Bonne-Nouvelle section, a monopolizer of essential goods and hosiery; she said she was motivated "by the scarcity that the people endure and the high price of all commodities."

7. A.P.P., AA 77, 17–18, Prairial Year III; AA 148 f. 388; A.N., F⁷ 4752 d. Julien; *Archives parlementaires* 69, p. 84.

She was arrested in Prairial Year III for this denunciation. When her home was searched, the documents found included the rules of the Society of Revolutionary Republican Women, a letter confirming her admission to the club, an address given by the club to the Convention on 17 July 1793 on the death of Marat and the ode read over his tomb, the speech of congratulations by the Parisian authorities to the Revolutionary Republican Women, and issue 17 of Leclerc's *L'Ami du Peuple* of 30 August 1793. She was freed on 30 Thermidor Year III.

WIFE OF DUBOUY (OR DEBUIS), CALLED THE MÉRE DUCHESNE

The wife of Dubouy lived at Rue Beaujolais in the Temple section.[8] She was an unemployed cook who worked as a nurse's aid. She was separated from her husband, a servant.

She was denounced at the end of the Year II in a letter delivered to Tallien, and then on 8 Prairial Year III by two neighbors who testified against her at the surveillance committee in the sixth arrondissement (a district of Paris). The first denunciation accused her of having been "the satellite and missionary to all women under Robespierre's orders, a most ferocious woman . . . who corresponded with this monster regularly by telling him which victims to sacrifice to his savagery." And she had said to one of her denunciators of 8 Prairial that she "had loved only two men at the Convention, Marat and Robespierre." All accused her of having gone to the galleries, "to the revolutionary tribunal in the morning, in the evening to the Jacobins or to city hall." She had been known at the Jacobins "by her clamouring and her threatening gestures," and by the various denunciations that she had "howled" from the women's gallery. She spoke highly of 31 May 1793 and said "that there were still more than one hundred villains in the Convention, the enemies of Robespierre, whom it was necessary to get rid of, as well as thirty thousand in Paris." In Thermidor Year II, she supported the insurgent city hall and said that "they should not have killed [Robespierre] without having heard him." In the Year III, she grew indignant over the return of the Girondin deputies to the Convention, saying that since 9 Thermidor only patriots were incarcerated, that Collot, Barére,

---

8. A.N., F⁷ 4664 d. Debuis, F⁷ 4683 d. Dubouy.

and Billaud were honest men, and that the wrong was not done directly by the Convention, but in its committees.

WIFE OF DUBREUIL

The wife of Dubreuil resided at 10 Enclos du Temple in the Temple section.[9] She had lived in Paris for fifteen years. When her husband was a servant for the king's brother, they lived at the Palais du Temple; when he lost his position, they moved to the Gravilliers section and then returned to the Temple section at the beginning of the Year III.

She was declared under arrest by the Temple general assembly at the request of the Gravilliers assembly, who accused her on 7 Prairial Year III of being "a dedicated terrorist, having regularly corresponded with Marat," of having been a secretary of the Society of Revolutionary Republican Women, of having carried a dagger "in order to strike those who wished to dissolve women's societies," and finally of being "very dangerous according to all reports, eloquent, audacious, and wicked." The Temple police commissioner added that "this was one of those women for whom the guillotine has always been a satisfying spectacle." She acknowledged having written three times to Marat (to "give him advice about the methods used by *émigrés* to return to France, . . . to propose to him the means . . . appropriate to prevent fires in the offices of ministers," and in June 1793 to warn him "that the guards of the king who had emigrated had just been promised important places in the armies of the Republic") and having been secretary of the Revolutionary Republican Women. But she denied having threatened anyone with her dagger. She rejected the first charge ("dedicated terrorist") by asserting that "for eight months this term has been squandered with as little circumspection as that of *aristocrat* once was," and the fifth ("very dangerous, . . . wicked") by remarking that, even if these accusations were true, they "could not be included among the crimes of state that the Convention had wished to punish."

She was one of those revolutionaries who did not pardon Robespierre and the committees of the government for having, according to her, "wished to assume without right the sovereignty of the people." And in the evening on 9 Thermidor, she urged the company of the Gravilliers section not to join city hall, for fear of "setting off civil war within the Republic"

---

9. A.N., F⁷ 4683 d. Dubreuil; F⁷ 4604 d. Bochard; *Journal des débats des Jacobins,* no. 302 (3 October 1793).

and because Robespierre was a "dictator [who] made laws," as the law of 22 Prairial Year II proved. She said that it "was necessary that Robespierre, Couthon, and Saint-Just take their heads to the scaffold." At the end of September 1793, she wrote to the *Journal des débats* to defend the Revolutionary Republican Women. She remarked that the enemies of the club were "ignorant and servile" women "who were besotted with prejudice" and men "who realized that to the degree that women become enlightened, their marital despotism will appear like that of the former king, and they will be obliged to renounce their despotism so as not to blush, under the Republican regime they wished to maintain. Women are beginning to see that they are not created to be more debased than men." She proposed finally that women possess, like men, citizenship cards after having sworn an oath "so that bad female citizens can be distinguished from good," because she thought that "women who do not hold to good principles are as dangerous as men."

CONSTANCE EVRARD

Born in 1768 in the Vosges, in 1791 Constance Evrard had been a cook for three years at the home of a former treasurer of France, who lived at Rue de Grenelle in the Fontaine-de-Grenelle section.[10] She knew how to read and write.

In January 1791, she was mentioned in the *Révolutions de Paris* because she had congratulated the newspaper for its article on "tyrannicides" and had asserted: "If you need a tyrannicide to complete the batallion, count on me; I would quickly throw off my women's clothes and don the garb of a sex whose courage I feel in myself," adding that she would shed "with pleasure all her blood in order to spill the blood of enemies of the fatherland." A neighbor of Pauline Léon, she went with the latter in February 1791 to smash a bust of La Fayette at the home of Fréron. She was with Léon when they were taken to task by a troop of royal bodyguards on 21 June 1791. On 17 July, she went with Léon to the Champ-de-Mars where, "like all good patriots," she signed the petition—which she had not read, but which she knew "aimed to organize the executive power differently." After returning home, angered by the fusillade, she attacked a neighbor who was in the national guard. She said to him that "La Fayette will be fired," called him a murderer, an executioner "who killed everyone at the Champ-de-Mars,"

10. A.P.P., AA 148 f. 30, AA 90, 31 1793; A.N., microfilm AE II 37, AE II 1252 C I 90; *Les Révolutions de Paris* 81, 22–27 January 1791, p. 157.

and threatened to stab him and to strike his wife and his mother-in-law. She was questioned and it was learned that at this period she sometimes went in groups to the Palais-Royal or the Tuileries, frequented the Cordeliers, subscribed to the *Révolutions de Paris*, and also read Marat, Audouin, Camille Desmoulins, and *L'Orateur du Peuple*. On 6 March 1792, she signed the petition that asked that women have the right to bear arms. In 1793, she joined the Revolutionary Republican Women's club and participated in the anti-Girondin days of 31 May to 2 June. After that date, we find no more trace of her and we do not know what became of her.

GENEVIÉVE ANTOINETTE JULIE GAUTHIER

Geneviéve Gauthier lived at 36 Rue Transnonain in the Gravilliers section and worked as a pastry cook with her parents.[11] She was the only daughter. Her father was arrested on 9 Prairial and released on 19 Fructidor Year III. She knew how to sign her name.

She was arrested by order of the Gravilliers general assembly on 9 Prairial Year III. She had always "shown Jacobin opinions." On 9 Thermidor, she agreed with her father that "Robespierre will vindicate himself." Her denouncers asserted that "often she was seen running through the streets with a pike in her hand, taking the lead of all the rebellions." During the Year III, along with her parents, she "exhorted and roused" her neighbors to revolt. She was very close to the Barbot sisters, her neighbors, and "attended their secret meetings." On 1 Prairial, she was at the head of women who went to the Convention, forcing recalcitrant women to follow them. Having learned that her daughter was to be arrested, her crippled mother convinced her to hide and escape arrest. The Committee of General Security decreed her released on probation on 3 Fructidor Year III.

FRANÇOISE BORNE, WIFE OF GRIMONT

Françoise Borne was born in 1741 in the Côte-d'Or.[12] She lived at 53 Rue Beauregard in the Bonne-Nouvelle section. Unemployed, she lived on the pension that she received from the nation as a wife and mother of soldiers (160 livres per year) and the help in kind that her section gave her because she was destitute. Her husband was a head driver in military transport. Her

11. A.N., F⁷ 4720 d. L.J. Gauthier.
12. A.N., F⁷ 4733 d. Grimont, F⁷ 4714 d. Gaillard.

son had been in the army since 1792. She knew how to sign her name but not very well.

On 3 August 1793, she wrote to the Bonne-Nouvelle general assembly in order to put herself under its "protection": having supported the Jacobins in May 1793 and having cried over the death of Marat, she had been persecuted and threatened by her landlords and dared no longer return to her home. Referring to the Declaration of Rights, she asked the general assembly for "safety for herself" and that her landlords be ordered to no longer cause her "the least annoyance." On 26 Nivôse Year II, the revolutionary committee of the section asked her to go to the shop of a pork butcher to see if he obeyed the maximum price law; she informed the committee that the pork butcher had refused to serve her.

In the Year III, she declared that she went "very often" to the galleries of the Convention. She was arrested there on 9 Pluviôse for having screamed in the corridors that she was going to die of hunger while her son and her husband were at the front, "that tyranny reigned, that all good patriots were imprisoned, and that the guard was only composed of aristocrats." She was freed on 17 Pluviôse Year III thanks to the intervention of a deputy. But in the evening of 3 Prairial, she "heatedly" accosted two armed soldiers, saying to them "that they were bloody idiots, that they had been summoned to protect monopolizers and merchants and oppress honest and destitute citizens," that the day before they had behaved like villains, "that without them it would have been all over for the Convention whose intention was to kill the destitute of Paris," "that it was unfortunate that the day before had not been a success, and that Parisians behaved like jackasses because it was entirely up to them to have bread." She added that the Convention, composed of "villains worthy of destruction," "only sought to provoke us and to make us die of hunger," which was her case, whereas her son could be killed from one moment to the next in the army, and that the Convention had promised to provide for the parents of soldiers. Asked to withdraw, she "refused and lay down on the ground, screaming" that she was on a "public road of the nation" and was "free to stay there." Although she appeared drunk, she was taken to prison. On 14 Messidor Year III, she asked to be released, claiming that she had been arrested by two citizens who were "enemies of the public good." She was released on 13 Fructidor Year III.

CLAIRE LACOMBE

Claire Lacombe was born on 4 March 1765 at Pamiers (Ariège) of merchant parents.[13] She was an actress. She lived at the Rue Neuve-des-Petits-Champs in the Lepeletier section with the female citizen J. Thibaut. She knew how to write.

At the beginning of the Revolution, she was working as a successful actress in Marseille, Lyon, and Toulon. On 30 March 1792, she left Marseille, where she had lived for a year, to come to Paris where, without work, she dedicated herself to the Revolution, living on her savings. On 25 July 1792, dressed as an amazon, she read a speech to the Legislative Assembly, offering to go fight the tyrants (but asking that mothers not leave their children to follow her example) and asking for the arrest of Dumouriez. With arms in hand, she took part in the assault on the Tuileries on 10 August 1792, eloquently encouraging the other insurgents. On 19 August, in homage to her bravery, the *fédérés* offered her a national sash and a civic crown, which she gave to the Assembly on 25 August. In spite of an advantageous contract that she signed with a Mayence company of actors in April 1793, which promised three thousand livres per year to play "the leading tragic and comic roles," she remained in Paris, where on 3 April she proposed to the Jacobins that they take aristocrats and their families as hostages. She regularly attended the meetings of the Jacobins and joined the Fraternal Society of Patriots of Both Sexes.

But it was her name that was linked above all with the Revolutionary Republican Women's club. At first she played only a secondary role. Then her personality imposed itself during the summer, and she became successively secretary and president. After the inauguration of the obelisk in honor of Marat on 18 August, Lacombe, then secretary, announced to the Jacobins that the Revolutionary Republican Women were going to occupy themselves with public safety; she also read the petition of the club on 26 August to the Convention. Linked to Leclerc (she was accused of being his mistress), in September she urged the club to defend opinions that were close to those held by him. Through her, the women's society in which she had become the major figure was called into question. On 16 September, Chabot attacked her at the Jacobins: "Madame Lacombe, for she is not a female citizen," had asked him to arrange the release of the mayor of

13. A.N., F⁷ 4756 d. Lacombe, T 1001 1–3 W 76 no. 45; *Archives parlementaires 47*, p. 144; *Archives parlementaires 48*, p. 714; Alphonse Aulard, *La Société des Jacobins*, vol. 5 (Paris: 1889–1897), p. 123; Joachim Vilate, *Les Mystères de la Mère de Dieu dévoilés* (Paris: Pluviôse Year III); *La Feuille du salut public*, n. 81, 23 September.

Toulouse, who had dared to call Robespierre "Monsieur Robespierre." First Bazire, then Renaudin, tried to outdo each other: "The female citizen Lacombe, or Madame Lacombe, who loves nobles so much, is offering refuge to a noble at her home" (Leclerc!). She was then accused of "intruding everywhere" and of having asked for "the Constitution, the whole Constitution, and nothing but the Constitution." A Jacobin exclaimed, "The woman who is being denounced is very dangerous because she is very eloquent; she speaks well at first, but then attacks the constituted authorities." Refused a chance to speak and threatened by the women of the gallery she occupied, Lacombe promised, if they dared to touch her, to show them "what a free woman can do." She was arrested on the Jacobins' motion and freed the next day, for the authorities had found only letters that "breathed the purest patriotism" at her home. On 23 September, *La Feuille du Salut Public* wrote that she was "harmless" and called her a "counterrevolutionary bacchante" who liked wine, food, and men very much. She vindicated herself before the Revolutionary Republican Women, asserting that she was far "from comparing the citizen Robespierre with the Bazires of the day." "Beware, Robespierre!" she cried "I perceive that those who have been accused of corrupt practices believe that they will escape this denunciation by accusing those who denounce them of having spoken ill of you. Beware that those who need to protect themselves through your virtues don't drag you with them over the precipice." She also justified herself before the Jacobins on 8 October and continued to head the women's club until its dissolution.

On 13 Germinal Year II, without resources and not finding employment in Paris, she was arrested on the basis of denunciations by former members of the Society of Revolutionary Republican Women as she was preparing to rejoin the theater troupe at Dunkirk. During her imprisonment, her friends continually demanded her release (making use of seven documents). She herself, who always signed her name as "Lacombe, free woman," sent many of them: in not one did she renounce Robespierre or the government of the Year II, nor did she exploit in order to gain her freedom the fact that she had been arrested before 9 Thermidor. On 7 Vendémiaire Year III, her friend Victoire Capitaine wrote that "her health and her spirits were strangely fatigued." Four months later, Vilate, held prisoner with her in Luxembourg, presented her in another light: "Do you remember the famous Lacombe, the renowned actress and president of the fraternal society of revolutionary amazons? She has become a shopkeeper providing small pleasures to prisoners of the state, her companions in misfortune. . . . Before taking this course of action, she walked with her head high, and she looked so proud, you could imagine her on stage, ready to play her roles; now she is simple, neat as a pin, gracious to the buyers, only a small, modest, bourgeois woman who knows how to sell her merchandise at the highest price."

She was freed on 1 Fructidor Year III, after fifteen and a half months in prison. Three months later, she left Paris for Nantes, where she had an engagement to play the "great leading roles, in tragedy as well as in comedy and drama, queens, noble mothers, great coquettes." She received in gold coins (not paper money) 183 livres per month. She stayed there until spring of the Year VI, corresponding occasionally with her former Parisian comrades, who urged her to return to Paris and who tried to find her employment in a theater of the capital. But she seems to have abandoned all political activity in order to dedicate herself to her work and to her loves. In Prairial Year VI, she returned to Paris with an actor, her companion, in debt 386 livres to her landlady, and from this time no more is known of her.

MARIE FRANÇOISE VICTOIRE GUILLOMET, WIDOW OF CASTEL, WIFE OF LANCE

Marie Guillomet was born in 1731 or 1732.[14] She lived on the Rue du Faubourg-Saint-Antoine in the Montreuil section. She was a linenworker and former shopgirl at the home of a notions dealer. She owned a home at Poissy, inherited from her first husband. She had been separated since 1767 from her second husband, Pierre Lance, a "mechanic." She received 320 livres in yearly income from her house and 180 livres in pension from the nation. She knew how to sign her name.

She was mentioned on 5 Nivôse Year III by the surveillance committee of the eighth arrondissement in a report on "dangerous individuals who do not appear at all inclined to wish to change their behavior": "Excessive female Jacobin having professed openly their principles. . . . emissary whom the Jacobins maintain in the faubourg . . . has bragged of having caused the imprisonment of eighteen people in Poissy, has complained that the court of blood does not sacrifice enough victims, and has proposed, if necessary, to pull the cord of the guillotine. . . . Dangerous because of her principles, which she will propagate if she has the opportunity."

14. A.N., F⁷ 4736 dd. Guillomet and Guillouet, F⁷ 4660 d. Damoye, W 77 d.5 no. 321, F⁷ 4775³⁴ d. Pampelun.

On 9 Prairial Year III, the surveillance committee of the eighth ar-rondissement opened an inquiry on her. She went to the Jacobins every day, "to learn," she said. She took her work there, in the company of friends, and in particular the widow Lagon, wife of Pampelun. She stayed from 10:00 A.M. to 11:30 P.M. When she was reproached for abandoning her household, she responded: "It is absolutely necessary that I go there; the galleries have been invited to go there." She was also a regular in the galleries of the Montreuil section popular society, where she had met the wife of Pampelun. She had become "the intimate friend and confidant of Bernard," a revolutionary commissioner of the section who was guil-lotined on 10 Thermidor Year II. During the Year III, she supported the sansculottes when they went in force to the general assembly. Several people described her as "one of those maniacs for whom blood is a food and crime a need," "an enraged Jacobin breathing only blood," and claimed to have heard her utter bloody remarks. She observed the carts of the condemned who passed under her windows with the help of a pair of opera glasses, rejoicing when their number was considerable ("There's a good crop today") and saying "discontentedly" in the opposite case, "That's all there is; it's not worth going." According to all witnesses, she had been particularly angry the day those who were guilty of an at-tempted assassination of Robespierre were executed: "As soon as the Re-naud girl appeared, she became a fury and poured out invectives against the condemned, crying loudly enough to be heard on the other side of the street, 'If I was down there, I would plunge my knife into all of their hearts,' 'Ah, the villains! There is still enough for ten days and after that it will be the merchants' turn; they will receive no mercy.'" When asked during her interrogation if she had not shown "a bloodthirsty joy" when she saw these carts pass, she responded "yes, because she had been a true believer." She denied having said that she was ready to pull the cord of the guillotine but acknowledged having asserted that "if her father was counterrevolutionary, she would denounce him." All the witnesses af-firmed that she was known and feared in her neighborhood as an "ex-aggerated Jacobin," "an *enragé* (follower of Jacques Roux)," who never ceased "to preach," "to propagate with all her power" her opinions. She had often been heard to "speak in solemn praise of Robespierre, Collot, and others of this sort"; when Collot was wounded, "she took a very spe-cial interest in his health and felt sorry for him."

"On 9 Thermidor in the evening, uncertain of the fate of her dear Robes-pierre, she left the Jacobins to rush to the general assembly, where she stayed from one o'clock in the morning until four o'clock while keeping the most profound silence. All the grief and the sorrow that she felt showed on her face." Retired to Poissy after 1 Floréal Year III, she did not take part in the insurrection of Prairial. She was arrested on 15 Prairial Year III; she was still in prison on 4 Vendémiaire Year IV.

PAULINE LÉON

She was born in Paris on 28 September 1768.[15] She was a chocolatemaker and merchant with her parents on the Rue de Grenelle in the Fontaine-de-Grenelle section, at her mother's home. She was married on 28 Brumaire Year II (18 November 1793) to the *enragé* Leclerc. She knew how to read and write. She had four brothers and sisters.

She explained her revolutionary behavior in a written statement on 16 Messidor Year II. Her father, a "follower of the Enlightenment," gave her a rather careful education but died in 1784. On 14 July and the following days, she was in the street, rousing men and putting up barricades. From the beginning of the Revolution, she sided with the foremost patriots; she distrusted La Fayette in particular, especially after his actions on 5 and 6 October 1789. In February 1791, with female friends who were "patriots," she smashed a bust of the general at the home of Fréron. On 21 June 1791, in the company of her mother and Constance Evrard, she just missed being "assassinated" by a troop of royal bodyguards in retaliation for their indignation at the flight of the king. On 17 July 1791, once again with her mother and Constance Evrard, she was fired on by the national guard at the Champ-de-Mars, where she had signed the petition asking for the dethroning of the king. On returning to their section, they called a neighbor who was in the national guard a brigand and assassin and threatened to stab him. On 6 March 1792, she read a petition to the Legislative Assembly, asking for the right for Parisian women to form a female national guard. She tried to put her ideas into practice; on 10 August 1792, after having passed the night at the general assembly of her section, she joined the batallion armed with a pike, which she relinquished however to a sansculotte "at the request of all these patriots." Shortly thereafter, she signed a document asking for the death of the king and "many other patriotic petitions."

Beginning in 1791, she was "introduced" to the Cordeliers club, to the Fraternal Society of Patriots of Both Sexes, and to the (sexually mixed)

15. A.N., F⁷ 4774⁹ d. Leclerc, F⁷ 4756 d. Lacombe, BB³ 72 N. 69, AE II 1252 C I 90, microfilm AE II 37; A.P.P., AA 148 f. 30.

popular society of Luxembourg. In 1793, she was one of the founders of the Society of Revolutionary Republican Women, where she participated in the struggle against the Girondins. At the end of May, in the faubourgs Saint-Antoine and Saint-Marcel, at the central committee of the sections at the Archbishopric, she preached "the Holy Insurrection with all the energy she possessed." On 2 June, as president of the club, she appeared at the bar of the Convention with the insurgents. The personality of Claire Lacombe came little by little to impose itself in the women's club, but Pauline Léon did not lessen her activity as a member of the Revolutionary Republican Women. In September 1793, she denounced a grocer who was the author of counterrevolutionary words. In the club, she defended the same "enragé" positions as Claire Lacombe and demanded that the Convention be replaced; she recalled that Rousseau had written that "the prolongation of power is often the death of liberty," and, repeating the words of Leclerc, insisted that the members of the Convention had "hung onto their benches" for too long.

On 28 Brumaire Year II, twenty days after the banning of the women's club, she married the enragé Leclerc and resumed the management of her mother's chocolate business. The banning of the Society of Revolutionary Republican Women, her marriage, and her business removed from the political scene this active militant woman who henceforth, according to her, "dedicated herself entirely to caring for her household and providing an example of conjugal love and domestic virtues that are the foundation for love of the fatherland." In Germinal Year II, she went to Lafère (Aisne) where Leclerc was stationed to "embrace once again her husband" before he left for the front. They were both arrested in this town by order of the Committee of General Security on 14 Germinal Year II. They were released on 4 Fructidor Year II, and there is no more trace in the documents of Pauline Léon (sometimes known as Anne Pauline Léon), the wife of Leclerc.

WIFE OF MONIC

The wife of Monic lived at 978 Rue du Rempart-Honoré in the Butte-des-Moulins/Montagne section.[16] She worked with her husband as a merchant of notions and snuffboxes. She was married to Monic, a police informer during the Year II, whose reports have been saved and who participated in all

16. A.N., F⁷ 4774⁴⁸ d. Monic; A.P.P., AA 96, 29 Pluviôse Year III; Proussinalle, *Le Château des Tuileries*, II, 35; Pierre Caron, *Paris pendant la Terreur: Rapports des agents secrets du Ministère de l'Intérieur* (27 août 1793–germinal an II), 6 vols. (Paris: 1920–1949), vol. 1, introduction.

the revolutionary movements from 14 July 1789 to 31 May 1793. She knew how to sign her name.

A member of the Society of Revolutionary Republican Women, she had given a speech there that concluded "that women were worthy of governing, I would say almost better than men. "In Nivôse Year III, she was accused of holding gatherings of Jacobins at her home. On 29 Pluviôse her husband was arrested as a Jacobin and "distributor" of the *Tribun du Peuple*; he was released on probation on 17 Floréal Year III, at the request of Rolin, a former colleague who was still a police informer, whom he served unknowingly as an informer. But the general assembly of the section declared the arrest of the couple as Jacobins on 5 Prairial Year III. Monic escaped arrest by running away. His wife was set free on 6 Thermidor Year III at the request of the general assembly (who had been assured that there would be no danger in freeing her "because she would be sufficiently watched by all her neighbors") and of the civil committee (who explained that she had deserved her incarceration).

MARIE PIERRE DEFFAUT, WIFE OF PÉRIOT

Marie Pierre Deffaut was born at Charleville circa 1755 and lived at 18 Rue des Lavandières in the Louvre/Museum section.[17] She was a merchant of small notions, keeping a small stall on the Quai du Louvre. Her husband was a journeyman goldsmith who was arrested on 8 Prairial Year III and released on 25 Messidor Year III. She knew how to sign her name very well.

She was declared under arrest by the general assembly of her section on 8 Prairial Year III, along with her husband, who was accused "of having shared the atrocious opinions of his wife, of not having repressed her excess, and even of having supported her and applauded her conduct." On 10 Prairial, neighbors sent accusatory letters about her to the general assembly, after which she was sent before the Military Commission.

In the Year II, she went occasionally to the Jacobins, inviting her female neighbors to come with her. She acknowledged before the Military Commission that she had believed they were "good." One of her accusers wrote, "I became unhappily aware of the joy of this shrew who only showed it when there passed before my shop and hers the victims driven to execution, when this woman did not stop barking at them until she no longer saw them; she was only seized by sadness when she learned that

17. A.N., F⁷ 4665 d. Deffaut, F⁷ 4774⁶⁷ d. Périot, F⁷ 4774³⁹ d. Mauger, W 546 no. 29; A.P.P., AA 185, 17 January 1793, AA 187 f. 188.

there was to be no guillotining or that the number [to be executed] was not sizeable." She responded to these accusations "that when people were led to their execution, she like many others had gone there to see, but had never shown either joy or sorrow." She insulted well-dressed people who passed before her shop, calling them aristocrats and royalists. She "oppressed the neighbors of her shop to an astonishing extent by the terror that she inspired until 9 Thermidor," asserted one of them. She said to a man who did not wish his wife to accompany her to the Jacobins "that she was married, but that she would rather kill her husband than live with someone who was not of her opinions." Around her neck she wore portraits of Marat and Robespierre, whose "maxims she had preached to different groups." In the night from 9 to 10 Thermidor, she "provoked the people against the Convention." She acknowledged before the Military Commission that she "had wept over the fall [of Robespierre] because she believed him to be an honest man."

On 13 Vendémiaire Year III, she lodged a complaint against a neighbor (one of the fiercest against her in Prairial) who had several times incited citizens against her by calling her a Jacobin. During the trial of Carrier, she formed groups in which she took his defense, "always threatening the Convention with impending dissolution and the merchants with certain pillaging." She subscribed to *L'Ami du Peuple* of Lebois "and informed all the public who wished to hear the remarks of his infamous journal." She called women who wore green ribbons "Charlotte Corday" and spat while passing the shop of one of her female denouncers, saying that "this stinks of Fréron." At the end of Floréal, she said, "Patience, the brigands will not always have the upper hand. The Montagnards will recover. The moment is not distant. . . . The gilded *mignons* and the *muscadins* will pay one day." On 1 Prairial, she followed the women who went to the Convention, asserting that even if there were ten cannons waiting for them, the Constitution of 1793 and bread were necessary. During the insurrection, she exhorted women "not to give up until they were given the Constitution of 1793 at once." "Courage," she said, "today the Montagnards are going to triumph. We must crush the moderate toads. . . . We must ask for Billaud, Collot, Barère, and the Montagnards who are under arrest and besiege the Convention until they are returned to Paris. The merchants will have their turn later. Yes, we have on our side the troops, the brave gendarmes, and the faubourgs. There are complaints about the guillotine, but the guillotine will be called *muscadin* from now on. . . . Yes, we must have the traitors' blood." On 2 Prairial, she went with a female friend to see "the faubourgs march." She said that at four in the evening she went to the Rue Saint-

Antoine, probably to go see what was happening in the insurgent Faubourg Saint-Antoine.

On 18 Prairial, she was found guilty by the Military Commission and condemned to six years of detention with preliminary exposure on a scaffold "for a period of two hours during three consecutive days" (the first day she was exposed at the Place du Palais-Egalité [Royal], the second at the Place de Grève, and the third day at the Place de la Révolution).

WIFE OF SAINT PRIX

The wife of Saint Prix lived at 158 Faubourg du Roule in the Bondy section.[18] She was a paintbrushmaker for miniaturists. She had no news of her husband, a prisoner of the Austrians since 1793. She had two sons who were volunteers in the Army of the North. She knew how to write.

She was the only woman arrested in Prairial Year III by the general assembly of the Bondy section. She was accused of being a Jacobin and responded in a written statement that she almost never went to the Jacobins but had attended all the general assemblies of her section. She was accused of having said that she would denounce "all those who do not think like the Jacobins." She defied anyone to find a denunciation by her. On 9 Thermidor, she asked "that Robespierre be returned to us." Although she was known to have supported Robespierre, she wrote that on the day of the Feast of the Supreme Being she had discovered "by his dictatorial air all his shrewdness and his perfidy" and had said that day to a neighbor whom she trusted: "He will fall soon; I detest him; I regard him as a reigning dictator." After 9 Thermidor, she "persisted in supporting the side of the former Jacobins." She was denounced on 28 Germinal Year III for participating in clandestine gatherings with former revolutionary commissioners of the section. On 1 Prairial Year III, she read in the street *The Insurrection of the People,* saying that "all the good citizens" must write on their hats "bread and the Constitution of 1793." From her prison, she wrote: "I could not protect myself from the powerful influence that was exercised over my mind by imposters whose apparent patriotism seduced me. I believed that by giving myself to their lying insinuations I served my country like my husband and my children serve it in the armies. The illusion is over; I recognize my error and beseech you to see in me only the wife and mother of three defenders of the fatherland." A report on the "terrorists" arrested by the

18. A.N., F7 4775[11] d. Saint Prix, F7 4775[29] d. Thomas, F7 4775[32] d. Toupiolle, F7 4648 d. Christophe.

section was very indulgent toward her: according to the report she was inclined toward error and it pointed out that she had welcomed in her home a woman without resources whose husband had been killed in the Vendée and had lavished on her all her friendship and "her affectionate and tender care," which "proves," said the report, "that in spite of the almost fanatic exaggeration to which she had given way, she was privately capable of being humane, sensible, and generous." She was released without conditions on 24 Messidor Year III.

BARBE AUDIBERT, WIDOW OF SERGENT

Barbe Audibert was born at Nancy and lived on the Rue Neuve-de-l'Egalité, formerly Bourbon-Villeneuve, in the Bonne-Nouvelle section.[19] She had lived in Paris since 1766. She married Sergent, a wigmaker, in 1789. She was a former servant who currently rented furnished rooms (mostly to prostitutes). She knew how to sign her name.

During the Year II, she went to all the Jacobin meetings with the women of her neighborhood. She was closely linked to Hébert and received his wife at her home. She was "well regarded" by the revolutionary committee of her section. On 3 Prairial Year III, she gathered people and incited women to save Tinel. After the failure of the insurrection, she abused all *muscadins*. She was denounced at the Committee of General Security for having been president of the Jacobins (!), receiving twenty-one livres a day in salary, and for having, on the order of Robespierre, "preached Jacobinism in the armies." Arrested on 4 Prairial, she was released on 22 Vendémiaire Year IV. A subscriber to the *Tribun du Peuple,* she was linked to the Babeuvists whom she received at her home and was occupied with a collection for the prisoners of Temple. It was then asked that she be watched without alarming her, because precious information could be gathered without her knowing.

MARIE MADELEINE SOLENDE (OR SOLANDE, SOLANDRE, SOLANGE), CALLED LABLONDE AND MARIE LOUIS VITECOQUE (OR VILDECOQUE, VAUDECOQUE)

Marie Solende and Marie Vitecoque were cake merchants who were partners on the Avenue de Neuilly (Champs-Elysées).[20] They belonged to

---

19. A.N., F⁷ 4775[18] d. Sergent, F⁷ 4276 pp. 231, 249.
20. A.N., F⁷ 4629 d. Bunon, F⁷ 4736 d. Guimard, F⁷ 4756 d. Lacombe, F⁷* 2473 p. 53, F⁷* 2476 4 Prairial Year III; A.D.S., VD* register 794, pp. 22 and 121; *Les Révolutions de Paris* 215, p. 210.

the Revolutionary Republican Women's club and were even denounced in the spring of the Year II for having been part of the "general staff" of Claire Lacombe. Moreover, their names are found at the bottom of the minutes of the meeting of 7 Brumaire Year II and a petition of 22 Nivôse Year III asking for the release of Claire Lacombe. After 9 Thermidor, they fought the government in several "crowds, notably on 11 and 13 Germinal" Year III. At the doors of bakers and butchers, they made "the most offensive remarks against the national representation." Consequently, on 4 Floréal the Committee of General Security asked the civil committee of the Champs-Elysées for information about them. On 2 Prairial Year III, the civil committee described them as "capable of harming the public good by their incendiary conduct and words, especially in the present circumstances." The next day, four women testified against the female citizen Solende: on the first of Prairial, she supposedly said "many things against the Convention, among others that it failed to provide bread," praised the Jacobins, and said that she wished "to see blood up to her knees" and that, to make the Convention fall, she "was going to get dressed up and go to Paris to seek its women, and if she found herself in the fight, she would do as the others." The two friends were arrested by the general assembly of the Champs-Elysées on 5 Prairial Year III for having "constantly preached murder and assassination," for having "displayed openly the principles of excessive Jacobinism," and for their behavior during the Year III, particularly during the insurrection of the previous days. They were released on 23 Fructidor Year III.

Index

Printed in the United States
129887LV00001B/148-162/A